ENCOUNTERING MARY

ENCOUNTERING MARY

VISIONS OF MARY
FROM LA SALETTE TO MEDJUGORJE

SANDRA L. ZIMDARS-SWARTZ

AVON BOOKS ◆ NEW YORK

AVON BOOKS
A division of
The Hearst Corporation
1350 Avenue of the Americas
New York, New York 10019

Copyright © 1991 by Princeton University Press
Published by arrangement with Princeton University Press
Library of Congress Catalog Card Number: 90-46215
ISBN: 0-380-71885-5

The Princeton University Press edition contains the following Library of Congress Cataloging in Publication Data:

Zimdars-Swartz, Sandra, 1949–
    Encountering Mary : from La Salette to Medjugorje / Sandra L. Zimdars-Swartz.
        p.   cm.
Includes bibliographical references and index.
1. Mary, Blessed Virgin, Saint—Apparitions and miracles—History—19th century.
2. Mary, Blessed Virgin, Saint—Apparitions and miracles—History—20th century.
I. Title.
BT650.Z56   1991
232.91′7′09034—dc20   90-46215

First Avon Books Trade Printing: December 1992

OPM   10   9   8   7   6   5   4   3

To Paul Zimdars-Swartz and Diane DeArmond

I AM THE MOTHER OF THE POOR, OF THE NEEDY,
MOTHER OF THE WHOLE WORLD, WHO LOVES YOU
SO MUCH, SO MUCH MY CHILDREN!
DO NOT DOUBT YOUR HEAVENLY MAMA!

—*The Virgin Mary, according to Rosa Quattrini,*
5 August 1967

CONTENTS

ILLUSTRATIONS

ENCOUNTERING
MARY

M Y INTEREST in modern Marian apparitions began in the fall of 1982, when I spent the better part of a day exploring Lourdes, where the young Bernadette Soubirous reported an apparition of the Virgin Mary in 1858. I went to Lourdes on a whim, thinking that my interest in medieval popular religion would be enhanced by an encounter with modern medievalism: a thriving pilgrimage site dedicated to the Virgin and renowned for its healing powers. But I found Lourdes compelling in its own right, from the crowds of the sick and infirm in their wheelchairs to the innumerable souvenir shops filled with thousands of pious trinkets. Critics of Lourdes charge that the town and its mammoth shrine exploit the hopes of the desperately ill and that the chief beneficiaries here have been the thriving business community and the Roman Catholic Church. They also point out that between 1858 and 1980 only sixty-four miraculous cures were officially recognized. The impression that I had of the *malades* and those who accompanied and cared for them, however, was that under the ever-present image of Mary at Lourdes these people had achieved some kind of peace with themselves and their situation and that their suffering, if not physically alleviated, was at least being transformed into something meaningful. This impression has since been reinforced by conversations with a number of people who have told me stories of their own experiences or those of friends and relatives at various Marian apparition sites throughout the world.

The many stories which emanate from these sites are stories of encounters with Mary: a few of them report visions of the sort which originally called attention to these places, but the vast majority tell of less spectacular experiences, such as of the sun behaving strangely or of rosary beads changing color, phenomena which, for those who tell them and for many who listen, testify to the Virgin's continuing presence and intervention at these special places to bring healing to troubled people and to a troubled world. It is the process of the transformation of these ordinary places into holy places, where many thousands of people believe they have encountered the Virgin Mary and her healing graces and messages, that I have sought to understand and to present in these pages.

Since 1982 I have visited the sites of other modern Marian apparitions and have read a great deal of what has been written about them. While some of the literature is scholarly, most is popular and devotional and says much more about the beliefs of the persons who visit these sites than it does about the events that called attention to them. For most of the apparitions recognized by the Roman Catholic Church, some scholarly effort has been made to collect and edit materials that would shed light on these events—newspaper articles, notes or transcripts of interviews with the seers, journals, letters from local residents and early visitors to the site—and with these materials in hand one can, without too much difficulty, credibly reconstruct much of what happened in these apparitions, as well as the first public responses to them. For apparitions not recognized by the Roman Church, however, such scholarly collections are rare and this reconstruction is usually much more difficult. In only a few cases have cultural anthropologists, psychologists, and others especially trained to access the kinds of human data with which apparitions are concerned turned their attention to the study and reconstruction of these phenomena. While the scholarly study of apparitions is thus not a very well paved path, I am convinced that it is worth the effort, and that there is a particular need here for the collaboration of persons trained in a variety of scholarly and clinical disciplines.

This study is an introduction to modern Marian apparitions. It traces the transformation of private experience into public belief and the transformation of suffering, the suffering of particular people but also, finally, the suffering of a community and of the world, into meaning. This is a transformation which, as will be seen, is usually accompanied by a sense of pending crises of the sort that are commonly called apocalyptic, and as the study moves, therefore, from a focus on the apparition experiences of individuals to the religious worldviews which have grown out of these experiences, it will be increasingly concerned with apocalyptic motifs and scenarios.

The materials surveyed will no doubt suggest questions to the reader which have not been raised at what might seem appropriate points in the text. Why are so many of the apparition visionaries women? What affect here have the patriarchal thinking and institutions of the church had on the image of Mary, the content of her messages, and the demands which she makes of her devotees? What is the relation of these

encounters with Mary to unusual visionary phenomena outside of a
Catholic religious context, such as encounters with spiritual guides and
UFOs? Why do some apparitions become focal points for nationalist
movements, and the image of Mary associated with them a symbol for
a nation or culture? How do the apocalyptic speculations of the Catholic
devotees of recent Marian apparitions compare to those of non-Catholic
Christians? While I have attempted to answer some of these questions
in the final chapters and in the conclusion of the study, others simply go
far beyond the scope of this work. I am convinced that no one school of
thought, method, or approach can uncover all that these phenomena
have to teach us, and I hope this introduction will inspire other scholars
to ask their own questions of Marian apparitions and to seek to answer
them according to the rules of their own disciplines.

The University of Kansas has supported my research in several ways.
The Hall Center for the Humanities provided funds for travel to the
Republic of Ireland in the fall of 1985 to study the apparition at Melleray. The General Research Fund provided summer stipends in 1986
for additional work on the Melleray apparition and in 1987 for a study
of the apparition at Necedah, Wisconsin. A sabbatical leave in the fall
semester of the 1987–1988 school year allowed for the initial organization and drafting of this manuscript. I thank my colleagues in the
Department of Religious Studies for their support and encouragement
of this project. The readers of the manuscript provided valuable suggestions which I believe improved the quality of the work. Cathie Brett-
schneider was very helpful in guiding the manuscript through the long
process of publication.

Two people deserve special thanks for their contributions to this
book. Diane DeArmond's unwavering belief in me and in the project
made the task of research and writing less formidable and more enjoy-
able. Paul Zimdars-Swartz was present at every stage of the project and
provided patience, encouragement, and love. He read each draft, made
insightful suggestions, and painstakingly edited each page. I am grateful
for his participation in this project.

ENCOUNTERING
MARY

INTRODUCTION

Modern Marian Apparitions, Their Background, and Their Religious Milieu

AT VARIOUS TIMES in the past two centuries, millions of devout Christians, most of them Roman Catholics, have gathered at rural sites scattered throughout the world to catch a glimpse of one or more persons who claim that they have been seeing and receiving messages from the Virgin Mary. Some have gone to these out-of-the-way places simply out of curiosity or at the urging of family and friends. Probably the majority, however, have gone in faith, hoping in some way to encounter the figure whose presence and special graces have presumably been manifested there.

Few of these persons have expected to see or hear the Virgin themselves, which is generally regarded as a privilege granted only to a very few. Many of them, however, have hoped to see the seers in ecstasy as Mary appears and speaks to them. Many have hoped to hear these persons deliver some of her messages. And many have hoped to experience one or more of the signs that have come to be associated with these events and that would confirm for them the reality of the Virgin's presence and graces: rosary beads changing color, plants blooming out of season, rose petals falling from heaven, the sun spinning or otherwise acting strangely, or a miraculous healing or alleviation of a serious illness.

While it would be difficult to estimate the number of persons in recent years who have returned from these pilgrimages convinced that they have experienced one or more of these signs, the number is surely very large. Reports of experiences such as these have today become almost commonplace, for example, among visitors at the site of the ongoing Marian apparition at Medjugorje, Yugoslavia, which began in 1981 and has continued for more than eight years. Such experiences mirror the often more diffuse but still very important experiences of the millions who visit the sites of apparitions which have long since ceased but where pilgrims still assume and sense a supernatural presence, such as Lourdes and Fatima.

Before looking more closely at these curious events and the meanings that have become associated with them, it is important that the meaning of some basic terms be clarified and that these events be placed in some historical context.

An apparition is best understood as a specific kind of vision in which a person or being not normally within the visionary's perceptual range appears to that person, not in a world apart as in a dream, and not as a modification of a concrete object as in the case of a weeping icon or moving statue, but as a part of the environment, without apparent connection to verifiable visual stimuli.[1]

Apparitions have been reported and seen as important for many centuries in many different cultures. In modern times, the figures who have "appeared" in apparitions have more often than not been identified as actual historical persons separated from the visionaries either in space or in time. There have been many reports, for example, of relatives residing in a distant place suddenly appearing in a room or at someone's bedside, or more commonly, of persons recently deceased appearing in such settings. Apparitions usually involve an important communication—about the death of a loved one, for example, or about a valuable object that has been lost, or about what needs to be done in an impending crisis. This communication usually assumes a particular importance in the case of religious apparitions in which the being or beings who appear are understood by the seers and their communities as important figures in a clearly defined religious tradition.[2]

The apparitions with which this study is concerned are all apparitions which have been understood and defined within the context of Roman Catholic Christianity. The literature of Christianity from its origins up to the present abounds in reports of presumably supernatural apparitions or visions—in premodern reports it is often impossible to make the distinction—of Jesus, the Virgin Mary, and other holy persons and angelic figures. Since the eleventh and twelfth centuries, however, when devotion to the mother of Jesus began to flourish in Western Christianity, the figure who has most often been seen and who has assumed the most importance in Christian apparitions and visions has been the Virgin Mary. Reports of appearances of the Virgin seem to have sharply declined in most places early in the sixteenth century, evidently as a result of the Protestant Reformation and the Inquisition. In the nineteenth and twentieth centuries, however, there has been a revival of interest in such reports, and public attention has been focused on some of these in such a way as to draw great masses of people to certain sites where appearances of the Virgin have allegedly taken place. For Roman Catholics, these modern "Marian apparitions" have become focal points for what appears to be a significant revival of interest in the supernatural in many parts of the Christian world.

The peculiar importance that has become attached to some of the Marian apparitions of the past two centuries can be explained, in part, by the fact that many of these have been both "serial" and "public." A serial apparition is one in which the seers have been led in an initial experience to expect that this experience will be repeated, and when they speak about it to relatives and friends and suggest that it will happen again, word spreads and people gather around the seers at the announced or expected time. The subsequent experiences of the seers, then, occur in the presence of anywhere from a few to several thousand people, giving rise to public events of sometimes immense proportions. A public apparition is simply one in which people surround the seers during their experiences. While those gathered may witness a sign, such as a sun miracle, generally speaking they do not see (or expect to see) the Virgin themselves.

The public apparition, in which a number of people gather to observe a seer in ecstasy, seems to be, at least in the context of the history of Christianity, a phenomenon peculiar to the last two centuries. The subjects of the many recorded Christian visions of premodern times, who were usually persons known for their disciplined religious lives, were almost all temporarily separated from their communities or households and alone at the time of their visions. Book Seven of Caesarius of Heisterbach's *The Dialogue on Miracles*, for example, an important thirteenth-century collection of medieval miracle stories, recounts some sixty-four visionary encounters with the Virgin Mary, most of them experienced by members of the Cistercian Order but some by priests, clerics, knights, and pious women. In the vast majority of these stories the visionaries are alone at the time of their visions, and when they are not, as for example when a lay brother is said to have seen the Virgin among the monks in the choir, there is no indication that anyone else present was aware of the vision.[3] This is also the case for the later apparitions studied by William A. Christian, Jr., which were visions reported by laity in Catalonia and Castile from the fifteenth to the early seventeenth centuries.

Christian has shown very clearly the place and the importance of apparitions, most of which were Marian, for the public life of a number of different communities in these regions during these particular centuries. The visions which he uncovered in local archives were all social in nature, in the sense that particular communities became very interested in them, investigated and found collaborating evidence for the visionaries' claims (sometimes in the claims of other visionaries), and were very concerned for some time with what they understood as the Virgin's requests. In some of these cases, the Virgin reportedly appeared to seers more than once, for example to remind a community that they were not heeding her initial requests; but these reappearances, like the initial appearances, were private experiences, and there is no suggestion as yet of a reappearance of the Virgin being expected in advance or of people gathering to observe an apparition seer in ecstasy.[4]

While the serial and public nature of recent apparitions is thus, apparently, a peculiarly modern development, the expectations associated with modern Marian apparitions have for the most part been inherited from the Marian piety and Marian visions of the Christian middle ages. Fundamental here are the themes of the Virgin's exceptional powers in times of crisis and her loyalty to those who place themselves in her care. Between 1000 C.E. and 1200 C.E., faith in the powers and patronage of Christian saints, which had grown up around particular tombs or relics, began to give way in many Western Christian communities to faith in the presumably more effective and accessible powers and patronage of the Virgin, leading to a widespread belief that devotion to the Virgin in and of itself could protect or save persons anywhere facing a crisis. According to Caesarius of Heisterbach, for example, a half-witted priest who could do little more than say the Virgin's Mass was kept from losing his vocation when the Virgin herself appeared to him and sent him to the bishop with the message that he should be reinstated. She gave the priest a sign which the bishop could not fail to recognize as miraculous and as a clear indication of the reality of the priest's vision and the importance of his work.[5] And when Beatrice, a devotee of the Virgin and custodian of a convent, ran away with a clerk to lead a life of licentiousness, the Virgin herself reportedly took her place so that her absence was not noted until the woman returned, repentant, fifteen years later.[6] Caesarius also describes other cases in which the Virgin "intervened" on behalf of persons devoted to her who had led evil or useless lives, saving them from the fires of hell at the last possible moment by allowing them a deathbed confession and reception of Communion.

Most of the visions related by Caesarius speak of the Virgin's intervention in purely personal crises, but some speak of her intervention in crises of the social order or of the world as a whole. This is the case, for example, in the vision which begins Book Seven of the *Dialogue*. In his own province, Caesarius says, people were worshiping in their parish church when a terrible storm arose, and while the priest was celebrating the divine mysteries, an image of the Mother of God was seen to be sweating violently. A person who had been thought to be possessed by a demon gave the explanation of this prodigy that came to be the accepted one. It was that Mary's son had stretched forth his hand to strike and that if she had not actively restrained him, the world would have been destroyed.[7] Another popular medieval legend sounds a similar apocalyptic theme, with the Virgin's activity likewise contrasted, initially, to that of her son, but with the link between the Virgin and the Cistercian Order, implicit in Caesarius's tale, now transferred and explicitly applied to the two new Mendicant Orders. According to this legend, the young Dominic had a vision of an angry Christ who was aiming three lances at the world, when his mother intervened, falling at her son's feet and begging him to be merciful. When Christ replied that justice had to be served and that wickedness could not go unpunished, Mary said that there was a way in which people could be brought back to him. She then introduced him to her two servants, Dominic and Francis, and said she would send them out to effect true repentance. The legend ends by recounting the miraculous meeting of these two founders.[8]

Often in these medieval miracle tales, Mary's interventions address the situation of a particular community which is suffering or under threat. A popular theme here is that an individual's sins are bound up with, and are symptomatic of, the sins of the community. Caesarius tells the story, for example, of a pious matron of twelfth-century Friesland to whom the Virgin appeared in order to explain that the flooding that was threatening the province was a chastisement from Christ, who was offended by the inhabitants' disregard for his Body in the form of the Communion host. Sometime before then, a man known for his drunkenness and wife-beating had knocked the pyx out of the hands of a priest with a stein of beer, scattering the consecrated hosts across the floor. The Virgin reportedly made it clear to the matron that this action was only a particularly blatant example of a sin rampant in the community and that only the building of a chapel and showing it "as much reverence as the Holy Sepulcher" would suffice to turn away chastisement.[9]

The appearance of Mary that is described in this tale is typical of shrine-establishment apparitions, of which there have been hundreds since the early middle ages and which have functioned chiefly, it seems, to give legitimacy to a local Marian devotion. It introduces, moreover, the main themes of the major modern Marian apparitions, which, while giving rise to some immense shrines, have come to be understood as proclaiming not a local but a universal message. Mary appears to a member of a community that is suffering or whose existence is threatened; she explains or clarifies what lies behind the suffering or threat; and she recommends a remedy. More often than not the problem is identified as the sin of the community, defined in terms of ritual transgressions: a host has been desecrated, prescribed prayers have not been said, people have not been going to confession or to Mass. The remedy offered by the Virgin is also, typically, a kind of ritual: the establishment of a new shrine, the rebuilding of an old one, or the promotion of a particular devotional practice or exercise.

Recognizing that the only direct witness to the supernatural reality that may be manifest in a vision is the visionary, communities and Church officials have for centuries sought and found indirect confirmation of the claims of a visionary in various kinds of signs. Some of these signs, such as weeping icons, became associated with the sites of apparitions and with the images often erected at these sites; others, such as the ability to read consciences, became associated with apparition seers; and still others, such as healings, were often associated with both the sites and the seers. Most of the visions reported in the first millennium of the history of Christianity were experienced by persons known for leading exceptionally disciplined religious lives (monks, nuns, hermits) and reputed to be holy. Other Christians sought and found signs of the sanctity of these persons and the truth of their visions in their presumably miraculous powers, such as their ability to heal, to read consciences, to give wise advice to kings and popes, and later, as the Eucharist became an important focal point of piety, the ability to distinguish consecrated from unconsecrated hosts. In the later middle ages, a number of men and especially women who had made no formal commitment to the religious life began to acquire reputations as visionaries, and the expectations that had long been associated with holy seers were transferred to these persons as well. While it is unclear whether the seers of the fifteenth- and sixteenth-century apparitions studied by Christian were a part of this tradition, most of the seers of modern Marian apparitions have inherited the role and have been expected during the course of their experiences to conform to the type of the late-medieval visionary. Modern seers are seen as persons who prior to their visions were not especially talented or devout, who are given prophetic gifts and certain paranormal powers at least for the duration of the apparition, and who are presumed in the wake of their experiences to be destined for a religious life.[10]

While apparitions have thus had a long history and have long been an important part of devotional life in Western Christianity, their official status for Roman Catholics was unclear until Pope Benedict XIV (1740–1758) specifically addressed this matter in the treatise *De servorum Dei beatificatione*. It was noted here that the approval that the Roman Catholic Church might give to a private revelation (which includes apparitions)[11] meant only that after a careful investigation permission might be given to publicize the revelation "for the instruction and good of the faithful." Such revelations, even when thus approved by the Church, should not be given the assent of catholic faith (*fides catholica*). Rather, the pope said, they should be given the assent of human faith (*fides humana*) according to the rules of prudence by which such revelations are probable and piously believable. He then went on to draw the logical conclusion: one can refuse assent to these revelations providing that one does this with the modesty that comes from having good reasons and without the intention of being derisive. Later statements of the Church's position have been little more than commentaries on and reaffirmations of this statement.

This eighteenth-century pronouncement is not, of course, a comprehensive statement of doctrine about everything that the Catholic faithful may expect and may do in connection with an apparition. Since at least the fourth and fifth centuries, teachers and bishops of the Roman Church have sanctioned and encouraged belief in the intercessory powers of departed saints in general and the special privileges accorded to the Virgin Mary in particular. While the powers of departed saints have been emphasized less and less in official Roman Catholic teaching since the early middle ages, however, the special privileges and by implication the special powers of the Virgin Mary have been emphasized more and more. The official proclamation of the Virgin's bodily assumption into heaven, made by Pope Pius XII at the end of the Marian Year of 1950 and hailed by the Swiss psychologist Carl Jung as one of the most significant events in the whole scope of Roman Catholic history, is generally seen as the culmination of this long period of Mary's ascendancy. All of this has given considerable impetus to the belief that evidently lies at the root of a great deal of Roman Catholic interest in Marian apparitions: the belief that one can obtain special privileges or graces through devotional exercises which express or help to establish a special relationship with the Virgin Mary.

The prerogative of investigating an apparition and of deciding whether or not it is worthy of "the assent of human faith" belongs officially to the bishop in whose diocese it has occurred. It should be noted, however, that the majority of apparitions reported in the past two centuries have not been investigated by diocesan commissions. Some of these alleged appearances have simply failed to sustain widespread public attention for very long, and their sites have faded from memory or have ceased to attract anything more than local attention. Others, however, have thrived in spite of a lack of formal recognition, and their sites have attracted pilgrims from beyond local and regional boundaries. The apparition at Knock in the Republic of Ireland is a case in point. On 21 August 1879, a group of villagers saw under the gable of the village church a tableau of the Virgin, John the Evangelist, and Joseph around an altar on which was the figure of a lamb. Two commissions investigated this apparition, one immediately after the event, the other in 1936. No formal declaration of approval has been given, but the worship of ecclesiastical authorities (including Pope John Paul II) at the site, the donation of gifts to the shrine by such persons, and the recent dedication of a major airport by the local bishop have been understood as informal declarations of approval. Knock is today one of two premier pilgrimage sites in Ireland.[12]

Sometimes a commission's negative decision, that is the proclamation that an apparition should not receive even the assent of human faith, discourages pilgrims and keeps a shrine from being established. This was apparently the case at Fehrbach (Kreis Pirmasens) in West Germany, for example, where an apparition reported in 1949 is now little more than a diocesan file and a memory among some local families.[13] Sometimes, however, a negative decision and the active opposition of the bishop seem to have relatively little effect on popular feeling or may even spur apparition devotees into successful independent efforts to maintain and promote a cult. The latter seems to have occurred, for example, at Garabandal, Spain, and at San Damiano, Italy, both sites of apparitions in the early 1960s. Pilgrims still come to these sites in considerable numbers, and there are groups of people today dedicated to the task of convincing Roman Catholic authorities to reverse the earlier negative decisions that were made with respect to each of these apparitions.

Of the hundreds of apparitions that have come to the attention of Roman Catholic authorities in the past two centuries, seven were investigated by diocesan commissions, were approved by the local bishop and went on to gain international attention: Rue du Bac (Paris, France, 1830), La Salette (France, 1846), Lourdes (France, 1858), Pontmain (France, 1870), Fatima (Portugal, 1917), Beauraing (Belgium, 1932–1933), and Banneux (Belgium, 1933).

It is common parlance in the literature of and about apparitions to speak of people accepting or rejecting an apparition, and it is important that the meaning of such terms be clarified. To accept an apparition or to believe it to be authentic generally means, and will mean in this study, to judge it to be of divine origin, whereas to reject it or believe it to be inauthentic means to judge it to have a purely natural or perhaps even a demonic origin. It will be assumed that the judgment of whether to accept or to reject an apparition, while it may be based on empirical data, is not ultimately an empirical judgment but a judgment of faith. While scholars in the secular academy who want to study apparitions without religious bias will make this assumption simply as a matter of course, scholars working in the context of Roman Catholicism may and often do make the same assumption, since it is quite consistent with the Church's official position as sketched in the treatise *De servorum* of Pope Benedict XIV.

Marian apparitions are not simple events with self-evident meanings, as much of the popular apologetic literature that has grown up around them would suggest. Persons seriously interested in these events, whether from a perspective that assumes the real possibility of supernatural interventions or from a perspective that assumes a purely human and natural explanation, will learn from an examination of the earliest accounts of apparitions that these are very complex phenomena that have been pared down and subjected to a considerable amount of interpretation by those who have sought to make them publicly accessible. It may not be easy to see this, however, in the case of apparitions where the initial accounts are no longer extant or not easily accessible, or in the case of very well known apparitions, where interpretive constructs, reinforced for decades in the apologetic and devotional literature, have so shaped people's perceptions of the event that they have come to be treated as facts. To illustrate the interpretive process through which some of the original data of an apparition becomes a manageable unit of public meaning, which may begin to attract the attention of persons far beyond the boundaries of the local community, it will be useful to examine a recent apparition about which few readers at this time are likely to have any preconceptions.

Melleray, 1985: A Case Study in the Development of an Apparition Narrative

In mid-August 1985, at a Lourdes-style grotto near the Cistercian monastery of Mount Melleray in the Republic of Ireland, two young boys claimed that on five consecutive nights they had seen and had received messages from the Virgin Mary.[14] The experiences of Tom Cliffe and Barry Buckley lasted for approximately two hours each night. On the second night friends and neighbors began to flock to the grotto, and by the end of the week several thousand people had gathered around the boys. Tom and Barry described to them what they were seeing and hearing with the aid of a public address system that had been brought in after the first night. While no one but the boys reported seeing the apparition itself, there were numerous reports of other peculiar phenomena. Some saw the statue of the Virgin Mary in the grotto move, and others saw superimposed on the statue the faces of Jesus, Padre Pio, and other locally popular figures.

Shortly after these events began, the boys' parents and others who had either experienced something unusual themselves or whose relatives or friends had such experiences began to meet in order to publicize what was happening at the grotto and to make provision for the comfort and safety of visitors. After the apparitions ceased, this "grotto committee" continued to meet to promote and encourage interest in the grotto, to plan for physical improvements, to organize public devotions and special events, and to encourage church authorities to conduct investigations that they hoped would lead to official recognition of the apparition.

One of the concerns of this committee was the gathering and recording of information about what had already occurred and what might continue to occur at the Melleray grotto. Each night, after the apparition had ended, Tom Cliffe's mother, Cait, sat down with the boys and wrote down all that they could remember of what they had seen and heard. While Cait Cliffe's journal proved to be perhaps the most important source of information about what Tom and Barry had experienced at the grotto, the committee sought to gather information from other persons as well. Sometime during the week of the apparition, for example, a notice was posted at the entrance of the grotto which asked anyone who had had an extraordinary experience there to send the committee an account of what had happened to them.

The Melleray grotto committee was also concerned with the production of written accounts of what had transpired at the grotto that could be used to inform visitors and to publicize the messages that they believed the Virgin had delivered there. The production of these accounts proceeded in several stages. Several days after the apparitions had begun, a committee member wrote a half-page account of what had been reported at the grotto, stressing that the Virgin's message to the world was "peace and prayer." This hastily written account apparently served the need felt by this committee for a brief statement that could be quickly reproduced and handed out as a leaflet to the many visitors. A second edition of this leaflet, which was prepared shortly after the boys' experiences ended, brought the account of the apparition up to date and also corrected the grammar and what some had seen as inaccuracies in the first version. This leaflet, which unlike the first was typeset and illustrated with a reproduction of a small devotional image of the Virgin, contained a somewhat longer summary of the Virgin's messages. These messages, moreover, were put in a rather different light than in the first leaflet by the inclusion of the Virgin's statement that God was angry with the world and that people needed to improve, behave, and pray if a catastrophe were to be averted in the next ten years. When it became clear that more copies of this leaflet would be needed, a third edition, differing only slightly from the second, was printed and sent to the grotto for distribution.

The difficulty of producing a statement of what had transpired at the grotto that was satisfactory to all persons concerned apparently convinced the committee members that special skills were needed, and they turned to William Deevy, a local veterinarian whose daughter had been among those who had seen extraordinary things there. Deevy interviewed the boys at length during the fall of 1985, and on the basis of these interviews he wrote an account of events at the grotto which ran to about twenty typed pages in length. A little later he assisted reporters from the *Cork Examiner* in preparing an account of the events for the Christmas edition of their newspaper. Then in March 1986, he helped prepare another account, which was apparently the first attempt to fit most of the phenomena reported in and around the apparition into clear chronological sequence. This chronicle traces events from Friday, August 16, when members of a local family first saw the statue of Mary "come alive," through the five days of the apparition itself (August 19–23), up to Saturday, August 24, when Tom Cliffe heard the last of Mary's messages. This account, which was prepared for distribution at the grotto like the earlier leaflets, took the form of a four-page printed brochure.

There is, of course, no minute-by-minute report of the events at the grotto, nor even of what was heard and seen by the two boys in the apparition itself. Moreover, a comparison of the early unpublished records of the apparition, that is, the transcripts made by Cait Cliffe and Deevy, with the aforementioned brochure makes it clear that a considerable amount of material in the earlier records did not make it into the brochure that was publicly distributed several months later. Some of this material is of a personal nature, pertaining to one or both of the seers or to particular persons in the crowd, and was evidently judged to be of private concern only. Most of the remaining deleted material seems to make little sense and was evidently excluded for that reason. None of this private or enigmatic material, in fact, has been included in any of the accounts distributed to the public at the grotto. Messages that were understood as specifically addressed to the public, however, have not only been included but have been at the core of all three accounts, appearing in the March brochure, for example, in bold type. This brochure, then, like the leaflets that were distributed earlier, was an official account of the apparition that included and emphasized what committee members, looking back over the many events and reported messages, thought to be of public importance and relevance.

In their production of an account of what had happened at their grotto, the Melleray grotto committee went through a process that no doubt reflects what has taken place among the first devotees of most other modern Marian apparitions, but in most cases only a few glimpses of this process may be evident in the available written records. The basic task of such communities is to simplify the complex web of events in which they have participated and to shape it into a meaningful, memorable, and engaging narrative. Public interest in particular aspects of these events, which is influenced by an awareness of previous apparitions and other similar phenomena associated with popular Catholicism, impinges on this process both in formal interviews and in many informal conversations and functions as a touchstone for those who assume the task of constructing the narrative. This interest becomes the guide, as it were, which leads them to select and to highlight some material and to reject other material as irrelevant. While the words and actions of the seers that pertain to what the narrators perceive as the central theme of the apparition are of primary importance in this construction, the testimonies of others who have experienced one or more of the traditional confirmatory signs (sun miracles, healings, conversions) are typically used to supplement the narrative and to reinforce the drama of the encounter with the supernatural that it presents. What has begun as an oral process within a community responding to some unusual experiences thus leads, finally, to a written account, which is usually printed and often widely distributed and which tends to be accepted as canonical by persons who are subsequently drawn into the believing community. Such accounts are usually devotional, which is to say that they can be used by persons who already accept the apparition to rehearse its drama, and apologetic, which is to say that they present the apparition in terms that will probably be meaningful to other Roman Catholics and that may encourage its recognition by Church authorities.

The task of producing this account typically falls to an educated person, sometimes a member of the local community but more often an outsider. This individual is usually an educated layperson or priest who has an active personal interest in such phenomena, considerable leisure time, and the financial means for travel and for underwriting the costs of publication. While the official account of the apparition may technically be the work of this person and may reflect some of his or her biases, it is more properly understood as the work of the believing community which has gathered around the apparition site.

In June 1986, the Melleray grotto committee with the help of Mr. Deevy was negotiating with Mercier Press for the publication of a book that would include both an account of the Melleray apparition and testimonies to other presumably supernatural phenomena witnessed at the grotto. They were also making plans for the production of a videotape. With respect to their goal of obtaining official church recognition for their apparition, members of the committee spoke with both optimism and studied realism. They were prepared to wait, they said, "as long as it took at Knock."

Contexts of the Melleray Apparition: From Moving Statues to Medjugorje

From the perspective of the social historian or anthropologist, the event at the Melleray grotto was scarcely an isolated phenomenon. About six months earlier, in February 1985, newspapers in the Republic of Ireland had begun to note scattered reports of moving statues of the Virgin Mary in various churches and grottos, chiefly in the southern part of the country. These reports continued into the spring and summer, and in July, in an incident that was widely publicized and attracted a considerable crowd, several women reported that a statue of the Virgin at a roadside grotto near Ballinspittle was rocking back and forth and lowering its hands, and that images of saints and popes could be seen on its face. While Ballinspittle received the most publicity and drew the greatest crowds, moving statues had been reported at more than thirty sites throughout the Republic of Ireland by the time of the events at Melleray.[15]

Some observers suggested that the revival of Marian devotion in Ireland that presumably inspired the reports of these moving statues was an anxiety-induced reaction to some conditions and events that were troubling many people in the Irish republic at the time, especially in the rural areas. Most often mentioned here was a perceived loss of the Church's ability to influence government policies with respect to matters of personal morality, as reflected in a 1984 action of Parliament legalizing the over-the-counter sale of some kinds of contraceptives. Also noted, however, were such factors as an impending accord with the counties of Northern Ireland and the exceptionally wet spring and summer, which had reportedly threatened crops and the tourist industry and frayed many people's nerves.[16]

The members of the Melleray grotto committee were certainly not oblivious to and indeed some had some personal encounters with the "moving statues" at other sites in Ireland before the events that took place in their own neighborhood. But while they saw what happened at their grotto as related to these moving statues, they believed that it was of a higher order. It was, they insisted, an apparition, which they interpreted not in the context of conditions peculiar to Ireland but in the context of other Marian apparitions of recent years. It was an extraordinary expression of the Virgin's love and concern for the Irish and indeed for all people in the troubled times before Christ's Second Coming and a reminder that the messages of other Marian apparitions, about which they were quite knowledgeable, had to be taken seriously. Of particular importance for them—so important in fact that in the minds of some the two apparitions could almost be said to be a single event—was the ongoing apparition in Medjugorje.

Since June 1981, several million people from Europe and America, most of them Roman Catholic, have visited the tiny mountain village of Medjugorje, Yugoslavia, where six children (ranging in age from ten to twenty in 1981) have been reporting almost daily appearances of the *Gospa* (Madonna). Irish pilgrims had been going to Medjugorje for some time before the Melleray apparition, and on 7 November 1985, the *Irish Catholic* reported that when the Yugoslavian seers asked the Virgin about the events in Ireland, they were told, "The Irish are to be the messengers of my messages."

That the apparition at Medjugorje has had a considerable impact in Roman Catholic circles in the United States as well as in Ireland became clear on 15 August 1988, when about fifteen thousand people gathered outside the church of St. John Neumann, a charismatic Catholic parish in Lubbock, Texas, in anticipation of a miracle. Three parishioners, who had been to Medjugorje, began to meet on Monday nights, beginning in February 1988, to pray the Rosary. In March they began to report "inner locutions" at these meetings, that is, they heard a woman's voice, presumably that of the Virgin Mary, delivering messages. While some of these messages were personal or concerned the parish, others seemed directed to the wider public, and some of these suggested that a crowd would gather and that the Virgin would perform a miracle on the Feast of the Assumption. This feast would come in 1988 on their regular meeting day, and since this day would also mark the culmination of the Marian Year declared by John Paul II, the rosary group and the parish began to plan some special events to mark the occasion. Word spread in charismatic Catholic circles throughout the United States and while the crowd that gathered that day was not as large as the group leaders, the parish, and even the Lubbock police had expected, many of those who came and sat in the late-afternoon sun on the east side of the church, hoping to see a miracle, were not entirely disappointed. During prayers and during the outdoor Mass shortly before sunset, many in the crowd reported seeing "sun miracles," and a number of people said that they had seen visions of Jesus and Mary in and around the parting clouds.[17]

The informal network of apparition devotees that exchanges and distributes information about such phenomena throughout the world was much in evidence at Lubbock. During this day-long event a visitor could, for example, after reading through one of the everywhere-available newsprint editions of the Virgin's messages at Lubbock, browse through the large makeshift bookstore in the parish hall and buy books containing the Medjugorje messages or pick up pamphlets about an apparition in Nicaragua. There were also leaflets about a much less publicized apparition in Louisiana.

While Medjugorje has undoubtedly been the focal point of most American and European interest in apparitions in the 1980s, much attention has been drawn to Medjugorje in the United States through events such as Lubbock and, more recently, some instances of weeping or moving statues which many have associated with the events in Yugoslavia. Recent lesser-known apparitions such as that at Melleray, one in Egypt, and several in the Ukraine are not satellites of Medjugorje in the same sense as these recent American phenomena, but they have joined forces with it in many persons' minds. The considerable public attention that has been given to some of the apparitions of the past several decades has created the impression that apparitions are proliferating—an impression that inspires different responses from different quarters.

Skeptics have suggested that cultural malaise and anxiety or the particular difficulties to which Catholics in certain countries are subjected have prompted an epidemic of "imitative" experiences. Believers, however, have understood this proliferation of apparitions as evidence of the nearness of the end of time and an expression of a divine plan which God is revealing today through Mary at various sites throughout the world. Small Catholic presses in many different places have published hundreds of books and pamphlets which give voice to such ideas, usually focusing on what are understood as the Virgin's messages in a particular apparition but at the same time linking these to the messages of a number of other apparitions. These are related to historical events both of the distant and the recent past in such a way as to yield a relatively coherent dramatic scenario of "the last days." The basic theme of this scenario is usually the battle between the forces of good and evil, with Mary portrayed as issuing an almost irresistible maternal call to join her forces. On a personal level, Mary is seen as a tender and concerned mother who calls her children away from the brink of disaster and offers them safety and comfort under her sheltering mantle. On a social level, however, Mary is presented as the leader of a mighty army of spiritual warriors ready to do battle with the forces of evil. These two images of Mary, set in the context of the last times, have very frequently led to a militant Marian ideology united with conservative political forces.[18]

Plan of the Study

This study is basically a study of experience and its interpretation, of the movement from private experience to public meaning, and from individual stories of encounters with Mary to all-encompassing accounts of world history. The experiences of a seer which, interpreted in a Roman Catholic religious milieu, have been understood as a Marian apparition, are in themselves probably inaccessible and indescribable. By studying the earliest reports of these experiences, however, and by putting them in what appears to be their appropriate personal and social contexts, it is usually possible to see and to represent these experiences much more accurately than they have been represented in the devotional and apologetic accounts. Indeed, it is usually possible to see when and under what circumstances additions or deletions in the descriptions of these experiences have been made and thus to follow the movement from experience to interpretation in and through which the public face of an apparition has come to be defined. This study will sketch that movement and show how the interaction of important individuals and groups has shaped the interpretation of six important apparitions of the past two centuries.

The apparitions addressed in this study have been chosen, first of all, to illustrate and illuminate the development in modern popular Roman Catholicism of a transcultural apocalyptic ideology of Marian apparitions that has grown up around the maternal imagery of many of the apparition messages. I have summarized this ideology in the final chapter. A second consideration in the selection has been the accessibility of documents that permit the kind of reconstruction of the interpretive process that has just been described.

La Salette, Lourdes, and Fatima are pre–World War II apparitions,

all recognized by the Roman Catholic Church. They have been extremely important for millions of Roman Catholics throughout the
world and are the prototypes for the later postwar apparitions. Lourdes
set the pattern for modern Marian healing shrines, while La Salette and
Fatima have defined the themes of the apocalyptic worldview that per-
vades the messages and the devotional literature of most of the later
apparitions. There are numerous references to these three "classic" apparitions in the messages reported by later visionaries, and it is chiefly
by references to these three that devotees of other apparitions, as yet
unrecognized, have sought to present their case to Roman Catholic authorities.

San Damiano, San Sebastian de Garabandal, and Medjugorje are all
post–World War II nonrecognized apparitions for which there are documents of the sort that are required in this study. These three later cases
illustrate and illuminate the most recent developments in the transcultural ideology of apparitions that it is my ultimate goal to describe.
While negative decisions of one kind or another have been made by
commissions or local bishops with respect to all of these apparitions,
this does not mean that they are uniformly rejected by all Roman Catholic authorities or that the future holds no possibility of a reevaluation.
Each of these three apparitions is distinctive and illustrates specific aspects of the modern Marian apparition that are not so evident, or perhaps only latent, in other examples.[19]

Part 1 of this study is concerned with apparitions as religious experience and with the tension between the apparition as religious experience
for the seer and as religious experience for the public. The opening
chapter examines the interaction between the seers and the public in
those earlier recognized apparitions (La Salette, Lourdes, and Fatima)
that have set the pattern for the apparitions of more recent years. Chapter 2 examines one of these more recent apparitions (San Damiano), in
which the catalyst for the apparition was apparently a crisis in the physical health of the seer and in which health became a focal point for public
interest and an important metaphor in the messages. Chapter 3 examines the early interaction between the seers and the public in the recent
apparition at Garabandal, where, for most, "experiences of the supernatural" in encounters with the seers soon replaced the seers' own experiences as the central phenomena of the apparition.

Part 2 of the study is concerned with apparitions as religious knowledge and with the struggle over the interpretation of an apparition once

it has become a public event, a struggle which comes to focus most clearly in the efforts of the seers, the public, and Church authorities to control or to have access to the "secrets" that the seers claim the Virgin has confided to them. The opening chapter of this section, Chapter 4, sketches the history of the so-called secrets of La Salette, which were the first secrets to be associated with modern Marian apparitions and which set the pattern for secrets and responses to secrets in the later apparitions. Chapter 5 examines the process of the formation and gradual publication of the so-called secret of Fatima and the struggle over access to the presumably not yet published third part of it. Chapter 6 examines secrets in the post–World War II apparitions (Garabandal and Medjugorje) and points out how in these apparitions, as in the later history of Fatima, these secrets have been associated with apocalyptic expectations, not the least of which has been the expectation that the seers would be heralds of events of world-historical significance.

The final chapter, Chapter 7, discusses, in summary form, some of the fundamentals of modern Marian worldviews, sketching first the basic elements of the transcultural apocalyptic ideology that can be seen today in most of the popular apparition literature and then some examples of modern Marian views of history, the first three of which assume the Virgin's triumph in the last stages of a divine plan of history and the last, an evil conspiracy against which she seems to offer only limited protection.

PART ONE

Apparitions as Religious Experience

CHAPTER 1

Personal Experiences and Public Demands

LA SALETTE, LOURDES,

AND FATIMA

THE EXPERIENCES that constitute apparitions and that attract attention to them are best expressed in stories. The more time one spends with the reports of such experiences, the more the sense and the importance of this axiom becomes clear. To represent apparition experiences, at least initially, in any other way than through the narratives in which the seers and devotees have themselves represented them would in all likelihood be to miss the symbolic contexts that have defined these experiences, and it is precisely these contexts that we want to discern and to understand.

There is, unfortunately, no systematic way to get at these symbolic contexts. The central narratives of an apparition, which seem to speak most directly of what the subjects have seen and heard and around which the devotional literature tends to be organized, are distillations, which in themselves may not cue us in to the symbols out of which these experiences have crystallized. When these narratives, however, are read in the light of other narratives, selected not because they are religiously edifying but because they tell us much that we would not otherwise know about these persons, the persons around them, and their general environment, the symbolic context in which a particular apparition experience has occurred may begin to emerge with some clarity. Generally speaking, this context has been one of suffering, suffering with which the subjects, through their special experiences, have begun to come to terms.

The goal of the chapters in this section will be to present, in a sequence of appropriate narratives, a glimpse into the experiences of the seers and first devotees of five important modern Marian apparitions, to trace the crystallization around these experiences of particular interpretations, and to show how certain interpretations (sometimes after intense competition with alternative ones) gave to each apparition a particular character and a particular place in modern Roman Catholic piety.

The choice of the first apparitions to be treated here calls for some explanation beyond that sketched in the introduction to this study. If by modern Marian apparitions we mean those of the nineteenth and twentieth centuries, and if the criterion for selecting apparitions from the first part of this period is understood as an apparition's enduring importance for piety and devotion in an international Roman Catholic framework, the obvious choices will be those that took place at the Rue du Bac, La Salette, Lourdes, and Fatima.

The first Marian apparition of the nineteenth century to receive widespread attention and to be formally recognized by Roman Catholic authorities was the apparition reported by Catherine Labouré in the convent of the Sisters of Charity of St. Vincent de Paul on the Rue du Bac in Paris, in July and November of 1830.[1] The most important feature of this Rue du Bac apparition was the purported revelation of an image of the Virgin which Catherine said she was instructed to have struck into a religious medal, over which was to be written the prayer, "O Mary, conceived without sin, pray for us who have recourse to thee." This medal began to be minted in 1832 and quickly became very popular. While it is generally acknowledged that the great popularity of this "Miraculous Medal" helped prepare the way for Pope Pius IX's proclamation of the dogma of the Immaculate Conception in 1854, it would seem that it also contributed substantially to the Church's formal approval of the authenticity of Catherine's visions in 1836 and to Catherine's beatification in 1933 and canonization in 1947.

The Rue du Bac apparition was unlike all of the recognized apparitions to follow it in one very important respect. It took place in a cloistered religious environment, and the seer was not subjected to public scrutiny in the aftermath of her experiences. Indeed, it was not until many years later that the public even learned her name. The meaning which became attached to the Rue du Bac apparition was not, therefore, the malleable product of an interaction between the seer(s) and the public, as were the meanings which grew up around other modern Marian apparitions. It was, rather, a more quickly defined and static devotional artifact, not unlike the medal with which it was associated.

An examination of Catherine's experiences and of how this more or less fixed meaning became attached to them would require a very different approach than that which has been chosen for these chapters, and it would not contribute substantially to an understanding of the interaction of personal experience and public demands in the modern apparitions, which is one of the basic goals of this study. It makes sense, therefore, to exclude Rue du Bac from the sequence of apparitions here investigated.

La Salette: The Experience, the Miracles, and the Prophecies

The apparition at La Salette, high in the French Alps near Grenoble, where in 1846 two shepherd children reported a single meeting with a figure assumed to be the Virgin Mary, was the first Marian apparition of modern times outside of a cloistered religious environment to attract widespread attention and to be officially "recognized" by Roman Catholic authorities. While the sources needed for a critical study of the seers' experience are not as abundant here as in the case of the later public serial apparitions, there is sufficient material at least to sketch the seers' experience and some biographical contexts for it. There is also a fair amount of material about the early miracles and prophecies through which public attention began to be drawn to this experience and to the site where it occurred.

François-Mélanie Mathieu, or Mélanie Calvat, was the older of the two seers of La Salette. She was born on 7 November 1831; her parents were Pierre Calvat (Mathieu) and Julie Bernaud, and she was the fourth of their ten children. Her father, reportedly, had no regular employment and worked variously as a day laborer, sawyer, and mason to support his large family. Little is known about Mélanie's early life, except that before her tenth birthday she had been sent out to work for the farmers of the region, and for the next four years she lived at her parents' home only during the winter. It was said that by the time of the apparition in the fall of 1846, when she was only fourteen, she was already a seasoned shepherdess.[2] Her employer at that time, Baptiste Pra, described her as extremely lazy, disobedient, and sullen, saying that she would not respond when spoken to and would often hide in the fields near the house all night.[3] Mélanie could not read, spoke only the dialect of the region, and understood French only imperfectly.

Just what kind of relationship the young Mélanie had with her family is difficult to establish, but it would seem that it was not particularly good. In her autobiographies she said that when she was very young she had been rejected by her mother, told that she was no longer a member of the family, and locked out of the house for days at a time. In these times of isolation, she said, she was kept company by her heavenly brother, Jesus.[4] Mélanie is given to hyperbole in her writings, and this must be taken into account when reading her description of mistreatment at the hands of her mother. It is clear, however, that as a child she was rejected and probably emotionally isolated, and as an adult her relationships with family members remained troubled and painful.

Pierre-Maximin Giraud was born on 26 or 27 August 1835, the fourth child of a wheelwright. His mother had died when he was just eighteen months old, and his father had remarried four months later. As Maximin was growing up, his father was reportedly absent from the family for long periods of time, either working or relaxing in the local tavern, and Maximin was, again according to report, made the object of family scorn and abused by his stepmother. Like Mélanie, Maximin could not read, and his father said that he had been able to teach him a few prayers only with a great deal of difficulty. He was described as a reckless child, an innocent without malice but also without foresight. In September 1846, Maximin had been indentured to Pierre Selme, a farmer at La Salette, to watch his cattle in the place of his regular shepherd, who had fallen ill.[5]

Although they lived in the same region, Maximin and Mélanie did not know each other and did not meet until one or two evenings before the experience that made them famous.[6] It was on a Saturday morning, 19 September 1846, that Mélanie and Maximin led their cattle up the slope of Mount Planteau, some distance above the village of La Salette. Each had four cattle, and Maximin also brought his dog and his father's goat. When they returned that evening, Mélanie went, as expected, to her employer's barns to return her cattle to the stable. Selme, however, who had been working in a field near where Maximin had been pasturing the cattle (so that he could keep an eye on his novice shepherd) had noticed something unusual about the boy's routine that day. He had not returned to the pasture as he was supposed to do after taking the cattle up the ravine for a drink, and when Selme saw Maximin that evening, he asked him about this. The boy, he recalled, said something like, "Then you don't know what happened!" and told him that he and Mélanie had seen a beautiful lady who had entertained them with conversation for a long time. Selme then took Maximin over to see Mélanie's employer, Pra, and in the presence of the two farmers Maximin repeated his story and Mélanie confirmed it.[7]

What had happened, according to the account which the children gave to their employers and to some other people as well during the next few days, took place a couple of hours after they had taken the cattle to drink at the "beasts' spring," which was up a small ravine on the southern slope of the mountain. They said that they had gone there after the Angelus had sounded, and while their cows rested they ate their lunch of bread and dry cheese and then went for a drink to the "people's spring" a little farther up the ravine. Three other shepherds joined them there for a few minutes before returning to their animals farther down the mountain. Mélanie and Maximin then returned to their own animals and settled down on the grass for a nap. They slept for about an hour, when Mélanie awoke, and seeing that their cattle were gone, she woke Maximin and they climbed to the top of a small knoll from which they could see their animals. When they returned to the spot where they had left their knapsacks, however, Mélanie saw a bright light, and when she called Maximin's attention to it, he came to her side and saw it too.

In several lengthy interviews about five months later with the Abbé François Lagier, a native of the region and curé of Saint-Pierre-de-Cherennes, Mélanie described in some detail what happened next.[8] She said that the light whirled a bit and seemed to turn on itself, rising to the height of a person. She began to make out an oval face and hands inside the light, but she couldn't see anything very clearly. She said she cried out, "Oh, my God!" and dropped her shepherd's stick, which prompted Maximin to say that they should both keep their sticks in hand. He said that he would give the figure "a good whack" if it tried to do anything to them.

Mélanie said that while neither she nor Maximin could make out what sort of person was in the light, they could see an oval face, hands, arms, and elbows, and while they couldn't see the rest of the figure, it seemed to be seated. Suddenly, then, it stood up and folded its arms across its breast. Mélanie said it looked like a woman because of the hands and face, but the manner of dress left them puzzled. The woman then came toward them, walking as if she were following the brook, and she began to speak, saying, "Come near, my children, don't be afraid! I am here to tell you great news."

On the day after the apparition, in an interview with the two employers and another man of the area, Mélanie reported in some detail the conversation she and Maximin had had with the woman, this account being substantially the same as those which both children gave in later interviews.[9] She said that the woman began to speak to them in French, issuing a warning that if her people would not submit, she would no longer be able to restrain the heavy hand of her son:

> For a long time I have suffered for you; if I do not want my son to abandon you, I am forced to pray to him myself without ceasing. You pay no heed. However much you would do, you could never recompense the pain I have taken for you.
>
> I have given you six days for work; I have reserved the seventh day for myself and no one will grant it to me. It is this which weighs down the hand of my son. Those who drive the carts cannot swear without introducing the name of my son. It is these two things which weigh down the hand of my son.
>
> If the harvest is spoiled, it is your fault. I warned you last year about the potatoes, but you have not heeded it. On the contrary, when you found the potatoes had spoiled you swore and you introduced the name of my son. They will continue this year so that by Christmas there will be none left.

At this point, Mélanie said, she was confused by the French word for potatoes (*pommes-de-terre*). She was about to ask Maximin what it meant when the woman said, "You do not understand, my children; I will say it in a different way," and she began then to speak in the local dialect.[10]

> If you have wheat, it is not good to sow it. All that you will sow, the beasts will eat, and that which remains the beasts will not dare to eat. In the upcoming year it will fall into dust.
>
> A great famine will come. Before the famine comes, the children under seven years of age will be seized by trembling and they will die in the hands of those who hold them.
>
> The others will do their penance in the famine. The walnuts will be worm-eaten and the grapes will rot. If they are converted, the stones and rocks will become heaps of wheat, and the potatoes will sow themselves in the fields (in the year that comes). In the summer only some old women go to Mass on Sunday and the rest work, and in winter the boys only want to go to Mass to mock religion. No one observes Lent; they go to the meat market like dogs.

Then, Mélanie said, the woman asked them if they said their prayers well. When they replied, "Not very well, Madame," she reportedly told them that they must pray in the evening and in the morning and must at least say an "Our Father" and a "Hail Mary," if they could not do better. The woman then asked them if they had seen spoiled wheat, and Maximin replied that he had not. The woman reminded him, however, that he had once seen some when he had gone to Coin with his father. Mélanie said that the woman then described that incident, and Maximin said that now he could remember it. The woman then said twice, in French, "Now, my children, make this known to my people."

Mélanie said that the woman then turned and crossed the brook and walked up the knoll and that she and Maximin followed her. When the woman reached the top of the knoll, she rose into the air and began to disappear, her head first, and then her arms and her feet. The two children then returned to pick up their knapsacks and locate their cattle.

In her interviews with Lagier early in 1847, Mélanie recounted her conversation with Maximin after the woman had risen into the air and mentioned several ideas they had had at the time about who the woman was. Mélanie said that she and Maximin had thought that perhaps the woman's rising into the air meant that she was a great saint.[11] She also told Lagier that when the woman had spoken about her son, she had thought that perhaps the woman had a husband who wanted to kill her son and that she had mentioned this then to Maximin: "If I hadn't seen her rise up into the air, I would have believed that it was some woman whose husband wanted to kill their children."[12] She also recalled that when Maximin had seen the woman weeping and had heard her say that the arm of her son was "so strong and heavy that she could no longer restrain it," Maximin had thought of a woman "whose son had beaten her and then left her." She said that Maximin had told her later that he had thought about telling the woman to be quiet and not to cry because they would help her, but that he had not said anything because the woman kept talking.[13] Maximin, in his one interview with Lagier, said only that he thought the woman could have been someone from the nearby town of Valjouffrey.[14]

Something of the personal contexts in which an apparition figure assumes meaning for a seer can often be discerned in the seer's initial thoughts about that figure's identity, and this would seem to be the case in these early reflections of the La Salette seers about the woman who had appeared to them. What is most striking here is Mélanie's (and perhaps also Maximin's) initial reference to situations of family violence. Both children were from troubled homes, and it seems safe to conclude that there was a connection between their own family experiences and this encounter with a weeping woman who spoke about restraining her son and about coming chastisements. Persons who understand La Salette as a supernatural event which the children have accurately reported might say that their family backgrounds simply gave them a special sensitivity to the woman and her message; the more skeptical might say that those backgrounds influenced the children's perception of the apparition; and still others might say, of course, that the apparition was nothing but a reflection of, and an attempt to come to terms with, those backgrounds.[15]

When the two children told their employers that evening about their encounter and conversation with the woman, they spoke only of a "beautiful lady." At that time, it seems, no one placed much stock in their story except the mother of Mélanie's employer, who suggested that the children had seen the Blessed Virgin.[16] This suggestion apparently led other members of the two families to take the children's story more seriously, for it was agreed that the next morning, Sunday, the children should tell their story to the parish priest. The elderly curé of La Salette, Abbé Jacques Perrin, was so impressed by the story that he used it as the basis for his homily that morning.[17] From that point on, word of the alleged apparition of the Virgin spread quickly through the area, and by that evening, Mélanie, who had remained with her employer while Maximin had returned to his father in Corps, was being subjected to the first of a long series of interviews.

In the Marian apparitions of the past two centuries, the initial identification of the apparition figure as the Virgin Mary by someone other than the seers is not uncommon and indeed is the general rule. Once this identification is made, reports of the apparition often spread very rapidly; the seers often become instant celebrities; and persons with an intense interest in the apparition, or persons in authority, move in quickly "to protect" the seers and to learn as much as they can about their experiences and their private lives.[18]

The site of the La Salette apparition soon became a focus of both curiosity and devotion for people in the region, and reports of miraculous events were not slow to follow. The best sources of information about early interest in the site are the letters of the Abbé Pierre Mélin, curé of Corps, to the bishop of Grenoble, Mgr. Philbert de Bruillard. Mélin, who interviewed Maximin perhaps a week after the apparition and made his first visit to the site a few days later, around September 28, was quickly captivated by the story of the two seers. He first wrote about the apparition to the bishop on October 4, and he then became the bishop's regular correspondent, keeping him well-informed about all that was being reported concerning the hallowed spot.[19]

In his first visit to the site, Mélin discovered that people were breaking up the rock on which the Virgin was thought to have been seated and had pulled out all the grass where she was thought to have walked. They were preserving all this debris, he wrote the bishop on October 4, with "religious respect." Mélin then immediately told his young sacristan, Felix Blane, and Maximin, to remove what remained of the rock and to take it back to the parish house at Corps.[20] There, according to an early pamphlet, he himself zealously guarded it.[21]

On October 12, Mélin wrote the bishop again, answering several questions that the bishop had raised. He added that the event was producing some marvelous effects: more people were coming to the Sunday offices, and more had begun to observe the Church's mandates with respect to work prohibited on Sundays. He reported, moreover, that a steady stream of visitors had been making their way up the mountain, stopping to pray along the path. He himself had now acquired, he said, both the rock that had been a seat for the Virgin and the two canvas knapsacks in which the young seers had carried their daily provisions. He assured the bishop, however, that he personally had seldom spoken of the apparition, either publicly or privately, so that the event itself and the children's very naive reports of it might have more effect.[22] Mélin, by this time, had apparently established himself as a sort of administrator of the supernatural at La Salette. His right to this position, however, as symbolized by his possession of the precious rock, was contested by the new priest at La Salette, and he was eventually forced to return most of the rock to the La Salette parish.[23]

The smaller pieces of the rock on which the Virgin was thought to have been seated were also highly prized, and one of these was associated with an event that was considered a miraculous proof of the apparition. Accounts of this event, differing only in minor details, are found in the private correspondence of some of the early visitors to the area and in some early brochures. In late October, two lieutenants passed through Corps with some military recruits. They had heard of the apparition, and at a local café they had occasion to meet and talk to Maximin. When they asked for a souvenir of the apparition site, Maximin said that he knew people who had pieces of the rock on which the Virgin had been seated. He then left the café and returned a few minutes later with a rock about the size of four fingers. One of the lieutenants was given a hammer to split the rock, and when it was broken, half of it was found to have been imprinted with the face of Christ, "in a manner that could not be mistaken." The face, according to some accounts, was in the style of the "Ecce Homo." The officer then made a rubbing of the face for the proprietress of the Café, which she then put on display. The accounts of the incident note that this event was witnessed by as many as thirty people.[24] Clearly, in the wake of the La Salette apparition, there was a great deal of interest in tangible and visible evidence of the presumed supernatural intervention.

The two seers themselves claimed to have had other extraordinary experiences at the site. Mélanie, for example, said that she had returned to the site on Monday, September 21, when she had taken her cattle up to pasture. She told Lagier that since people had said it was the Virgin that she and Maximin had seen, she had been eager to return and look around, but that now she could see nothing unusual. Before she left, however, she broke her stick in order to make a cross, which she erected at the place where the woman had risen into the air. The next day, as she was again taking her cattle up to pasture, one of them broke the cross. A little later, however, she returned and found that the cross was again standing upright with only a broken piece beside it.[25]

About three or four weeks after the apparition, Maximin and three or four other boys reportedly also went to the mountain to erect a cross there. As they approached the site, they said they saw in the distance a woman dressed in black whom they thought might have been one of the Sisters of Providence from Corps. When he returned to Corps, however, Maximin found that none of the sisters had been on the mountain that day, and this led him to conclude that he had seen no ordinary person but someone from "the other world," perhaps his deceased mother.[26]

While Church authorities gave little credence, finally, either to the miraculous face of Christ on the rock or to these later experiences of the seers on the mountain, many stories such as these apparently circulated in the aftermath of the apparition, along with many small tracts and pamphlets, spreading and strengthening belief in the site's miraculous powers. An engraved broadsheet from these years, for example, shows the Virgin and the two shepherd children surrounded by four smaller images depicting miracles associated with the site, one of which was the miraculous face and the other three, miracles of healing (see figure 1).[27]

Healing miracles in fact played an important part in the early spread of La Salette's reputation, but these were closely connected with La Salette's "miraculous spring" and should be seen in that context.

The story of the discovery of the miraculous spring illustrates how, in the immediate aftermath of the children's experience, perceptions of the supernatural began to take shape around the apparition site itself. There were several springs that fed the little brook where the shepherds led their animals to drink, some of which flowed only after a rain. Mélanie and Maximin had agreed that they had seen no spring at the spot where they had placed their knapsacks, taken a nap, and then spoken with the woman. They also, apparently, had seen no water at this site when they returned to it after following the woman up onto the knoll. It is unclear whether anyone visited the site on Sunday, September 20, but Mélanie told Lagier that it had rained that day and that that was why she had not returned to the site until Monday. It was then that she first noticed the spring at the very spot where she and Maximin and spoken with the woman. She said that she told her employer, Pra, about the spring that evening, asking him if there had been a spring there before, and that he said he was not sure of the spot but would go up with her someday to look at it.[28]

Pra, however, told Lagier that he had gone up the mountain on Monday and that he saw the spring at that time. He said that he remembered a spring being there before but that when he had been there on the preceding Friday, he had noted that it was then dry. While he agreed with Mélanie that it had rained that Sunday, he didn't think that it had rained enough to account for the water that he saw there afterwards.[29]

In any case this spring now flowed quite regularly, and the idea that it should have curative powers seems to have occurred very quickly to persons inclined to believe in the apparition, including the Abbé Mélin. Indeed, Mélin acted as the catalyst for one of the first cures associated with the spring's water.

In a letter written to the bishop several months after the apparition, Mélin recounted the healing of his friend, Madame Aglot, a member of a leading family of Grenoble, who had become bedridden and could not retain any food.[30] Shortly after he had visited the site of the apparition, Mélin said, it had occurred to him that he should take some water from the spring back to his friend, because he knew of "her faith and merit." He had already begun his descent of the mountain, however, and so he commissioned Maximin and another boy traveling with him to return to the spring to fill the bottle with water. Apparently, Mélin told them to deliver the water to him later that day at Corps, and when the two boys reached Corps, according to him, they were seen by a cousin of Madame Aglot who asked them what they were carrying. When she learned that it was water from the apparition site, she apparently told Madame Aglot about it immediately, for a few minutes later the cousin came to Mélin's house seeking some of the water at the request of the invalid, who said that she "thought it would do her some good."

Madame Aglot drank the water in the course of praying a novena, Mélin said, and after the nine days she joined her family at the table and ate without indisposition. Mélin said that this was the first bottle of water brought from the spring to Corps, suggesting that the practice soon caught on, and he told the bishop that he had been all the more impressed with what had transpired because he had not yet said anything to anyone in Corps about why he had had the water brought there.

A healing was also reported in connection with Maximin's first return to the mountainside about a week after the apparition. Maximin's father had apparently charged his stepmother to examine the site to see if anyone might have hidden there and deceived the two children. On this occasion, therefore, Maximin was accompanied by four persons, including his maternal grandfather, his stepmother, and a cousin who had been disfigured by an eye disease associated with smallpox. Maximin led them to the site and there told them the story of the apparition. Then, reportedly, the fifth member of the group, a young woman, told Maximin's cousin that she should wash her eyes with water from the spring. Two days later, it was said, Maximin's cousin was healed.[31]

It was not till early the following year (1847) that an account of this girl's healing appeared in some literature relating the story of the apparition and extolling the site's supernatural qualities, and by this time several other very similar miracles had been reported. An inhabitant of Corps, writing to his brother late in November of 1846, noted that more than fifteen people with eye diseases who had washed with water from the spring had been healed. More specifically, he said that his brother-in-law, who had lost his sight as a result of smallpox, had washed his eyes in the water and had been healed two or three days later.[32] A similar healing was claimed in connection with a pilgrimage to La Salette of the Confraternity of the Penitents of Corps on November 28. On this pilgrimage, it was said, sight was restored to a ten-year-old child who had been blind for two years after contracting smallpox.[33]

A particularly well known healing attributed to La Salette's water was that of Marie Laurent, of Corps. She had been disabled for some twenty-three years, suffering first from rheumatic pains and then from injuries incurred by falls, and for about sixteen years she had been unable to move without crutches. She reportedly made some soup from water drawn from the spring and drank this each day during a novena, which she began on November 17. By November 24, she felt well enough, it was said, to go to confession without her crutches, and the next day, to Communion. Mélin, in reporting this cure to the bishop on December 2, said that at that time the woman was still weak but that she was so pleased with her recovery that she was forgetting to eat.[34]

Many of La Salette's healings, particularly those that were said to have occurred at the site itself, were associated with mass pilgrimages involving very large numbers of people, and this suggests that psychological factors could have played a considerable part in these healings. Particularly significant were the pilgrimages of the Confraternity of the Penitents of Corps. A pilgrimage of this group, for example, reportedly brought about seven hundred people to the mountain on November 17, the day Marie Laurent had begun her novena, Mélin noting that the group had included her that day in their petitions. About a thousand people reportedly made the pilgrimage with this group on November 28, the day on which the healing of the blind child was said to have taken place. Another healing grew out of this occasion: that of a woman who had been suffering from dropsy. Something of what one might call the dark side of the supernatural was noted in connection with this incident. In gratitude for her cure, according to the account, the woman removed the cross from her rosary and hung it on the cross which had been set up at the apparition site. As the pilgrims were leaving, however, a man took her cross, ostensibly to prevent it from being stolen. On the way down the mountain this man injured his foot, and people saw in this a divine chastisement for his act of sacrilege.[35]

Another story suggesting that sacrilege with respect to La Salette could have dire consequences grew up around the tragic death of a young girl on November 27. Her mother, people said, wanted to go on a pilgrimage to La Salette but her father had responded to this with an outburst of anger. One account attributed to him the statement, "The Virgin was a woman like other women." His wife reportedly warned him to mend his evil ways, lest he bring misfortune on them. It was not long after that their daughter fell into a pot of boiling water. It was said that her father immediately saw the hand of God at work in this tragedy, and the day after the burial he and his wife were both on the mountain asking pardon from the Virgin.[36] Stories such as these may have led some persons already favorably inclined toward the apparition to take it more seriously, but they also led many others to think that what was happening at La Salette was little more than superstition and clerical manipulation.

Mélin's correspondence with Bishop Bruillard testifies to the rather rapid growth of interest in the apparition site. Some of the mass-pilgrimages and alleged healings that took place on the mountain eight to ten weeks after the apparition have already been noted, and Mélin's letters make it clear that the stream of visitors to La Salette had begun some weeks before then. Mélin wrote to the bishop on November 4, about six weeks after the apparition, that he was being inundated with letters unaccompanied by return postage and that the Corps parish was flooded with pilgrims. In the preceding three weeks, he said, he himself had played host to more than fifty people, and he complained that he did not have the resources to cover the necessary expenses. He estimated that from the date the apparition had occurred, two or three hundred people had visited the site and three or four hundred had questioned the children.[37]

It should be noted here that while many of those who interviewed Mélanie and Maximin were not impressed with their general demeanor, finding them lacking in manners and refinement, it was often reported that when they spoke about their experiences, they were transformed and seemed to speak with simplicity, seriousness, and a "certain religious respect."[38] Clearly, the children were acquiring the aura of the age-old motif of the humble shepherds blessed with a holy visitation.

Two weeks later, on November 18, Mélin wrote the bishop that six or seven hundred pilgrims had climbed the mountain in the preceding week alone, a figure that apparently did not include the six or seven hundred who had made the mass pilgrimage the day before. "The mountain seems to lower itself," Mélin wrote to the bishop, "and the difficulties disappear. Children, old men, old women, pregnant women, all rush up there, arriving sweating and panting, drinking at the spring, and descend again joyous and content. Their prayers and their confidence purify the water; it has harmed no one."[39]

Mélin was certainly one of the most enthusiastic proponents of the apparition and the devotions taking shape around it. If there were those who strongly disagreed with his endorsements, they chose, for several months at least, not to make a public issue of their dissent. When, early in 1847, criticism did begin to surface in the public media, it was criticism not so much of the apparition itself and its credibility as of how it was being reported and used by the clergy.

On November 26, a Lyon anticlerical journal had printed a brief and rather neutral account of the alleged apparition which noted, in closing, that a Lyon priest had written to La Salette asking to be informed about the truth of the matter.[40] On 27 January 1847, however, an article appeared in this journal which maintained that the exploitation of the supposed miracle was instilling panic in the imagination of the rural populace and which lamented that neither civil nor ecclesiastical authority thought it appropriate to suppress such a disturbance. Accompanying the article was the letter to the editor that had apparently prompted it. The writers of the letter had heard the apparition extolled from a Lyon pulpit, with quotations from the prophecies reported by the children, and they were concerned that these prophecies were frightening the least-enlightened part of the populace, fomenting unrest among those already overwhelmed by economic distress. The journal, they said, should publicize the facts about the apparition, in order to counteract the rumors being propagated by Church authorities and the abuses that sprang from these rumors.[41]

Particularly disturbing to the writers of this letter were two of the prophecies supposedly reported by the children: that the potatoes would rot before Christmas and that it was useless to sow wheat because it would be eaten by insects or fall into dust. The 1840s had seen a famine in Europe, which by the fall of 1846 had reached southeastern France, bringing serious food shortages and high prices. The writers of the letter were saying that in such a situation, these prophecies could be very disruptive.

An article in a Parisian newspaper on 16 February 1847, which mentioned La Salette along with two other reported miracles, made virtually the same point.[42] La Salette had caused a great stir in the provinces, the article said; then citing the same two prophecies, it observed that these had added to the disquiet created by the food shortages. There was a community of women at Montpellier, the article continued, who believed that since a famine was inevitable, they should accustom themselves to not eating, and as a result, in the course of several days the rations distributed to them had been considerably reduced. One of the women, reportedly, could not adapt to the discipline and had chosen to leave the community to await the famine. This sort of thing could become contagious, the article suggested, and there was a need, certainly, for a more solid foundation in such matters. The article noted, finally, that the bishop of Grenoble had ordered an investigation of La Salette, but that thus far the commission had been able to find no proof for the event.

There was some firm support for how the Church was dealing with La Salette from the pro-Catholic sector of the public media. On 9 January 1847, for example, a Lyon "legitimist" journal, the *Gazette*, printed a response to the critical article that had appeared two days earlier in the anticlerical journal of that city.[43] The editors of the *Gazette* wrote that they did not consider themselves commissioned to control miracles, whether genuine or pretended, nor to decide whether a miracle was authentic or contrived. This was a matter for ecclesiastical authority, which had always shown itself prudent and wise in these matters. As Catholics, the editors said, they believed in the miracles described in the lives of the saints, and they believed that others were possible. The latter were rare, however, and merited confidence only when verified and attested by the bishop, which did not mean, however, that belief in them was obligatory. The editors of the *Gazette* took pains to distinguish the apparition itself from the two prophecies that were being cited as stirring up the populace. In the accounts of the apparition that they had heard or read, they said, there was nothing about potatoes rotting before Christmas, and in the accounts that were deemed most genuine, nothing ridiculous. The bishop of Grenoble had acted prudently in having already established two commissions to investigate the apparition, and these commissions had concluded that thus far nothing had been proved. Moreover, the bishop had quite properly warned his clergy not to become too involved in the piety surrounding the apparition.

While papers such as the *Gazette* sought to make La Salette more palatable by excising the most troubling of the apocalyptic prophecies that were being associated with it, others were adding to the list of these prophecies. In an article appearing on 16 January 1847, the *Journal de Rennes* reported that the Virgin had announced to the children four great chastisements for the year 1847—war, disease, famine, and floods—and that these prophecies had been widely accepted by the inhabitants of Corps. This article was reprinted in two other journals later in the month.[44] While there were, in fact, no prophecies of war or flood in any of the accounts of the messages given by the children, these prophecies no doubt seemed to many a natural extension of what was in these accounts. It is hard to avoid the conclusion, moreover, that it was the association of La Salette with such prophecies that had finally led newspapers throughout France, in January and February of 1847, to bring La Salette to the attention of the nation as a whole.[45]

Meanwhile, at least one of the commissions which the bishop of Grenoble had appointed to investigate the apparition had been having its own problems with the prophecies delivered by the children. In the first of its reports, issued on 15 December 1846, this commission, consisting of professors from the seminary at Grenoble, raised but did not answer a number of questions about these prophecies. Did the lady really announce that there would be no more potatoes at Christmas, and did she actually mean to forbid planting wheat? Did she mean that all children would die as they are "seized by trembling" or only a great number? Did she mean that adults would die from hunger or only that they would suffer from hunger? What was the time frame of the prophecies, and to what geographical area or areas did they refer? And what was the meaning of the promise that if people were converted the rocks would turn into wheat and the potatoes would plant themselves?[46]

As newspapers both publicized and lamented the effects of the prophecies associated with La Salette and as Church officials struggled to understand the prophecies that the children had indeed reported, secular authorities made some attempts to check the spread of interest in the apparition that was legitimating these prophecies. Some brochures containing accounts and depictions of La Salette, for example, were confiscated by government officials.[47] It was not a time, however, for keeping such things in check. The year in which the La Salette prophecies began to spread throughout France was the year before the revolution of 1848 and the end of the so-called July Monarchy, and the Church that was to emerge in the first years of the Second Republic with an improved official status was a Church that knew how to build on popular needs and interests to consolidate its support and authority. Thus, while the appointed commissions continued for several years after the 1848 revolution to ponder the difficulties of the La Salette apparition, and while very strong opposition to its cult had developed among some of the French clergy,[48] on 19 September 1851, the fifth anniversary of the event, Bishop Bruillard issued a statement formally authorizing devotion at the site and the continued publication of the story of the apparition and its accompanying messages.

France's woes were not yet over, and in the years that followed, the La Salette prophecies continued to be publicized and to create controversy, somewhat overshadowing the fact that the site had originally attracted attention and had become a popular place of pilgrimage because of its miraculous healing spring. This spring, however, was not forgotten by French Catholics, who a few years later would begin to travel to another source of the Virgin's healing waters in the south of France, one which would eventually eclipse La Salette as a pilgrimage shrine.

The Church's formal recognition of the La Salette apparition in 1851 marked the point, according to later Roman Catholic interpreters, at which the supernatural mission of the two children was assumed by the Church itself. This meant that from that time on, Mélanie and Maximin were to be regarded as ordinary persons with no special gifts or powers, whose subsequent lives, views, and visions (should there be any more) should cast no aspersions on, nor affect the understanding of, the apparition for which they had once been the instruments. Some of the events that led up to this remarkable determination will be described in a later chapter, where the so-called secrets of Mélanie and Maximin will be discussed in some detail. It will suffice here to give only a very brief sketch of the seers' later lives.

About two months after their encounter with the "beautiful lady," Mélanie and Maximin, with the authorization of Bishop Bruillard, were both taken from their homes and enrolled in the school of the Sisters of Providence at Corps.[49] Maximin attempted several careers, ranging from liquor dealer to priest, only to find himself unsuited for any of them. He spent the summer of 1874 in ill health, living on the charity of the new sanctuary of La Salette, and died there on 1 March 1875.[50] Mélanie lived an unsettled and unhappy, but very eventful, life in various convents in France, England, and Italy and became the focus of attention of a small but influential group of followers with a distinctive political and religious orientation. She found herself increasingly at odds, however, with Roman Catholic officials, particularly after the publication in 1879 of her "secret." She died at Altamura, Italy, on the night of 14–15 December 1904.[51]

Mélanie and Maximin, in the years immediately following the apparition, were apparently not seen by the public as saints in the traditional sense, that is, as persons who were thought even from an early age to have manifested special abilities or to have lived in an aura of the miraculous.[52] As people sought to get in touch with and to appropriate their presumably miraculous experience, the seers did, however, come under intense public scrutiny, and the many days of questioning and interviews to which they were subjected set a pattern which was repeated as people sought to understand later public apparitions where crowds gathered around the visionaries during their experience. There was one feature, however, of the way in which the experience of the La Salette seers had been appropriated by others that gave Church officials pause and was not repeated in the Church's dealing with subsequent apparitions. The charges of manipulation and exploitation that were directed against the local clergy who were the earliest supporters of La Salette led Church authorities and most clergy to take a more cautious and reserved approach to such reports in the future.[53]

Lourdes: The Background and the Ecstasies of a Young Saint

In 1858 at Lourdes, France, in the foothills of the Pyrennees, the young Bernadette Soubirous reported a series of appearances of a young woman who quickly came to be seen as the Virgin Mary. Today, because of the immense popularity of Lourdes as a pilgrimage site and because its seer is a canonized saint, Bernadette's experience is probably the best known and most studied of all modern Marian apparitions. This is not to say, however, that what transpired at Lourdes is in general well understood, or that it has been adequately studied from the standpoint of the phenomenology of religion or as a mode of religious experience. Almost all published accounts of the Lourdes phenomenon are very selective with respect to the materials presented, and many contain a number of statements that stand in rather clear contradiction to the earliest sources. The extensive edited collections of these sources, moreover, must themselves be used very carefully, since, as is common with such collections, the editors have arranged and annotated the materials in accord with their own apologetic assumptions.

While the La Salette and Lourdes apparitions were separated by only twelve years and arose in somewhat similar environments, there were some significant differences. The most important of these is that while the La Salette apparition was single and private, the Lourdes apparition was serial and public. Bernadette had a series of ecstatic experiences at a specific site, all but the earliest of which came at more or less predictable times and were witnessed by others, and some of the latest of which were witnessed by a great number of people.

Bernadette (Marie Bernarde) Soubirous was born at Lourdes on 7 January 1844, the first child of François Soubirous and Louise Castérot. Bernadette's early life, like that of her parents, would seem to have been characterized chiefly by misfortune, ill health, and poverty. Almost all of the extant materials pertaining to her early life and the life of her family, however, represent a selection which has probably been governed more by hagiographic than by strictly historical interests, and thus an attitude of reserve is called for with respect to the conclusions toward which these materials seem to point.

Shortly before Bernadette's first birthday, her mother, who was then only eighteen, became unable to nurse her, and Bernadette was sent to a farm at Bartrès, near Lourdes, where Marie Laguës, whose infant son had recently died, took charge of her and kept her until April 1846. While Bernadette's mother later told an investigator simply that she had suffered a change in health and that despite her willingness to do so, she could no longer nurse the child herself,[54] devotional accounts of Bernadette's life embellish this occasion with an incident that functions as a sort of introduction to the family's misfortunes and that sounds as if it could have been concocted by the writer of a dime novel. Her mother was dozing in a corner by the fireplace, it was said, when a resin candle fell on her, igniting her clothes and burning her breasts.[55]

François and Louise Soubirous, shortly after their marriage, moved in with Louise's mother and sisters so that François could help run the Castérot family mill. While they seem to have fared rather well there at first, their fortunes reportedly declined with changing circumstances, accidents, illness (Bernadette developed chronic asthma), and the births of three more children, and soon they were both reduced to working as day laborers at various menial tasks, while Bernadette cared for her younger siblings. She and her sister Marie (or Toinette) also gathered wood, scrap iron, and bones, the sale of which helped support the family. At about the age of twelve, she lived for a while with her Aunt Bernarde, caring for her aunt's children, and then again with her one-time nurse at Bartrès, where she cared for the children, tended the sheep, and did other chores.[56]

At about this time, in the spring of 1857, Bernadette's family, who by now were, according to the accounts, rather well known for their indigence, were turned out of their rented lodgings, and no one was very anxious to take them in. François, however, had a cousin who leased and lived in the building that had housed what was once the town jail. His cousin's family lived on the second floor, below which was a room known as the *cachot* (dungeon) that had been abandoned by the city some thirty years earlier because of its unhealthiness. It was described in a report of March 1858 as a "foul, somber hovel," looking out on a courtyard filled with trash and poultry manure. François's cousin had been renting it to itinerant Spaniards, and he admitted that he was reluctant to let the Soubirous live there, fearing that he would end up providing them not only with lodging but also with food. Nonetheless, since they were "out on the street," he agreed to take them in.[57]

It is not easy in matters relating to the Soubirous' poverty at this time to separate fact from pious fiction. In the aftermath of the apparition, some of the inhabitants of Lourdes told stories that clearly romanticized both the poverty of Bernadette's family and their own generosity towards them. Two of these stories involved Bernadette's younger brother, Jean-Marie. One of the earliest enthusiasts of the apparition, Emmanuélite Estrade, said that during the winter of 1856–1857, she had been praying in church when she saw a little boy scraping candle wax from the floor and eating it. She had asked the boy why he was doing this, suggesting that he was hungry and might prefer something else, and had then taken him to her home and fed him on the landing of the stairs, since he was reluctant to enter the house. During the fortnight of the apparition, she said, when she saw Bernadette with members of her family, she recognized the little boy she had fed the preceding winter as Jean-Marie.[58] Questioned about this incident decades later, Jean-Marie disavowed any knowledge of it, and with some irritation he called the suggestion that as a child he had ever eaten wax "absurd."[59]

In a similar vein, the wife of the Lourdes police commissioner recalled that when her five-year-old daughter had completed her first knitting project, a pair of white stockings, she had told her daughter to give them to the first poor child to come along "even if it's a Spaniard." Her daughter went down to the street, she said, and immediately saw Bernadette, leading by the hand one of her little brothers. Thus the little Soubirous boy supposedly became the recipient of the stockings. There were also other simpler and less romantic stories, however, which testified to the Soubirous' poverty; it was recalled, for example, that the women of Lourdes and Bartrès sometimes gave Bernadette wheat bread, fruit, and potatoes.[60]

It is clear that by this time, if not earlier, the Soubirous were regarded by the more settled and more influential residents of Lourdes as representatives of a marginal class, whose activities, values, and general demeanor were poorly understood and often suspect. In March 1857, a Lourdes baker reported the theft of two sacks of flour and told authorities that he believed the thief to be François Soubirous. The baker told the prosecutor that François had worked for him hauling flour the previous September and that at that time he had no reason to complain about his integrity. François's present "miserable state," however, suggested to him that he had been responsible for the recent theft. On March 27, François was arrested and jailed for theft, not of the flour but of a wooden plank that authorities had found during a search of the Soubirous' premises and that François said he had picked up while gathering sticks on his way home from Bartrès.[61] On April 4, he was released from jail "for humanitarian reasons," and the charges against him were eventually dropped.[62]

About a year later, the Lourdes prosecutor commented on the presence of Bernadette's parents at an episode of the apparition in a way that illustrates very well the bourgeois class-prejudice against the Soubirous that appears in many of the early records. His comments also show, however, how this prejudice could highlight contrasts that might—if one failed to pick up a sarcastic tone—be mistaken for awe and give impetus to hagiography. He spoke of the Soubirous as "miserable people" and said that "their language, especially their habits and their reputation" were such as to "destroy the charm [of the story that the Virgin was appearing]," inspiring "not only doubt but disgust." These were, he said, "the very vile intermediaries for the one who is regarded as pure being *par excellence.*"[63]

In January 1858, Bernadette rejoined her family in the *cachot* at Lourdes. There were apparently two reasons why she left her work with the Laguës family at Bartrès. First, Marie Laguës had apparently treated her harshly, and the situation had worsened after the death of the Laguës' youngest child in December 1857. Second, Bernadette, who was then fourteen, had not yet completed catechism lessons or made her First Communion, and it was said that one of the conditions for her employment with the Laguës family had been that she attend the lessons offered by the Bartrès parish priest. Marie Laguës, however, had decided not to send Bernadette to these lessons and had attempted to teach her the catechism herself. This arrangement was not very successful, however, and Marie had concluded that Bernadette was stupid and incapable of memorizing her lessons. Thus, Bernadette left Bartrès ostensibly in order to attend catechism lessons and make her First Communion at Lourdes.[64]

The first written account of Bernadette's early experiences at the grotto near Lourdes was made by the Lourdes police commissioner, Jean Dominique Jacomet, on 21 February 1858, ten days after the commencement of those experiences on February 11. Jacomet had stopped Bernadette as she was leaving the parish church after vespers and had taken her to his apartment, where, in the presence of several witnesses, he asked her to tell her story. Jacomet took notes as she spoke and then used them to compile a brief account of her experiences, an account which gives only a few details and little information about the contexts in which those experiences took place.

Bernadette told Jacomet that her experiences began on Thursday, February 11, a market day at Tarbes, as she was gathering bones along the shore of the river with a friend, Jeanne Baloume (Abadie) and her own sister Marie (Toinette). Before she had crossed the channel near Madame Lafitte's mill, Bernadette said, she heard a very loud rustling in the hedge above the grotto called Massabeille. She looked up and saw the hedge moving and something white behind it. This "something white" had the shape of a young girl, which in subsequent statements Bernadette called *aquerò*, a local dialect term meaning "that one." She stared at it for a moment and then knelt down and began to pray. *Aquerò* smiled at her, she said, and then disappeared into the grotto. Just then her companions appeared on the other side of the river, and she asked them if they had seen anything. They said they had not, and when they asked her what she had seen she replied that it was nothing and set about gathering wood. A short time later, however, when she was alone with her sister, she told her about her vision, and later that afternoon she also told her friend Jeanne. When Bernadette told the story at home, she said her mother told her it was undoubtedly a dream, and her Aunt Romaine said it was an illusion.[65]

Bernadette's next experience, according to Jacomet's account, was on Sunday, February 14. After the High Mass, she had returned to the grotto with several young girls, including her sister Marie, two of them having taken a bottle of holy water from the church. Bernadette said that when they arrived at the grotto they knelt down and were saying the Rosary when *aquerò* appeared to her again above the grotto's entrance. Jeanne Baloume, who had followed at a distance and had stopped above the grotto, then threw a stone which frightened the other girls and caused them to run away. Bernadette said she was going to ask *aquerò* if she was there on behalf of God or on behalf of the devil, but she said the figure disappeared before she could do this.[66]

After vespers that evening, according to Bernadette, she described everything she had seen that day to a local woman who had come to see her. Then, on Monday, she spoke about her experiences with the superior of the hospice, where she had begun to attend a school for indigent girls, and with one of the sisters. Bernadette said that both of them told her that her vision was only an illusion.[67]

On Tuesday, February 16, according to Jacomet's account, Madame Millet, a well-known resident of Lourdes, sought Bernadette out and listened to her story, and the two of them then made plans to go to the grotto the next Sunday morning. Millet, however, reportedly couldn't wait that long, and on Thursday morning, February 18, she and her assistant came to the *cachot*. Bernadette said that the three of them went to the grotto, knelt, and recited the Rosary, and that then *aquerò* appeared to her again and made a sign for her to approach. Millet told Bernadette to give *aquerò* the paper and pen she had brought along so that she could show by writing what she had said to her. *Aquerò* said, however, that this was not necessary, and she then told Bernadette "to have the grace to go to see her for fifteen days." At Millet's request, Bernadette asked *aquerò* if Millet's presence was appropriate; *aquerò* replied that it was not too disagreeable. Millet then took Bernadette home with her, and Bernadette ate and slept there for the next two days. Bernadette told Jacomet, however, that she had since returned to her own home because her aunt didn't want her staying with Millet.[68]

In her early discussions of her experiences at the grotto, Bernadette consistently referred to the figure of her vision as *aquerò*. Others, however, speculated about more specific possibilities. Millet, for example, thought that it might be Elisa Latapie, a child about Bernadette's age who had died the previous October. Elisa had been a devout member of the Children of Mary and had impressed many of the people of Lourdes by her piety. Bernadette had described the figure of her vision as being about her own age, wearing a white dress with a blue waistband and carrying a rosary on her arm. This description, Millet thought, seemed to fit Elisa, and it was apparently her desire to confirm this that led her to accompany Bernadette to the grotto on February 18. What Bernadette said about *aquerò* that day, however, led Millet to dismiss her initial idea that the figure was Elisa.[69]

It is not clear from the documents just who first concluded that *aquerò* was the Virgin Mary. Bernadette, following *aquerò*'s reported instructions, went to the grotto each morning of the fortnight from February 18 to March 4 around seven o'clock and reported appearances of the figure on all but three of these days. The number of people accompanying her increased each day. By the time the first article about her experiences appeared in the local weekly (perhaps on February 22), it was clear that many people understood the figure whom Bernadette was seeing as the Virgin and thought that Bernadette herself suggested this identification.[70]

According to this newspaper article, Bernadette, on the occasion of her first experience, had called to her two companions, "See! See this lady dressed in white! She comes to speak to me. This is the Mother of Angels. There can be nothing for me on this earth; she has promised me a place in the kingdom of the elect if I come each morning for fifteen days to offer her my prayers in this same place!" Her companions, it was said, had then hurried to tell their parents the words of the poor visionary. The article noted, however, that there were a thousand versions of this story in circulation. Each morning now, in any case, the young girl was going to the grotto, a candle in hand, accompanied by more than five hundred people. This event, the article continued, which had so piqued the curiosity of the Lourdes populace, was thought to be nothing less than an apparition of the Holy Virgin. There was also another opinion in circulation, however, which, to judge from the article's introduction, was the opinion favored by the author: that the young visionary was afflicted with catalepsy.

Evidently Bernadette did basically the same things on her morning visits to the grotto during the fortnight following February 18 as she had done on the morning of her first encounter with *aquerò*. She left Lourdes about six o'clock, walked to the grotto carrying a candle, knelt down, lit the candle, and began to pray the Rosary. According to the second article in the local newspaper, which appeared sometime toward the end of that fortnight, Bernadette was stiff and unmoving during her ecstasies, her eyes open and fixed on a spot just above the grotto. Her lips sometimes moved as if to speak, and she sometimes leaned forward as if to salute her vision; sometimes she smiled, and sometimes her eyes were moist. When she was ready to leave, the article said, she might make a sign, at which the crowd, now estimated to be between eight hundred and twelve hundred people, would kneel. Those who were most impressed by Bernadette agreed that during her ecstasies her body was immobile and her gaze fixed, but they commented also on her pallor and her pose, and they noted that her few movements, such as making the sign of the cross, were made with vivacity or grace.[71]

According to the newspaper accounts and even the observations of the local priest, many and perhaps most of the people who accompanied Bernadette to the grotto or sought her out at the *cachot* early in this fifteen-day period already saw and treated her as if she were a saint. When she held up her rosary during one of the earlier episodes of the apparition sequence, those in the crowd who had rosaries held them up also. When she left the grotto, many people tried to kiss her, and many who could not do so reportedly scraped up earth from her path and kissed this instead. Bernadette had become for the masses, the local paper concluded, "the interpreter if . . . not the image of a superior power."[72]

Of the apparition episodes that Bernadette reported during this period, those on February 25, March 2, and March 4 were especially important. On February 25, the crowd watched as Bernadette crawled on her hands and knees to the back of the grotto, where she dug in the ground and uncovered some muddy water. After several tries, she managed to drink some of it and smeared some on her face. When asked to explain her actions, she said that *aquerò* had directed her to drink at the spring and to wash in it.[73] Later that day, some people dug deeper at the spot where Bernadette had been digging, found a spring there, and took bottles of the water back to Lourdes, suspecting it of possessing special powers. By March 4, when Antoine Clarens, a cousin by marriage of Bernadette's father, wrote one of the first lengthy accounts of the events at the grotto, cures were being attributed to water from this spring, and many people were carrying away samples of it.[74]

In preparing his account, Clarens had interviewed Bernadette at length on February 28, and one of the questions he had asked her at that time was whether she had been given some mission. Her reply had been, "No, not yet," but two days later, on March 2, in the presence of an estimated sixteen hundred people gathered at the grotto, Bernadette reportedly received her mission: *aquerò* directed her, she said, to go to the priests and tell them that a chapel should be built there, and that people should come there in procession.[75]

The directive to have a shrine erected at the site of a heavenly being's visitation is an ancient motif which, not surprisingly, is often explicit in premodern reports of Marian apparitions remembered and preserved as a result of their association with the establishment of local shrines. In these reports, the effort of a seer to convey this directive to persons in a position to implement it and to convince them of its authenticity is often a *leitmotif* of the shrine-establishment drama. At Lourdes, this motif emerged in the guise of a "mission" that seemed to involve something more than the building of a shrine, and this expansion of the seer's role helped set the stage for the various missions claimed by and for the seers of Marian apparitions in the twentieth century.

Immediately after the episode of the apparition on March 2, Bernadette went to the local rectory accompanied by her aunts Basile and Bernarde. Her Aunt Basile reported some years later that the curé of the parish, Dominique Peyramale, gave them a rather hostile reception. He called Bernadette a liar, she recalled, and complained that it was unfortunate to have a family in the town that created such disorder. Bernadette managed to tell him that *aquerò* wanted a procession, but nothing else.[76]

Because she had conveyed only part of the message that *aquerò* had given her, Bernadette returned to the rectory again that evening. Since no member of her own family wanted to go with her, she was accompanied on this occasion by a sister of her father's employer, Dominiquette Cazenave. There were several priests at the rectory that evening, including Bernadette's confessor, Abbé Pomain. According to Dominiquette, Bernadette told them about *aquerò*'s request for a chapel and was in turn questioned by them, and Peyramale instructed Bernadette to ask *aquerò* her name. Either this evening or the next, Peyramale also reportedly told Bernadette to ask *aquerò* to make the rosebush in the grotto bloom—presumably a miracle that would be at once recognized as attributable only to the Virgin. As they left the rectory, Dominiquette recalled, Bernadette told her that she was content because she had fulfilled her mission. Dominiquette said she too urged Bernadette to ask the lady her name, because without it the chapel would not be built.[77]

It was during the apparition episodes of March 3 and 4 that Bernadette said she asked *aquerò* to state her name and to make the rose bush bloom. But, she said, *aquerò* only smiled at her each time and repeated her request for a chapel. When she told this to Peyramale, he told her that *aquerò* was playing with her.[78] He asked her if she had the money for the chapel, and when Bernadette said that she did not, he said that he did not either and that she should tell the lady to give it to her.[79]

Estimates of the crowd on March 4, the final day of the prescribed fortnight, ranged from five thousand to twenty thousand people. Many had come that day, it seems, in anticipation of a miracle, for a rumor was circulating that Bernadette had predicted "a revelation of the Virgin" on that day.[80] Many apparently also expected that everyone present on the occasion would be able to see and hear the Virgin themselves. Others hoped that in response to Peyramale's request, *aquerò* would reveal her name and that the rose bush would bloom. A reporter for one of the major newspapers was not very favorably impressed by the piety and credulity of the crowd that day. He noted that all streets, paths, mounds and fields from which one could see the "mysterious grotto" were literally covered with people. Above the din of the crowd, he said, one could sometimes hear piercing cries, dares, insults, invocations, and prayers. In the swarm of humanity there was a woman worried about her crinolines being crushed by peasants and a man ready to avenge himself for having his foot stepped on. The trees were full of urchins gamboling about like monkeys, and the police were powerless to keep order. Such was the conduct of the people, he observed, when Bernadette finally appeared and the cry was heard, "There is the saint! There is the saint!"[81]

Persons who observed Bernadette's actions at the grotto on March 4 reported little that differed from her actions on previous days: she knelt, lit her candle, began to pray the Rosary, stopped praying for a time while staring at a spot above the grotto, then resumed the Rosary, blew out her candle, rose, and departed. On her way out, however, she stopped to embrace Eugénie Troy, a partially blind child from Barèges. According to the newspaper account, when pressed for what she had seen and heard that day, she said that she had seen the same thing as before: a pretty lady wearing a white dress with a blue sash and with yellow shoes. The lady had not spoken, she said, because she was angry with people's disbelief.

While there were no reports that day of the specific signs that Peyramale had requested or that others had expected, rumors of other signs and wonders did circulate in the crowd, testifying to the emergence of a schema of expectation and fulfillment built around "signs," the kind of schema that would come into play in most subsequent serial Marian apparitions as well. Some said that a dove had hovered over Bernadette's head during her ecstasy that day. Others observed Bernadette's embrace of Eugénie Troy and said that the young seer, by breathing on the child's eyes, had restored her sight. Others said she had healed a child whose arm had been paralyzed. Such reports, it should be noted, seem to be taking as their model the signs and healings recorded in the New Testament.

But not all of the "signs" followed the New Testament models quite so closely. An especially bizarre rumor concerned the fate of a peasant from the valley of Campan who had boasted that he was not fooled by these scenes of hallucination. That very evening, it was said, through the agency of the young seer, the sins of this irreverent man had been changed into serpents, the serpents had devoured him on his way home, and no trace was ever found of him thereafter.[82] According to another version of the story, though, some of this man's skin had been left behind, which was found and put on display in Lourdes at the historical museum.[83] This story shows clearly the degree to which popular imagination had been stimulated by the events at Lourdes and the dramatic ways in which nascent belief was being reinforced.

While Bernadette did not return to the grotto for three weeks after the apparition on March 4, reports of miraculous events associated with her on that day, especially the healing of Eugénie Troy, created such excitement in the area that her reputation as a "young thaumaturge" was now firmly established. The report of the healing of the blind child had spread through the crowd, in the words of Peyramale, "with the speed of an electric spark," and later that day and on subsequent days Bernadette was besieged by people who wanted to see and to touch her, and to have her touch their rosaries, their medals, and innumerable other objects.[84] At this time also, stories began to circulate about miraculous incidents in her youth. According to one of these stories, when the young Bernadette was tending sheep at Bartrès, a stream, swollen by rain, had parted so as to let her and her flock pass through safely.[85]

Rumors were also circulating now, however, that were not so favorable toward Bernadette and her family and that would seem to have been fed by the class prejudice noted earlier. After the incidents of March 4, Commissioner Jacomet dispatched a report to Baron Massy, prefect of the Haute Pyrénées, describing the events of that day and taking note of a rumor that Bernadette's parents were collecting fifteen centimes from each person who came to see her. Jacomet said that while he was inclined to believe this, he had not been able to confirm it thus far, and that with respect to such matters he was maintaining a policy of constant surveillance.[86]

Bernadette herself seems to have been careful not to accept the gifts that visitors were offering to her. This is evident, for example, in her description, given about two weeks later to several government officials, including Jacomet and the mayor, of the scene that took place on March 4 when she returned from the grotto to the *cachot*, where she and her family had been living. Many more women than men had come there to see her, she said, and a great number of children. She was taken to her aunt's rooms on the second floor, and people filed before her in a long line. They wanted to touch her, shake hands with her, kiss her, or have her touch their rosaries. People offered her money, but she refused it, she said, and one man offered her two oranges, but she did not want to accept those either. After briefly describing the content of her vision that day, she told her interrogators that she did not know if she would return to the grotto or not.[87]

Bernadette tried, apparently, to distance herself, both in such interviews and elsewhere, from the rumors that she had performed miracles and from the adulation that many were now showering upon her. In an interview with town officials on March 18, she said, for example, that she had not previously known Eugénie Troy or the two other children whom she had reportedly healed, that her touching them had been a simple response in each case to a request from the child's relatives or friends, and that she did not think she had healed anyone. Bernadette's cousin, Jeanne Védère, recalled some years later that Bernadette had been somewhat perplexed and perhaps annoyed by the demands of the crowd at that time, and that she had preferred not to touch the rosaries of others herself but simply to mingle them with the one she had used at the grotto. On March 4, when Jeanne joined the line of people waiting to present their rosaries to Bernadette, she recalled that her cousin had exclaimed, "You too! What in heaven's name do you want me to do? I'm not a priest!"[88]

On the day after Bernadette's March 18 interview, Commissioner Jacomet sent another report (his fourth) to the prefect of the district. He concurred here with Bernadette's description of the people that came to see her; they were mostly women and children, and a few working-class men. The visits had tapered off after March 4, but had then begun to pick up again with renewed zeal. On the day he was writing, which was a market day, many people from places other then Lourdes had come to see Bernadette, but, he noted, she had received no one and the door had been closed to all. Town officials had apparently ordered the Soubirous on the previous day to turn away all visitors.[89]

While the authorities thus made some attempt, beginning on March 18, to isolate the young seer, they could do little to dampen the excitement that the events at the grotto had already created, especially in view of the growing conviction that these events were not yet finished. On March 21, Adélaïde Monlaur, a young woman living with her father in the vicinity of Lourdes, wrote to her cousin, a priest, to bring him up to date on what had been happening. She mentioned several rumors that were current at that time, one of which was that Bernadette would return to the grotto on March 25, the Feast of the Annunciation.[90]

Bernadette did return to the grotto on that day, but it was apparently very early in the morning, and only about twenty people were waiting there or had accompanied her. Those who were there said that she conducted herself much as she had before: she knelt, said the Rosary, bowed and smiled to her invisible visitor, and then left.[91]

In her own account of what transpired then, Bernadette said that she asked *aquerò* several times to have the kindness to say who she was. *Aquerò* at first only smiled, but then she opened her hands "in the manner of the Miraculous Medal," clasped them again to her breast, raised her eyes to heaven, and said, "I am the Immaculate Conception."[92] After leaving the grotto, Bernadette, accompanied by her Aunt Basile and apparently her cousin Jeanne Védère, went to see Peyramale, who reportedly responded with irritation to what Bernadette told him. Basile recalled that he mocked the young seer and said, "Your lady could not have that name!" Jeanne, however, said that he merely told Bernadette she was mistaken and asked her the meaning of "immaculate conception." Bernadette, according to Jeanne, replied that she did not know and that that was why, as she left the grotto, she kept repeating the words to herself in order to remember them.[93]

In Catholic tradition, the words "immaculate conception" refer to the Virgin Mary's preservation from the guilt of original sin from the very moment of her conception in the womb of her mother Anne. Belief in the Immaculate Conception had been common in many parts of the Western Church since the later middle ages, as attested by many theological treatises, several papal decrees, and the widespread popularity of the liturgical feast celebrating the doctrine on December 8. It was not until 1854, however, just four years before Bernadette's experiences, that the doctrine of the Immaculate Conception, through a proclamation of Pius IX, became an official and obligatory dogma of the Roman Church. It has been argued that Bernadette, who was illiterate and who was having trouble learning the catechism, could have known nothing of this doctrine without supernatural intervention. As Thomas Kselman has observed, however, by 1854 this was already a very popular doctrine, supported and advanced by many prophecies, apparitions, cures, devotional cults, and pious tracts.[94] The doctrine was, for example, already explicit in the prayer of the Miraculous Medal ("O Mary, conceived without sin, pray for us who have recourse to thee!"), which had been a staple of popular Roman Catholic devotion for nearly two decades before the 1854 proclamation. Bernadette's mention of the Miraculous Medal in her description of her March 25 experience would suggest that she knew this prayer and that this, as well as the iconography of the medal, may have helped shape this experience.

Apparently, what Peyramale found difficult to accept in Bernadette's initial report of the March 25 apparition was not the term "Immaculate Conception" but the peculiar expression, "I am the Immaculate Conception," given in response to the request for *aquerò*'s name.[95] This expression seems to have been quickly modified so as to make more sense and so as to fit into the context of other reported messages, such as that of March 2, that reflected a specifically devotional interest. On March 26, Marie Dufo, a resident of Lourdes, wrote to her younger brother that Bernadette had told her about her experience of the preceding day and had reported that the lady had raised her eyes to heaven, saying: "I am the Virgin of the Immaculate Conception. I want a chapel built on this very spot."[96] She reported that Bernadette then said that the lady should perform a miracle, after which the lady smiled but said nothing more. When Adélaïde Monlaur wrote on April 8 to her cousin to inform him of the latest developments at Lourdes, she too reported a more elaborate message. According to Adélaïde, the lady said to Bernadette, "I am the Mother of God, the Immaculate Conception," and had told her that the chapel that was to be built there should be called the "Chapel of the Immaculate Conception."[97]

The reaffirmation of the doctrine of the Immaculate Conception in Bernadette's report of her March 25 encounter with the Virgin at Lourdes apparently fit very well into the rather apocalyptic Marian piety of French Catholics during this period and was to contribute a great deal toward making Lourdes the most popular Marian shrine in France within a very few years.[98]

Later Experiences at Lourdes and the Development of the Cult

Bernadette reported two more appearances of *aquerò*: on April 7, the Wednesday after Easter, and on July 17, the Feast of Our Lady of Mount Carmel. She brought back no messages from either of these appearances.

On April 7, however, Pierre-Romaine Dozous, a local physician who for some time had maintained a skeptical interest in the events at the grotto, said that he himself saw something quite extraordinary there. Bernadette was holding her lighted candle and had cupped her hands around it to protect it from the wind. It seemed to Dozous that the flame was brushing her hands without her being aware of it, but when he examined her hands afterwards, he could find no burns on them. The excited doctor then apparently proclaimed this "prodigious event" to everyone he encountered.

While some persons who had been at the grotto and had seen Bernadette with her lighted candle suggested that the doctor had misperceived and misinterpreted the event, Jacomet's report of Dozous's story noted that this had become the topic of much conversation, and it would seem that Dozous's conversion signaled a sort of turning point in the attitudes of some of the more important persons of the area, including some of the clergy, towards the Lourdes phenomena. Writing to the prefect of the district on April 11, Jacomet said that Dozous had sought him out to tell him about the candle incident and in the process had observed that the clergy were "shaken" by what had happened and had "accepted the fact." Jacomet said that when he pressed Dozous several times to explain just what he meant by this, Dozous told him: "If the little one [i.e., Bernadette] did not go to the grotto to bring about some miracle, if, for example, she did not succeed in obtaining some healing, whether by touching or by prayers, what does it matter! The great world-plan which brought her to the grotto would itself suffice to convince the higher clergy that there was something miraculous there!" Dozous, finally, told Jacomet that in not many days he too (i.e., Jacomet) would want to go to the grotto in procession.[99]

The grotto was in fact, by this time, well on its way toward becoming an important goal for local pilgrimages.[100] At the end of March, Jacomet began recording in a notebook the money and other objects that had been left there by pilgrims as votive offerings. On March 27, for example, he found there a total of eight francs and thirteen centimes, a half-pound of linen, and six candles.[101] About two weeks later, on April 11, the same day on which he wrote to the prefect about Dozous, he found fourteen francs and sixty-one centimes, four lighted candles, and a framed picture of Our Lady of La Salette, the latter attached to a structure that had been erected at the entrance to the grotto and decorated with garlands of artificial roses and other flowers. This picture, according to Jacomet, bore the inscription, "The arm of my son weighs heavily on sinners; I can no longer hold it back," and on its corners were depicted four miracles, including the miracle of the rock imprinted with the face of Christ. Clearly it was a copy of the La Salette broadsheet noted in the preceding section.[102]

The presence of this broadsheet at the Lourdes grotto, twelve years after the events at La Salette and only about a month after the end of the fortnight of Bernadette's ecstasies, suggests that the messages and miracles of La Salette played an important part in shaping people's expectations and experiences at Lourdes. While belief in the "miraculous rock" of La Salette, for example, had been discouraged by the bishop and did not become a permanent fixture of La Salette piety, this miracle was apparently well known throughout France at this time, and it seems to have been replicated at Lourdes in various forms. Some people said, for example, that the dove that had been seen fluttering over Bernadette's head on the morning of March 4 had left its image on the rock wall above the grotto, and on April 8, Jacomet noted in his journal a rumor that a man who had picked up a rock at the grotto and taken it home had discovered, when he showed the rock to his family, that it had assumed the shape of Christ.[103]

For the most part, though, it was the miracles depicted on the other three corners of the broadsheet—i.e., the healings attributed to the water of La Salette's "miraculous spring"—that struck the most responsive cord in the perceptions and piety of those who were coming to the grotto at Lourdes. Access to the spring allegedly discovered by Bernadette at the Lourdes grotto had been made much easier in mid-April, when a channel was dug for the water and a zinc basin with three spigots was installed; and from this time on, reports of healings ascribed to the water increased dramatically. The popularity of the stories of these healings is attested by the considerable efforts of Commissioner Jacomet to refute them. Jacomet investigated a number of these alleged healings himself and collected testimonies with respect to others, and he was convinced that the evidence showed in all cases either that the suffering person had not improved or that the person's condition had never been very grave in the first place.[104] Few of these early alleged healings, in fact, were recognized by the episcopal commission which was set up to investigate them.[105]

Although local government officials tried to discourage people from going to the grotto, their efforts met with little success. On June 5 the grotto was declared "off limits," and on June 15 it was barricaded. People soon demolished the barricades, however, and when they were set up again on June 18, they were once again demolished—this cycle repeating itself several more times in the weeks that followed. It was on October 5 that the barricades were finally ordered removed by the emperor.[106]

The frustration that Jacomet felt over the state of affairs early that summer was reflected in his report to the prefect on June 25. The resistance offered to the authorities by "the simple and all-too-credulous people" was due largely, he said, to the encouragement of others from some of the town's leading citizens, men and women of good family and high intelligence. These well-born devotees could be seen every hour of the day, he complained, kneeling and praying along the path that led to the grotto or on the other side of the river. He was especially bitter about the propaganda distributed by educated persons such as Dozous, extolling the virtues of the grotto's water. Without such incitement, he thought, "everything would eventually return to order."[107] Jacomet's report suggests that what finally gave legitimacy to and established the Lourdes grotto as an important pilgrimage site was perhaps not so much its popularity with the common folk as with some of the town's educated elite.

At about the same time that Jacomet had written to the prefect about the miracle of the candle reported by Dozous and had seen the La Salette broadsheet, the grotto became the center for another series of unusual events that lasted for about three months. Persons other than Bernadette were claiming to have had visionary experiences at the site beginning on or about April 11, when five women decided to explore the opening in the cliff above the grotto where Bernadette said she had seen *aquerò*. Several of these women gave accounts of what happened on that occasion to Jacomet, about five days later.

While she had apparently not instigated the project, Marie Cazenave, a twenty-two-year-old dressmaker from Lourdes, was the chief spokesperson for this group. She was accompanied on the expedition, she said, by Honorine Lacroix, Madeleine Cazaux, and two women whom she did not know. They climbed into the opening, two of them carrying lighted candles, and entered a sort of vault, where they examined everything in detail. As they were about to leave, however, something suddenly occurred to Marie, and she said to the others, "Although the Virgin left heaven in order to come here, we are not worthy to walk here, but since we have come, let us at least pray." Her idea met with some resistance (Madeleine, for example, declaring that she was afraid to do so), and the majority of the group favored descending to the main part of the grotto and saying the Rosary there. Marie, however, said that she would stay there alone to recite the Rosary, and the others, to her surprise, then decided to stay with her.

According to Marie, when they had finished saying the first decade of the Rosary, she saw a white rock and then, suddenly, a little to the right of the rock, the form of a woman, of ordinary height, carrying a child in her left arm. She could see this figure perfectly, she said. The woman had curly hair falling to her shoulders, with something white above her head, and she smiled most of the time. She was wearing a white dress. Marie said she could barely see the child, and after her first glance, in fact, she could not see it. When the women reached the third decade of the Rosary, Madeleine tugged at Marie's dress, embraced her, and said that she saw the Virgin and wondered if Marie saw her too. It was then, Marie said, that she first spoke out loud about what she saw. Honorine then asked them what they were seeing, and they raised their candles to show her, but as they did this, the figure disappeared. When, however, the candles were returned to their former positions, it appeared once again. The women recited more prayers and then climbed down to the main part of the grotto.[108]

A second group of women, led by Suzanne Lavantès, a fifty-year-old servant, climbed up to the opening a few days later, on April 14. Suzanne said that she had obtained a ladder from a farm at Espeluges, and that four other women had joined her: Marie Samson, Bérènice Curés, Paulette Marthe, and Paulette's mother. When they climbed up to the opening, however, Paulette's mother had stayed behind, and another woman whom Suzanne did not know took her place. When the five women had all reached the opening, they recited the Rosary and other prayers, and Suzanne said that when she raised her head she saw a white figure. She said that the figure was vaporous and vague, and that she could not say just what the object was without returning to the grotto and examining things there more closely. The sight of it made her weep and tremble, she said, but when her companions looked to see what was affecting her, they could see nothing. Then, when Paulette approached her with a candle, she herself could no longer see the figure. After they descended, Suzanne told the others what she had seen and, Jacomet noted, she never ceased to talk of it from that time on. Everyone, she said, came to see her to get the details about what she had seen, and she "satisfied their curiosity."[109]

Jacomet and several other men, including a local architect, had explored the area of the grotto where these visions were taking place, and when he reported the visions to the prefect, he described the locale as well. The rock which bordered on and covered the interior gallery of the opening, he said, had "very bizarre, very irregular" forms. The play of light and shadow on these rough rocks was such, he thought, that, "with a little compliance," one could see in them "the image that one was seeking and with which one was preoccupied."[110]

Jacomet also commented on the moral character of some of the women experiencing these visions or associated with them. He described Marie Cazenave as a virtuous girl with an ardent faith and an overactive imagination, Madeleine Cazaux was a "bad woman devoted to drink," and Honorine Lacroix was a prostitute with "disgusting morals."[111] Suzanne Lavantès was, he admitted, a rather devoted servant, but he noted that she was given to bad language and as a youth had had the reputation of being tempestuous.[112] Of these women, he thought only Marie Cazenave was such as to inspire confidence. His reports to the prefect indicate that Jacomet was concerned for a "sane appraisal" of the rumors that were "agitating" the public at this time and that he himself was very skeptical about all of the supposedly miraculous events taking place at the grotto.[113]

The most celebrated of the so-called new visionaries was Marie Courrech, who reported appearances of the Virgin at the grotto from mid-April through December 1858. Marie was in her mid-thirties, worked as a domestic servant for Lacadé, the mayor of Lourdes, and was well known for her piety. Abbé Peyramale, writing to Bishop Laurence, described her as a "holy girl if there ever was one" and reportedly gave her a more cordial reception than he had given Bernadette.[114]

Marie said she had been present at some of Bernadette's ecstasies and had been impressed by them. While others told her that Bernadette was bewitched, or was hallucinating, or was simply a fool, Marie said she had never had a bad impression of her, and she admitted that Bernadette had affected her own piety. Marie's first visionary experience was on April 17. Some friends had stopped by to ask her to accompany them to the grotto, she said, but she had not wanted to go because she had a great deal of work to do. Her friends, however, urged her employer to let her accompany them.[115] Dominiquette Cazenave, who had known Marie for some time, remembered that the group had wanted to go to the grotto because it was being said that everyone who went there saw the Virgin. She said that Lacadé, who did not believe in such things, had finally told his servant to go, saying that if she saw something he would believe.[116]

Marie said that when she arrived at the grotto she knelt down about ten paces from the niche where the figure had appeared to Bernadette and began to recite the Rosary. She had not yet finished when she saw on the right side of the niche a person, fifteen or sixteen years old, dressed in white. She said she then became unaware of her surroundings, and when the figure disappeared, she was astonished to find herself again in the grotto with her companions. The next Sunday she felt a great desire to return to the grotto and went there early in the morning before Mass. Again she saw "the Virgin," who smiled, she said, except when she told her to pray for sinners. Over the next eight months, Marie reported about ten more such experiences, most of them on religious festivals. On these occasions, she said, the Virgin told her things like, "Drink three times from the water," or "Wash yourself in the water." On the Feast of the Immaculate Conception (December 8), the Virgin told her, "It is here that I will distribute my graces."[117]

In the late spring and early summer of 1858, the number of people reporting visions at the grotto grew steadily, until by mid-July more than fifty people could be counted among the visionaries. Included here were a number of school children, many from neighboring towns, who in mid-June had begun to visit the site and to report that they experienced visions there. The power which some of these young seers exercised over the other pilgrims who were coming to the grotto emerges very clearly in a description of a visit to Lourdes on July 11 of the curé of Saint-Méard.[118] The curé had gone to the grotto, he said, because a rumor had spread through the district that seers from Lourdes and from the nearby town of Ossen would be encountering the Virgin that day.

The curé found a considerable number of people from the region gathered near the grotto, but the police were not allowing people to enter at that time. It began to rain, he said, and quickly the place became deserted, but he noticed people from the Ossen area beginning to gather around a seer from Ossen. He estimated that about a hundred people assembled around this person, and when the group withdrew to the shelter of a barn not far away, the curé went with them. They were there for about forty-five minutes, and for the first half hour, he said, everyone was silent, and the seer was "calm but dreamy." Then the seer suddenly announced that they should recite the Rosary, and the curé said that it fell to him, as the "most informed" of the group, to lead the prayers, while others made the responses. When they had finished the Rosary, the seer said they should go to the grotto, and since it was still raining a little, the curé was given the privilege of sheltering the seer with his umbrella and leading the "processional march."

They had no trouble entering the grotto, because the guards had left. The seer then knelt facing the opening where Bernadette said she had seen the "Immaculate Conception." He took his rosary and began to recite a decade, but suddenly stood up, exclaiming, "Ave Maria!" Then he put his rosary in his pocket and hastened to the base of the grotto, his arms open as if to grasp what he was seeing. He then ran back and forth as if chasing something, emitting little cries of joy and moving so quickly that the others crowded into the small area had difficulty following him. Once he slipped and fell on the wet rocks, but he did not seem aware that he had fallen; he rose quickly and continued moving as before with astonishing deftness. When the object of his pursuit seemed to stop on a rock near the miraculous spring, the child cried out, "Ah! Ah! Ah!" with his arms extended, the curé said, "as if he had before him an object of ravishing beauty."

The young seer then put together his thumb and forefinger as if he had seized something and turned to the crowd as if to show it to them. "The rose bush of Mary! The rose bush of Mary!" he exclaimed, but it was useless for people to look, the curé said, for they saw nothing.

In the meantime, four or five young seers from Lourdes, seven to ten years of age, had arrived at the grotto, some accompanied by their parents. The curé said that they all rushed quickly toward the place which was fixing the attention of the first seer, and staring in the same direction, they all cried, "Ah! Ah! Ah!" Then, lighting their candles and turning toward the rock wall, they directed their gaze toward the cavity that opened up into the vault of the grotto. In unison, they knelt, then rose and went farther into the grotto, where the crowd heard them weeping and lamenting.

One of these seers then suddenly left the group, the curé said, and took hold of a child in the crowd. This child, reportedly, had fallen from a cherry tree the day before and had broken or sprained his arm. The young seer led the child to the miraculous spring, unwound the linen, and removed the wood splint from the child's arm. Then, looking to the side at whatever it was that he saw, he smiled and washed the limb four times. When he released it, it appeared to the assembled crowd to be healed. The other seers had gathered around to watch this, and the one who had performed the healing then returned to their ranks.

The young visionaries then returned to the position where they had originally gathered, prostrated themselves, and indicated to the crowd that they should do the same. If someone failed to do as they requested, they seemed impatient, the curé noted, but they said nothing and communicated only with gestures. This went on for about two and a half hours.

One of the seers eventually asked the curé to lead the crowd in the litanies of the Virgin, which he did, the crowd responding, he said, "with an enthusiasm difficult to describe." When these were finished, this seer (the same one who had performed the healing) came up to the curé and told him to add the phrase, "Sancta et immaculata Conceptio Beatae Mariae Virginis"—this, observed the curé, from a child who was poorly dressed and barefoot and who could barely speak the local dialect. All of the seers except for the first then left; the curé took up his post beside him, sheltering him with his umbrella as he had done before; and they left the grotto "entirely dumbfounded" at the things that they had seen.

In his reflections on the origin and meaning of the experiences of these young visionaries, the curé of Saint-Méard recalled first that a professor noted for his theological rigor had spoken of them as "monkeyshines of the devil." But the priest himself rejected this notion and said that he thought them to be of a divine origin. He did not think it possible that such innocent, naive children would or could participate for so long in a prank. While he admitted that he might not have the knowledge required to distinguish the true from the false in this situation, he was predisposed to think that these seers had been given the task of continuing the mission first conferred on Bernadette.

These young visionaries were not, however, so well regarded by everyone. Some thought that they were being manipulated for personal gain, while others thought that their purpose was to cast doubt on the visions of Bernadette and that it was perhaps the devil who had appointed them to do this.[119] Furthermore, some of the messages which these seers were reporting seemed to be inspired chiefly by a kind of rivalry between the surrounding towns. Such a message was reported, for example, by a resident of Omex, who was present one day at the grotto along with some of the young seers from Ossen and Lourdes. Suddenly, from within the grotto, this woman said, there came a very high (fine) voice, like that of an affected child, saying, "In the valley of Batsurguere and especially at Ossen there are many worthy people; at Lourdes there are only scoundrels." The woman who reported this did not believe, as some presumably did, that this "high voice would be that of the Virgin." She recalled saying to those who were gathered there, "The one who speaks is more the devil than the devil himself."[120]

Abbé Peyramale was quite skeptical about the ecstasies of these juvenile seers, and he was apparently careful not to do anything that could be seen as encouraging visits to the grotto. In a letter of July 9 to the bishop of Tarbes, he noted that these children sometimes made crazy, twirling motions, and that their visions were taking place in circumstances that were "for the most part bizarre and burlesque." Peyramale, believing that he was acting as the bishop would wish, wrote that he had dismissed one of the best known of the young seers from the choir and that he had forbidden all of the children in his catechism class from visiting the grotto. He was refusing publicly, moreover, to bless the candles that people wanted to take to the grotto.[121]

The bishop of Tarbes himself took two significant steps during the month of July with respect to what had been happening at Lourdes. Early in the month, he formally condemned the reports that were coming from the "false visionaries," and on July 28, he established a commission to investigate Bernadette's claims to have seen the Virgin and the claims being made for the water at the grotto.[122] After this, the reports of "new visions" at the grotto ceased, except for the visions of Marie Courrech, which, as already noted, continued until December.[123] Marie's reputation for piety evidently shielded her from some of the pressure that suppressed the visions of the other seers, and it was said that when Bernadette was asked if anyone else had seen the Virgin, she referred to the common opinion, without however specifically endorsing it, that "the maid of the mayor" had seen her.[124]

Bernadette herself did not seem to have been directly involved in the struggle between local government officials and devotees of the cult that began to develop around the grotto in the wake of her apparition. She was sometimes confined to bed because of her asthma, and for several weeks in May she was absent from Lourdes, having been taken for convalescence to the waters at Cauterets. Her enrollment at the hospice school at Lourdes operated by the Sisters of Charity of Nevers also apparently gave her some respite from the many visitors who sought her out at her home.[125]

In September 1858, the Soubirous family moved from the *cachot* to better lodgings in the house of some other relatives, and at the beginning of the next year they moved to a mill where Bernadette's father had some promise of steady employment. In 1860, arrangements were made by Lacadé and Peyramale for Bernadette to become a boarder at the hospice school, and she remained there until 1866, when she moved to Nevers to become a member of the religious order under whose care she had already been for six years. She lived at the motherhouse of that order until her death on 16 April 1879.

Bernadette appeared twice before the episcopal commission appointed to investigate the Lourdes apparition: once on 17 November 1858 and again on 7 December 1860. Thirteen months after the second of these interviews, on 18 January 1862, Bishop Laurence issued a letter officially declaring the apparition worthy of the assent of the faithful and sanctioning the cult of the "Immaculate Mother of God" at the Lourdes grotto.[126] Bernadette was beatified by the Roman Catholic Church on 14 June 1925 and canonized on 8 December 1933.[127]

One can see at Lourdes, in the spring and summer of 1858, the development of a considerable variety of ways of "public access" to the sacred. Bernadette, like Mélanie and Maximin, had been subjected to intense public scrutiny in the aftermath of her experiences, but unlike them, whether by virtue of her personality or simply because of the needs and expectations of those attracted to her experiences, she had quickly gained the reputation of a young thaumaturge and saint. She herself, and not simply the water of the grotto where her experiences had occurred, had, in spite of her disavowals, become associated with reports of healings, and stories circulated which endowed her even as a child with an aura of sanctity. The public's tendency to closely associate the miracle at Lourdes with its seer was transferred, evidently, in the months immediately after her experiences, to the other young persons who began to have visions at the grotto and gave rise to the small cults which formed around them. There were also, as has been noted, a number of more immediate perceptions of the sacred at Lourdes: visions inspired evidently by unusual rock formations, phenomena such as the alleged image of the dove on the wall above the grotto, and of course the grotto's healing water—all of these giving people access to the sacred in direct and concrete ways apart from the presence of any seer.

Manifestations of the sacred similar to these have been noted in connection with most subsequent Marian apparitions. Some of these have been what we might call Rorschach tests: material objects or surfaces in (or on) which people of faith discerned sacred images, presumably testifying to a divine presence at the apparition site. Others were of the nature of signs, events expected and then perceived on particular occasions (as on March 4 at the Lourdes grotto), which confirmed the devotees' beliefs that something of a divine plan was unfolding.

At Lourdes, however, as at La Salette, one can also trace the development of a canon of officially sanctioned means of access to the sacred (the revelations to Bernadette and the healing water), surrounded by a fringe area of tolerated means of access and the gradual suppression of those stories and relics which would draw attention away from this canon.

Approaching Fatima: Lucia and Her Childhood Memories

The apparition at Fatima, Portugal, where in 1917 three shepherd children reported a series of appearances of the Virgin Mary, like the apparitions at La Salette and Lourdes, has rarely been approached from the standpoint of the phenomenology of religion or religious experience. One of the first things that such an approach to Fatima requires is that we address some widely held assumptions about just what materials should be studied by the person who seeks to understand this apparition. While a devotional approach to Fatima will usually focus attention on the so-called Fatima messages, regarding these as the center around which the other aspects of the apparition revolve, a phenomenological approach requires, rather, that attention be focused on the human processes and interactions that have led up to the seers' communication of those messages and that have affected how those messages have been understood. The Fatima messages will thus not be dealt with directly in this chapter at all. They will, however, be discussed in two later chapters, one of which is concerned with the so-called secret of Fatima, and the other, with understandings of history which have commonly been associated with modern Marian apparitions, the most popular of which give considerable prominence to some of these messages.

Lucia dos Santos, the only one of the three Fatima seers to grow to adulthood—in 1988, she was still alive, residing in a Carmelite convent in Coimbra—has played a particularly important part in defining the character and the meaning of the Fatima apparition. It has not simply been Lucia's longevity, however, that has lent her this significance, for it is clear that she played the leading role in the scenario of the apparition itself. All accounts agree that she was the only one of the three seers to interact with both her vision and with the crowd, carrying on conversations with both while her two cousins stood by silently. She has said, moreover, and probably not incorrectly, that Francisco and Jacinta had been accustomed to follow her directives before the apparition began, that they turned to her for guidance afterwards, and that it was she who convinced them that they had to be very careful in speaking about their experiences. Lucia's leading role in the events surrounding the Fatima apparition, and indeed during the apparition itself, is the first important matter with which the student of Fatima has to come to terms. The second is the fact that much of what devotees today accept as the content of the apparition comes from four memoirs written by Lucia in the convent between 1935 and 1941, many years after the series of experiences that constitute the apparition event.

It is difficult to establish precisely what the children said in the immediate aftermath of their experiences in 1917. The most important early sources of information here are the interviews conducted and recorded by interested clergy such as Dr. Manuel Formigão, canon of the patriarchal see of Lisbon and professor at the seminary and lyceum of Santerem, and Fr. José Ferreira de Lacerda. Also important is Lucia's first written account of the apparition, composed on 5 January 1922, about four and a half years after the events, at the request of her spiritual director, Mgr. Manuel Pereira Lopes.[128] This, of course, is significant as testimony to Lucia's own earlier understanding of the apparition, and it should be noted that there is a gap of about fifteen years between this document and the first of Lucia's memoirs.

Each of Lucia's four memoirs was composed in response to a specific request of the bishop of Leiria, Dom José Correia da Silva, to whom each memoir was then formally addressed. Between 1925 and 1929 Lucia reported a series of experiences in which the Virgin and Christ had appeared to her and had requested special devotions to the Virgin's Immaculate Heart. It was apparently these experiences, in conjunction with the bishop's requests, which convinced her, in 1935, that additional commentary on her 1917 experience was necessary. Each of the four memoirs which she subsequently wrote presumably provided some details not previously available concerning the events of that crucial year. Lucia wrote her *First Memoir* in December 1935; her *Second Memoir* in 1937; her *Third Memoir* in August 1941; and her *Fourth Memoir* in November 1941.

Lucia was born on 22 March 1907, the youngest of the seven children of Antonio and Maria Rosa dos Santos. One child had died in infancy; of the six who survived there were five girls and one boy. Lucia was five years younger than the next oldest, her sister Carolina. Lucia remembered being the family pet during her first six years, her siblings often arguing about who could caress and play with her. When this happened, she said, her mother would take her, and if she was too busy to give her affection, she would give her to her father.[129]

Lucia described herself in her memoirs as having three talents which she manifested even when very young: a sharp memory, an ability to entertain (especially other children), and an ability to get people to do what she wanted. Her memory, which in her *Second Memoir* she called a gift from God that enabled her to recall in great detail the apparition of about twenty years earlier, was apparently something of which she was proud even as a child. She had always been able to remember and repeat things after one hearing, and her mother, knowing that she could repeat "like a parrot" everything that she heard, made her a sort of chaperone for her two oldest sisters. Her sisters, who were, it seems, "leading lights" among the young people of the village, evidently accepted this arrangement fairly well, for Lucia said they took care to dress her properly and taught her to sing and dance. This, Lucia recalled, she loved to do and did with rare skill even when she was very young. Her sisters would place her on a crate at festivals, where she would sing and dance to the admiration of all.[130]

Lucia's entertaining and storytelling talents evidently made her popular with the younger children of the village. Since her two oldest sisters
worked at home, she recalled, neighbors would leave their children at
the dos Santos home in the morning before going to work in the fields.
While this informal day-care center was supervised by her sisters, the
young Lucia was put in charge of entertaining the children and keeping
them away from the pond in the yard. It was in this context that her
younger cousins Francisco and Jacinta Marto became especially attached to her. Lucia told the younger children stories that she had heard
in the evening from her family: fairy tales told by her father and sisters,
and biblical stories and saints' lives told by her mother. Any story she
had heard at least once, she said, she could repeat in all its details, and
she recalled in particular telling her cousins the story of "Our Lord's
Passion," which moved Jacinta to tears.[131]

Lucia described her mother as a serious woman on whom the neighbors relied for nursing skills but who herself preferred reading to visiting. Everyone believed that what her mother said was "like Scripture"
and that she was "worth more than all her daughters put together."[132]
Lucia remembered especially that at siesta time her mother gave them
catechism lessons, which became especially intense during Lent. "I don't
want to be ashamed of you," she told her children, "when the priest
questions you at Easter on your catechism."[133]

At the age of six, Lucia said, she had already learned the catechism
along with the older children, while sitting on her mother's lap listening
to this instruction. In the spring of that year, when the date was set for
some of the children of the village to make their First Communion, her
mother sent her and her older sister Carolina to the catechism lessons
given by the parish priest. While ten was the usual age for a child's First
Communion, Lucia said, her mother thought that she might already
know enough to be ready. The priest apparently did not object to her
presence, and indeed, he seems to have been impressed by her knowledge. Lucia recalled that he would summon her to his side when one of
the older children did not know an answer and would have her respond
in order to shame them.[134]

Twenty-four years later, Lucia remembered her experiences in this
class as being charged with intense emotion.[135] The events of that
spring, as she recalled them at least, reflect already the drama of adulation and humiliation, revelation and secrecy, that would characterize her
life in subsequent years. She had begun the catechism lessons, she said,

"radiant with joy, hoping soon to be able to receive my God for the first time." She was thus greatly disappointed when, on the evening before the appointed day, the priest told her that she would have to wait another year. Immediately she began to cry and laid her head on his knee. At that moment, however, a visiting priest entered, and when he found out why she was crying, he took her into the sacristy and examined her on the catechism and the mystery of the Eucharist. This priest then took her by the hand and told the other priest that he should allow her to go to Communion because "she understands what she's doing better than the others." The visiting priest said that he would take responsibility for her.[136] Lucia was filled with inexpressible joy, clapped her hands with delight, and ran home to tell the good news to her mother.

It was at Lucia's first confession that she apparently learned something of the importance of secrecy. According to her account, she had been prepared for this event by her mother, who accompanied her to the church, gave her some last bits of advice, and then sat down before the altar to wait for her. Lucia went by herself to the sacristy, where the priest who had interceded for her earlier was hearing confessions; there she waited her turn. When she entered the sacristy, however, she apparently failed to close the door, and when she emerged afterwards, she saw that everyone was laughing. Her mother then told her that confession was a secret matter which ought to be done in a low voice and that everyone there had heard what she said, except for one thing. Her mother then tried to get her to tell her "the secret," but Lucia's response was complete silence.

Lucia's mother seems to have been interested in something the girl had said to the priest. But when Lucia went on to describe "the secret" she had withheld from her mother, she recalled it as having more to do with what the priest had said to her. What she remembered was a sort of personal encounter, inspired by the priest's words and framed in almost formulaic devotional language, with the religious figure who was to become so important for her a little later, that is, with the Virgin.

The priest, she said, had told her that her soul was the temple of the Holy Spirit and had told her to keep it pure so that God could work within it. Lucia recalled being filled then with respect for this "interior," and she asked the priest what she should do. He directed her to kneel down before the Virgin and ask her with great confidence to take care of her heart, to keep her heart for the Lord, and to prepare it to receive him worthily the next day. Lucia said that she then went to the altar before the statue of Our Lady of the Rosary, the care of which had been entrusted to her sisters, and asked "with the ardour of her soul" that her heart be kept for God alone. As she said this prayer, it seemed that she saw the Virgin smile, and with "a loving look and kindly gesture" she assured Lucia that she would do this.

Lucia's experiences on the next day, at least as she remembered them twenty-four years later in her *Second Memoir*, revolved around the words that her mother spoke to her when she left that morning for the church. Maria Rosa dos Santos, playing on the family name, told her daughter that she should ask God, above all, to make her a saint. At the church she spent a few minutes before the altar of Our Lady of the Rosary and felt again the numinous atmosphere of the preceding day. She was the first to receive Communion, and when the host was placed on her tongue, she felt "an unalterable serenity and peace." Indeed, she felt so bathed by the divine that "the presence of our dear Lord became as clearly perceptible to [her] as if [she] had seen and heard Him with [her] bodily senses." She prayed as her mother had taught her, asking God to make her a saint and to keep her heart for God alone. Then, she recalled, it seemed that from the depths of her heart God spoke to her this bene-diction: "The grace granted to you this day will remain living in your soul producing fruits of eternal life."

Reflecting on these pious memories, Lucia remarked that she did not know whether all this was reality or just "a little child's illusion," sug-gesting that she herself may have been aware that these memories should not be taken too literally. Nevertheless, it is apparent that Lucia's first confession and communion were intense experiences which made a lasting impression upon her, and something of her mother's voice was undoubtedly echoing in her mind as she thought back on them. These early events had, she said, a "great influence in uniting [her] to God," which may be her way of saying that they provided her with patterns of meaning and satisfaction that would sustain her through the less-happy years that followed. In the second part of her *Second Memoir*, Lucia de-scribed those years of malaise, which she saw as directly preparing her for the apparition of the Virgin. She remembered them as years in which she lost her privileged position in her family and in which her family's problems began to mount.

Lucia lost her special status in the family in the year that she turned seven, which was, it should be noted, the year of the outbreak of the Great War. It was then, she said, that her mother decided she was old enough to care for the family's sheep. While her father and her sisters were so fond of her that they wanted her to be exempted from this work, her mother held that she was "just like all the rest." When the news spread that Lucia was to be a shepherd, almost all of the other young shepherds, according to her, offered to pasture their flocks with hers and to be her companions. At first she said yes to all of them, but she soon discovered that she wasn't comfortable in the midst of such a crowd. She then quietly chose just three girls as her companions, and for a time she and these three girls watched their flocks together on the slopes opposite those used by the other shepherds.[137]

It was with these three girls that she shared, in the following year, 1915, a series of extraordinary experiences. She recalled that she and her companions usually ate lunch around midday and that then she would invite them to pray the Rosary with her. One day, they had hardly begun the Rosary when they saw, poised in the air above the trees, a figure which was like "a statue made of snow" and was "rendered almost transparent by the rays of the sun." Lucia decided to say nothing about this to her family, but as soon as the children returned to the village, her companions told their families what they had seen. The news spread quickly, and Lucia's mother, in fact, heard about the vision from others. When she asked Lucia about it, the girl told her that the figure looked like a person wrapped in a sheet and that she could not make out any eyes or hands. Her mother, she recalled, made a gesture of contempt and exclaimed, "Childish nonsense!"

The children saw the strange figure on two other occasions; and again Lucia's mother learned about it from others, which made her very unhappy. People started making fun of the girls, and Lucia said that her sisters, who remembered that after her First Communion she had been "quite abstracted," began to ask her scornfully if she was seeing someone wrapped in a sheet. Because she had been used to "nothing but caresses," she felt these contemptuous words and gestures very keenly.[138]

Not long after these events, Lucia's cousins, Jacinta and Francisco, received permission from their parents to start taking care of their family's sheep. Lucia said that her two cousins could not bear to be separated from her and had persistently pressed their mother until this permission was given. Lucia was apparently not very pleased at first to have them as her companions, but once the matter was settled her feelings seemed to have changed. To avoid the chaos of the other children, Lucia said, she, Jacinta, and Francisco arranged to use the pastures which belonged exclusively to their two families.[139]

In the course of the following year (1916), Lucia said that she and her two cousins had several extraordinary experiences. These experiences, however, were apparently never publicly announced until 1937, when Lucia recorded in her *Second Memoir* that in 1916 she and her cousins saw and took communion from an angel. Ever since the humiliation she had suffered on the occasion of her First Communion, Lucia had become very reluctant to speak about any of her special religious experiences, and her reticence had increased in 1915 when family and friends had ridiculed her for the strange vision her companions had reported. In her *Second Memoir*, she said that after the first appearance of this angel, she convinced her cousins to tell no one.[140] In her *Fourth Memoir*, however, she said nothing about urging her cousins to keep silence but instead attributed their silence to the apparition itself. It did not occur to them to tell anyone, she said, the experience having been so intimate that "it was not easy to speak of it at all."[141]

The experiences of Lucia, her friends, and her family need to be seen in the context of the peculiar turmoil that had come upon Portugal during these years. Under the liberal monarchy of the later nineteenth century the economy had long been on the decline, and the republican revolution of 1910 had only made it worse. While life in the countryside was probably more secure than in the cities, where food riots had erupted, it is doubtful that many families even in rural areas found these years very comfortable. Probably just as troubling for many of the common folk as the new government's failure to right the economy, however, were its policies with respect to religion. Not since the French Revolution had a European government made such determined efforts to stamp out religious institutions, and the groundswell of support for these institutions that arose in reaction to government persecution seems to have surprised even many Church officials. One need not subscribe to the view that religious phenomena are simply a reflection of an economic or social matrix to note that the religious experiences of Lucia and her cousins began as a part of this groundswell and that they became, in 1917, the nucleus for one of its most powerful expressions.[142]

These experiences cannot be understood, however, without a somewhat closer look at the Marto and dos Santos families. It appears that the Marto family was somewhat better able to cope with the difficulties of these years than was Lucia's. The Marto family was a large one. Olimpia, the sister of Lucia's father, was caring for two children from a previous marriage when she married Manuel Pedro Marto in 1897. Nine children were then born to Olimpia and Manuel, the youngest of whom were Francisco, born in 1908, and Jacinta, born in 1910. The Martos were described as a hard working couple, who could provide their large family with the necessities of life and sometimes even a few luxuries. They are said to have treated their children with a great deal of affection.[143]

By 1917 the dos Santos family was experiencing, to judge from Lucia's recollections in her *Second Memoir*, some very hard times. Her two older sisters had married and left home, and her father (in Lucia's oblique terminology) "had fallen into bad company and let his weakness get the better of him," resulting in the loss of some of their property.[144] Others, however, noted more bluntly that he had begun to drink heavily and to gamble.[145] Evidently in an attempt to regain some financial security for the family, Lucia's mother had insisted that the two oldest daughters who were still at home go out to work as servants. With Lucia's father absent from the home most of the day, this left only Lucia's brother to work the remaining fields, her mother to care for the home, and Lucia herself to care for the sheep. Lucia said that her mother was miserable during these years, and that in the evening, while waiting for her husband to return for supper, she would tearfully exclaim, "My God, where has all the joy of our home gone?" Lucia and her brother often joined their mother in this lament.[146]

The stress, Lucia said, took its toll on her mother's health, and when she became unable to work, one of the older daughters was summoned home to care for her and for the house. Consultations with the doctors of the area, who prescribed various remedies, and a difficult journey to a doctor at Leiria for treatment were all reportedly to no avail. Finally her mother was diagnosed as having "a cardiac lesion, a dislocated spinal vertebra, and fallen kidneys," and a rigorous therapy involving treatment with various medications and red-hot needles did at last bring some improvement.

An additional threat to the dos Santos family came in the spring of 1917 when Lucia's brother became eligible for military service. Since he was in excellent health and since many young men were being drafted at this time for service in the war, it seemed that he was very likely to be called. Lucia's mother, nearly frantic, called for the second of her daughters to return home. An exemption was eventually obtained for her brother, however, her mother thus being granted "this small measure of relief."

Though only a child at the time, Lucia understood very well the precariousness of her family's situation and felt their misery acutely, according to her memoirs. The scene, repeated on many evenings, of her mother and brother weeping together was, she said, the saddest she had ever witnessed, and this, along with her own longing for her older sisters (before they were called home) made her feel as if her heart were breaking.

Lucia sustained another blow around this time: the proscription of one of the activities she had most enjoyed in her earlier years. The parish had undergone a change of leadership, and the new priest had begun to preach against dancing, denouncing it in his Sunday sermons as a pagan custom. As soon as her mother heard this, Lucia said, she forbade her daughters to attend any dances. Others eventually followed this example and dancing soon died out in the village, even the little dances that had been popular with the young children.[147] While Lucia does not directly describe how she felt about this development, one senses that it was a particularly poignant expression for her of the end of an exceptionally happy childhood.

The attitude which Lucia was beginning to adopt with respect to the losses of these years is well summarized by what she later recalled as the words of the angel during his second appearance to her and her cousins in the summer of 1916: "Above all, accept submissively the sacrifices the Lord will send you." While it is impossible on the basis of Lucia's recollections to correlate precisely the alleged appearances of the angel with difficult moments in the life of the dos Santos family, it is clear that the angel and the difficulties were closely connected in her memory. When she felt her heart was breaking, she said, she would think of the angel's words and withdraw to a solitary place so as not to add to her mother's suffering. There she would weep and offer her own suffering to God, and when her cousins would come and find her thus engulfed in sorrow, they too would weep "copious tears." Then Jacinta would give voice to their offering with some form of the following prayer: "My God, it is as an act of reparation and for the conversion of sinners that we offer you all these sufferings and sacrifices."[148]

It is difficult to imagine a six-year-old peasant girl either using or understanding such a prayer; perhaps it was later superimposed on these experiences by the adult Lucia. It is quite possible, however, that she and her cousins did at this time have conversations and pray together in ways that helped them find meaning in their unhappiness, and whatever their words might have been, it is important that Lucia would remember them in just this way. It would seem that before 1917 Lucia had developed a way of seeking and finding religious meaning in the midst of adversity, that is, by sharing unusual experiences in near-secrecy with a few friends—and this set the pattern for what was to become the apparition of Fatima.

Assessing Fatima: The Apparition and Its Effect on the Seers

The six "appearances of the Virgin" reported by Lucia and her two cousins began on Sunday, 13 May 1917. Curiously, Lucia, in her memoirs, passed very quickly over these six incidents which constitute the Fatima apparition, on the grounds that they were already well publicized. In her *First Memoir* she did note, however, that she and her cousins had originally agreed to keep the matter to themselves and that it was Jacinta who betrayed that agreement. Jacinta, according to Lucia, had been so impressed by what she had seen on that first Sunday that for the rest of the afternoon, as the children sat with the sheep, she kept breaking into ecstatic exclamations, such as "Oh, what a beautiful lady!" Lucia remembers having warned her that if she continued in this state she was sure to tell someone, but Jacinta insisted that she would not.[149]

Jacinta and Francisco's mother, Olimpia, recalled that when she and the other members of their family returned home later that day from the fair at Batalha, Jacinta ran to meet her, clutched her around the knees in an unexpected way and exclaimed that she had seen "Our Lady" at the Cova da Iria. When her mother made light of this, Jacinta persisted, insisting that she had seen, earlier that day, a beautiful lady surrounded by a dazzling light who had told them to recite the Rosary every day. At dinnertime, her mother had her repeat the story to the rest of the family, Jacinta adding that the lady had promised to take them to heaven and had said other things that she could not remember but "which Lucia knows." Francisco, then, confirmed what Jacinta had said.[150]

The next morning the story spread quickly through the village. Maria dos Anjos, one of Lucia's married sisters, remembered hearing it from a neighbor, who had heard it from Jacinta's mother, and she said she went to Lucia right away to see if it was true. When Lucia heard that Jacinta had broken the silence on which they had agreed, she reportedly said nothing for a while and then said, "And I told her so many times not to tell anyone!" Lucia explained to her sister that she had not wanted to make the experience public because she was not sure that the "pretty little woman" they saw was really the Virgin. Lucia told her further that the woman had asked the three children to go to the Cova da Iria once a month for the next six months and that she would there reveal to them what she wanted. She had asked the woman where she came from, and the woman had answered, "I come from heaven." Her sister recalled that Lucia seemed unusually sad and didn't want to talk about the experience.[151]

Lucia, in her *First Memoir*, recalled receiving the news that their experience had become public knowldege not from her older sister but from Francisco. She said that she had been very upset that her younger cousins had broken their silence and that she had been especially critical of Jacinta, reminding her that this was just what she (Lucia) had predicted. Jacinta, who was then on the verge of tears, answered that there was something in her that just would not let her keep quiet. Lucia then told her cousin not to cry but also not to reveal to anyone what the lady had said to them. Jacinta confessed that she had already repeated some of what the lady had said (i.e., that she had promised to take them to heaven), and Lucia recalled that she responded to this with shock, saying something like, "To think that you told them that!" At that point Jacinta promised her that she would not "tell anybody anything ever again."[152]

The day on which the children expected the second episode of the apparition, June 13, was the Feast of St. Anthony, which was customarily celebrated in the parish with great festivities. Lucia had always looked forward to festivals, and her mother and sisters now taunted her with this: "We've yet to see if you'll leave the festival just to go to the Cova da Iria to talk to that lady." Lucia recalled feeling "cut to the heart" by their mockery.[153]

Her distress was apparently heightened when she discovered early on the morning of June 13 that people were arriving from neighboring towns who wanted to see her and accompany her to the apparition site. She had just brought her sheep to the pasture when her brother came to tell her that some people wanted to talk with her. While she had planned to attend the ten o'clock Mass and then go to the Cova da Iria, she decided now to ask the visitors to go with her to the eight o'clock Mass. When she returned home after the Mass, still more people were waiting for her in the yard. About eleven o'clock, she went to get Jacinta and Francisco, and the three children then left for the Cova da Iria, accompanied by people asking them "a thousand questions."[154]

Leopoldina Reis and Maria dos Santos Carreira (Maria da Capelinha), both of whom were present that day, recalled the events many years later, in the mid-1940s, in interviews with Fr. Jaoa de Marchi. Leopoldina, who was about Lucia's age, said that she and about fourteen other children who had been with Lucia at her First Communion decided to accompany her that day. "When Lucia proposed something no one contradicted her," she said; but she remembered Lucia's brother, nonetheless, trying to bribe her not to go to the Cova da Iria that day. Lucia refused the bribe, saying she simply wanted to go and did not care about the money. When they arrived at the Cova da Iria, Leopoldina recalled, she and the other children began to play and eat their lunches, but Lucia became very thoughtful and serious. After a while then, she said Lucia told Jacinta, who had been playing with the others, to be quiet since "Our Lady" would soon be coming.[155]

Maria da Capelinha claimed to be the first to reach the Cova da Iria that morning. She said that while she had been in poor health, she wanted to go, in order to find out if the events of which she had heard were true. Her handicapped son, John, agreed to accompany her. They sat down by the road to wait for the children to arrive, and they were soon joined by other people from neighboring villages. Around eleven o'clock the three seers arrived, accompanied by some friends and a number of others, and when they asked Lucia where the lady had appeared before, Lucia pointed out the spot. Maria remembered that the day was calm and still. Some people began to eat their lunches, and a girl from Boleiros began to read aloud from a prayer book. Because she was feeling weak and tired, Maria asked Lucia if she thought it would be long before the Virgin came, and Lucia replied "not long," after which Lucia began to watch for signs of her coming. Meanwhile, some members of the assembled group were reciting the Rosary. The girl from Boleiros was about to begin the Litany when Lucia interrupted, saying there wouldn't be time. She called to Jacinta that the Virgin must be coming, for "there's the lightning."

At that point, according to Maria, Lucia and her cousins ran to the oak tree, where the lady had appeared to them before. Lucia lift~ ' her hands as if in prayer and said, "You asked me to come h tell me what you want." Maria's account reports that th something like the "buzzing of a bee," which she thought must have been a "tiny little voice" responding to Lucia (Maria could not make out the words). After a while, Lucia got up very quickly, and with her arm outstretched she cried, "Look, there she goes! There she goes!" There had been a sound "rather like a rocket, a long way off, as it goes up," but all that they could see was a little cloud a few inches from the tree. This cloud rose slowly and moved away toward the east. The three seers stood silently and looked in that direction, until Lucia said, "There, now we can't see her anymore. She has gone back into Heaven, the doors are shut!" Maria said that when the people present looked again at the oak tree, the shoots at the top, which had been standing straight up, were now bent to the east. Some members of the group began to pull off twigs and leaves from the top of the tree, but Lucia told them to take them from the bottom, where the Virgin had not touched them.[156]

On July 13, Jacinta and Francisco's father, Manuel, was present at the Cova da Iria for the third episode of the apparition. He described what happened on that day in terms similar to those Maria da Capelinha had used a month earlier. The crowd was much greater in July, and Manuel said that he had some difficulty making his way through it. Two men had positioned themselves in such a way as to keep Jacinta and Francisco from being crushed, and Lucia was kneeling a short distance away, leading the crowd in the Rosary. When the prayers were completed, she stood up very quickly, looked to the east, and cried out for people to close their umbrellas (used for shade) because "Our Lady" was coming. Manuel said he looked hard and could see nothing at first, but then discerned a little grayish cloud resting on the oak tree and felt the sun's heat lessen a little and a "delicious fresh breeze" spring up. Then he began to hear a buzzing sound, like "a mosquito in an empty bottle." Lucia, who was now kneeling, became "pale as death" and cried out in terror, calling "Our Lady" by name. Then there was a sound like a clap of thunder, and Lucia rose suddenly to her feet, pointing at the sky and crying, "There she goes! There she goes!" He heard her say a few moments later, "Now you can't see her anymore." Manuel was by now convinced of the genuineness of the apparition.[157]

Other accounts of the events that took place at the Cova da Iria on the thirteenth of each month throughout the summer of 1917 offer descriptions very much like those of Maria da Capelinha and Manuel Marto. This suggests that a fairly well defined pattern developed in these months in terms of which the apparition transpired and was perceived. This pattern included the children's approach to the tree, the recitation of the Rosary, Lucia's sudden announcement of the Virgin's coming, her presumed conversation with her while kneeling, and finally her standing up and announcing the Virgin's departure toward the east. Many people also heard the sounds of the buzzing and the thunder (or rocket) and saw the little cloud over the tree, at the appropriate times. In the course of this scenario, Jacinta and Francisco would kneel near Lucia, not saying anything but apparently gazing in the same direction. Something of the significance of this pattern became apparent on August 13. On that day, even though the children were absent, a number of people who had gathered at the apparition site said that they heard the clap of thunder and saw the cloud descend and rest over the tree, then rise again and disappear. The Virgin had come to the Cova da Iria, they believed, even though the children had not.[158]

While it is clear from the report of August 13 that by late in the summer, for at least some of the religious seekers at Fatima, the apparition was no longer dependent on the seers, it is also clear that for others, the seers were in a certain sense no longer dependent on the apparition. Almost as soon as their experiences had become public knowledge, some people began to look upon the children as saints, who through their privileged relation to the Virgin could obtain special graces and favors for the faithful. Lucia recalled several incidents, for example, in which people who met her and her cousins on the street would throw themselves at their feet, presenting petitions. She and her cousins, she said, would kneel down, pray some portion of the Rosary with them, and then convey to them some kind of reassurance (for example, "Our Lady is so good! She will surely grant you the grace you are asking!"). When crowds gathered at the apparition site on July 13, September 13, and October 13, the children found it hard to reach their accustomed position near the oak tree because so many people were falling at their feet, beseeching them to present their requests to the Virgin. Many others, Lucia recalled, had to call out their requests from a distance Most people asked for a cure or for the safe return of a male relative who had gone to war.[159] Lucia remembered that on these occasions and on August 15, she presented many of these requests to the Virgin in the course of her conversations with her. The answer that she received from the Virgin was always the same: that some would be granted within the year and some would not, and that it was necessary for people to amend their lives, ask forgiveness, and pray the Rosary.[160]

On 13 October 1917, about seventy thousand people gathered at the Cova da Iria in anticipation of the Virgin's last visit, at which time, it was widely believed, she would perform a miracle. Lucia said that sometime before then she had asked the Virgin to perform a miracle so that people would believe that she had really been appearing to her and her cousins. The Virgin had replied that she would do this in October. Thus, in spite of a heavy downpour on October 12 and 13, the curious and the devout streamed into the Cova da Iria on the morning of the thirteenth to see what would happen. Late in the morning, Lucia and Jacinta, dressed in new dresses provided by a devout pilgrim and wearing white wreaths in their hair, and Francisco, were led through the crowd to the apparition site.

Maria da Capelinha, who was among the thousands present at the Cova da Iria that day, recalled that a priest who had been praying at the site all night asked the children, when they arrived, what time the Virgin would appear. Lucia replied that she would arrive at midday, at which point the priest looked at his watch, noted that it was midday, and that the Virgin does not lie. Some minutes passed, after which, according to Maria, the priest announced that the time was past, that the apparition was all a delusion, and that the children should run along. When he tried to push them away, Lucia was almost crying and said that those who wanted to leave could leave but that she would stay. The Virgin had come the other times, the child avowed, and she would come this time too. Lucia then looked to the east and told Jacinta to kneel down, saying that she had seen the lightning and that the Virgin was approaching.[161]

Others present that day said that Lucia had cried out, "Be quiet, be quiet, Our Lady is coming!" At about this time, in any case, the rain stopped, the clouds began to part, and Lucia suddenly exclaimed, "Look at the sun!" Her cry was picked up by the crowd, and as people looked up, many began to weep and to ask each other what they were seeing. According to a number of reports, some of which came from professional journalists, a majority of those present said that they had seen the sun tremble and dance, and spoke of a variety of colors issuing from the sun and illuminating the crowd. Some, however, said that they had seen the face of the Virgin, and some that the sun whirled like "a giant Catherine wheel," falling toward the earth as if to burn it up in its rays. Many also declared that the sun radiated a great deal of heat, so that by the time the sign had ended (by some accounts, about ten minutes later), everyone who had been soaked by the rain was dry. Reports of these phenomena, according to the accounts that soon appeared in the Portuguese newspapers, came not only from persons gathered that day at the Cova da Iria but also from others as far away as forty kilometers.[162]

In her own account of that day in her *Fourth Memoir* (1941), Lucia said that after she arrived at the Cova da Iria, she was moved by an interior impulse to tell the crowd to close their umbrellas and to say the Rosary. A few minutes later, she and her cousins saw the flash of light that signaled the Virgin's arrival. She recalled that at the end of her conversation with the Virgin, Mary opened her hands and "made them reflect on the sun, and as she ascended, the reflection of her own light continued to be projected on the sun itself." It was at this point that an interior impulse had moved Lucia to cry out about the sun. She had not intended, she said, to tell others to look at the sun, for she was not really aware of the crowd at that moment. She recalled that she then saw a series of figures: first Our Lady of the Rosary, then St. Joseph and the Holy Child, then Our Lord blessing the crowd, then Our Lady of Sorrows, and finally Our Lady of Mount Carmel.[163] Her two cousins saw only St. Joseph and the Child.[164]

All accounts agree that Francisco and Jacinta said nothing during each episode of the apparition and as little as possible afterwards. Persons who interviewed them reported that while Jacinta could both see and hear the Virgin, Francisco could only see her. Whether Jacinta could have conversed with the Virgin if she had wanted to became a matter of some conjecture. Maria da Capelinha said that she once asked Lucia, in Jacinta's presence, why the Virgin did not speak to Jacinta also. Lucia replied that if Jacinta would speak to the Virgin, the Virgin would speak to her, but Jacinta was too tongue-tied. Maria said that Jacinta then looked at both of them and smiled shyly.[165]

Lucia's experience of being rejected by family and neighbors in 1915 paled in comparison to the experiences of rejection that she remembered after the first episodes of the 1917 apparition. She recalled in her *First Memoir* that her mother was worried about the gossip and was determined to make her deny that anything had happened, sparing "neither caresses, nor threats, nor even the broomstick" in her efforts to achieve the desired retraction. Lucia recalled that on one especially distressing day she was in tears when she joined her cousins with the sheep. When Francisco heard that Lucia's mother was bent on forcing the child to admit that she was lying, he reportedly turned to Jacinta and said, "You see, its all your fault. Why did you have to tell them?" Lucia said that Jacinta then began to cry, knelt down, begged their forgiveness, and promised once again that she would never tell anything to anyone.[166]

However much the three seers might have wished that they had never spoken of their experiences to anyone, there was now no turning back. They were constantly in demand and had to deal every day with reactions ranging from requests for intercession with the Virgin to attempts to discredit them and outright contempt. Jacinta and Francisco, to judge from both Lucia's recollections and some other sources, received a measure of support and protection from their parents. Lucia's family, however, and especially her mother, apparently became all the more determined to make her confess that she had lied and heaped all the more abuse upon her. Lucia seems to have found some satisfaction in recalling and relating the various kinds of abuse to which she and her cousins were subjected at this time. Her memoirs thus give a vivid picture, overlaid with what might be called a theology of sacrifice and reparation, of the stresses placed on a young person whose religious visions have suddenly been thrust from the private into the public sphere, in a volatile religious and political environment.

Some of her most difficult experiences, Lucia recalled, involved the priests who quizzed them in the aftermath of their visions. Not long after the second episode of the apparition on June 13, for example, the priest of the local parish summoned the three children and their parents to meet with him. Lucia recalled that her mother had told her that the priest could do anything he wanted to, as long as it was for the purpose of obtaining her confession that she had lied, and her sisters invented endless threats to frighten her about the forthcoming meeting. When she told Jacinta and Francisco what her mother and sisters had told her, she recalled that they tried to console her, saying that while their mother too had said that they must see the priest, she had not hinted at any such ordeal. If the priest beat them, her cousins told Lucia, they would "suffer for the love of our Lord and for sinners."[167]

The meeting the next day was in fact conducted in a calm and kindly manner, and Lucia found it not so much frightening as tiresome. The priest, however, had reportedly been struck by her reluctance to speak, and he took this as evidence that her experience was probably not a revelation from heaven. In the case of a divine revelation, he thought, God would in all probability command the visionary to give an account of the events to the local religious authority, but Lucia had tried to keep everything to herself. What they were dealing with might very well, therefore, be a deceit of the devil, he said, and only time would reveal its real nature. This left Lucia in an acute state of doubt, and shortly thereafter she was paralyzed with fear by a nightmare of the devil laughing as he tried to drag her into hell. It was not until the third episode of the apparition on July 13, she said, toward which she had been impelled "by a strange force," that her doubts left her and peace returned to her soul.[168]

Her mother's conviction that Lucia was lying and that the affair had to be stopped so that people would not be led astray led to her being taken to the priest a second time. He questioned her this time "with the greatest kindness and even . . . with affection," trying different strategies to catch her in contradictions. He finally let her go, however, with a shrug of his shoulders. Lucia recalled that other priests were not so kind in their interrogations. They would subject her and her cousins to the most rigorous cross-examinations, leave, and then return and repeat the process. She remembered these meetings as the harshest of ordeals and said that soon, whenever she and her cousins found themselves in the presence of a priest, they would prepare themselves "to offer up their greatest sacrifice." They tried at that time to avoid priests as much as possible, and this led even the local priest, who had previously been kind to them, to complain and to grow more suspicious.[169]

The idea that the apparition was a deceit of the devil was apparently circulating among the populace in general in the summer of 1917. Maria da Capelinha, for example, recalled that while she had heard this rumor and had been upset by it, she was not dissuaded from going to the Cova da Iria on August 13. A woman from Santa Caterina had told her that "it was the devil who came and that he would wait until many people were gathered and then open the earth and swallow them up." She reasoned, however, that since so many people would be praying there, nothing very bad could happen; and so she went.[170]

It is likely that acute tensions between the Church and the Portuguese state had led many persons, unsure of just what expressions of religion the government would tolerate, to be very much afraid of what was happening at the Cova da Iria that summer. Such fears may have been an important factor in the ambivalent attitude of the local clergy towards the children's experiences and in the more-consistently negative attitude of Lucia's family. Conscious or unconscious fear of government reprisal may also have lent support to the idea that the devil lay behind the Cova da Iria phenomena, as well as to the rumor that the young seers' lives were in danger.

Lucia recalled hearing a poor man, who had boasted of ridiculing, insulting, and even beating the children, ask her mother what she thought of her daughter's visions. Her mother replied that it seemed to her that her daughter was "nothing but a fake who is leading half the world astray." The man then warned her mother not to say such things aloud, since there were people around who would be only too glad to kill her daughter.[171]

The negative attitude of Lucia's family toward her experiences may, however, have had less to do with their fear of official or unofficial persecution than with the financial strain that her role as visionary had begun to place on the family. Lucia's sisters, whose normal duties included sewing, working in the fields, and caring for the house, found themselves, after the onset of the apparition, spending a large amount of time dealing with the people who wanted to speak with Lucia and watching the sheep in her place so that she could spend time with these people herself. The family garden, moreover, which was near the apparition site, was reportedly so overrun by people that both harvesting and replanting had become impractical. These were matters of considerable importance, at a time of general economic distress, for a family who had only limited resources to start with, and Lucia said that her family was now blaming her for its financial problems. Her mother told her that when she was hungry she should go ask the lady for something to eat, and her sisters told her to eat what she could find at the Cova da Iria. Lucia said that she then became afraid even to ask her family for bread.[172]

The dos Santos family apparently had no way of gaining any significant financial recompense from the visitors who were unwittingly destroying their livelihood. Lucia gave the impression in her memoirs that her mother was opposed in principle to her accepting any of the money or other small gifts that visitors sometimes offered her. Possibly, however, it was not so much Lucia's acceptance of these donations as her mother's suspicion that she was attempting to keep some of them for herself that made them such a bitter source of conflict between mother and daughter.

Lucia recalled, for example, that a neighbor once "took it upon herself" to remark to her mother that Lucia had accepted some money from a gentleman. Her mother asked her for the money, and although she denied having received anything, her mother did not believe her and beat her with a broom handle. It was not until the "dust had been well beaten out of her clothes" that her sister Carolina and another girl intervened to say that they had seen the incident and that the gentleman had not given anything to Lucia.[173] Maria dos Anjos remembered the incident somewhat differently, but she agreed that their mother had not believed Lucia, had beaten her, and had said something like, "People who tell little lies are likely to tell big ones too." Maria's account suggested that it was Jacinta and not Lucia on that occasion who had been given a coin, but by the time their mother realized this, "even St. Anthony couldn't take away Lucia's bruises."[174] Manuel Gonçalves, a resident of Fatima, told Formigão in the fall of 1917 that the children sometimes did accept things from visitors, but not willingly.[175]

One of the most stressful times for the young seers and their families came in early August, when Lucia, her cousins, and their respective fathers were summoned to appear before the mayor of Ourém. Lucia remembered that what hurt her most about this incident was the contrast between her parents' attitude and that of her aunt and uncle. She said that her uncle sent word to the mayor that while he would appear himself, he would not bring his children. He thought that the nine-mile trip was too long for small children and that it was senseless, moreover, to bring such children before a court. Her aunt and uncle treated their offspring with affection, Lucia felt, putting themselves at risk to defend them, while her own parents handed her over to others with what seemed to be the utmost of indifference. Her consolation was to think that she was suffering "for the love of God and for the conversion of sinners."[176]

Apparently, the threat of death was felt keenly by all three children at this time. After it was decided that Lucia was the only one of the three who would be taken to Ourém, both she and her cousins were apparently afraid that she might never return. Her parents, moreover, according to her account, did nothing at all to alleviate her fear, but rather "took advantage of this situation to frighten us in every way they could." Before she and her father set out for Ourém, she went to say goodbye to Jacinta, and her cousin said to her, sobbing, "If they kill you, tell them that Francisco and I are just the same as you and that we want to die too." Later that day Lucia's sister apparently teased Jacinta and Francisco, for when she returned, Lucia said, her cousins were astonished to see her, telling her they had been weeping and praying for her and that her sister had told them that she had been killed.[177]

What happened at this meeting with the mayor, and at another which followed on August 13 in which all three of the seers participated, will be described in a later chapter that looks closely at the interaction between the seers (especially Lucia) and the public in connection with the matter of secrets. The present chapter has focused on the apparition itself and its more general effects on the seers, and some attempt can now be made to summarize those effects.

Since they wrote nothing and said so little that has been recorded, it is impossible to say much that is exact about how the apparition affected Jacinta and Francisco. It is clear, nevertheless, that they as well as Lucia suffered great physical and emotional strain in the summer of 1917, as great numbers of people began to intrude on their formerly very private world. When Formigão spoke with the seers about a week after the final episode of the apparition on October 13, he said that they were exhausted, and that Lucia in particular was unable to reply to his questions with the care and attention he desired. Her answers were mechanical, he observed, and she could not recall the circumstances of her experiences as clearly as she had a month earlier. He concluded that if the children were not spared the ordeal of such long interviews, their health would be in jeopardy.[178] A similar observation was made at about this time by Rev. Laçerda, director of the weekly *Leiria Messenger* and chaplain to the Portuguese Expeditionary Force. Lacerda's notes, however, seemed to confirm Lucia's recollections that the Martos made at least some efforts to protect their children from the public's intrusions. Lacerda said that Jacinta and Francisco's mother had not "greeted [him] with open arms" nor had she given him immediate access to the children. Their father, meanwhile, chided him for not believing the children's story.[179]

The following year, 1918, when a flu epidemic struck the area, Jacinta and Francisco both became ill and were confined to bed. Reports suggest, however, that neither the children's illness nor the efforts of their parents to shield them detered the visitors who continued to come to see them, and indeed, since they were now physically unable to escape, the strain on them was worse than before. On 4 April 1919, Francisco died, and in the fall of that year Jacinta had major surgery at Ourém. Lucia recalled that she endured this and the difficult treatments that followed with few complaints. Jacinta continued, however, to be distressed by the frequent visitors and understood this suffering, Lucia said much later, as a sacrifice "for the conversion of sinners."[180] She died on 20 February 1920. De Marchi, writing a quarter of a century later, reflected that it might have been better for the children if they had been removed from the scene, since their parents did not seem to have had enough "firmness and authority to prevent the least important visitor from plaguing them."[181]

The tensions to which Lucia remembered being subjected in the wake of the apparition were, to a remarkable extent, tensions with members of the community and with her own family. Lucia's problems with the community first became evident in her alienation from the village priest during the course of the apparition and became quite serious when this priest, who was evidently very popular, left Fatima, reportedly so that he would not be associated with what was happening there. People blamed her, Lucia said, for his departure.[182] While Lucia does not say much more than this about her relations at this time with her friends and neighbors, it is clear that she was receiving little support from these quarters and that she felt this acutely.

Lucia's difficulties with her family during the period in which the apparitions took place and in the months that followed seemed to be chiefly difficulties with her mother. It is clear that there had been problems in Lucia's relationship with her mother some years before the apparition, and these were apparently sharpened and magnified by the events of the summer of 1917.

Lucia's mother was not in good health at that time, and indeed, that summer she once again became seriously ill and was thought to be on her deathbed. Lucia recalled that each child was summoned to her bedside to receive her last blessing, and that she had said to Lucia: "My poor daughter, what will become of you without your mother! I am dying with my heart pierced through because of you." She then began to cry bitterly and clasped Lucia in her arms. Lucia's eldest sister then took Lucia into the kitchen and told her not to return to the sickroom, saying that her mother was dying of the grief that Lucia had caused. Sometime later, two of her sisters reportedly told Lucia that if she had really seen the Virgin, she should ask her to make their mother well, and that they would do whatever the Virgin asked. Lucia said that she then went immediately to the Cova da Iria to offer this petition—and that when she returned, her mother was feeling better. When her mother was told about this, however, Lucia said that her response was "How strange! Our Lady cured me and somehow I still don't believe! I don't understand how this can be."[183] She is said to have responded in a similar way to the signs reported during the apparition.

Lucia's recollections of her mother's insistence, on several important occasions, that her daughter was lying and was responsible for the family's troubles, and of her mother's beating her, have already been noted. When Maria Rosa was told, for example, that some people were ready to kill her daughter, Lucia recalled that her mother said that she did not care "so long as they force her to confess the truth," and went on to boast that she always told the truth herself, no matter whom it might affect.[184] On the other hand, her mother was also sometimes very kind to her, particularly when Lucia became pale and weak herself as a result of the stress she was enduring. Lucia was very careful in her memoirs to exonerate her mother for this duplicitous behavior and saw it as a special grace from God that she never felt the slightest resentment toward her mother for the times she was treated badly. Her mother had been right, she said, to say that she was unworthy of such a favor as an appearance of the Virgin and therefore to conclude that she was lying, which is why she had beaten her.[185] Apparently, Lucia had accepted beating and other mistreatment as lessons in humility and as occasions for the offering of sacrifices and reparations for the sins of others.

The apparition at Fatima, which was declared worthy of the assent of the faithful by José Correia da Silva, bishop of Leiria, on 13 October 1930, is the most important of the three recognized twentieth century apparitions, in the sense that it has profoundly affected how most of the subsequent apparitions have been perceived and understood. Fatima was not widely publicized and in fact was barely known outside of Portugal for more than two decades. In the early 1940s, however, as Roman Catholics in many lands struggled to make sense of the war, the messages which Lucia reportedly received at Fatima, some of which had only recently been revealed in her memoirs (and which will be discussed in later chapters of this study), began to attract international attention. In the postwar years, the Catholic world was deluged with Fatima literature, including some of the presumed Fatima messages, as the "Virgin of Fatima" became an important ally of the Church in its struggle against socialism and communism.

Many of the apparitions reported in the postwar years repeated the dramatic scenarios that were prominent at Fatima or in these Fatima messages: the dancing sun, Communion from an angel, the promise of a visible sign foreshadowing chastisements, and warnings about Russia. Indeed, paradigms associated with Fatima became so much a part of the consciousness of devotees of these later apparitions that many expected their seers to meet a premature death, as had Jacinta and Francisco. One later visionary reported seeing Jacinta and Francisco in the company of the Virgin.[186] Supporters of another apparition sought to authenticate their devotion with a story that some of Lucia's relatives had been divinely led to visit their site and had found what had been reported there to be credible.[187] In many of these later apparitions the Virgin is reported to have said that she had returned because people had neglected or forgotten the messages she had conveyed at Fatima. For the many Roman Catholics who believed and found meaning in the Marian apparitions that followed the Second World War, Fatima, along with La Salette and Lourdes, had become a model by which the authenticity of a later apparition might be tested, and those who have seen the later apparitions as authentic have usually understood them as extensions of the mission which the Virgin had inaugurated at Fatima.

CHAPTER 2

Personal Crises of Health, Public Crises of Faith

SAN DAMIANO

Physical and Spiritual Interventions for a Dysfunctional Body

THE history of the apparition at San Damiano, Italy (1964–1981) is to a considerable extent the history of the seer who reported it and who, for its duration of almost sixteen years, stood at the center of the considerable amount of attention it received. Except for a period of about ten years, Rosa Quattrini was ill for much of her adult life. Her period of good health, which she believed she owed to a miraculous healing, coincided with the time in which the Roman Catholic Church was undergoing the tremendous changes wrought by the Second Vatican Council. Rosa's understanding of physical and spiritual illness and health, which she communicated, along with her apparition experiences, to the many visitors to San Damiano, became important for many Roman Catholics who were troubled by those changes. The cult which grew up around her reported apparitions of the Virgin was influenced by another healing cult surrounding the Italian stigmatic, Padre Pio (1887–1968),[1] and in the later stages of its development overlapped to some degree with the resistance, led by the traditionalist archbishop Marcel Lefebvre, to the reforms instituted by Vatican II. To understand Rosa Quattrini, her concerns, and her visionary encounters with the Virgin Mary, it is important to begin with a brief sketch of her earlier life.

Rosa was born on 26 January 1909 to Federico and Giacomina Buzzini, at Sentimento di Rottofreno, in the province of Piacenza in north-central Italy. Of the seven children born to this couple, four daughters survived childhood, Rosa being second to the youngest. The family was a part of the Buzzini clan, headed by Federico's father Paolo; and after Rosa's father died, when Rosa was only two, Giacomina and her daughters continued to live near Paolo, following him when he moved to rent a farm at Guzzano. The daily life of Rosa and her sisters was comprised of school and farm work. But while her sisters were apparently inclined to study, Rosa herself showed little interest in it and left school as soon as possible, attending only up to the third grade. Indeed, her older sister Anna recalled that Rosa had seldom attended school even when enrolled. There was much to be done, Anna said; their grandfather wanted them to work; and since Rosa did not like to study, the family was content to let her watch the flocks.[2]

All three of Rosa's sisters decided on religious vocations, two becoming foreign missionaries and one a Carmelite nun.[3] Rosa, however, remained and continued to work at home. In her spare time she taught children their catechism and was involved in Catholic Action for Youth. On 7 October 1937, at the age of twenty-eight, she married Giuseppe Quattrini, a young man who at that time was working in a brickyard.

Rosa and Giuseppe Quattrini lived and raised their three children at various places in the province of Piacenza, their circumstances being marked, it seems, by considerable mobility, financial insecurity, and chronic ill health. Not long after their marriage they moved in with Rosa's paternal aunt, Adele, whose son had died suddenly, leaving her alone on a rented farm at Villo di Vigolzone. From there the Quattrinis moved to Gornegliano, where they rented a farm that had belonged to Guiseppe's family. Difficulties with their landlord forced them to leave there in 1943, however, and they moved to the little town of San Damiano. In 1954 they moved to a small farm at Villo, and in 1960 they returned to San Damiano to be close to their daughter, Giacomina, who was married and living in a nearby town.

Rosa's poor health appears to have been precipitated by her first pregnancy in 1938 (Giacomina) and aggravated by the two which followed in 1943 and 1952 (Paolo and Pier Giorgio respectively). All three children were born by caesarian section. The first surgical intervention apparently led to a ventral hernia, which doctors attempted but apparently failed to correct at the time of the 1952 surgery. It is clear, at least, that Rosa's health problems persisted, and in 1958 her symptoms worsened. At this time, in spite of her wearing a prescribed corset, she reportedly suffered from severe abdominal pain and intestinal blockage, and acquaintances said that she could not eat properly, was very weak, and soon became bedridden.[4]

Rosa's condition became acute in 1961, in which year she was hospitalized twice. She was admitted to a hospital in Ponte dell'Olio on March 6, after having suffered for twenty-four hours from violent abdominal pains accompanied by vomiting and anorexia. The hospital record noted that her abdomen was the site of a "large eventration due to three previous caesarian interventions." She was dismissed on March 14.[5] Three months later, on June 30, she was admitted to a hospital in Piacenza for essentially the same problem and remained there until July 8.[6] The published literature does not specify what treatment she received during these hospitalizations, nor does it say whether any special regimen was to be followed at home.

Rosa herself, her Aunt Adele, the parish priest of San Damiano, and some neighbors all testify that Rosa's ill health ended suddenly in the fall of 1961. While she had been virtually bedridden from the time of her last hospitalization until September 29, after that date she reportedly resumed a normal routine.[7] Rosa attributed her sudden recovery to an encounter with an unknown woman who was collecting alms for Padre Pio.

Rosa's own descriptions of the encounter that allegedly led to her recovery can be found in transcriptions of interviews, all of which were conducted some years later, after Rosa had begun reporting apparitions of the Virgin Mary. The earliest of these was an interview with the Italian writer Dino Buzzati in 1966.[8] Rosa told Buzzati that she had been sent home from the hospital because there was no hope for her recovery. Once home she felt a little better, but then she fell ill again and was worse than before. On September 29, the Feast of St. Michael the Archangel, she was at home in bed with only her Aunt Adele to attend to her. Giuseppe, who was himself scheduled to be hospitalized soon for treatment of a hernia, was out gathering chestnuts for the family. Around noon a young woman came to the house, whom Rosa described as about twenty-five years old, very beautiful, more blonde than brunette, and dressed in poor clothing. She wore a bluish-grey dress and carried a black purse, and she said she came from far away.

The woman first talked with Adele, Rosa said, and told her that she was seeking a contribution for candles for the sanctuary of Padre Pio at San Giovanni Rotondo. When she asked for a contribution of fifteen hundred lire, Adele replied that they were poor and that they only had a thousand lire, which they had borrowed. When the woman said that they should nonetheless make a contribution, Adele said that while she had always made offerings before, this time she could not. Her niece was ill; she had to be cared for; and the family, she insisted, had only the thousand lire. The woman then asked to see her niece and Adele directed her to Rosa's bed.

The woman entered the room, Rosa said, greeted her, and asked her what was wrong. She told the visitor that she was "terribly wounded" and had been sent home from the hospital because there was no hope. At that moment, Rosa said, the noon bells rang. The woman then told her to get up, but she replied that she was unable to. The woman told her to hold out her hand; when she still could not rise, even with the visitor's help, she was told to hold out both her hands. Grasping both of the woman's hands, Rosa said, she felt a great shock. The woman told her again to get up, and this time she rose. When she began to exclaim, "I am healed! I am healed!" the woman told her to be quiet and to recite an Agnus Dei and five Paters, five Aves, and five Glorias according to the instructions of Padre Pio. She recited these prayers; then the woman placed her hands on Rosa's wounds, and the wounds were suddenly healed.

In an interview in 1968, Rosa gave a somewhat different and more elaborate account of the events that brought about her healing. The woman told her to recite the Paters, Aves, and Glorias seven times, she said, in honor of the wounds of Jesus. The woman also told her to recite another prayer, apparently a special form of the Ave Maria, seven times, in honor of Our Lady of the Seven Sorrows.[9] Each time she recited the cycle of prayers, the woman placed her hands on her stomach; when the prayers were finished, the wounds were healed.[10] The woman also asked for a glass of water and put in it five grains of holy earth, an olive leaf, and a bit of a candle consecrated on the preceding February 2 (The Feast of the Purification of the Virgin, or Candlemas). She had Rosa drink a little of this mixture and told her to place what was left outside on the window ledge. The woman told her that for the next three mornings she was to rise at five o'clock, the hour at which Padre Pio said Mass, and drink a little of this water.[11]

The woman then (returning to the account given to Buzzati) told Rosa that she was to go as soon as possible to see Padre Pio. When she asked her how she could do this, since their landlord had taken all their money, the woman replied that they should find another place to live and that then she should make the trip. When Rosa said that she did not even have money for food, much less for proper clothes for the trip, the woman told her not to worry: when the time came, she would have everything she needed. In the meantime, her aunt, she said, had gotten five hundred lire, which she gave to the woman, and the woman then left. There were some people outside, including her little boy, Pier Giorgio, who was playing. He alone saw the woman leave.

In two interviews in 1968 and 1974, Adele, who had lived with the family for many years and who had been largely responsible for their care during Rosa's illness, basically echoed her niece's account. She added that during Rosa's 1961 hospitalizations, a doctor had warned her that her niece was in constant danger of death. He told her that Rosa had five wounds in the stomach, and a case of "perforated peritonitis," that her intestines were pushing out through the wounds, and that she would require much care. Adele recalled telling the doctor that she had placed her niece in the care of the Madonna. She would do what she could for her, she said, but she also had the rest of the family to look after.[12]

Adele said that while Rosa had had confidence in the woman who had come to collect alms for Padre Pio, she herself had at first been skeptical. To judge from the transcripts of the later interviews, her initial skepticism pertained not just to the woman's mission and her claims but, in some measure at least, to the healing itself. She explained her giving of the money to the woman by saying that she had given it "for the grace received" (that is, for Rosa's healing) and in honor of the Madonna and that she was not really thinking about Padre Pio at all.[13] It should be noted that belief in the healing powers of the stigmatic Padre Pio had by this time become one of the most widely held tenets of the folk piety of the Italian penninsula.

Adele recalled in fact that she had had an open disagreement with the woman about the powers of Padre Pio.[14] She did not at that time, she said, share this woman's faith in those powers, but she told her that if Rosa were healed, then "one would see." Indeed, when the woman pressed her on the matter, Adele conceded that if her niece were healed, she would believe. After the woman left, however, she expressed her reservations to Rosa, lamenting that they had given her five hundred lire without knowing who she was and whether Padre Pio had really sent her. Rosa tried to reassure her and insisted that she had indeed been healed. Adele then went into her room, where there was a statue of the Madonna, and she asked the Madonna to make sure that the money she had given the woman really went to Padre Pio. At that she heard a very strong voice say, "Have confidence, your sick one will be healed." It was at this time, apparently, that Adele began to share Rosa's confidence that she would soon be in good health and that her healing was a miraculous event attributable to the intervention of Padre Pio and his mysterious messenger on this particularly auspicious day.

While it seems clear that Rosa's health did suddenly improve at about this time, not everyone who knew her interpreted this improvement as she and her aunt did. Some apparently said that Rosa began to wear a new corset on this day, and that it was this that improved her health. Roland Maisonneuve and Michel de Belsunce, who collected and edited the documents pertaining to these events in 1983, make a point of refuting this, maintaining that it was not until six months later that an anonymous benefactor bought a new corset for Rosa. During the fall of 1961, they say, she had continued to wear an old and apparently dilapidated one.[15] With respect to the allegedly miraculous healing itself, they refer to the testimonies of two doctors and a nurse who is said to have cared for Rosa after a second period of ill health which began in 1970. These attest to the perfect closure of the scars from Rosa's caesarian sections and the absence of any eventration. There is, however, no direct medical evidence available from the fall of 1961 that would collaborate these testimonies to her healing.[16] The clearest contemporary evidence for the healing is the testimony of acquaintances that she suddenly resumed her normal activities without any indication of pain.

Dom Edgardo Pellacani, the parish priest of San Damiano during this period, gave an account of Rosa's healing which says nothing directly about what was said or done at Rosa's bedside on 29 September 1961, but from which some crucial features of the event can be deduced. After Rosa began reporting her visions of the Virgin in 1964, Pellacani became the center of a great deal of controversy, being accused, among other things, of having orchestrated Rosa's healing and even some aspects of the apparitions.[17] In preparing their collection of documents, Maisonneuve and De Belsunce submitted a questionnaire to Pellacani, and his response, which apparently came sometime after his dismissal from the parish in 1969, is basically a defense of his own activities during the several years that followed Rosa's sudden and purportedly miraculous recovery.

Pellacani recalled that Rosa had asked him to bring her Communion because of her poor health, which, he noted, was due to an eventration connected with caesarian interventions. He said that she had sometimes suffered from sharp pains in the stomach, fell to the ground unexpectedly, and vomited frequently, and that her sole nourishment was a little puree of fruit and cooked vegetables. He found out about her recovery, he said, sometime during the following week through a local woman, Maria Mazzoni, who, convinced that Rosa had been healed through the intercession of Padre Pio, told him that she had sent an account of the miracle to the editorial staff of the bulletin published by the hospital at San Giovanni Rotondo. Pellacani then met Rosa herself going toward the church, inquired about her health and the rumor that she had been healed, and was then told about her encounter with the mysterious stranger. Pellacani, who was himself the spiritual advisor to Padre Pio prayer groups in the area, said that he was perplexed that a woman would be collecting alms for Padre Pio without his knowledge and told Rosa that she should have sent the woman to him.[18]

Padre Pio and Rosa's Service to the Sick

In the fall of 1961, Rosa became active in the parish in ways that had apparently been impossible for her earlier because of her illnesses, and in view of the way she now understood (or at least was beginning to understand) her remarkable recovery, it is not surprising that one parish activity to which she gave very particular attention was a Padre Pio prayer group. In May 1962 she went with a group of pilgrims led by Pellacani to San Giovanni Rotondo. Clearly, this pilgrimage was for Rosa a kind of thanksgiving for her healing, and she recalled it later as having been surrounded by an aura of the miraculous. She told Buzzati in 1966, for example, that sometime before their scheduled departure she had received an anonymous letter containing the money she needed for the trip and had understood this gift as the fulfillment of the promise made by her mysterious visitor on September 29, that when the time came she would have everything that she needed.[19]

Rosa recalled three incidents at San Giovanni Rotondo that gave her a sense of a special connection to Padre Pio.[20] First, while the pilgrimage group was gathered in the church near the altar of the Sacred Heart, a Capucin brother approached them and asked "in the name of Padre Pio" where he could find the *miraculé* (the one who had been miraculously healed) from San Damiano. When Rosa was pointed out to him, he reportedly told the group that despite the stormy weather they must go outside and make the Stations of the Cross along the boulevard. This incident was confirmed by a pilgrim from Piacenza, who recalled that about midafternoon, after the benediction, a father from the convent had sought the group out to tell them that Padre Pio wanted them to make the Stations of the Cross with the *miraculé*.[21] Rosa recalled that their group went outside in the rain, but that by the time they had finished their prayers the sun had come out and their clothes were dry.

The second incident was an encounter with a woman whom Rosa identified as the one who had come to her house on September 29. Rosa said that on Saturday morning, the day after the group had been told to say the Stations of the Cross, she was sitting on the church square with a companion, reciting the Rosary. When she had finished, she suddenly saw the woman "who had healed her." Her companion, however, and others standing nearby apparently saw no one. Rosa said that the woman asked her if she recognized her and she replied that she did, telling the woman that she knew she (the woman) was the Madonna but that "you have not wanted me [before now] to say it." The woman then reportedly said that she was "the Mother of Consolation and the Afflicted" and that Rosa should tell this "to the professor and to those at San Damiano who have not wanted to believe in your healing." She then told her that after Mass the two of them would meet at the altar and she would take her to Padre Pio.[22]

The third incident was Rosa's alleged meeting with Padre Pio himself. Rosa recalled that after the Mass she found herself standing with the woman near the altar. The woman (whom Rosa in these later recollections now referred to as "the Heavenly Mama") opened the door which led to the sacristy, and there they immediately encountered Padre Pio. Rosa said she knelt before him and told him that she did not know what to make of "all this." Padre Pio responded by pointing to the woman and saying, "There is the one who will confirm it for you." Then, she said, he told her that she should go home and care for the sick.

In another account of this incident, Rosa said that Padre Pio pointed to the woman and told her (Rosa) that she would need to be very strong in order to carry the cross and that it would be very heavy.[23] But he reassured her that with Jesus in her heart and the Heavenly Mama to hold her hand she would be able to endure everything. He also told her to tell her family that they should allow her to care for the sick wherever she was called. Rosa said that she told this to her aunt and to her husband and they gave her their permission.

Pellacani, in responding to the questions of Maisonneuve and De Belsunce, recalled that Rosa was one of forty persons on this diocesan pilgrimage. He said that while he was not present on this occasion when Rosa met Padre Pio, he learned of the encounter later. Rosa had also told him that Padre Pio had advised her to care for the sick at Piacenza. He recalled being a little perplexed about this since Rosa was not a trained nurse and could not be separated for very long from her family. He also said that Rosa had told him that in San Giovanni Rontondo she had seen the woman who on September 29 had come to her house and healed her, and that this woman was the Virgin Mary.[24]

When she returned to San Damiano, Rosa began her "service to the sick" by offering practical assistance such as feeding and bathing, and sometimes also companionship, to people she encountered who seemed to be in need. Her accounts of this activity indicate that she understood herself as directed to each of her patients by divine guidance and that she saw each one as in a kind of spiritual need that she was able to meet.

Rosa said, for example, that one Monday she went to a civil hospital, where she encountered a member of a religious order in the elevator. She told this brother that she had been sent by Padre Pio to care for the sick, but that she did not know where to go. He told her that he had been waiting for her, and he took her to the room of a man who was facing a serious operation. This man's two daughters had been looking for someone to care for him, and they were worried not only about his health but about the state of his soul, since he "was not reconciled to God." The brother told the two women to entrust their father to Rosa who, he said, would offer many prayers for him. Rosa recalled that after five terrible days, during which the man was quite hostile and during which she prayed constantly for him, he was converted. The man then underwent his operation and recovered from it very well, Rosa said, after which he and his family were all very grateful to her and supportive of her and her family.[25]

On another occasion, Rosa said, she was leaving her house when suddenly Padre Pio "appeared" to her and told her to go to the hospice Victor Emmanuel, because "there is there another soul to care for and to save." She went to the hospice as directed and told the mother superior that she had been sent there because they needed someone to assist one of the inmates. Rosa said that the mother superior told her that there was indeed such a need but that she had not yet spoken of it to anyone, and she then entrusted Rosa with the care of an elderly man known as "Colonel P." He was initially difficult and violent, Rosa said, and did not want anyone near him, but she prayed over the case intently, and eventually he began to understand her purposes, to rely on her, and to develop an affection for her. He was then willing to confess to a priest and was converted. According to Rosa, she cared for him for five or six months before he died.[26]

Rosa's services to sick strangers ended after a few years, when her aunt became ill with bronchial pneumonia and her assistance was needed at home. Rosa's new responsibilities became clear to her, apparently, in the course of another pilgrimage to San Giovanni Rotondo. There, she said, in mid-September 1964, she went to Padre Pio for confession, and he told her that her mission was finished, that she should return to San Damiano to care for her aunt, and that a great event awaited her. He advised her to pray at a small chapel in San Damiano and to invoke the archangel Michael for assistance. He told her to prepare herself for her mission and never to be discouraged because Michael, her "Mama in Heaven," and he himself would always be near her. She said that he told her, "Pray much. Be very humble. Carry the cross with Jesus."[27]

During this period, Rosa very clearly understood Padre Pio to be the main agent through which God intervened in and guided her life. Her accounts of the encounter with the woman purporting to collect alms for him show that she believed that he was primarily responsible for her healing, a belief encouraged, no doubt, by persons close to her who had been drawn into the Padre Pio cult, such as her aunt and the woman who reportedly had sent an account of Rosa's healing to San Giovanni Rotondo. While on her first pilgrimage to San Giovanni Rotondo, Rosa said she met for the second time the mysterious woman who had cured her, and although she said she then recognized her as the Virgin Mary, it was not this woman but Padre Pio whom she considered to be directing her life. It was he who instructed her to care for the sick and then, a few years later, when her aunt became ill, to return home to care for her aunt. It was only when the "great event" which he had predicted actually came to pass that Padre Pio moved away from center stage for Rosa and was replaced by the figure who in her earlier experiences of the supernatural had seemed to be merely his messenger.

Light and Joy from the Heavens

It was on 16 October 1964 that this momentous event took place. On that date, according to Rosa, the Virgin Mary appeared to her—under very different circumstances and in a very different way than she had appeared before—and gave her a message for the public. This appearance was the first of many that Rosa was to report over the next decade that would attract international attention and that would bring pilgrims to San Damiano from France and Switzerland, as well as from Italy. The earliest written account of this experience is a transcription made sometime later that day by Pellacani of what Rosa herself had related to him.[28]

Rosa told Pellacani that at about 11:30 that morning a neighbor stopped by to ask a favor. She and this woman talked for a while, and when the noon bells sounded, the woman left.[29] Rosa said that when the bells sounded she went to pray and that when she reached the "Ecce Ancilla Domini," she heard a woman's voice say, "Come, come, I am waiting for you!" She left the house, but she continued to hear the voice calling to her. She followed the voice, and when she reached the first trellis in the vineyard near her home, she saw a beautiful light. As she came closer the light grew stronger, and the voice became sweeter and more penetrating.

Rosa said that at this point she began to weep and tremble but also to rejoice. At first she connected these manifestations with her sister Anna who was then doing missionary work in Sri Lanka. Rosa had recently received word that her sister had been with a group of nuns who had been attacked on a road, that the mother superior had been killed, and that Anna had been tied to a tree and not found until five days later when, unconscious and apparently near death, she was taken to a hospital. Rosa had just finished saying a novena for her, and she wondered if the strange experiences that followed were signs that some further misfortune had befallen her sister.[30]

When she reached the second trellis in the vineyard, she sat down on a small footstool and made the sign of the cross with her rosary. This, she said, was her way of asking the Madonna to let her know the meaning of the light and of the voice. Looking toward the heavens, she saw a cloud descend with stars of gold and silver dancing and turning around it. Then she saw a great shower of roses and rose petals, but none of them reached the ground. The cloud, she said, covered all the foliage of a plum tree until she could see only a bit of the trunk. Then she saw a red globe alight on the branches of a nearby pear tree, at which the white cloud disappeared, and over the trunk of the plum tree she saw the Virgin Mary.[31]

Rosa described the Madonna as wearing a white cloak and a blue gown tied at the waist with a white sash. A rosary with shining white beads hung from this sash on the left side and ended with a crucifix on which there seemed to be a living figure of Jesus. Circling her neck was a round necklace of shining stars. Rosa said that the Virgin's arms were open and that luminous rays radiated from the palms of her hand, rays which struck Rosa on her face and body.

Rosa said that she fell to her knees and exclaimed, "Oh! My Mother! I am not worthy enough for you to come to me, but say a word and I will listen!" She described the Virgin as beautiful but sad and said that she left the plum tree and moved to the red globe above the pear tree. Then the Virgin told her, "Listen, my daughter. I have come from afar to announce to the world that it is necessary to pray, to pray much, for Jesus can no longer carry the cross. You [must] help him carry it."[32]

Rosa said she asked the Madonna to give her the strength to bear her appointed burdens. Then the Madonna told her to go promptly to the priest with the message she had been given, warning that if no one believed or prayed then great scourges and chastisements would come.[33] "Go, go, act quickly!" the Madonna told her, but Rosa responded by saying that she was not capable of announcing these things, that no one would believe her, and that people would think she was a fool. She asked for a sign that everyone could see and believe. Then she began to cry.

In her later recollections of this experience, Rosa elaborated on what she had felt.[34] She remembered that three years earlier no one believed that she had been healed. She felt that she was only a poor ignorant peasant, and she was afraid that if she reported her experience and delivered the Madonna's message, she would be judged evil and thrown in prison. These were the motivations that led her to implore the Madonna for a sign. In a later account she said she told the Madonna, "Give me a sign and I can go with serenity, with love. I will do everything. Only give me a sign."

In response to her request for a sign, Rosa said, the Madonna told her that in departing she would cause the trees to flower, and that everyone would see and would believe. She told Rosa to proceed along the road, and there she would find a child. She should send this child to find the young woman (that is, the neighbor) who had been with her a little earlier, and Rosa herself should go to the priest. The Madonna took first the rosary and then the crucifix, blessed her, and told her goodbye. She then rose and, at a height of about two meters, moved in the direction of the church. Showers of rose petals fell from her hands, and when she reached the belfry, she rose still higher and continued to move away, always in the direction of the church.[35]

Later Rosa added some details to this description of her experience. She said, for example, that there was a great deal of light when the Madonna departed and that as she rose over the pear tree she smiled at her. Rosa said she felt as if the Madonna had strengthened her.[36] In another account, Rosa said that the "rays of the Madonna" covered her with light and gave her "so much joy, sweetness, and love." She also said that when she asked the Madonna why the rose petals were falling, she was told, "these are all the nations of the world that will come here."[37]

As she departed, Rosa said, the Madonna left the sign which she had promised: the pear tree, which had previously been bare, came into full bloom, and one branch of the plum tree on which the Madonna had briefly rested her feet also began to flower. Reports of these events spread quickly. Among the first to hear them, apparently, were some Italian and American pilots at the air base adjacent to the Quattrini home, and according to some witnesses it was they who, led by an American general, joined Rosa later that day for the first public recitation of the Rosary at the tree. Later devotees saw this as significant insofar as this day was the feast of aviators, and in later interviews Rosa said that the Madonna had specifically directed her to take the message to the air base.[38]

On the afternoon of October 16, people from the area gathered in the orchard behind the Quattrini home. Some of them recalled that the pear tree was entirely white with blossoms although it still had some summer fruit on its branches. They remembered and were impressed by the fact that even though there was a considerable amount of rain that fall, these blossoms lasted for about twenty days. On October 18, an article describing the events appeared in the Piacenza daily newspaper, and after this people began to come to San Damiano from Piacenza and other more distant places. When the visitors asked Rosa if she had really seen the Madonna and if she would see her again, Rosa told them that she had indeed seen her and that the Madonna had assured her that she would return.[39]

It was apparently the blossoming pear tree and not the report of the apparition as such that attracted the most attention at the time, although most visitors, like Rosa herself, seemed to view the blossoms as a physical sign of a supernatural or spiritual event. On October 19, another Piacenza newspaper reported that hundreds of cars had lined the roads leading to San Damiano and that thousands of people had gathered around the tree, some taking the flowers to keep as relics, and some then making their way to the seer's house to speak to her, to pray, and to recite the Rosary.[40] On October 20, a newspaper reported that a metal fence had been constructed around the tree to protect it and that Rosa and her aunt stood inside the fence to receive objects that visitors wanted put in contact with the tree of the "miracle." People also threw money into the enclosure, which they understood, according to this report, as donations for the work of Padre Pio with which Rosa was connected. The newspaper accounts noted that people had come to the site from a variety of motives—faith, simple curiosity, hope for spiritual or corporeal graces—and that the sick had been observed raising their arms or crutches toward the pear tree.[41]

Rosa's report of the appearance of the Madonna on October 16 and the sudden surge of interest in the miraculous pear tree apparently brought mixed responses from her family. Her husband, Giuseppe, seems to have been supportive, but other members of the family reportedly reacted with fear and even anger. Adele remembered opposing Rosa and asking her over and over whether she knew what she was doing: "Don't you know that all this will spread? That so many people will come?" She was worried, she said, about what "people would do to us."[42] Rosa's daughter, Giacomina, who lived not far away, recalled hearing from a neighbor about her mother's experience and the flowering pear tree. She did not want to go to her parents' house to verify the report, she said, but her husband did so, and after he had seen the tree, he believed. When he told her that her parents' house was full of visitors, she was furious, and she became even more angry when she finally went there herself and saw how many people were there. For two months, she said, she was unwilling to listen to anyone speak about her mother's visions and the other presumably miraculous events.[43] Rosa remembered that her son, Paolo, was also angry and left the house for a long time, telling her, "You make us look like fools; we are all fools!"[44]

Pellacani heard about Rosa's experience of October 16 later that afternoon, when he returned to the parish from Piacenza. In an interview given in 1981, he recalled that an elderly woman had knocked on his door and told him to hurry to Rosa. When he arrived at her home, he found her kneeling in the garden under the pear tree. Others had gathered also and were talking about the miracle, and he recalled feeling it was "too much" and fearing that an avalanche of ridicule would descend upon the village. However, Pellacani himself was later accused of having instigated the publicity surrounding the apparition by alerting the newspapers,[45] so one should consider the possibility that this recollection might be one-sided and not entirely disinterested. Pellacani admitted that he had spoken with journalists from Piacenza, but he said that this was only to urge them not to print a single line about the matter. He had had no previous experience with journalists, he said, and although the reporters listened to him politely, they did not respect his (presumed) wishes that the incident not be publicized. After that, he noted, the course of events was out of his control.[46]

Pellacani mentioned that it was his uncertainty about the authenticity of the apparition that led him to take Rosa to San Giovanni Rotondo the following spring (1965) to confess once again to Padre Pio. He reasoned that the Capuchin stigmatic, whom he considered to be a saint and able to read consciences, would be able to discern the origin of Rosa's experiences. Since San Damiano and its visionary were now quite well known, particularly among Padre Pio's followers, Pellicani supposed that if Rosa were lying or inspired by some evil spirit, Padre Pio would refuse her absolution and would publicly rebuke her. Rosa reportedly did not have to wait long after arriving in San Giovanni Rotondo for this meeting with the stigmatic. Pellacani himself took her into the church and he sat with his eyes on the confessional. Indeed, he said he saw Padre Pio's hand giving her absolution, and shortly after this Rosa told him that the holy man had confirmed the heavenly origin of her experiences.[47]

Rosa had indicated to those who came to see her in the days after this first apparition that she expected the Virgin to return, an expectation that appears to have been based on the Virgin's parting words ("So long, until I see you again!") rather than on any announced date. In later interviews, Rosa remembered more specific directives being given during this first appearance, perhaps reflecting the pattern of her later communications with the Virgin. In 1966, she told Buzzati that the Virgin had told her, "I will return each Friday. I will give you messages and you will announce them to the world."[48] In 1968, she said the Virgin had promised, "I will come always, as long as you live, every Friday. Every day I will be with you, as well as my Son, Jesus."[49] During this interview she also said that the Virgin had told her to dress in black as a token of sharing the suffering of Jesus. Indeed, by the time a year had elapsed, Rosa, dressed in black, was going to the pear tree each Friday and sometimes on special festivals, and conveying the Virgin's messages to large crowds of assembled pilgrims.[50] This continued for about four years, through February 1968, when Rosa was ordered by the bishop of Piacenza not to appear in public. She then moved indoors and used loudspeakers to convey the Virgin's messages to the waiting crowds. In 1970, in response to the bishop's threatened sanctions, Rosa ceased reporting the messages publicly.[51] To those who sought her out, however, she had become a spiritual mother, who could read troubled souls, recognize religious vocations, and direct people onto a spiritual path. In her reception of pilgrims to San Damiano, she was carrying on the "service to the sick" which she had begun after her healing, under what she believed to be Padre Pio's direction. In devotional literature, she is affectionately called "Mama Rosa."

Graces and Comfort from the Earth: San Damiano's Healing Water

It was about a year after the appearances of the Virgin began that Rosa said she received from Mary the revelation that a source of miraculous water would be found at the apparition site. On the 6th and 13th of August, 1965, Mary reportedly told her that people should come to this spot because from it would issue a great source of graces, a pure water that would cleanse both body and soul.[52] The following year, on October 21, Rosa said that the Madonna had confirmed that water would be found here and that it was necessary for a well to be dug. Then, eight days later, Rosa said that the Virgin, accompanied by several angels, appeared and held in her hand a rosary made of white roses, symbolizing graces, which ended in a cross having two red roses, symbolizing suffering. With this rosary, the Madonna traced a circle over the spot where a well was now being dug. Then she herself descended into the circle and said, "The water will be very clear, very fresh, and miraculous."[53]

On November 18, the Virgin again spoke to Rosa of the water and said that the digging should continue. She said that people should wash and purify themselves with the water, drink it, and have confidence in it. Many people would be healed from physical illnesses, and many would be sanctified. The water should be taken to the seriously ill, to the dying, to suffering souls, and into homes. The Virgin promised that people would obtain infinite graces from it.[54]

At this point, Rosa appealed to an engineer, Antonio Pelagatti, to take charge of the digging of the well. Pelagatti said that he had had occasion to meet Rosa before then, but that he did not know her well. Yet when Rosa unexpectedly asked him to assume this task, he agreed to do so. The work was done by hand, because Rosa told him that the Madonna wanted it that way.[55]

Rosa was aware in advance, it was said, of the various layers of rock that would be encountered as the well was dug, and it is clear, at least, that she was very much concerned with the well's progress. On December 2, about two weeks after Pelagatti assumed the task of supervision, the first water began to flow, at a depth of a few meters. At this point, however, a businessman from the province of Reggio who was an expert in this kind of work was contacted, and soon he joined the project. The well was deepened, and water began to flow in sufficient supply to meet current needs. But, according to Pelagatti, Rosa insisted that the well be dug to a depth of twelve meters: the "Heavenly Mama" had told her that at this depth there was a peculiar rock formation where a particularly abundant vein of water would be found.

On December 16, digging had to stop at a depth of five meters because the pump could not cope with the abundant supply of water and because the water made it impossible for the workers to penetrate a particularly hard layer of rock. Some weeks later, however, the water supply lessened, and the work of digging began again. Reportedly, at a depth of twelve meters the peculiar rock formation was found, and when this shelf of rock was struck with a pickax, a crevice opened from which water began to flow. Rosa insisted that the digging continue for another five meters where the "vein of water" itself would be found. A drill was brought in to cut through the rock and, at a depth of seventeen meters, the vein was reportedly discovered, just as Rosa had predicted.

It was apparently not until late in 1967, however, that the well was finally completed to Rosa's and the Madonna's satisfaction. Several times that year, Rosa said, she had received instructions from heavenly persons about how water should be withdrawn from the well and distributed. On May 26, the archangel Michael appeared along with the Madonna, and speaking in the name of the Eternal Father, gave orders that everyone should prepare plastic casks suitable for carrying large quantities of water, as well as smaller bottles. He said that when "the terrible moment of discouragement" would come, because "no one had heard his word," people should take the water from the bottles and put it on their faces, and they would then be safe. The archangel also gave some very specific directions for drawing water from the well. Only one person at a time should draw water from the well, and no one else should enter the enclosure. When families came to draw water they should first recite ten Ave Marias and say, "Heavenly Mama, save us and free us body and soul." With this prayer, he said, much water would pour forth, and by means of it people would recover their health and be saved. A few days after that, Rosa said, Michael appeared again and described the water as bringing light, love, peace, and health into homes and families. He exhorted people to let it be their strength and power against all the diabolical powers that were unleashed against them.[56]

The healing qualities of the water were also noted and emphasized in messages from the Virgin. On 13 October 1967, for example, Rosa said that the Heavenly Mama had told her that drinking large quantities of the water would restore health to body and soul and would purify and free one from obsessions. When bathing afflicted parts of the body with the water, one should recite three Ave Marias and one Credo. Rosa said that the Madonna promised to bless with faith those who did this and confer upon them all graces and comfort.[57]

New Bodies and New Problems: Rosa's Institutional Legacy

A well was not the only thing, however, that the Virgin called for at the site. In the summer of 1965, more than a year before she ordered the digging of the well, Rosa said that the Madonna named the place where she had appeared her "garden of paradise" and envisioned there a "City of Roses," with charitable foundations to care for orphaned children, for the elderly who had devoted themselves to religious service, and for the sick. The details of these foundations and whom they were to serve were spelled out in various messages over the next several years.[58]

Several different organizations prepared the way for the Virgin's "City of Roses" or were formed for the specific purpose of building it. In 1965 a group of Italians formed the Comitato Madonna di San Da-miano, whose primary concern was to publicize the events at San Da-miano and the messages that Rosa said the Virgin had entrusted to her. It was this group which, during the few months of its existence, pub-lished the first brochure on the San Damiano phenomena. Apparently no property was ever bought by this group as such, though a member did buy, near the San Damiano church, a small house, which was placed at the disposal of pilgrims. This group was officially disbanded in the fall of 1965 after the bishop of Piacenza, on September 7, issued a negative opinion concerning the apparition's supernatural origin, and a few years later the house set aside for pilgrims was sold and put to another use.[59]

The vision of the City of Roses was revived, however, in 1967, with the formation of an association called Pro San Damiano, which, while it sought to be international in scope, was in fact primarily Swiss. Rosa gave this group permission to collect the offerings of the faithful who wished to contribute to the building of the City of Roses, and she turned over to it the offerings she herself had already received.[60] Members of the association soon began to purchase lands and houses designated by Rosa as the sites where the Madonna wished her charitable foundations to be established.

This association, however, was plagued by dissention. There was apparently tension between the different nationalities in its constituency, and the development of the properties acquired by the members was delayed while an international legal agreement was sought that would guarantee the project's completion. Several consultations and studies were called for, but the association equivocated, and one solution for the completion of the project which gained the support of the majority of the members was rejected by Rosa in the name of the Virgin. At this point the foreign members withdrew, and the Swiss president resigned.

G. de Lutiis has credited the Swiss supporters of Rosa in this association with her rather rapid rise to fame and, more importantly, with the sustained attention directed toward San Damiano and its seer by European Catholics, in the face of the opposition of the local bishops. The Swiss had not only acquired property in and around San Damiano, but they began to publish monthly magazines in French, German, and Italian, and were apparently also instrumental in the publication of several books. What de Lutiis has called the "finely tuned propaganda" generated by these Swiss supporters and the international network of relationships they formed seem to have spread the message of San Damiano throughout Europe and to have brought thousands of non-Italian Catholics into the circle of its devotees.[61]

Most of Rosa's Swiss supporters in the 1970s were apparently also supporters of the traditionalist leader Mgr. Marcel Lefebvre, former archbishop of Dakar and of Tule, whose complaints about some of the reform statutes of the Second Vatican Council began to attract attention after his founding of the Fraternity of St. Pius X in Fribourg in 1969 and a traditionalist seminary at Ecône in the Rhone Valley in 1971. This led to increasing tension between Rosa and her Swiss friends, Rosa having no desire in these years to complicate her already tenuous relationship with Roman Catholic authorities. In the fall of 1976, a crisis of sorts was approaching, when Lefebvre, who had just been suspended *a divinis* by Pope Paul VI, visited San Damiano with the intention of celebrating there a series of Latin Masses. His plans were thwarted, chiefly because Rosa was not very cooperative. At that point her relationship with the Swiss devotees of the San Damiano apparition sharply deteriorated.[62]

In the meantime, an Italian group had been organized which also had the goal of furthering the Virgin's charitable projects, the Ospizio Madonna delle Rose. When this organization was founded in the spring of 1974, the members of Pro San Damiano were invited to join and to turn over to this group the properties that they had acquired, but the majority refused. The Ospizio Madonna delle Rose was also plagued with legal problems and had difficulty, apparently, in gaining from the Italian government the necessary charters recognizing the organization and granting approval to develop the lands it had acquired.[63] Finally, Rosa herself was persuaded to assume the title to the properties acquired by the members of this group so that construction of the planned facilities could proceed. Envisioned now for the City of Roses were a hospital and medical center, a village for youth, foundations for orphans and the elderly, accommodations for pilgrims, and an ecumenical Marian center.[64]

In December 1978, a district attorney sequestered the assets titled under Rosa's name and the names of her children and opened a judicial investigation, charging Rosa, her children, her son-in-law, and two foreigners with perpetrating a fraud for personal benefit and with criminal intent in their publicizing of the appearances of the Virgin and her messages. While the sequester against the assets of Rosa's children was soon lifted, that against Rosa's own assets remained in effect, and the criminal charges filed in 1978 were still under investigation at the time of her death on 5 September 1981.[65]

Rosa's death did little, however, to settle the problem of the assignment of the assets intended for the City of Roses. In a will dated 27

March 1979, Rosa had bequeathed her properties to the pope. The pope was apprised of the terms of this will not long after it had been opened and registered, and on 4 November 1981, the bishop of Piacenza, acting in the name of the pope, announced to the press that the pontiff had refused to accept Rosa's bequest.[66]

Rosa's family, who had agreed to the terms of her will shortly after it was opened and registered, also refused at this time to assume the title to these properties. Some months after her death, at the request of her family, a curator was named to administer these assets. On 30 September 1982, on the recommendation of the district attorney, they were put in the care of an administrator named by the Tribunal of Piacenza, and shortly thereafter this Tribunal lifted the last sequester against them.[67]

One further legal problem remained but was resolved a few months later, on 7 December 1982, when a civil magistrate dismissed the still-outstanding charges of fraud against Rosa's family and two of her supporters. It had not been demonstrated, the magistrate ruled, that those who had donated money for the City had been led to do so by "artifices and maneuvers" arising from fraudulent intent. It had not been shown, in other words, that Rosa's visions and auditions had been staged for the purposes of monetary gain. It was noted, moreover, that Rosa's family had not profited from the projects that had been begun: the houses that had been purchased and remodeled had been used solely as hotels for pilgrims, with very modest charges, and had clearly not been profitmaking ventures. The family's support of an association which would be responsible for administering all gifts and offerings was also taken as additional evidence of their lack of any criminal intent.[68]

Both the will of 1979 and an earlier will had made it clear that Rosa wanted these assets to be used for the work she said the Virgin had requested, and the Ospizio, which Rosa had designated to oversee this work after her break with Pro San Damiano, was the logical group to take charge of the assets. In new statutes chartered on 23 August 1982, this organization, which now had the support of the Quattrini family, declared itself willing to abide by Rosa's wishes and to continue the work she had undertaken. At this point, therefore, it filed a formal request with the regional authority for legal recognition and authorization to accept Rosa's inheritance and to move ahead with the projects which she and those who had given her money and property had envisioned.[69]

The Ospizio thus obtained, at last, a clear title to the majority of the properties that had been purchased for the City of Roses. While it seems that not much building has been done since 1982, this organization still owns and administers the properties and in 1988 it was operating two houses for pilgrims, a home for the elderly, an infirmary offering medical services to the area, and "a center of spiritual studies for youth." Other works are said to be planned but are on hold "for financial reasons." The association also sponsors and hosts annual international youth meetings. To judge from the program of one of these meetings, this association, which is careful not to issue literature that could be construed as propaganda for a San Damiano cult and which has the status of a "non-profit apostolate," now promotes a Marian devotion that is international and post–Vatican II in character and that understands Rosa Quattrini as only one of a number of modern "suffering souls" who have been especially devoted to the Virgin.[70]

Maintaining the One Body: San Damiano and Post–Vatican II Politics

It is clear that most Roman Catholic officials almost from the very first doubted the authenticity of the San Damiano apparition and were troubled by the growth and the ongoing expressions of piety at the site. It would seem, however, that some officials were initially reluctant to speak out against the growing cult, and it is not clear if this was a result of some uncertainty on their part about the apparition or because of the fear of alienating the thousands of Catholics who were being swept up in the phenomenon. In any case, the cult seems to have attracted enough support in its first year or two to have insured a kind of political standoff with Catholic officials which, insofar as there are still many people visiting San Damiano who believe the apparition to be authentic, has lasted up to the present day.

The apparition at San Damiano began in 1964, when the Second Vatican Council was well under way, and for bishops suddenly confronted with implementing the Council's wide-ranging reforms, one might expect that San Damiano would be profoundly disturbing. A survey of almost twenty years of public statements from the bishops and other Church officials most concerned with this phenomenon will show that most of them have indeed found it very disturbing. More significantly, however, it will show that the standoff that developed between these officials and the seer and devotees of San Damiano involved more than a simple conflict of authority. It involved a conflict between the Church's need for a single, unified order and the human need for expressions of physical well-being that often crystallize around an apparition, and this survey will illustrate how hard it may be for a bishop and for the Church as a whole to prohibit devotion to such an apparition once this process of crystallization has begun.

In September 1965, the then seventy-five-year-old bishop of Piacenza, Umberto Malchiodi, issued a statement saying that the supernatural origin of the events had not been proven and requesting that the faithful abstain from going to the site. He reiterated this position in a second statement issued in August 1966, at about the time of Rosa's announcement that the Virgin was calling for the digging of a well. The now-popular pilgrimage to San Damiano, however, was not to be stopped by such admonitions as these from the local bishop.[71]

About eighteen months later, however, in February 1968, Malchiodi issued a lengthy pronouncement on San Damiano which, quite unlike the earlier ones, included some rather specific prohibitions.[72] He began by noting that the earlier statements had been based on a careful and thorough examination of the facts; yet Rosa Quattrini, apparently disregarding the published judgment of the bishop, did not cease her activities, and her supporters had continued to distribute "propaganda" about the alleged apparitions. While he had no doubt about the validity of the earlier decisions, Malchiodi thought it opportune, in order to restore the peace, to conduct his own personal investigation into the events at San Damiano and the people who had been interested in them. The determination of this investigation was that "there exists no positive fact permitting affirmation of the supernatural character of the events."

Malchiodi went on to remind people that Church doctrine had consistently given the bishop the power of judgment concerning the authenticity of any extraordinary phenomena in his diocese. Then he declared that (1) the affirmations of Rosa Quattrini concerning the supernatural character of the apparitions and messages were without valid foundation, and (2) that the "disordered usage" that was being made of the apparitions and messages could no longer be tolerated. In order to put an end to Rosa's public religious displays, including those regularly held on Friday, and to the diffusion of materials by her followers, he was obliged now, he said, to issue several decisions: first, that

Rosa cease to hold public displays on Friday or any other day; second, that Rosa's partisans cease distributing propaganda concerning her life and the messages she was attributing to the Virgin; and third, that anyone acting contrary to these decisions would be considered to be disobeying ecclesiastical authority. Malchiodi said that he had confidence that his decision would be obeyed and that he would not have to speak on the subject again. He concluded by warning priests and the religious of other dioceses who should learn of this pronouncement that if they disregarded it they would be deprived of all powers in the diocese of Piacenza, including authorization to say Mass.

It is interesting that while this proclamation threatens sanctions against professional religious who continue their association with San Damiano, these were probably very hard to enforce, and there is as yet no penalty specified for laypersons visiting the site or indeed for those who were said to be "disobeying ecclesiastical authority" by promoting the cult.

Special efforts were made to publicize Bishop Malchiodi's proclamation outside of the diocese and indeed outside of Italy. About two weeks after this proclamation was issued, the vicar general of Fribourg addressed a letter to the "Friends of San Damiano" in the Lausanne-Geneva-Fribourg diocese, apprising them of the statement, asking them to read it carefully, to make it known to groups to whom it had not been specifically addressed, and to observe its directives.[73] About nine months later, in November 1968, the Holy See sent the statement to bishops in various countries with the directive to inform their constituencies of its content and to ask priests and laity not to go to San Damiano or to give credence to things "that are not worthy of confidence." Apparently in response to this directive, a Swiss diocesan newsletter printed on 19 December 1968 a statement of Mgr. Charrière, bishop of Lausanne, Geneva, and Fribourg, while a similar French periodical printed in January 1969, a statement of Mgr. Elchinger, bishop of Strasbourg. Both of these documents substantially reiterated Malchiodi's position and advised members of these dioceses to obey its directives, noting that it had come not simply from the bishop of Piacenza but also from the Holy See itself.[74]

It is clear, however, that such directives as these were not very effective in stopping the flow of Swiss and French pilgrims to San Damiano. About two years later, on 19 February 1970, Charrière, whose diocese was the home of virtually all French-speaking Swiss Catholics, published another statement in his diocesan newsletter. Here he reminded his readers of his previous publication of the directives of the bishop of Piacenza and said that while the majority had obeyed these directives, some had not, apparently believing rumors that they were going to be modified. Charrière said that these rumors were false and that he had received a new directive from the chancery of Piacenza that affirmed the earlier one of February 1968. It was not devotion to the Virgin or praying the Rosary that was in question, he said, but the fact that at San Damiano these things were accompanied by acts and words "of a nature to disorient the faithful." As an example, Charrière cited a message reported by Rosa several months earlier suggesting that receiving Communion in the hand would be a sacrilege. Noting that no one was obliged to receive Communion in this way, Charrière reminded the faithful that the Supreme Pontiff had nonetheless approved this form of Communion as acceptable. The Vicar of Christ could not authorize a sacrilegious act, he argued, and thus the Virgin could not have inspired the words which Rosa had attributed to her. He concluded by emphasizing that it was "our duty" to obey ecclesiastical authority and not to give credence to events "that do not merit confidence."[75]

Later that year, in the fall of 1970, an editorial written by Cardinal Deacon Journet, a professor of theology at Fribourg, appeared in the periodical *La Suisse*; it took a somewhat different tack in trying to dissuade the Catholic faithful from visiting San Damiano.[76] Journet contrasted the apparition reported by Rosa and the pilgrimage which focused on it with "true mysticism" and "true pilgrimage." The true Christian mystic, he held, leads a normal (although rare) religious life, opening a new way that everyone may follow. In a true pilgrimage, a profound Christian faith triumphs over the "sociological element" that is always present, and in such a pilgrimage the center or heart of the pilgrimage is something specifically acknowledged by the Church. Such a center was absent at San Damiano, where the Church had not been able to discern the authentic mark of a supernatural revelation.

It is interesting to see how Journet defined the sociological element that he saw dominating the events at San Damiano as distinct from the religious element that he saw in a true pilgrimage. All that the Church could affirm of San Damiano, he said, was that its power to attract pilgrims was based on the credulity of an anguished world rather than on supernatural intervention. The messages reported by Rosa pretended to address the (presumably legitimate) need of persons to know the state of their relationship with God, a need which becomes particularly intense at times of chaos and uncertainty. But what, in fact, people seek to know in such times is what day the world will end and what form their death will take—which is precisely what God has willed that they shall not know, so that they may live responsibly each and every day. It was this "negative need to know," he argued, that was bringing people to San Damiano. Journet did, however, have one positive thing to say about the San Damiano pilgrims. They were seeking a remedy for their anguish not in an easy form like drugs but in prayer, and their faith and their desire for Christian living could be admirable.

Journet described Rosa as a sincere woman who experienced an insurmountable need to speak and who without doubt possessed an exceptional rhetorical gift. He judged her, however, to be the victim of an illusion. What she believed to be the voice of the Virgin was only an interior voice, perhaps the voice of her own subconscious, and there was nothing extraordinary about her messages. The San Damiano phenomenon rested first on the illusion to which Rosa had fallen victim, and second, on the conviction of a number of Christians that the present world was moving toward its destruction. While he could not condemn either Rosa or her followers, he was less indulgent "with the organizers and propagandists of these pilgrimages" and "ecclesiastics whose role is to clarify and not to follow." These persons, he concluded, "do not act in a Christian spirit of obedience to the Church."

Journet's editorial was a candid sketch of how many in the Post–Vatican II Catholic hierarchy understood the "problem" of San Damiano some six years after the pilgrimages had begun. Another document appeared about this time, however, which shows much more clearly what the local Church authorities felt compelled to do about San Damiano and the cautious and deliberate manner in which they were proceeding. This was a lengthy statement of the new bishop of Piacenza, Enrico Manfredi, which appeared in the Piacenza diocesan newsletter on 1 November 1970.[77]

Manfredi began by noting that he had been occupied with the events of San Damiano ever since he had assumed the office of bishop, and that since these events were believed by some to have a divine origin, it was necessary for the bishop to express his judgment on them. Manfredi said that he had of course informed himself completely on the measures taken by his predecessor and had read all the materials that preceded and followed Malchiodi's declaration of 2 February 1968. All that his predecessor had done, he said, had been done with prudence and diligence, and the Holy See, particularly the Sacred Congregation for the Doctrine of the Faith, had been kept well informed. As evidence that the Sacred Congregation had approved his predecessor's actions, he cited a letter of 29 December 1969, in which the declaration of 2 February 1968 was described as "proof of a pastoral wisdom and of praiseworthy moderation."[78]

Manfredi also praised the clergy and the laity of the diocese for following the directives of their bishop without hesitation. This showed, he said, "the veneration that they have for their pastor, their obedience to the authority of the Church, and thus their clear-sightedness on the events in question." But, he added, such respect for the authority of the Church had not been showed by the faithful from other dioceses. "Agitators of the manifestations" and the seer herself had not obeyed the bishop, causing the events to be prolonged. A vast "propaganda" had continued to bring people to San Damiano, most of them from foreign countries. It was painful, he said, that people pretended to honor the Holy Virgin by a "cunning disobedience" to the Church. Many who had come in good faith had been led into error, endangering both the Christian faith and true Christian piety.

The bishop was particularly critical of priests from other dioceses who disregarded the local bishop's "legitimate" directives and took part in or directed prayers and processions. The disobedience of these priests was a bad example for the faithful and a very serious matter, he said, as were their attempts to justify their conduct "by affirming things clearly contrary to the established teachings of the Church that had been confirmed by Vatican II."

One of Manfredi's main concerns was clearly the challenge presented by these outside clergy to the authority of the local bishop. They had dared to claim that he had no authority over them because they did not belong to his diocese, he said, although they knew very well that this was contrary to the laws of the Church concerning public order. They had also challenged the bishop of Piacenza's right to judge the alleged supernatural occurences, arguing that since these had become well known far beyond the limits of the diocese, only the Holy See was in a position to render judgment on them.

In his defense of his predecessor's judgments and presumably also his own, Manfredi appealed to the statements of Vatican II concerning the function of a bishop. The Council had described the bishops as "heralds

of faith" and "authentic teachers," who were "invested with the authority of Christ" and who were to be "attentive to weeding away all the
errors that menace their flock." The faithful, on their part, according to
the Council, were to be attentive to the bishop's expressed judgments
and give him the "religious assent of their spirit." Concerning the events
at San Damiano, Manfredi insisted, the bishop had the authority both
to issue a judgment and to publicize it widely. Indeed, he saw this as
one of the duties imposed on a bishop by Vatican II in its statement
about the "solicitude" that the bishops, "as members of the episcopal
college and legitimate successors of the apostles," should have for the
whole Church, a solicitude profitable for the universal Church, "even if
it is not exercised by an act of jurisdiction."[79] The wide distribution of
his predecessor's judgment on the events at San Damiano, Manfredi
said, had given his brothers in the episcopate a valuable instrument for
forming their opinion and avoiding error. It was unfortunate, therefore,
that this had not been welcomed by everyone and that the partisans of
San Damiano had continued to sow trouble by favoring disobedience
to legitimate authority.

Manfredi then spelled out five specific conclusions which pertained to
the continuing demonstrations of piety at San Damiano. First, he reiterated the judgment of his predecessor that the events of San Damiano
had nothing of the supernatural about them, saying that the alleged
proofs of supernatural agency had no conclusive value, and that in fact
there were many proofs to the contrary. Second, he noted that although
Rosa had given evidence of increasing prudence in her expressions, she
was still, in substance, continually and publicly disobeying the bishop
by continuing to present herself as "a seer and instrument of the Holy
Virgin." She had been warned, he said, that if she persisted in this attitude the diocesan authorities would be obliged to refuse her access to
both the Church and its sacraments, noting that someone whose disobedience and rebellion disrupted the Church's unity could not be admitted to the Eucharist, "which is the center and source of unified charity." Third, Manfredi upheld the action of his predecessor, purportedly
confirmed by the Holy See, prohibiting Edgardo Pellacani from participating in any activity at San Damiano, adding that Pellacani stood under the threat of suspension should this prohibition be violated. Fourth,
Manfredi warned the partisans of San Damiano that if they persisted in
promoting the phenomenon, they would be denied access in the diocese
to the church and the sacraments, and that priests who so persisted

would be suspended. He urged Catholics from other dioceses to refrain from visiting San Damiano, both in organized pilgrimages and as individuals, noting that he reserved the right to "inform the ordinaries" of persons participating in activities there, and that these persons might even, if persistent in their disobedience, be denied access to the San Damiano church and to other churches in the diocese.

It is remarkable that this was the first time, apparently, that Church authorities had threatened specific disciplinary measures for Rosa and for other leaders and supporters of San Damiano (other than Pellacani) if they persisted in their activities. The elaborate defense in this statement of the authority of the local bishop, the remarkable restraint in the bishop's threats of discipline, and the return again and again here to the theme of disobedience, suggest that the ongoing manifestations of piety at San Damiano had become a very delicate political matter and a sort of touchstone in disputes over the nature and scope of the authority of bishops.

While the bishop of Piacenza, in this 1970 declaration on San Damiano, had followed and further developed the tendency of his predecessor to focus on issues of authority and obedience, a French bishop a few years later issued a statement that appealed chiefly to reason and that showed more respect for the basic motives of the San Damiano pilgrims. This was a statement of the archbishop of Chambéry, Mgr. Bontems, which appeared in a French diocesan journal on 1 March 1973.[80]

Bontems urged the devotees of San Damiano to reevaluate and redirect their piety into more appropriate expressions of Marian devotion. He reminded his readers that he had already intervened several times to discourage interest in San Damiano, but that, in France, fervor for the apparition had periodically been rekindled. He admitted that simple faith and hope merited respect and said that one should not be surprised that the Virgin should seem near at hand when the humble ask her to help them and place their hope in her. With regard to the alleged apparition itself, however, Bontems adopted the views of Cardinal Journet. The messages reported by Rosa were appealing because their direct style was adapted to the sensibilities of the simple listener, but, Bontems observed, "they are so abundant and of such great banality." Rather than manifesting marks of the supernatural, they gave "an impression of trouble and ambiguity," which was why the diocesan authorities, with the approval of the Holy See, had warned people about them several times and had finally forbidden pilgrimages and other demonstrations of piety. Contrary to rumor, Bontems said, the bishop of Piacenza had assured him in a lengthy letter that his attitude toward the events at San Damiano had not changed. The diocese of Piacenza was simply not particularly concerned with the phenomenon anymore, and it was in the French-speaking countries that propaganda for San Damiano had recently been most troublesome.

The most remarkable part of Bontems's statement, however, was its brief conclusion, where he invited his readers, as it were, to join him in a little self-critical reflection. How much better would it be, he mused, if the devotees of San Damiano would spend less time on pilgrimages and more time serving the Church, carrying the richness of their love for Our Lady to various groups and Christian communities. But then the Church in general, he suggested, needed to give serious thought to its celebrations. While these had been much improved (apparently a reference to the liturgical reforms of Vatican II), the fact that some ceremonies had been stripped to "coldness and unworthiness" meant that one should not be surprised if people looked to other places for comfort. He asked his readers, then, to be concerned about the "human quality" of the Church's celebrations and create appropriate channels for devotion to the Virgin Mary that were in line with the pronouncements of Vatican II. Here, then, Bontems came close to saying that San Damiano might have been a reaction to liturgical reforms that in some ways might have been insensitive to human needs.

In the years that followed, while Church officials became somewhat more willing to openly discuss and criticize the increasingly evident resistance to Vatican II reforms, they apparently went no farther than Bontems in conceding that the devotees of San Damiano might been motivated by some legitimate concerns. Indeed, after the incident with Lefebvre in 1976 and again after Rosa's death, there seems to have been a hardening of the Church's opposition to the cult, and the themes of authority and unity, which had always underlain the majority of the official statements on the subject, were again expressed in open and uncompromising language. These themes are clear, for example, in a statement about San Damiano by Mgr. Coffy, bishop of Albi, published on 13 October 1983.[81]

It was common for alleged apparitions and private revelations to be multiplied in troubled times, Coffy said, recalling that prophecies had flourished, for example, during the war. Seers and prophets make "good box office" during such times, he suggested, because people have a need for security and when faced with questioning and doubt, will welcome clear and precise messages which confirm what they are already thinking. This was why the Church, out of concern to safeguard the faith of its people and their ecclesiastical communion, had always been very careful about apparitions and prophecies. Many people, Coffy suggested, had been abused by fraudulent apparitions and had left the Church to follow false prophets. The Church recognized apparitions, he noted, only after long and minute investigations, and at San Damiano the local bishop, after undertaking such investigations, had in fact demanded the closing of the parish church. This, Coffy insisted, was not a mere caution but an interdiction. Could one remain faithful to the Church, he asked rhetorically, and not take account of this? He recalled that on the Feast of the Assumption that year (15 August 1983), Pope John Paul II, in an address to the pilgrims at Lourdes, had asked French Christians "to consolidate their unity around their bishop," and Coffy then asked those French Catholics who go to San Damiano to consider what sort of witness they are giving by their actions to the Catholic faithful in the diocese of Piacenza.

Coffy contrasted the messages of the Virgin reported by Rosa with those reported by Bernadette at Lourdes. In the latter case, he noted, the Virgin's messages could be summarized in a few words and were basically only a reminder of the requirements of the Gospel. By contrast, the accounts he had read of the apparition at San Damiano and of other apparitions publicized by its partisans gave him the impression, he said with some sarcasm, that the Virgin was very prolix. Some of the messages at San Damiano, moreover, were very clearly in contradiction to the practices of the primitive church. He insisted that he did not wish to judge the piety of those who go to San Damiano, granting that their intent may be to deepen their devotion to the Virgin. But what was at issue here was the judgment of the Church. Some of the devotees of San Damiano, he thought it necessary to add, had been people who had had difficulty welcoming and putting into practice the reforms of Vatican II.

This survey of the ecclesiastical statements on San Damiano shows very clearly that Church officials, at least until quite recently, have approached San Damiano from a very different perspective than the apparition's supporters. It would seem that the standoff between these two groups has been largely the result of their failure to appreciate each other's concerns. The bishops seem almost from the beginning to have focused on threats to the integrity and proper functioning of the Church as a body, fearing the effects, in particular, of disobedience to those in authority and the irregularity of allowing in one diocese practices that are prohibited in another. Perhaps because many of those who supported the San Damiano cult also sympathized with Lefebvre, the bishops perceived its popularity to be a threat to the unity of the "Body of Christ" and for the most part were unsympathetic to the devotees, downgrading their interest in the apparition to a matter of needing "simple answers in troubled times."

The devotees of San Damiano, however, have been less concerned with the welfare of the corporate Body of Christ than with the physical and spiritual health of individual Christians. They have understood the site as offering purification and protection of both body and soul and a refuge from apocalyptic dangers. Water from the San Damiano well, they believe, will heal, sanctify, and protect even in the face of the "terrible moment of discouragement." In their concern for the health of the individual, they have kept alive Rosa's (or, as they believe, the Virgin's) vision of a city of physical and spiritual care and healing for the less fortunate, a precedent for which was established by the hospital at San Giovanni Rotondo; and in spite of internal conflicts and the lack of ecclesiastical support, they have managed to put in place at least a beginning of this "City of Roses." While leaders of the association still speak of the delicacy of their situation and seem to be afraid that publicity could be injurious to their relations with the Church, pilgrims visiting San Damiano today, many of whom are French, attend Mass faithfully in the parish church; and they are hopeful that the Church may soon look more favorably on their devotion and their healing mission.[82]

CHAPTER 3

Can the Testimonies of
Thousands Be Wrong?

SAN SEBASTIAN DE
GARABANDAL

THE APPARITION at San Sebastian de Garabandal, a small village in Cantabria in northern Spain, began on 18 June 1961, when four young girls reported that they had seen an angel. In the next two weeks there were nine more appearances of the angel, after which, in the next two years, came more than two thousand reported appearances of the Virgin Mary. The paranormal abilities claimed for the seers during the course of the apparition, two "public messages," and a distinctive end-time scenario of warning-miracle-chastisement have been widely publicized in a number of languages by devotees of this apparition. Indeed, today, more than twenty-five years after the apparition, Garabandal Centers around the world are still disseminating information about it and working for its official recognition by the Roman Catholic Church.[1]

Two documents are particularly important for reconstructing the events of 1961–1963 at Garabandal and how they have been understood by devotees. The first of these is the *Diary* of Conchita González, the seer who played the central role in the unfolding of the apparition event. It is not quite correct to call this a diary, however, since it is not a record made by Conchita in the immediate aftermath of her experiences. Conchita began to write this account in September 1962, a little over a year after the apparition began, and she finished it sometime during the summer of 1963.[2] Although it contains some discrepancies in dates and details, this account is important as a record of the seer's own recollection of the chronology of events and of her own perspective on their importance.

The second important document is a collection of accounts of the apparition gathered by Ramon Pérez from the villagers of Garabandal in 1971. Pérez asked each of his subjects twenty-five questions and then taperecorded, transcribed, and published their responses. These accounts are biased in the sense that all of Pérez's subjects believed that the apparition was of supernatural origin. According to Pérez, however, this bias was not intentional; villagers who did not believe that the experiences were supernatural, he said, refused to be interviewed.[3] Pérez himself defended the authenticity of the apparition and took care to summarize and refute the points made by its opponents. In spite of these biases, however, the accounts collected by Pérez are of considerable value. They are essentially firsthand accounts of the events that transpired in Garabandal during the two years of the apparition, and in addition they clearly sketch the meaning that believers saw in these events about a decade later. These two documents will form the basis for the discussion of Garabandal that follows.[4]

First Phase: 18 June–26 July 1961

The apparition at Garabandal began on Sunday evening, 18 June 1961, when María Concepçion (Conchita) González González, who was then twelve years old, had the idea of taking some apples from the trees belonging to the local schoolmaster. These apple trees were in the *calleja*, a rocky lane leading from the village up to a group of nine pine trees (commonly known as "the pines"). As Conchita recalled later in her *Diary*, she and her friend María Cruz (Mari Cruz) González Barrido, who was almost eleven, were in the process of gathering the apples when they were joined by two other twelve-year-old girls, Jacinta González González and María Dolores (Mari Loli) Mazón González. Another girl who had joined them was shortly called away. When Jacinta protested about the theft of the apples, Conchita replied, "Keep quiet! The schoolmaster's wife will hear you and she'll tell my mother!" According to Conchita, all four of them were eating the apples when they heard a noise like thunder. Conchita then said that she was overcome by remorse over stealing the apples and lamented that the devil would now be happy and their guardian angel sad. To relieve their guilty consciences, they began to pick up stones and throw them to the left where the devil was said to be. Tiring of this, the girls then began to play marbles. Suddenly, said Conchita, "there appeared to me a very beautiful figure that shone brilliantly but did not hurt my eyes at all."[5]

Conchita was crying, "Oh! Oh!" and the other three girls thought she was having a fit. But no sooner had they decided to return to the village to tell Conchita's mother than they too saw the figure and found themselves in the same state. All four were silent for a while, Conchita said, but then the figure suddenly disappeared and they returned to normal. Thoroughly frightened, they ran toward the village church, meeting another girl from the village along the way. When she noted that they looked pale and scared and asked where they had been, they admitted that they had been taking apples but said that what had made them so upset was that they had seen an angel. Conchita recalled that while they had originally intended to enter the church, they changed their minds and went around to the back "to cry." There they encountered more children, whom they also told about the angel.[6]

The story quickly spread through the village. One person who heard it was the schoolmistress, who sought out and found the girls behind the church and asked them if the story she had heard was true. When they assured her that it was and rejected her suggestion that they had imagined it all, she suggested that they go into the church and say a Station "in thanksgiving to Jesus in the Blessed Sacrament." When they finished this, Conchita said, it was late and she was upset, first, because of the experience itself, and second, because her mother had told her to be home before dark. She reported that when she told her mother she had seen an angel, her mother exclaimed, "In addition to coming home late, you come and tell me a thing like that!"[7]

Despite the taunts of some of the villagers, the girls returned to the calleja on the days that followed. Some people wondered why they went to an alley to pray instead of to the church, and the local boys threw stones at them. When the angel did not appear to them on the next day, Monday, they were disappointed, Conchita said, but the schoolmistress reassured them, suggesting that the angel hadn't come that day because it was very cloudy. That night while Conchita was saying her prayers, she said that she heard a voice say, "Don't worry. You shall see me again."[8] While the angel did not appear to the girls on Tuesday either, they reported that as they were leaving the calleja that day they seemed to be surrounded by a dazzling light that momentarily hid them from one another. They were terrified and began to scream, but by then the light was already fading.[9]

On Wednesday the girls asked a woman from the village to accompany them to the calleja as a witness. According to Conchita, this woman, Clementina González, did not then believe in the apparition. She had asked another woman to accompany her, and on their way to the calleja other people joined them. When the girls had finished the Rosary without seeing the angel, some people laughed and told them to say a Station of the Cross. It was as they were completing the Station, then, that the girls saw the angel. When the appearance ended, Conchita said, people were very excited and began to cry, telling the girls that when they saw the angel again they should tell him to forgive them for not believing. Clementina González, reportedly, was the most excited of the group and, in spite of the urging of other women present, could not curb her emotions.[10]

In 1971 Clementina gave to Pérez an account of her own recollection of this incident.[11] She said that she had been reluctant to go to the calleja alone because she was afraid that the villagers would say she was "as crazy as the girls themselves." Thus she told the girls to ask the schoolmaster and his wife to go also. The schoolmaster's wife joined them, as did another woman, and it was only after the apparition had begun that more people joined them. They had arrived at the calleja, she recalled, at about 8:30 P.M. The girls began to recite the Rosary but then stopped. Clementina said she called this to the attention of the others, saying "They're not praying! They're not praying!" She was told to be quiet. When the girls were asked by the women what they had seen, they replied that they had seen a large frame but could not make out what was inside. Clementina said that she suggested that they finish the Rosary, but the girls decided to say a Station instead.

When they had finished reciting the Station, according to Clementina, the girls "had another ecstasy" that lasted until about 10:00 P.M. Toward the end of this ecstasy Clementina, to the amusement of the other women, began to call to the girls. The girls, however, did not respond, and Clementina, who was now quite excited, said that she then told Conchita, "Call Our Lady of Mount Carmel; call upon the Sacred Heart of Jesus; tell Him something! Ask Him what He wants of us." She recalled that the others laughed at her, told her not to jump to conclusions, and said that the phenomenon might be the work of the devil. She wanted to summon others, including the local priest, and she told the women, "If you don't believe in this, you don't believe in God." Then she said she heard Conchita saying, "Holy Virgin, they do not believe us!" She replied, "Yes, Conchita, we do believe you; everybody believes you." When the ecstasy ended, the girls were questioned about what they had seen, and, according to Clementina, they said they had seen the angel but that he had not spoken. When they had said "Holy Virgin," however, he had smiled and bowed his head. Word of this event spread quickly, and by the next day people from nearby villages were coming to Garabandal.

The girls reported appearances of the angel on eight of the next eleven days, and these occurred in the presence of a considerable number of people.[12] Not everyone who was present, however, was convinced that the experiences had a divine origin. Conchita reported that a Professor Marín was present on June 22, for example, and that after the appearance he took the girls to the home of a villager for questioning. This apparently led some to suspect him of using hypnosis to prepare the girls for their experiences, and these people, reportedly, wanted him arrested.[13] Others accused the girls of putting on an act, suggesting that the lack of appearances on certain days could be explained by their fear of feigning these experiences before a crowd.[14] Conchita attributed both of these attitudes primarily to people who were not from Garabandal.

The local priest, Don Valentín Marichalar, according to Conchita, was cautious but supportive. He had seemed nervous, she said, when he questioned her about her first experience.[15] He was present, however, for the appearances on June 22 and 23, and immediately after the appearance on the twenty-third he questioned each of the four seers separately at the sacristy. Then, according to Conchita, he went outside and told the crowd that because the girls had agreed perfectly in their statements about what they had seen, it seemed that "so far everything was from God."[16]

On six of these eight days in which the angel appeared to the girls, his only communication with them was a smile. On June 24, however, Conchita said that the angel had a sign beneath him. She said that they did not pay much attention to this sign and later could recall only that the first line began with *Hay* (it is necessary that) and that the second line contained some roman numerals.[17]

On July 1, according to Conchita, many people had assembled in Garabandal with the expectation that the Virgin would appear, since it was "her day." While the four girls did not see the Virgin this day, they did see the angel again, and he spoke to them for the first time. He said that he had come to announce that on the next day the Virgin would indeed appear to them as Our Lady of Mount Carmel. The girls said that he again had the sign with him and told them that the Virgin would explain to them what it meant.[18]

The appearance of the Virgin to the girls on the next day, July 2, was the first of more than two thousand reported by them in the next two years. On that day the girls left for the calleja, according to Conchita, at about six o'clock in the evening to say the Rosary. They had not quite reached the calleja when the Virgin appeared with two angels, one on each side. These angels looked like twins, Conchita said, and were dressed alike. She identified one as St. Michael (apparently the same angel who had been previously appearing to the girls), but neither she nor the other girls recognized the other angel. Beside the angel on the Virgin's right side was a large eye that Conchita said seemed to be the eye of God.[19]

Conchita said that they spoke to the Virgin at length during this first appearance and told her about their daily lives (working in the fields, putting up hay, being bronzed by the sun). The Virgin reportedly laughed as they described these things; she taught them the proper way to recite the Rosary, and then, after promising to return the next day, she left them. This reported content of the seers' conversation with the Virgin became a point of controversy among the observers. Apparently some did not believe that the Virgin would appear merely to hear about the daily lives of four young girls. Others, however, defended the report of the conversation and compared the relation between the seers and the Virgin to that between a daughter and mother who had been separated for some time. The daughter would naturally tell her mother everything, they said, and in this case the Virgin was a heavenly mother whom the seers had never seen before.[20]

In these first appearances, as in those that would follow, Conchita clearly played the central role. It was she who conceived the idea of stealing the apples and of relieving their guilty consciences by throwing stones to the left, and she who was the first to "fall into ecstasy." On the following day, after the girls had failed to see the angel, she was the only one to hear a voice that said, "You will see me again." It was she, moreover, who announced and was the subject of the so-called "little miracle" of visible Communion on 18 July 1962 (described later in this chapter). Conchita's experiences extended through 1965, two years longer than those of the other three girls, and it was some of her experiences that became for believers the crux of the Garabandal apparition: the so-called second message and the scenario of warning-miracle-chastisement (see Chapter 6).

Conchita's leading role was apparently noticed by Church officials not long after the apparition began. At the request of diocesan authorities, on 26 July 1961 she was taken to Santander for a period of time, accompanied by her mother, Aniceta, and a priest, Don Luis, who was also a relative. There was, she said, some suspicion that she was the one who was influencing the others. While in Santander she reported one appearance of the Virgin. This occurred on the first day and allegedly at the same time that the other three girls were seeing the Virgin in Garabandal.[21] In Santander Conchita was examined by members of the diocesan commission that had been established to investigate the apparition. She said that those who examined her determined that she was healthy, told her that the appearances had been a dream, and said that after she had been in Santander a while they would cease.

Conchita's mother, convinced by those who examined her daughter that she was fine, left her in Santander and returned to Garabandal alone. However, she reportedly found that the atmosphere in the village was "literally poisonous." She was harassed, she said, because some villagers thought she had chased Conchita out of the house. She was accused of having removed the Virgin from the village and of having suppressed "everything." Her sons found themselves isolated. Because of all of this, she returned to Santander two days later to bring Conchita back to Garabandal.[22]

Aniceta's decision to bring Conchita back to Garabandal, however, apparently did not please some members of the diocesan commission. Conchita's aunt, Maximina González, who had accompanied Aniceta to Santander, recalled an unpleasant interview with Dr. Piñal, a member of the commission. He had threatened Conchita, she said, warning her that if she did not deny everything people would think that she was crazy, and she would be put in an asylum and her parents and family jailed. If, on the other hand, she denied her experiences, she would be considered a *señorita* and could perhaps be admitted to a college. Conchita, she said, perhaps because she was frightened, admitted that her visions might not be "real" but said that she thought this was not the case with the visions of the other girls. Piñal then asked her to sign a declaration to this effect, which she did. Maximina thought that this might have been simply a blank piece of paper, but she was not sure of this.[23] Conchita herself remembered Piñal being very angry that she was leaving Santander and saying many things in an effort to convince her to remain there. She recalled telling him that she was not seeing the Virgin anymore but that she supposed that the other girls still were and thought that what the Virgin had told them was true. When he asked her to sign a statement to that effect, she agreed to do so. Her recollection of what she was affirming thus differs somewhat from her aunt's.[24]

Conchita's ten days in Santander clearly brought to an end the initial phase of the apparition. Before Conchita left, the girls appeared to have shared a common experience; that is, the appearances began and ended at about the same time, and the girls reported seeing the same things. Now, however, the appearances began to become more individualized. At first the three seers remaining in Garabandal reported common experiences not shared by their absent friend. This continued for a while after Conchita's return, but about two weeks later, on August 19, some of the seers began to have experiences not shared by any of the others. It is important to note, however, that some shared experiences were still reported after this, sometimes by all four girls, sometimes by two or three.[25]

The individualizing of the apparition experiences which marks the second phase of the Garabandal event is reflected also in the places and times of these experiences. The early appearances all took place in the calleja, where a *cuadro* (corral) had been quickly built to protect the girls from the crowds. Now, however, after Conchita's return, the appearances began to occur at other places in the village, and this site became less important. Individual seers, guided as it were by their visions, began to lead groups of the devout and curious around the village and into various houses. While the early appearances had all taken place late in the evening, the time that the angel had first appeared to the girls, now they began to occur at all hours of the day and night. Finally, in this second phase of the apparition, various paranormal phenomena began to be reported which became, for those who were on the way toward becoming "believers," an important part of the public aspect of the apparition and a means for personally contacting and appropriating something of its supernatural character.

The Formation of a Cult of the Paranormal at Garabandal

Phenomena which are perceived by visitors as paranormal or as bordering on the miraculous are an important but as yet little-studied aspect of most Marian apparitions. In the second phase of the apparitions at Garabandal, such phenomena were frequently reported. These later perceptions of the miraculous at Garabandal cannot be properly understood or appreciated, however, without first examining some peculiarities of the seers' own accounts of their earlier experiences and some of the earlier perceptions on the part of others of the seers' presumed supernatural abilities. To direct attention to these peculiarities and perceptions will be to enter into the first stages of the mind-set and logic of those who were becoming "believers" in the Garabandal apparition.

In the initial appearances of the angel and of the Virgin, as has been noted, the four seers appear to have shared a common experience: the appearances began and ended at about the same time for all four, and all reported seeing the same thing. The appearances of the angel to the Garabandal seers were unannounced and in a sense unanticipated; that is, while the girls returned each day to the site of the initial appearance, they had been given no assurance that this experience would be repeated. The appearances of the Virgin, on the other hand, they described as having been announced by three interior calls (*llamadas*). Conchita said that the first call was like a "weaker feeling of joy," while the second call was stronger. She said that they left for the site of the apparition only after this second call, because there was often a long delay between the first call and the second. The third call, she said, made them very excited and happy, and shortly after this call the Virgin would appear.[26]

Conchita said that they had told their parents about these calls prior to the second appearance of the Virgin. In their eagerness to see the Virgin again they had gone to the cuadro on that day immediately after school but although they said the Rosary, the Virgin did not appear. They were not disturbed, however, for they remembered that the earlier appearances had all occurred later in the day. That evening when they were all together again, at about the time they had seen the Virgin on the previous day, their parents suggested that they should go to the cuadro. The girls replied, however, that they had not yet been "called" and explained to their parents what they meant by this. Some who were present could not accept this, Conchita recalled, and they suggested separating the girls to test these alleged calls. If the separated girls came to the cuadro simultaneously, they thought, then the reality of the calls would be established. On the advice of Marichalar, who was among those present, two girls were put in one house and two in another. A half hour after these arrangements had been made, Conchita said, they received the second call and all four arrived at the cuadro at the same time.[27]

The testimonies of a number of villagers seem to collaborate Conchita's description of these calls and her recollection that attempts were made to test or verify these calls. The villagers differ, however, in their recollections of the circumstances under which this was done. Most of the inhabitants simply remembered that shortly after the appearances began the girls would be separated in different houses and still arrive at the cuadro at the same time.[28] A few, however, specifically remembered a testing in which not just villagers but also the Civil Guards were involved. The Guards placed each girl in a different house, they recalled, and then watched the houses to prevent any collusion among the girls and their supporters. Even under these circumstances, the girls reportedly met at the cuadro at the same time.[29] Several people remembered and described incidents in which one of the seers, while engaged in some routine activity such as eating dinner, would say that she had received a call and would suddenly leave for the cuadro.[30] Pepé Diez, who did not want to miss a chance to be present at any of these events, said that he would stop by the girls' homes during the winter to ask them whether they had been told that there would be an appearance that night. They would answer either "no" or "yes," he said, and if "yes," they would tell him how many calls they had received.[31]

Second Phase: A Shift in Attention

The paranormal abilities that the girls were perceived as manifesting in their ecstasies rather quickly became the proof, for the growing number of believers, of the authenticity of the apparition itself. In their criticism of the negative decision rendered by the ecclesiastically authorized investigating committee, devotees of Garabandal have focused most often on the committee's failure to interview witnesses who could offer firsthand testimony to these abilities. The devotional literature on Garabandal distributed by and for these devotees is filled with such testimonies, most of which seem to be built around the perceptions (1) that something about the seers has surpassed the capabilities or expectations of those who have encountered them, and (2) that as a result, these persons have been personally touched and moved to faith in the apparitions. These perceptions are particularly evident in the testimonies recorded by Pérez that are most typical of the second phase of the Garabandal apparitions: testimonies to the girls' increased weight or speed during their ecstasies, to their ability to return objects to their owners and to find things that had been hidden, and to their ability to recognize priests dressed in secular clothing.

During their ecstasies, observers would see the four girls tilting back their heads, looking upwards, and speaking. Those who were close enough said they could hear what the girls were saying. It was said that during these ecstasies the seers' faces were transformed and became serene, happy, and beautiful (see figure 5).[32] They became so heavy that it was hard to lift them even a few inches off the ground,[33] and when moved or pushed they would retain the positions, however uncomfortable, which they had been forced to assume.[34] The girls reportedly did not interact at all with their observers once their ecstasies had begun, and witnesses said that nothing could be given or communicated directly to them. They were, however, seen communicating with each other at these times. Indeed, it was said that a seer whose ecstasy had already begun could be attentive to the others who had not yet entered into this state and could accept from them a variety of objects for the Virgin to bless.[35]

Not long after the appearances began, doctors came to Garabandal to examine the seers. Most of their experiments seemed to be designed to measure the girls' sensitivity to pain during their experiences. Conchita said that many doctors were present during the appearance of the angel on June 25. On this occasion, she said, her family doctor lifted her up and dropped her on her knees from a height of about two and a half feet. Others told Conchita later that on this occasion they heard a noise like cracking bones, but Conchita said that she herself heard nothing. The doctors also pinched and scratched the girls' legs and pricked them with pins. The girls felt no pain, Conchita said, either during these operations or afterward, although the marks from the pricks and scratches remained on their legs.[36] It is not clear from either the witnesses' accounts or those of the girls themselves just how many times such experiments were performed.

Pepé Diez has provided an interesting description of one such session. While the girls were kneeling in the cuadro, he reported, one of the physicians directed a strong electric light on them and examined their eyes and faces, while another began pricking their legs with a needle. At the same time, Diez said, he saw the girls smiling and heard them saying to their vision, "What? They are pricking us? . . . But we don't feel anything!" From these remarks Diez concluded that the Virgin was informing the girls of what the doctors were doing to them.[37]

Similar conclusions were drawn by persons who placed small objects on the girls during their ecstasies so that these objects would be blessed. Conchita's aunt, for example, said that she once, while Conchita was in ecstasy, slipped into her pocket a ring, at the request of its owner, a mere acquaintance. She immediately heard Conchita say, "I have a ring in my pocket? Who put it there? Ah! well, kiss it." Conchita held up the ring and then returned it directly to its owner. Conchita's aunt, like Diez, concluded that the seer's knowledge of what was happening around her was conveyed to her by the Virgin. In this incident, as in a number of similar ones, this belief became part of the basis for, and reinforced, the conviction that the seers were manifesting paranormal abilities.[38]

The claim that the girls became heavier during their ecstasies was reportedly tested by "men of the Spanish countryside" who were used to lifting very heavy loads. Pepé Diez recalled seeing a number of young men in their twenties and thirties fail in their attempts to lift the girls during their ecstasies and remembered one in particular who had tried unsuccessfully to lift Jacinta. After the apparition he was challenged to lift her again, but he demurred, saying that he was frightened by the whole thing. When challenged again, however, he lifted Jacinta "as if she were a doll." He was then quite upset, according to Diez, and said that now he was convinced the apparition was true, but that he dared not say so because no one would believe him.[39]

Many people, to judge from the testimonies recorded by Pérez, were impressed by the seers' speed in reaching the apparition site and, in the second phase of the apparition, in going from house to house. While Diez conceded that observers had not precisely measured the girls' speed during their ecstasies, he was sure that it was extraordinary since eighteen- or twenty-year-old boys used to running and traversing the mountain paths could not keep up with them. Diez said that to his eyes their stride was extraordinary, and that while the rhythm of their legs seemed like a normal running pace, the girls moved forward at a speed that was at least three times that of anyone else. Diez was about thirty-five at the time and was himself a fast runner, he said, but even he could not catch up with the girls until they stopped.[40]

Observers also reported that, in contrast to those who tried or were forced to keep up with them, the girls showed no shortness of breath, fatigue, or other signs of physical exertion after their "ecstatic marches."[41] Laura González recalled that Conchita once fell into an ecstasy while clinging to a monk. He reportedly could not extract himself from her grasp and was forced to run with Conchita that night for as long as her ecstasy lasted. Witnesses found the scene hilarious, Laura said, and she was told later by the neighbor at whose house the man was staying that he had to change his clothes that night because they were soaked with perspiration.[42]

Observers also said that they were unable to imitate the girls' way of returning from the cuadro near the pines to the village: usually moving backward, sometimes walking upright, sometimes on their knees. Most impressive on these peculiar treks was the girls' alleged immunity to scratches and bruises on their knees or legs. Seeing his sister Conchita move in this way without injury brought Serafín González to faith in the apparition. He said that it would be impossible for the bishop to convince him that phenomena of that kind were natural and not from God.[43]

The practice of the seers' presenting various objects to the Virgin to be blessed (see figure 4) and then returning them to their owners appears to have begun spontaneously and to have gone through several phases. Precisely how it began, however, is not quite clear. In her *Diary* Conchita indicated that the practice began on 3 July 1961, when the Virgin appeared for the second time and had the Infant Jesus with her. People who were present gave the girls objects to be kissed by the Virgin, and the Virgin reportedly kissed them all. To amuse the Infant Jesus, the girls gathered pebbles, Conchita said, some of which she put in her hair, while Mari Loli put some in her sleeves. Jacinta offered her pebbles to the child, but he only smiled and would not take them.[44] As Conchita here described the event, the offering of objects to the Virgin to be blessed and the offering of pebbles to the Infant Jesus seemed to be two distinct activities.

When in 1970, however, Pelletier questioned Conchita about the origin of the practice of the blessing of sacred objects, she told him that this had begun when the Infant Jesus would not take the pebbles offered to him. The Virgin then reportedly took the pebbles and kissed them and told the girls to give them, presumably at random, to people in the crowd. In later ecstasies, according to Pelletier, the girls were told to give the pebbles to particular people whom the Virgin had singled out or chosen. When people heard that the Virgin was kissing pebbles, they began giving the girls rosaries and medals to be kissed and, according to Conchita, the Virgin agreed to their accepting these pious objects so that she could kiss them.[45]

The testimony of Laura González suggests that even at an early stage these practices were seen as testifying to the girls' supernatural gifts. González said that when the appearances of the Virgin first began, people would give the girls pebbles for the Virgin to bless for their sons or daughters. The girls would make a pile of the pebbles near their knees, and during their ecstasies they would hold the pebbles up and then drop them. After their ecstasies, she said, the girls would return each pebble to the person who had offered it.[46]

It is difficult to draw a distinction in the accounts between incidents in which people gave the seers objects to be blessed as a simple devotional exercise and incidents in which this was done as a test of the seers' alleged supernatural powers. Indeed, it seems that at least in the later stages of the apparition, these two motives cannot be clearly distinguished. Pepé Diez recalled that one day a man gave Mari Loli between twenty and thirty articles. The people in his group, the man said, wanted to have the Virgin kiss the articles, and they had authorized him to give them to the seer en masse. Some in the group, however, wanted Mari Loli to return each object directly to its owner. Mari Loli replied that she would ask the Virgin. Diez said that he watched the seers carefully that day and that Mari Loli had received many other objects besides those presented to her by this man. Nonetheless, during her ecstasy she singled out each one, held it up, and then returned it. The recipient would examine the article very carefully, saying something like, "Let me see if it's really my own rosary." Each one had been given the correct article, Diez said; Mari Loli had not made a single mistake.[47]

The reports of persons who believed that they had objects blessed by the Virgin's kiss miraculously returned to them by the seers suggest that these people saw themselves as having a special relationship to the seers and sometimes even a special role in the unfolding of the Garabandal phenomenon as a whole. Maximina González, for example, believed that she was the person responsible for starting the practice of presenting wedding rings to the Virgin to be kissed. One day, she said, when Jacinta was in ecstasy in Conchita's house, she (Maximina) handed her ring to Conchita and said, "Our wedding rings are blessed. Maybe the Virgin would kiss them." Conchita then went to Jacinta and told her to take the ring and give it to the Virgin. Jacinta took the ring, held it up, and said, "Here is this ring, please kiss it. Ah! It belongs to Maximina?" Jacinta, Maximina said, then came over to her and without looking at her, took her hand and put the ring on her finger.[48]

Wedding rings appear to have been used on various occasions by visitors seeking evidence or proof of the supernatural events that were reportedly taking place in Garabandal. Avelina González, for example, has described the visit to Mari Loli's house of a woman from Cosío who avowed that she believed in Garabandal but wanted to obtain proof. While Mari Loli was still absent, she took off her ring, gave it to another woman to give to the seer, and then disappeared into the crowd. According to Avelina, some people in the crowd thought all of this to be rather ridiculous. Soon Mari Loli arrived, in ecstasy, and was given the woman's ring "to be kissed." She then came up to Avelina and stood in front of her. Avelina said that this was at about two o'clock in the morning and that she was in a panic because she did not know what Mari Loli wanted at this late hour. She heard Mari Loli say, "It is not this one? Then tell me whose it is. Take me to her. Lead me!" Mari Loli then moved up to and into the crowd, which moved aside to let her pass so that finally she stood before the owner of the ring. She picked up the woman's hand and slipped the ring onto one of her fingers, saying, "Oh, that's not the right one? Which one then?" She removed the ring and put it on another finger. Avelina reported that the woman was left "in a terrible state" by this experience.[49]

Pilgrims, neighbors, and relatives also tested the girls simply by hiding objects for them to find. Maximina, for example, reported that she once hid some holy pictures in the corner of the kitchen chimney. She told Conchita she had some holy pictures for the Virgin to kiss, but she did not tell Conchita where they were. During an ecstasy later that day, Conchita reportedly went directly to the kitchen, found the pictures, and held each one up to be kissed.[50]

Thus an object such as a ring, rosary, or picture, initially used to put the seers to the test, often became the "miraculous means" whereby its owner was brought to faith in the apparition. There were also, however, reports of the conversion of such persons as a result of unmediated encounters with the seers or encounters mediated by objects that the seers themselves owned or carried. Piedad González recalled that one night her son hid in some bushes in their garden. According to her, he was thinking to himself, "If it is true that everything comes from the Blessed Virgin, may the young girl climb and reach my hiding place." That night, after Conchita had emerged from her home in ecstasy, she reportedly came to the garden and climbed through the brambles until she reached his hiding place. As a result of this, Piedad said, her son came to believe in the apparition. She also recalled that once she had given refuge in her attic to an exhausted pilgrim from Cabezon who could find no other room. Around three o'clock in the morning, the seers, in ecstasy, reportedly came to her home, and Conchita climbed the stairs to the attic and held out her cross for the man to kiss. He was so overcome with emotion, Piedad said, that he left with the girls and without even saying good-bye to her.[51]

Maximina González recalled a similar incident involving Fr. José Ramon Garcia de la Riva, a priest who had often stayed at her house when he came on pilgrimage. At two o'clock one morning, she said, Mari Loli came to her home with her brother, went to the room where Garcia de la Riva was sleeping, and gave him a crucifix to kiss. According to Maximina, the priest later told her that he had prayed for a proof, saying to himself, "If it is truly from God, let them come here and give me the crucifix, here in this very house."[52]

It is worth noting that the person involved in this report was a priest. Many people saw the seers as manifesting supernatural religious discernment and authority in their encounters with hidden seekers and challengers. This was felt to be particularly evident in their encounters with professional religious, some of whom wore distinctive garb which the seers presumably could not have identified by themselves, and some of whom came in secular clothing so as to conceal their identities and special vocations.[53]

Maximina recalled, for example, that during one ecstasy she heard the girls talking to their vision about a very nice priest whom they called "the white habit." This priest was sitting near the children, and he, as well as Maximina, reportedly heard them say, "Oh! it is a Dominican? Well, I shall not call him 'the white habit' anymore. Dominican? Well!" At these words the priest lowered his head, and when he raised it he was crying. Maximina recalled that a few days before, he and some other priests had been laughing about the "alleged apparitions" and had been reproved by a member of the crowd, who said that these were not matters to be laughed at.[54]

Priests and religious who came to Garabandal dressed in secular garb had little success, as the authors of the testimonies saw it, in concealing their vocations from the seers. Aniceta, for example, recalled that once a young couple came to Garabandal on a rainy day when a large crowd was present. The young man gave Aniceta a cross which, at his request, she laid on Conchita's hands during one of her ecstasies. Conchita held up the cross, and she was heard to say, "What a shame! While the Dominican habit is so nice . . . what a shame that he dresses like that." They later learned, Aniceta said, that the young man was indeed a Dominican, the young woman with him being his sister.[55]

It should be noted here that members of religious orders, and especially Dominicans, have been and still are some of the persons most interested in and supportive of Garabandal. While an analysis of the ecclesiastical politics of apparitions is not the primary concern of this study, it does seem that members of particular religious orders (or the monastic clergy in general) have been particularly visible among the supporters of many modern apparitions.[56]

The Little Miracle

In the light of the tendency of Garabandal devotees to seek and to find evidence for the apparition in paranormal events which they themselves (or other devotees) have experienced in encounters with the seers, it is not surprising that in the history of Garabandal one such event has a very special place. The so-called "little miracle" (*milagrucu*) that Garabandal devotees have seen as extraordinary evidence of supernatural intervention occurred in the context of an alleged angelic administration of Communion to the seers, not unlike that which had been reported at Fatima. During an appearance on 18 July 1962, a little over a year after the Garabandal apparition had begun and in accord with an announcement made by Conchita two weeks earlier, a Communion host reportedly became visible on Conchita's tongue. The memories of this event recorded by Conchita in her *Diary* (1962–1963), along with the accounts gathered by Pérez in 1971, illustrate how a religious experience can take shape for many people in an assembled crowd through a peculiar interaction of circumstances and expectations. To say that the formation of such an experience can be followed by giving careful attention to the historical records is not to say, it should be emphasized, that such an experience can or should have no religious validity.

It was on 1 May 1962, according to Pérez, that the seers began to say publicly that they had been receiving Communion from the angel, Mari Loli being the first to make this claim. During the appearance on that day, she had reportedly been told by St. Michael that he himself would give her Communion while the local priest was absent from the village. From this time on, Pérez said, "The four seers admit having frequently received Communion from the hands of the angel."[57] There is nothing in the testimonies collected by Pérez that either supports or contradicts his account of how and when these claims originated.

In her *Diary* Conchita has sketched a very interesting account of the origins of her and her companions' experience of receiving Communion from the angel. She said that soon after St. Michael began to appear to them he gave them "unconsecrated" hosts in order to teach them how the host should be received. At this time, she said, they had not yet been asked to fast. One day, however, the angel told them to go to the pines without eating and to bring another child with them, apparently as a witness. At this time, he reportedly told the girls, he would give them Communion with consecrated hosts. It was then, according to Conchita, that they first told others about their receiving Communion from the angel, which created some controversy. She said that some people, especially priests, objected, on the basis that an angel could not consecrate a host. When the girls raised this objection to St. Michael during a subsequent appearance, he reportedly told them that he had taken and given them hosts already consecrated, from tabernacles on earth. This explanation, however, did not satisfy everyone. Conchita noted that when they told people what the angel had said, "some doubted it."[58]

Conchita's account implies that the girls had "received Communion" in the course of an unspecified number of appearances of St. Michael for some time before they spoke about it publicly. The testimony of Jacinta's father, Simon González, given to Pérez in 1971, appears to substantiate such a view. Simon recalled that in some of their earlier ecstasies the girls made certain gestures—putting both hands together, extending their tongues, swallowing—that were meaningless until Jacinta explained that they were receiving Communion from the angel. It should be noted that at this point no one but the seers themselves claimed to see the hosts that they were being given. The gestures that Jacinta's father claimed were witnessed before their meaning was understood were seen by many people, however, after the girls spoke about their Communion, and indeed, many photographs were taken after that of the girls' "receiving invisible Communion."[59]

The miracle of "visible" Communion, according to Conchita, was announced to her during an appearance of the angel on Friday, 22 June

1962. Before then, she said, she and her companions had continually been pleading for a miracle. On this day, then, when she was about to receive Communion from the angel, he reportedly told her that God was going to perform a miracle "through his intercession and hers." When Conchita asked what this "miracle" would be, he replied that he was going to make the host visible on her tongue. When she expressed surprise at this, not yet having thought of the host as invisible to others, he explained that those gathered around her had not been able to see the host but that on the day of the miracle they would see it. She responded that this would be a tiny miracle, and the angel laughed.[60]

The basic chronology of events in Conchita's *Diary* from this announcement to Conchita up to the time of the so-called "little miracle" seems quite plausible, in spite of some inconsistencies in dating. During an appearance of the angel either on the following day (June 23) or a week later (June 29), Conchita said that she asked when the miracle would occur, and he told her that the Virgin would reveal this to her. Later that day, the Virgin appeared to her, and Conchita asked her when the miracle would occur. She was told that on the thirtieth she would hear a voice that would announce the date. On June 30, Conchita said, she did hear a voice, which told her that "the little miracle" (*milagrucu*), as she called it, would take place on July 18. Conchita said she had also asked the angel during one of his appearances (no date is specified) when she could announce to the public that there was going to be a miracle, and he told her she could announce it fifteen days in advance. On July 2, therefore, Conchita announced the miracle to the people of the village and wrote some letters about the expected event. The parish priest, however, warned her to stop writing letters, she said, because he doubted that the miracle would occur.[61]

Conchita said that she had told a few people about the anticipated miracle prior to this general public announcement, namely, the other three seers, Don José Garcia de la Riva, her mother, and her aunt Maximina González. Garcia de la Riva has reported an incident that occurred at this time that gives some insight into the tensions that can arise when several visionaries who have presumably shared an experience try to make decisions relating to its publication. It was on July 2, the priest said, that Conchita told him about the miracle. While he was not opposed in principle to their announcing the miracle to the public, he advised her to consult with the other three girls before specifying just what the miracle would be. But Mari Loli had already given this information to her father shortly after the girls had come down from the pines, and according to Garcia de la Riva, when Conchita learned of this, she became very angry and told her mother that because of Mari Loli's indiscretion the angel might cancel the miracle. This incident, taken along with Pérez's report that it was Mari Loli who first spoke of the girls' receiving Communion from the angel, suggests that there was some conflict between her and Conchita at this time about whether both of them had the authority to describe and interpret their apparition to the public.[62]

After Conchita's announcement, word of the expected miracle spread quickly throughout the region. On July 18 there were several thousand people crowded into the little village of Garabandal, some having gathered in anticipation of the miracle and some, no doubt, having come simply for a festival that happened to fall on the same day. For those who had gathered primarily in anticipation of the miracle, there were at least three sources of anxiety. Conchita noted that some were worried that the dancing of the festival might interfere with the miracle and wanted it to be stopped. She tried to reassure them, however, that the miracle would take place whether there was dancing going on or not. Then, as Fr. Pelletier has noted, a number of priests, including the local parish priest, were present on the occasion, and this too was a situation that many in the crowd found disturbing. It was well known—in fact, it was the theological rationale that had sanctioned belief in the angelic Communion in the first place—that the angel had heretofore given Communion to the girls only when priests were absent. Would an angel—indeed, could an angel—give Communion to the girls, whether visibly or invisibly, if priests were present? Pelletier said that Conchita tried to calm these fears also. Finally, then, there was the problem of just when the event would occur. By nightfall, Conchita had not yet had any ecstatic experiences, and people were becoming restless. At about ten o'clock, however, she received the first of the three calls that the girls had come to expect prior to an appearance of the Virgin, and, finally, at about two o'clock in the morning her ecstasy began.[63]

The impression given by Conchita's *Diary* is that her ecstasy both began and ended in a room of her house, where she was waiting with several other people. According to observers, however, after falling into ecstasy in this room, Conchita came out into the street and there dropped to her knees; and it was in the street that the event unfolded. Conchita said that the angel told her, just as he had on previous occasions, to say the "I Confess" and to think about whom she was to receive. After these admonitions, he gave her Communion, presumably placing the host on her extended tongue as he had done before. He then told her to recite the "Soul of Christ," to make her thanksgiving, and to leave her tongue extended until he was gone and the Virgin had taken his place. When the Virgin arrived, she told Conchita, apparently with reference to the crowd, "They still don't believe." Conchita's own recollection in her *Diary* of the crowd's response was that those who had seen the miraculous host on her tongue, or who placed confidence in the testimony of those who had seen it, believed immediately and firmly. But as time passed, she said, some came to doubt and to give credence to the rumor that she herself had placed the host there.[64]

Pepé Diez has left the most detailed account of Conchita's conduct and of the activities surrounding her on that day, along with a rather detailed description of his own emotional state.[65] He was with Conchita most of the day, he told Pérez in 1971, because her mother had asked him to accompany her daughter and protect her from the crowd. There was also, of course, his own desire, quite freely confessed, "to be in the first row" when the miracle took place. He said that he left Conchita for only about half an hour in order to go home to get something to eat, for he was thirsty and suffering from a lack of nourishment, and the wait was long and tiring.

While Diez was with Conchita when her ecstasy began, the crowd made it difficult for him to stay close to her when she went out into the street. Some people began to scream, he said, others fell, and still others tripped over those who had fallen. People grabbed at him "in order to take his place" and tore at his clothing, apparently ripping off his shirt and belt. He had seized Conchita's arm, but lost his grip when she fell to her knees in the street. When she began to speak, Diez recalled, he could not hear her because of the roar of the crowd. He did, however, fix his eyes on her face, illuminating it with the beam of a strong flashlight that he had brought with him.

When she extended her tongue, Diez said, he had "a terrible feeling of disaster." He had expected this to be the moment when he would see the host, but in fact he could see nothing on her tongue at all. He was all the more disappointed because he had followed the events of the day very closely. He was now only about eighteen inches from her face, and he was sure he had not missed anything. He had been hoping for so much, he recalled, and now Conchita's bare tongue left him with "a terrible feeling of failure." But as he watched, he saw a "neat, precise and well-formed Host" appear on her tongue. Diez described it as growing in volume and said that it remained visible for about three minutes. "I saw in that Host," he said, "a live force which reminded me of sea waves, sparkling and moving under the sun, when we see them from a distance."[66]

Others who were near Conchita also reported seeing the host, describing it, as Diez had, particularly in terms of "light." Felicidad González, for example, who was in front of Conchita, remembered that she saw a "white shadow . . . like when our tongue is covered with a white coating when we are sick."[67] Avelina González, who did not see the host herself but who said her brother had seen it, testified that he compared it in size to a five-pesetas coin and saw it increase in brightness "like the light of a carbide lamp."[68] And Benjamin Gomez, who was standing next to Conchita, said the host looked like a "snowflake upon which the sun's rays were striking," but noted that it did not hurt the eyes as the glittering whiteness of a snowflake might do.[69]

Some people, apparently, saw more than a host. Diez said that he had gone home after the event to replace the articles of clothing he had lost in the scuffle with the crowd and then had returned to find out what others had seen and to confirm his own perceptions of what had happened. He then met his brother-in-law, who was in a most agitated state, and who told him that he had seen a chalice, a hand coming down from heaven, and a light. When Diez asked his brother-in-law if he had really seen all that, however, the excited man admitted that he did not know what he had seen. Nevertheless, other people also told Diez that they had seen "a ray of light, a kind of chalice, something dark." Diez himself remained skeptical of these reports, concluding that many people, like his brother-in-law, gave witness in their elation to unusual or miraculous phenomena, when in reality "they didn't know what they had seen."[70]

Motion pictures were made of Conchita on this occasion, and many people believe that the camera captured the form of a host on Conchita's tongue. A single frame of this film purportedly showing this host has often been reproduced in devotional accounts of the events at Garabandal.[71] This photograph, in fact, figures prominently in the more recent arguments for the reality of the miracle. While belief in the *milagrucu* seemed to be fairly well established in the immediate aftermath of the event, doubts soon arose and spread, as Conchita herself has noted, because of the disparity in the accounts of it and the rumor that Conchita had put the host in her own mouth.[72] While Conchita has consistently denied that she in any way feigned or staged the miracle, she did admit, during a period of doubt, the possibility that autosuggestion could have played a part in people's perception of it. Conchita's mother, however, could not accept this possibility, reasoning that while people might succumb to autosuggestion, the camera could not.[73] Her confidence that the miracle has been captured once and for all by the camera seems to be typical not only of many who to this day believe in the apparition at Garabandal and hope for its eventual ecclesiastical recognition, but also of many modern believers in other alleged instances of the paranormal, for whom such photographs have become a kind of religious icon.[74]

It has not been difficult for believers to come to terms with minor inconsistencies in the unfolding of the "little miracle," such as the fact that the crucial event seems to have occurred not on July 18 as predicted but on July 19. They have pointed out, for example, that while July 18 came to an end officially at midnight, according to "sun time" it came to an end at 1:25 A.M. Since some observers placed the beginning of Conchita's ecstasy at 1:30 and the appearance of the host at 1:40, it could be said that these events came at the very end of July 18. Believers have also maintained that the interior calls should be considered the beginning of the miracle, which would mean that the miracle began on July 18, with or without reference to "sun time."[75]

Three Periods of Retractions

Conchita's stay in Santander, culminating in her signing of the statement for Dr. Piñal that she was no longer seeing the Virgin but that she thought her three companions were, was the first of three periods in which one or all of the visionaries at Garabandal retracted some earlier statements about their experiences. Indeed, it was apparently in the aftermath of Conchita's stay at Santander that believers began to find predictions of such retractions in the Virgin's messages. In the devotional literature, the later periods of retractions (in the spring of 1963 and the beginning of 1966), which apparently did little to discourage belief in the authenticity of the apparition, have been termed "periods of doubt." What transpired at Garabandal in this connection stands as an example of what can happen when an apparition that has been meaningfully ap-

propriated by believers is later questioned and challenged by the visionaries themselves.

Conchita has said in her *Diary* that at the beginning of the apparition
she and the other girls were told by the Virgin that they would come to
deny the appearances and to contradict one another, and that their parents would cease to get along well with each other.[76] While Conchita
did not note the day on which this prediction was made, her mother
and aunt recalled hearing of it for the first time on the day when Conchita returned from Santander. They were driving home, according to
her mother, when Conchita leaned over to a priest and said, "A day will
come when we will deny all that—absolutely all—and we will contradict
one another."[77]

Conchita's aunt, Maximina, however, remembered Conchita's return
somewhat differently. She recalled that when her sister Aniceta returned
from Santander with her daughter, her sister was convinced that the
apparitions were "absolutely false." Aniceta did not think the girls had
lied, Maximina said, but she thought that whatever was going on "did
not come from God." The other three seers had come to meet Conchita
on the road back to Garabandal, and the crowd accompanying them was
increasing. Maximina recalled that Aniceta sarcastically asked the people
if they thought there was a fair in Garabandal, and at this the girls lowered their heads, apparently in embarrassment or humiliation, and became silent. She said that at this point Aniceta wanted to remove her
daughter from the affair entirely.[78]

This is why, according to Maximina, her sister took Conchita home
when they arrived in Garabandal, whereas she (Maximina) accompanied
the other seers to the church to say the Rosary. There Mari Loli and
Jacinta fell into ecstasy. Afterwards, Maximina went to her sister's home
and found Aniceta scolding her daughter, saying something like, "You
naughty girl, now you can see your ecstasies aren't true! Why didn't the
Virgin call you today?" Conchita, however, told them that the Virgin
had spoken to her in the intervening two hours, describing to her the
ecstasies of the other girls, and she then proceeded, according to her
aunt, to recount exactly what her aunt had just witnessed at the church.
It was then, according to Maximina, that Conchita told them that the
Virgin had said that a time would come when the girls would deny their
experiences and would contradict one another.[79]

Others remembered hearing about the forthcoming contradictions
and denials during the course of an ecstasy whose date they do not spec-

ify. For example, Jacinta's brother, Miguel González, recalled overhearing the girls ask the Virgin "How can we deny that we saw you, since we are seeing you now?"[80] When, therefore, the girls did begin to issue denials in the spring of 1963, it came as no surprise to believers—at least, so they claimed in retrospect—but was seen, rather, as the fulfillment of a prophecy. Jacinta's mother, María, who recalled hearing about the forthcoming contradictions and denials and thinking that such things could not happen, was thus able to say later, "All this has come about [i.e., as prophesied]."[81]

Conchita's description in her *Diary* of this "period of doubt" which came upon all four of the seers is very interesting. Their public behavior, she said, had come into conflict with their inner conviction; interiorly they knew that they had seen the Virgin and the angel, but publicly they were denying some aspects of their experience. They told their parents, for example, that they had not seen the Virgin or the angel, but that they had never tried to deceive anyone and that the calls and the miracle of visible Communion were true. On the advice of Marichalar, Conchita said, they even brought up the matter at confession and received as a penance ten Rosaries and five Our Fathers.[82] This period of doubt lasted through the spring of 1963 and then, according to Conchita, she, Mari Loli, and Jacinta "returned to reality" and reaffirmed all their supernatural experiences. Mari Cruz, however, continued her denials.[83]

The third period of retractions began in February of 1966 when Conchita became a boarder at the Discalced Carmelite Mission at Pamplona. Her mother had come to the decision to take Conchita to Pamplona at least in part because the constant stream of visitors had made it impossible for Aniceta to work.[84] Conchita, on her part, harbored the desire to become a nun and eventually to go to Africa as a missionary. A week after her arrival at Pamplona, however, Conchita said she had a locution from Jesus, who told her that he had not called her to be a nun and that despite her desire for the cloister he wanted her to remain in the world. He also told her, she said, that before the "great miracle" (see Chapter 6) she would suffer much, because few people would believe her and her own family would think she had deceived them.[85]

As believers saw it, Conchita was put under pressure at Pamplona to deny her experiences. Her confessor did not believe in the apparition and reportedly refused her absolution if she did not issue a public retraction. Mari Loli visited her and expressed her own doubts about the reality of her experiences. Also, the new pastor of Garabandal encouraged Conchita's doubts and thus aggravated her distress.[86] All of this, coupled with guilt over having been the cause of the crowds and controversies at Garabandal and disappointment over her lack of a calling for the religious life, was more than enough to explain, as these persons saw it, why Conchita succumbed to the pressure.[87]

When she left Conchita with the Discalced Carmelites in Pamplona, Aniceta said, she had left instructions with the mother superior that no one was to be allowed to see her. Aniceta had heard that the bishop had summoned the other three girls, and she was taking precautions to protect her daughter. Three or four days later, however, the bishop and several priests went to the convent, she said, and in spite of the assurances the mother superior had given, they were allowed to see Conchita and, indeed, to interview her for seven hours. Conchita told her that she recited her *Diary* (which she had written about three years earlier) to the men from memory and that they wrote everything down. Then her memory "went completely blank, and she couldn't remember the least detail of what she had told them."[88]

While Aniceta's testimony implies that this occurred in February, records indicate that it was on 30 August 1966 that the bishop interviewed Conchita, and that interviews with the other seers followed, in September and October.[89] The seers apparently signed a document stating their retractions, and not long afterwards their parents were also asked to sign it. Believers in the apparition call special attention to the fact that the mothers of two of the visionaries apparently refused to sign, arguing for the priority of the witnesses' experiences over the girls' latest statements. The response of Jacinta's mother is noted as being especially clever and appropriate. According to Pérez's account, Jacinta urged her mother to sign the document, and she agreed on one condition, namely, that Jacinta fall into ecstasy at that very minute. When Jacinta said that her mother knew very well that this was impossible, her mother replied, "Then I do not sign."[90]

Aniceta, in spite of her daughter's urgings, also refused to sign the retractions. She said that it was of no consequence to her whether Conchita had denied everything or not. In the presence of both Conchita and the bishop, she described her daughter as now being "in a trance" and said that "an oblivious person does not know what has happened to her." Aniceta said that she knew what she herself had seen and whatever Conchita now had to say was "unimportant" to her.[91]

Fr. Rodrigo, a priest who was writing in defence of the apparition at about this time, agreed with these women that the seers' current denials were of no particular relevance for faith in the event. Indeed, he argued that believers in the divine origin of the apparition should not allow themselves to be affected by the statements of the children either during the epoch of the apparition itself or afterward. Belief in the events should be based on all the phenomena taken together and on what "other people fully worthy of faith" affirmed that they had seen. The ensemble of facts had been submitted to a severe critical analysis, he said, and it was clear that it could not have been invented by the children, nor was it the result of imagination or of pathological or demonic forces, although this did not exclude the possibility that occasionally the children might have indulged in fantasy. If belief in the supernatural character of the apparition rested on such duly established facts, Rodrigo argued, it could not be destroyed or weakened by whatever the children might currently or hereafter have to say. Should they deny their experiences, he said, "they will be in illusion, but not us."[92]

Judgments of Church Authorities

Bishop Vicenté Puchol Montis of Santander, however, took the retractions of the girls much more seriously. On 17 March 1967, he issued a statement, which began by noting that declarations had been received from the seers during the interviews conducted the previous fall. On the basis of those declarations, it followed that there had been no apparition either of the Blessed Virgin, the archangel Michael, or any other celestial being, and that there had been no divine messages. All the events at Garabandal had a natural explanation. He congratulated those among the clergy and faithful of Santander who had been obedient to the directives of the hierarchy. He regretted that others had acted imprudently and had undermined confidence in the religious authorities. Apparently referring to those who were encouraging the girls to hold to their original claims, he held that some had prevented "by formidable social pressure, that which began as innocent child's play from being demystified by the authors of the game themselves." He ended by reasserting that "the words of the Gospel, the Pope, the Councils, and the ordinary *magisterium* of the Church" were the means of transmission for the "real messages from heaven."[93]

The declaration of Bishop Puchol Montis was marked by none of the uncertainty or tentativeness of the statements that had been issued by his predecessors. Doroteo Fernandez Fernandez, who was bishop of Santander when the apparition began, had established a commission to investigate the events in Garabandal and had issued two statements pertaining to the apparition, on August 26 and October 7 of 1961. In both he called for prudence and asked that judgment on the nature of the phenomena be suspended pending future developments. He also asked religious and laity to refrain from visiting Garabandal. In the second statement he wrote, "So far none of the aforementioned apparitions, visions, locutions or revelations can be held as evidential or as having a serious foundation of truth and authenticity."[94]

A year later, on 7 October 1962, Eugenio Beita Aldazabal, who had succeeded him as bishop of Santander, published a note in the official bulletin of the diocese stating that he had received a report from the special commission investigating the phenomena at Garabandal. This commission, he said, which was qualified to assess these phenomena, maintained its previous position that they lacked a supernatural character and were due to natural causes.[95]

On 8 July 1965, however, Bishop Beita Aldazabel issued another statement. The see of Santander had gathered abundant documentation on the events at Garabandal, he said, and would always "receive with gratitude all the information anyone wants to send us to judge the same." Nothing had caused the commission to change its judgment that the supernatural character of the events was not self-evident. But no grounds had been found, he added, "either in the doctrine or in the spiritual recommendations that have been divulged in the events and addressed to the Christian faithful," for the publication of an ecclesiastical condemnation. These recommendations encouraged devotional practices that were traditional and praiseworthy, and they were also exhortations to a "holy fear of the Lord offended by our sins." Beita Aldazabal noted, however, the potential impact of priests actively participating and collaborating in the development of the cult, and he strictly forbade such assistance.[96] While not really changing his previous position or that of his predecessor and the commission, Beita Aldazabal appears here to have given the supporters of Garabandal a considerable amount of leeway.

This leeway was withdrawn or at least very considerably narrowed by Bishop Puchol Montis's statement of 17 March 1967, which bluntly declared that there had been no apparition and no message and deplored the imprudent conduct of at least some of the Garabandal supporters. José Cirarda Lachiondo, Puchol Montis's successor, issued a statement on 9 October 1968 affirming his support of the position of his three predecessors. The first two bishops, he noted, had been unanimous in their view that the phenomena under investigation manifested no supernatural character. His immediate predecessor, after having consulted with the Holy See about the whole matter, had affirmed that all the events in Garabandal had a natural explanation.[97] Then, about two years later, in June 1970, Bishop Cirarda Lachiondo issued a lengthy report to his fellow bishops that addressed the questions they had raised both with the diocese of Santander and with Rome with respect to Garabandal.

As one of the last and most comprehensive statements about Garabandal to bear the mark of full ecclesiastical authority, this report is worth summarizing.[98] Partisans of the alleged apparition, the bishop noted, had continued to publish books and articles (1) defending its divine origin, (2) challenging the bishop of Santander's authority to judge its authenticity, by contending that this was an affair that concerned the Holy See, and (3) arguing that there was a seeming contradiction on this matter between the Holy See and the curia of Santander. He then reiterated the conclusion reached by his predecessors: although the alleged message did not contain anything contrary to the traditional teaching of the Church on faith and morals, the phenomena at Garabandal had a natural explanation. He stated that on 7 October 1966 his predecessor Puchol Montis had sent the entire file on the apparition and the text of his proposed statement on the matter (the one subsequently published, on 17 March 1967) to the Sacred Congregation for the Doctrine of the Faith. Cardinal Ottaviani had replied in a letter dated 7 March 1967, in which he acknowledged receipt of these materials. After examining this documentation and that received from others, Ottaviani wrote, the Congregation had concluded that the question had been meticulously examined and settled by the bishop himself and that there was no reason for the Congregation to intervene.

Ottaviani's letter was important in the sense that it had made quite clear that high Church officials at Rome, to whom supporters of the apparitions had been appealing more and more in the face of the growing skepticism of the bishops of Santander, had no desire in this matter to give even the least appearance of questioning local episcopal authority. This may have been due, at least in part, to the local bishops' good

relations with the Vatican. Cirarda Lachiondo continued in his statement to say that he and his predecessors had always kept the Holy See
"well-informed regarding this problem." He had in fact made two visits
to Rome (January 1969 and February 1970) to discuss the matter with
the Sacred Congregation, the Chancery of State, and the pope himself.
He cited extracts from two letters he had received from Cardinal Semper
indicating that the Sacred Congregation had studied the matter more
than once, was content to praise the "prudence and pastoral concern"
shown by the curia of Santander, and saw no reason to intervene in a
matter which was in the bishop of Santander's jurisdiction. The Sacred
Congregation had thus in effect made no declaration on the events at
Garabandal. Bishop Cirardo Lachiondo further challenged the claim of
the visionaries that the pope had personally expressed his affection for
them.[99] Having duly informed himself on the matter, the bishop said,
he could announce that none of those claims was true and that the pope
identified himself with the Sacred Congregation and left the judgment
of the affair to the bishop of Santander.

Bishop Cirarda Lachiondo went on then to issue a prohibition of all
special manifestations of piety at San Sebastian de Garabandal. Priests
were forbidden to go to the village without special authorization, under
penalty of withdrawal of the right to exercise ministry in the diocese.
He also stated that the Sacred Congregation desired that this prohibition be observed everywhere, in accord with the disposition of the
bishop of Santander, and that this decree, which the diocesan bishop
had the right to issue, should be a sufficient motive for other bishops to
discourage all pilgrimages and exercises in respect to the alleged apparitions and communications in question. Cirarda Lachiondo concluded
his report expressing the wish that his communication would "serve to
clarify in its entirety, this irritating problem of the alleged apparitions."[100]

The Word of Five Men against Thousands

Supporters of Garabandal were not, of course, to be dissuaded from
their beliefs by a commission's report and a local biship's declaration,
however much these may have been sanctioned and supported by higher
authorities at Rome. They have continued to criticize the procedures
which the commission and the bishops of Santander used to arrive at
their position, denying that the commission did an adequate job of in-

vestigation and maintaining that some or all of its members were biased against Garabandal from the beginning. Garcia de la Riva, for example, remembered overhearing in the parish church several conversations between two priests whom he later discovered to be members of the commission. These conversations convinced him that these priests were predisposed to reject the apparition and were neither thorough nor responsible in their investigations. One said that he had been a professor of philosophy for five years and of theology for ten, but Garcia de la Riva was not convinced that this training was appropriate. Only a professor with a specialty in ascetical and mystical theology, he said, would be fully qualified to assess the phenomena at hand, and he further criticized the commission for not employing a professional photographer.[101]

Members of the commission were criticized in particular for failing to do an adequate on-site investigation. Some did not go to Garabandal at all, supporters of the apparition said, and others went there only once or twice. They were charged with failing to interview the visionaries and with taking testimony only from those eyewitnesses who did not believe the phenomena to be supernatural. Fr. Valentín Marichalar, the pastor of Garabandal until 1965 and a supporter of the apparition, said that the commission considered him of no importance and to get him out of the way had offered to arrange a vacation for him, if he himself would request it in writing. (This, he said, was to preclude people charging the commission with trying to get rid of him.) Fr. Materne Laffineur, one of the few supporters of the apparition who was interviewed, claimed that his testimony was taken in a restaurant by a mere clerk, acting as a procurator, lawyer, and assessor. He said that his answers to questions had been "pre-interpreted" in a way unfavorable to the apparition, and that when he refused to sign a statement the clerk had written, the clerk proceeded to sign his name for him in capital letters. He said that this document was used, then, as testimony against the apparition.[102]

The crux of these objections, to judge from what believers in the apparition found most disturbing, was that the commission had interviewed only a few eyewitnesses from among the believers' own ranks and had refused to take their testimonies seriously. Canon Porro succinctly expressed the issue for the believers: "Should the affirmations of the Commission be the only ones: that is to say, the word of five men against thousands of other persons? I say this with all my soul: that this is the absurdity of it all, that five commissioners should be infallible, whereas thousands of others must admit to being ignorant, deluded, or should we say, insane."[103]

Garabandal shows clearly that the devotion born of a particular series of visions is not inextricably tied to the ongoing lives of the seers. As the visions of such seers begin to acquire meaning for family members, friends and neighbors, and finally people from other, perhaps very distant locales, a cult of the supernatural often forms around the seers, as can clearly be seen in the case of Conchita and her three companions. As, however, those who have been drawn into this cult begin to realize the impracticality of spending their lives following the seers around on their daily routines, and as they struggle, at the same time, to distinguish between the seers themselves and what they believe the seers have experienced, a subtle but significant shift of attention seems to occur. At Garabandal it appears that even those who did for a time follow the seers around the village began very soon to transfer their attention to physical objects and eventually to remembered incidents and events that captured and brought to focus their contact with the seers and the powers they seemed to mediate. This shift of religious attention at Garabandal from the seers themselves to an ensemble of purportedly paranormal events associated with them in the memory of individuals and of the community of believers—the culminating event being the so-called "little miracle"—is apparently what allowed the community to flourish and to grow in the face of resistance not only from Church authorities but also, for a period of time, from the seers themselves.[104]

The story of Garabandal illustrates very clearly some of the permutations that traditional structures of religious authority may undergo in connection with apparition visions and associated experiences and shows also how hard it may be to say whether such visions and experiences affirm or deny these traditional structures. Priests and members of religious orders, for example, are clearly objects of special interest and attention in the Garabandal accounts. Their presence and participation in what are presumed to be supernatural events have clearly been seen by devotees as giving credibility to these events. On the other hand, some of the accounts are very critical of skeptical clergy and monks, and it is not clear whether the seers' presumed ability to recognize such persons when in secular clothing serves to affirm or subvert these persons' religious authority. Similiarly, the so-called Communion from the angel, which devotees see as important in the last phase of the Garabandal apparition, can be understood either as a kind of affirmation of the sacrament of the Eucharist, or (from the suggestion that it could not take place in the presence of priests) as a substitute for it. To make such judgments would perhaps be to take sides on the question of the apparition's authenticity. It may safely be said, however, that persons who use a religious symbol such as angelic Communion to understand Garabandal have found a remarkable and probably a personally satisfying way of reconciling the traditional authority of the Church with the authority of the apparition experience.

"Religious experience" is a much-debated expression today, and current thinking among American scholars who are concerned with such matters runs in the direction of doubting that any experience in and of itself can properly be called religious.[105] Even if it is granted, however, that there is no such thing as religious experience as such, this expression has the value of calling attention to the peculiar authority which some experiences, to which religious meanings have been attached, exercise over their subjects long after these experiences have passed. The materials surveyed in the past three chapters, which describe five different apparitions spanning a period of more than a century, show clearly that while the seers were influenced in their understanding of their experiences by the people around them, these experiences were not, for the seers, amenable to just any interpretation whatsoever. They retained for their subjects an independence and a religious autonomy which, to the extent that they were able to defend this publicly, significantly affected how these experiences were understood by others. These chapters have been concerned, for the most part, with the background of these five apparitions and the earlier stages of their interpretation, i.e., with those contexts most affected by the religious autonomy of such experiences and most important for understanding them. Thus, broadly speaking, they have been concerned with apparitions as religious experience. In the case of some apparitions, however, there have been some important interpretive developments which have gone well beyond the contexts sketched in the foregoing chapters. These interpretive developments provide the focus for the second part of this study.

1. A La Salette broadsheet, with illustrations of some of the best known of La Salette's miracles on the four corners. A copy of this broadsheet was reportedly posted at the entrance to the Lourdes grotto shortly after Bernadette's visions.

2. Bernadette Soubirous, the principal seer of Lourdes, who is now a canonized saint of the Roman Catholic Church.

3. José Correia da Silva, bishop of Leiria, Portugal, poses in 1948 with the envelope containing the famous "Third Secret" of Fatima.

4. The seers in ecstasy at Garabandal, Spain, holding up rosaries which people have given to them to be blessed by the Virgin.

5. Conchita González in ecstasy at Garabandal.

6. Melleray Grotto in the Republic of Ireland, where a Marian apparition was reported in August 1985.

7. A crowd surrounds the parish house in Medjugorje, Yugoslavia, where an apparition is in progress, 24 June 1986, the fifth anniversary of the first Medjugorje apparition.

8. People in the crowd point to what they probably understand as "sun miracles," reminiscent of Fatima, at an apparition-related gathering in Lubbock, Texas, 15 August 1988.

PART TWO

Apparitions as Religious Knowledge

CHAPTER 4

From Personal to Public

LA SALETTE

ECRETS are a particularly interesting aspect of modern Marian apparitions. Visionaries often indicate that the Virgin has told them things that they are supposed to tell no one. They are usually ambivalent about even mentioning such "secrets," however, probably realizing that they will be under pressure to reveal them. When people become convinced that a seer harbors secrets, speculation about their nature and content is inevitable, and the seer is pressed for anything and everything in the alleged secrets which might be of public relevance. Indeed, a seer's ability to withstand such pressure has often been understood as evidence of the authenticity of an apparition.

If most interested persons decide, finally, that a secret is purely a personal concern of the seer, interest in it eventually wanes. Such was the case of Bernadette of Lourdes, who insisted that the special prayer and three secrets confided to her by the Virgin during the fortnight of her apparitions of 1858 were for her alone and should not be told even to the pope.[1] If, however, a seer's secrets are thought to concern public figures, institutions, and events, interest usually increases, and the special knowledge presumably contained therein typically becomes the fulcrum of power struggles involving different interest groups (for example, clerics, bishops and rival bishops, members of religious orders, and the visionaries themselves), the drama of which may be very visible and may help maintain interest in an apparition and its presumed revelations for many decades.

The allure of secrets for apparition devotees and their great interest in what might be called the "public secrets" of certain apparitions—an expression that suggests both the importance of the revelation that has been given to a seer and the drama that accompanies its publication—shows very clearly the importance which most of these persons attach to such special knowledge. Most seers and devotees of modern Marian apparitions believe that when the Virgin appears on earth, she comes not just to alleviate personal suffering and impart grace to individuals but to alleviate communal or global suffering and impart grace to a particular community or to the world, through a message which brings understanding and illumination. The message of an apparition as sketched or summarized by its devotees will not, of course, to most non-believers, seem very illuminating or even very coherent. The person who studies these messages in their contexts, however, will see that they are not lacking in coherence and that as paradigms for religious illumination, they are no less compelling than the formulas set forth by the proponents of many other popular religious worldviews. The peculiarly autonomous experience of the apparition seer, when understood as the vehicle of such messages, can thus be seen as a manifestation or focal point of a tradition of special or privileged knowledge. While traditions of privileged knowledge are found and are of some importance in most religions, the scope and importance of such traditions in and for Christianity has yet to be generally recognized. In the case of Marian apparitions in a Roman Catholic milieu, the claim of privileged knowledge (which the Church has attempted to check but has in fact sanctioned by classifying apparitions as private revelations) has usually led to the rise of subgroups within the larger institution, with distinct patterns of belief and devotional practice. While persons in these subgroups participate in, and are often the staunchest supporters of, the Church's traditional rituals, they see themselves, by virtue of their apparition-based knowledge, as members of an especially privileged community, a church within a church, commissioned to impart their presumably crucial knowledge and understanding to the universal Church and to the world as a whole.

The history of the public secrets that form the core of the privileged knowledge claimed by many devotees of modern apparitions begins with the apparitions at La Salette and Fatima. The rather complicated history of the secrets reported by the seers of these apparitions is the framework in terms of which the secrets of more recent apparitions and the intense interest in those secrets must be understood.

Personal Secrets?

Mélanie Calvat and Maximin Giraud reported that when the Virgin Mary spoke with them on 19 September 1846, she gave each of them a secret. In his study, published in 1969, of the secrets of La Salette, Max

Le Hidec has summarized many of the events leading up to the transmission of these secrets to Pope Pius IX in 1851 and the issues surrounding the publication of the alleged secret of Maximin in 1871 and that of Mélanie in 1879.[2] In 1980 and 1984, Jean Stern published two volumes of documents concerning the apparition dating from September 1846 to April 1849.[3] Stern's publication of these documents makes possible a detailed study of the early development of public interest in and belief about the experience of the two children, including their secrets, only the later history of which has been sketched by Le Hidec. This early history reveals much about the function of these secrets both for the seers and for the public, and demonstrates how the secrets became both a locus of power and the carriers of apocalyptic expectations.

The children apparently made no reference to secrets in their first accounts of their experience with the Beautiful Lady. There is no reference to or suggestion of secrets, for example, in the accounts of Pierre Selme and Jean-Baptiste Pra, the children's employers, who were among the first to talk to them on the evening of the day of the apparition.[4] The determination that secrets were a part of the conversation between Mary and the two children was made by the Abbé Mélin, curé of Corps, in an interview with Maximin sometime between September 21 and 26.[5] There is no record of this interview from the hand of Mélin himself. But the Abbé Champon, who was involved with Maximin's education from 1853 to 1856, said that Maximin told him later that when he had finished telling Mélin of the apparition, Mélin had asked him whether there was anything else, and Maximin had replied "Yes, there is something, but the Holy Virgin has forbidden me to tell it."[6] Mélin then interviewed Mélanie, with the same result. In a letter of 12 October 1846 to Victor Rabillou, a librarian at Bourgoin (Isère), Mélin briefly summarized the conversation of the Lady with the children and noted that "a personal secret has been confided to them."[7] This is the first document to mention secrets, and it is important to observe that it is assumed here that the secrets are personal in nature.

The earliest written account of the apparition itself that makes reference to secrets dates from mid-October 1846 and comes from the Abbé Louis Perrin, newly appointed curé of La Salette.[8] Perrin based his account on notes taken during interviews with the children at the site of the apparition and in the presence of other witnesses. He reported that after Mary had advised the children to pray well each morning and evening and had conceded that if they could not do better, an Our Father and an Ave Maria were enough, she turned to Maximin and spoke to him alone. Although Mélanie could see the Virgin's lips move, she could hear nothing of what she was saying. This situation was reversed when the Virgin turned to speak to Mélanie. Perrin observed that the Lady requested them never to tell anyone "that which concerned only themselves." He refers to this as "wise counsel [*conseils de sagesse*]" and puts it clearly in the context of the Virgin's examination of the children concerning their personal devotion.[9] Perrin's account of the apparition reinforced the assumption of Mélin and others that the children's secrets were personal in nature, and his account was used as the basis for a number of others originating from Grenoble.[10]

Le Hidec speculated that the children initially refrained from mentioning their secrets for fear of being led to betray them.[11] If so, subsequent events demonstrated that their fear was not groundless. Investigators and pilgrims alike tried in various ways to wrest the secrets from the children. The earliest report of such an attempt comes from the Marquise de Monteyard, sister of the bishop of Moulins. The Marquise had occasion to interview Maximin while passing through Corps on September 29, and she wrote her account of the interview perhaps a month later.[12] Maximin referred to the secret at the end of his account, according to the Marquise, but refused her request to disclose it. The Marquise suggested that Maximin would at least tell the secret to his confessor, to which Maximin replied that the Beautiful Lady had forbidden him to tell anyone. The Marquise then asked if he could say whether that which the Lady had told him was "fortunate or unfortunate [*heureux ou mal-heureux*]." According to the Marquise, Maximin's face then assumed an ineffable expression, and he said in a low voice, "Ah, it is good fortune [*bonheur*]." To the remark of the Marquise's son that the secret would then be known by all some day, Maximin replied, "Yes, when all men will be judged."

The children were frequently subjected to such interviews and apparently quickly became adept at outmaneuvering their interrogators. Within a few weeks of the interview with the Marquise, for example, Maximin was reported to be responding thus to the notion that he would be obliged to tell his secret to his confessor: "No, it [the secret] is not a sin!"[13] Maximin also rejected the suggestion that he would be obliged to tell his secret to the pope, since the pope is God's representative on earth. The pope, he declared, was no more than other sinners, and like them would be rewarded or punished for his actions after death.[14] Threats of imprisonment and death, offers of money or other benefits, and tricks and ruses could not move the children to disclose their secrets.[15] The interrogators were impressed by such responses and tenaciousness. For example, the Abbé Chambon, superior of the boy's school of Rondeau, and several of his professors, interviewed the children sometime in late October. On November 10 he sent a report to Mgr. de Bruillard, bishop of Grenoble, stating with regard to the children and their secrets: "We have been truly struck by the astonishing resourcefulness that they find in order to defend themselves, when one presses them, notwithstanding their candor and simplicity."[16] With regard to Maximin in particular, investigators noted that although he was eleven years of age his lack of intelligence (that is, his failure to learn the catechism) had kept him even from making his First Communion. Nonetheless, they saw in his responses to the demands made for his secret "a precision, a reserve and a firmness entirely strange to his age and condition."[17] The children's preservation of their secrets in the face of such pressures became, for the investigators, an argument for the children's integrity and thus evidence for the divine origin of the apparition.[18]

The most tenacious inquisitor of the children with regard to their secrets was the Abbé Lagier, curé of St-Pierre-de-Cherennes. Lagier had been born in Corps, and because of the illness of his father he spent several weeks there again from the end of February through the beginning of March 1847. He thus understood the dialect of the area very well, and he devoted much of his time on the visit just mentioned to questioning the children, with the aim of finding some internal contradictions in their testimony and of testing Mélanie's fidelity in preserving her secret. Lagier placed before her a list of people (for example, a priest, her parents, a wise person, someone she could trust) to whom she might be willing to tell her secret, but she steadfastly replied that she did not want to tell it to anyone. Pressed for the reason, she replied, "Because it is forbidden for me to tell it; I don't want to tell it, and I will never tell it." She also refused to divulge anything concerning the nature of her secret. To detailed questions about what her secret concerned (for example, heaven, hell, the world, religion, something else), she responded, "It concerns that which it concerns; if I tell you this you will know it, and I don't want to tell it."[19]

On the basis of these remarks of Mélanie, the conclusion of an earlier investigator that "the particular revelation of the little girl concerns her

alone"[20] appears unfounded. As has been noted, most early accounts of
the apparition simply assumed that the children's secrets were personal
in nature. The Abbé Morel, pro-secretary to the diocesan office of Grenoble, was critical of such accounts in a letter of 4 June 1847 to the
Abbé Mathieu, director of a Catholic periodical. While reporting on
several matters relating to the apparition, he pointed out that "the children have never said, as some accounts have reported it, that their secret
regards only themselves. When someone asks them if their secret is
something that concerns only themselves or others, they elude the question with dexterity and one knows nothing."[21]

Public Secrets?

Morel's critical perception with respect to what could be known with
certainty concerning the children's secrets was not widely shared, and
while most early interpreters considered the secrets purely personal,
others expressed a very different opinion. The report of Armand Dumanoir, a Grenoble lawyer, written sometime during the spring of
1847, is the first document to contain the suggestion that Mélanie's and
Maximin's secrets were of public relevance. Dumanoir reported that the
Virgin conveyed secrets to the children after giving them advice concerning their personal devotion: "After these words the Lady gave to
each of them a secret which appears to consist in the announcement of
a great event, fortunate for some, unfortunate for others."[22]

Canon Rousselot also thought that the children's secrets might concern a great event, but he was more cautious in his assessment. On 19
July 1847, Rousselot, along with Canon Orcel, had been delegated by
Bruillard to gather documents and evidence concerning the apparition.[23] On October 15, on behalf of himself and his colleague, Rousselot sent to the bishop a report that was supportive of the apparition. He
argued that if one admitted the reality of the apparition then one would
also have to decide in favor of the innocence of the secret and the in-
junction forbidding the children to tell it; hence the intervention of
church authorities was unnecessary. The refusal of the children to divulge their secret should not be used, as some had done, to discredit
other parts of their story. Regarding the nature of their secret, Rousselot stated that it "could well be only the announcement of a future event,
fortunate or unfortunate, concerning themselves or others."[24]

The intense questioning of the children concerning their secrets, which continued through the year 1847, led to the determination that they had received them a bit earlier in the course of their conversations with the Lady than previous investigators had assumed. In a conversation with Lagier in mid-February, Mélanie remarked that the Lady had spoken to each of them separately at the time when she spoke of "the harvest [that would spoil] or of the children [who would be seized with trembling and die]."[25] Questioned by the Abbé Bez in May, Maximin stated that the secrets had been conveyed when the Lady spoke of the famine,[26] or, as he put it more precisely later, after she spoke of the spoiling of the walnuts and grapes.[27] The conveying of the secrets would thus have come at the end of the Lady's recitation of the sins that made her Son's hand so heavy and the prophecy of a coming famine, that is, *before* she questioned them about their personal devotional practices. This shift in context, although slight, was important and encouraged the notion that the secrets concerned matters of public interest.

The social and political turmoil in France in 1848, certainly, helped fire speculation that the children's secrets were crucial for understanding contemporary events. Mélin received numerous requests for confirmation of rumors based on this speculation. A letter from Corps to the Abbé Arbaud on 28 March 1848, which Mélin himself may have written, acknowledges that others were wondering, as Arbaud himself was wondering, whether there was a connection between La Salette and the recent "serious events." The author stated that, "If so, God is keeping the secret," for the children had divulged nothing and their behavior had not significantly changed.[28] Early in 1849, however, the rumor circulated that the nun who had received the revelation of the Miraculous Medal in 1830 had made a pilgrimage on foot from Paris to La Salette. There she had allegedly received a revelation that succinctly described a scenario of events reflective of the current turmoil and announced the imminence of the Second Coming.[29] A similar rumor circulated about a nun of Chateau-Thierry, in the diocese of Soissons, who had reported an apparition of the Virgin. She was said to have gone to Corps, and Mélanie and Maximin then allegedly told Mélin, "Monsieur le curé, hear this sister, for she too has a secret!"[30] In these contexts, clearly, the children's secrets were being understood as prophetic, that is, as describing the contemporary disturbances that were unfolding in France in ways that gave them a purpose in the divine plan. The rumored connections, moreover, between La Salette and other apparitions indicated that many people believed that God was revealing the details of this plan in various places and through various human agents.

Particularly interested in the children's secrets were persons who supported the restoration of the French monarchy and the elevation to the throne of Baron de Richemont, the alleged Louis XVII. According to Mgr. Ginoulhiac, successor to Bruillard as bishop of Grenoble, these persons had gone to Corps already in 1847 in order to interview the children and learn their secrets. Their attention focused on Maximin, with whom they could most easily converse but whose knowledge of French history and politics was apparently so poor as to leave them quite puzzled.[31] Despite initial disappointment, their efforts continued. On 17 March 1849, for example, one of these persons, E. de Leudeville, wrote to Mélin expressing his belief that "this impenetrable secret could well be tied more directly than one believes to the political and religious destinies of France."[32] According to Ginoulhiac, these persons employed a variety of means in 1849 and 1850 to uncover Maximin's secret. One tried to instruct Maximin about the life of Louis XVII and then surprise the boy into divulging his secret through skillful questioning. Then a man from Lyon, believed to be possessed of a demon and able to discern mysteries, was called in to confront Maximin. Ginoulhiac noted, however, that this attempt "failed against the ignorance or obstinacy of the child."[33] Finally the supporters of Baron de Richemont determined to take Maximin to the famous curé of Ars, Jean Vianney, a man renowned for his holiness and said to possess the ability to penetrate to the depths of a person's conscience. They convinced Maximin to accompany them to Ars on the pretext of consulting Vianney about Maximin's religious vocation. On 25 September 1850, they brought Maximin into Vianney's presence.

The encounter between Maximin and Vianney resulted in a misunderstanding that created a scandal both for the cause of La Salette and for the curé himself. After holding two brief conversations with Maximin that day, Vianney was convinced that Maximin had come to Ars to confess to him that he had lied about seeing the Virgin Mary at La Salette.[34] Maximin, however, denied that he had recanted his testimony concerning the apparition and maintained that Vianney had not heard correctly and had misunderstood him.[35] A year later Maximin explained to Mlle. des Brulais what he thought had brought about the misunderstanding. To Vianney's question about whether he had seen the Virgin, he had replied: "I do not know if it was the Holy Virgin. I have seen something . . . a Lady . . . But if you know, yourself, that it is the Holy Virgin, it is necessary to tell all these people so that they believe in La Salette."[36] Maximin said he had then mentioned to Vianney some lies he had indeed told to the curé of Corps. Vianney told him to recant the lies, but Maximin said those lies were not the problem, they were too long past, and he could not do it. Maximin said he had in mind lies about such everyday matters as not wanting to study or about where he was going, and Vianney, he conjectured, must have thought he was talking about the apparition. In any case, Maximin maintained that although the conversation had taken place at the confessional he had not said the "confiteor" and had not gone there to make a confession.

The incident was embarrassing to all concerned, including the partisans of de Richemont, who failed after all to learn Maximin's secret. Supporters of Vianney believed Maximin had behaved badly toward him and seized on the incident in an attempt to discredit the apparition.[37] As a consequence, however, the children's secrets were thrust even more into the public spotlight and became the object of even more ecclesiastical attention. Cardinal de Bonald, archbishop of Lyon, who had never been positive toward the apparition, now became convinced that it was only a deceit and decided to use his position to intervene.[38] Hoping that the children's secrets might serve as the key to reveal imposture, he determined to have them transmitted to the pope, with himself as the messenger.

Transmission of the Secrets to the Pope

Early in 1851, Archbishop Bonald began to make arrangements to obtain the children's secrets. He requested Cardinal Gousset, archbishop of Reims, who was making a trip to Rome, to inquire whether Pope Pius IX would be willing to have him (Bonald) transmit the secrets to him. Bonald then wrote to Rousselot, vicar general of the diocese of Grenoble, on March 21, inquiring whether "Marcellin and his sister [sic] would entrust to me their famous secret in order to send it to his Holiness."[39] Abbé Auvergne, secretary to Bishop Bruillard of Grenoble, was dispatched to interview the children to see if they would be willing to send their secrets to the pope. Maximin, who had been residing at the boys' school at Rondeau, resisted only slightly, first avowing that he would have to be in the presence of the pope in order to determine if he would tell the pope his secret or not. Then, however, he agreed that he would tell the pope his secret if ordered to do so.[40]

Mélanie, however, who was living in the convent of the Sisters of Providence at Corenc, was quite reticent about the matter. Auvergne interviewed her twice at Corenc, and each time she expressed reluctance to tell her secret to the pope, saying several times during the interview that the Virgin had forbidden her to tell it. Mélanie appears to have astutely perceived the politics of the situation. To Auvergne's argument that "the Virgin would have us obey the pope," Mélanie replied, "It is not the pope who requests the secret; other persons have told him to ask me for it."[41] Rousselot himself then went to see Mélanie and was told by the superior of the convent that the child had been greatly distressed. Auvergne had said nothing to her about the consequences of a refusal to communicate her secret to the pope, but she had drawn her own conclusions. According to the superior, Mélanie's roommate had heard her say in her sleep, "They want my secret . . . I must tell my secret to the pope or be severed from the Church," and she had been heard to repeat more than forty times, "to be severed from the Church."[42] Rousselot, however, had more success with Mélanie, and she agreed that she would tell the pope her secret herself or place it in a sealed letter entrusted either to Bishop Bruillard or to Rousselot himself. But she refused to entrust her secret to Bonald because, she said, "at Lyon they do not believe much in La Salette, and then I do not want them to unseal my letter."[43]

Bruillard reported to Bonald the conversations Auvergne and Rousselot had had with the children, and in June of 1851, he wrote directly to Pius IX appraising him of recent developments concerning La Salette, including the affair of Ars, and indicating the willingness of the children to reveal their secrets to him.[44] Bonald had received word in the meantime that the pope was willing to have the secrets transmitted to him. A few weeks later, Bonald wrote to Bruillard stating that he had been charged by the pope to send him "the secret and nothing else, the secret purely and simply." He instructed Bruillard to have the children write their secrets in the presence of a trustworthy churchman. The secrets were to be brought to Bonald unsealed, and he would affix his own seal on them and send them on to the pope.[45] Mélanie's attitude, however, seemed to Bruillard to preclude such an arrangement, and he decided to transmit the secrets to Pius IX on his own authority, without Archbishop Bonald's mediation.

According to the standard account of the transcription of the children's secrets, on July 2 Maximin was summoned from the boys' school at Rondeau to Bruillard by Dausse, a Grenoble engineer who had been interested in the apparition almost from the time it was first reported.[46] Bruillard placed Maximin at a desk with paper and pen and left him to write his secret under the supervision of Dausse and Canon de Taxis. Maximin first wrote a brief preface that he showed to Dausse, who commended it and encouraged him to continue. Maximin then applied himself to his task and wrote rapidly and without stopping. When he finished, he sat up and threw the paper into the air, exclaiming, "I am unburdened, I no longer have a secret, I am as others! One no longer has any need to ask me anything, one can ask the pope and he will speak if he wants!" The paper on the floor appeared to the two witnesses to be written sloppily, however, and they compelled Maximin to copy it neatly. Bruillard was then summoned, and he told Maximin to place his letter in an envelope and seal it. But Dausse intervened and suggested that Bruillard read the text to assure that they would not be forwarding to the pope a communication unworthy of him, and after hesitating briefly, Bruillard agreed and read what Maximin had written. Maximin then sealed the envelope, and the episcopal seal was affixed. Dausse and Taxis witnessed on the envelope that Maximin himself had written and signed his letter and had not been influenced by anyone while he was writing.

According to this account, Dausse went to Corenc that evening to repeat the process with Mélanie, but he found her quite ambivalent about transcribing her secret. After hesitating, promising, and then hesitating again, she finally agreed to write down her secret the next day. On July 3, in the presence of Dausse and the Abbé Gerente, who was the chaplain of her convent, she wrote down her secret calmly and without hesitation. She signed it and placed it in an envelope, which she sealed and addressed to Pope Pius IX. Mélanie became agitated a few hours later, however, and asked to see Rousselot, claiming that she had forgotten to write something. Rousselot agreed that she could write a new version, which she did on July 6 at the convent of the Sisters of Providence in Grenoble, with Auvergne and Dausse as witnesses.[47] She placed the text in an open envelope and, accompanied by the two witnesses, took it to Bishop Bruillard. She asked him to read it; he retired to his chambers to do so; and according to the witnesses, he emerged moved and in tears. He returned the envelope to Mélanie; it was sealed;

and Auvergne and Dausse certified that she had written the contents without external influence.

The children gave several reasons for their decision to transmit their secrets to the pope after almost five years of steadfast refusal to reveal them to anyone. The simplest explanation given by both was that they had not previously understood the position of the pope within the Church, the rights that he had, and their duty to obey him.[48] Conversations with the children, however, supply hints that people suspected and the children themselves believed that each had been given a special sign from heaven that permitted the transmission. Des Brulais, for example, asked Mélanie directly in September 1851 whether she had seen the Virgin again before she decided to reveal her secret to the pope. According to Des Brulais, Mélanie cast down her eyes, and a remarkable smile came over her features; but she remained silent. The assistant superior of the Convent at Corenc then repeated the question and directed her to answer, but Mélanie maintained the same attitude. Then Des Brulais rephrased the question and asked Mélanie to say at least whether she had somehow known, before revealing her secret to the pope, that she was permitted to do it. To this Mélanie replied, "Yes, Mademoiselle, *I knew*" (emphasis of Des Brulais).[49]

Maximin was also questioned by Des Brulais in September 1851, and on that occasion Maximin attributed his change of attitude to his new understanding that to obey the pope was not to disobey the Virgin. Someone had held a novena for him and prayed for him, after which he had gone to Mass, and it was in the wake of this, he said, that he finally decided to reveal his secret to the pope, since the Church had commanded it. Maximin rejected the idea that only a direct command from the Virgin herself could have sanctioned the revelation of his secret, and he denied that he had ever said he would never reveal it. He claimed that he had said "never or one day."[50] Some years later, Maximin gave another account of the motive for his decision. He said that when Taxis exhorted him to reveal his secret to the pope, Taxis used a phrase that was in fact a part of the secret, and this seemed to Maximin to be an authorization from God for the written transmission of the secret. It may be recalled, however, that it was Auvergne and not Taxis who had been sent to the children early in 1851 to urge them to reveal their secrets to the pope, and it may be, therefore, that Maximin's later recollection of these events was imperfect. It is clear in any case that in the later interview, Maximin wished to justify his decision by an appeal to a providential sign.[51]

Rousselot and the Abbé Gerin, curé of the cathedral of Grenoble, were designated to deliver the texts of the secrets to Pius IX. They left for Rome on 6 July 1851, arrived there on July 11, and were granted an audience with the pope on July 18. It was reported that they were cordially received, that they presented the envelopes containing the secrets, and that in their presence the pope opened the two envelopes and silently read their contents. Although he apparently later allowed selected officials to read them, Pius IX never released the texts of these documents to the public, and what became of the children's handwritten copies is unclear.[52]

New Speculation

This sequence of events put an end to the idea that the children's secrets might have been purely personal, assured that they would be understood now as concerned with public events, and set off a new round of speculation about them that had decidedly apocalyptic overtones. Important for the popular understanding of the secrets that was now emerging were reports and rumors about the transcription of the secrets, about the audience of Rousselot and Gerin with the pope, and about various conversations with important people who presumably knew what the secrets were.

The witnesses who observed Maximin and Mélanie while they were writing reported some features of the process that seemed to shed light on the content of the secrets. Maximin, it will be remembered, wrote a short preface that he showed to Dausse for approval. While inscribing the secret itself, he asked how the word "pontiff" was spelled. The format of his finished text was observed to consist of seven numbered paragraphs. The witnesses who observed Mélanie during the second transcription of her secret noted that she was very emotional while she wrote. She stopped suddenly in the middle of the task and asked what the word "infallibly" meant. She also asked the spelling of the words "soiled" and "antichrist." Her text was observed to be longer than Maximin's.[53]

Observers felt that certain comments made by Pius IX after he had read each of the children's secrets seemed to convey information about their contents. According to Rousselot and Gerin, the pope read Maximin's secret without any change in demeanor and then said, "Here is all the candor and simplicity of a child." While he read Mélanie's secret, however, the witnesses averred, his face changed and reflected great emotion. When he finished, he is reported to have said, "It is necessary that I reread these at more leisure. There are scourges that menace France, but Germany, Italy, all Europe is culpable and merits chastisements. I have less to fear from open impiety than from indifference and from human respect. It is not without reason that the church is called militant and you see here the captain."[54]

Finally, information thought to give insight into the nature of the secrets was gleaned from conversations between proponents of La Salette and various ecclesiastical figures who presumably had knowledge of the secrets. During his visit to Rome to deliver the children's transcriptions to Pius IX, Rousselot met with Cardinals Lambruscini and Fornari. Rousselot reported that Lambruscini, first minister to Pius IX and prefect of the Congregation of Rites, had told him, "I have known the fact of La Salette for a long time and as a bishop I believe it. I have preached it in my diocese and I have observed that my discourse made a great impression. Moreover, I know the secret of La Salette. The pope has communicated it to me." Cardinal Fornari, nuncio to Paris, told Rousselot, "I am terrified of these prodigies; we have everything that is needed in our religion for the conversion of sinners; and when Heaven employs such means, the evil must be very great." Rousselot had a second audience with Pius IX on 22 August 1851 and left Rome with the pope's blessing for the children, presents for Bruillard, and the message that the bishop "might do as he judged best as to La Salette."[55] Gerin, speaking with Mélanie after his return from Rome, told her that he did not know what she had written to the pope, but to judge from his reaction it had scarcely seemed flattering. Mélanie responded with surprise to the word "flattering," and Gerin asked her if she knew what it meant. She replied that the word meant "to give pleasure" and added, "But this [her secret] ought to give pleasure to the pope—a pope should love to suffer."[56] Some years later, Father Giraud, superior of the Missionaries of La Salette, is said to have asked about the secrets in a private audience with Pius IX and to have received the reply, "You want to know the secrets of La Salette? Ah, well, here are the secrets of La Salette: if you do not do penance, you will all perish."[57]

Persons convinced of the importance of the secrets gleaned what they could from these sources and assembled this material into meaningful constructs with the aid of assumptions, which may or may not have been justified, about the attitudes and states of mind of persons involved with the secrets, as well as assumptions about the crucial nature of the times. The comments of Lambruscini and Fornari and the approbation of the pope to the bishop of Grenoble reinforced the idea that nothing in the secrets was an impediment to belief in the apparition. Furthermore, certain words that were now believed to occur in the texts of the secrets ("pontiff," "infallibly," "antichrist"), the comment of the pope concerning scourges and chastisements, and his terse summary of the overall message all reinforced the growing conviction that the secrets spoke of and were addressed to a society, a Church, and a papacy facing imminent crisis. An important distinction arose now, however, between the respective secrets of the two children. With regard to Maximin's secret, it was unclear whether the pope's comment "Here is all the candor and simplicity of a child" concerned only the preface to Maximin's secret or the secret as such. But the fact that Maximin displayed no emotion while writing his secret and the pope displayed no emotion while reading it gave the impression that it was benign. Mélanie's great emotion while writing her secret was likewise understood as reflecting its content—whereas it might simply have reflected the fact that she had been pressured into surrendering it after so many years—and the fact that the pope was seen to be moved while reading it reinforced the idea that its message was ominous. It was on the basis of such evidence that Gerin, for example, concluded that Maximin's secret announced "mercy and the rehabilitation of things," while Mélanie's secret announced great chastisements.[58]

The reports of the transcription of the children's secrets and their transmission to the pope brought these secrets forcefully and irrevocably into the public realm and convinced many Roman Catholics that a knowledge of the secrets was crucial for understanding the critical times in which they lived. At the same time, however, the Roman Church had established itself as the official guardian of the secrets and the arbiter of their interpretation and significance. Anyone who speculated about them or presumed to reveal their content would have to come to terms with the teaching authority of this Church.

Publication of the Secrets

The fact that the secrets were now in the safekeeping of the person who was presumably best qualified to decide if and how they should be made public evidently did very little to prevent various persons from continuing to put pressure on the children to reveal them. Contrary to Maximin's explicit hope, he and Mélanie continued to be intently quizzed by people on the subject, and by 1854 texts were being circulated which purported to be the secrets of each of the two seers.

The earliest of these texts, which was identified as the secret of Maximin, predicted a series of events in which the seer himself would play a peculiarly exalted role. According to this text, Napoleon would die a tragic death. There would be a short period of anarchy and then a member of Napoleon's family would assume the throne. During this time there would be a persecution of priests, and the pope would die a martyr. Then Louis XVII would ascend the throne, and Maximin would be his prime minister. Louis would rule only a short time, and Maximin would succeed him. Through Maximin's efforts, Europe would gain peace, and Maximin himself would become a millionaire, conquering powerful enemies through the Rosary. England would be converted. Mgr. Philibert de Bruillard, bishop of Grenoble, would die a tragic death. These events, most of which would supposedly take place in 1856, would signal the end of the world. The antichrist would appear and kill Maximin. Finally, according to this text, the pope who would succeed Pius IX would be French.[59]

Most scholars today believe that Maximin offered these predictions simply to rid himself of the persons who had been pestering him. At the time, however, this text was taken seriously by at least some devotees and by many opponents of La Salette. The text had apparently been written down by one of Maximin's former classmates in August 1853, about a month after he had presumably heard Maximin himself say these things. He placed the text in an envelope and sealed it in the presence of several witnesses, saying that it would be opened when the events described therein began to take place. Needless to say, little of what was predicted actually came to pass.

There was another text, however, which gained considerably more acceptance as representing the actual secret of Maximin. According to Le Hidec, the public history of this second text began in 1871 with the publication by M. C.-Regis Girard of a brochure entitled "The Secrets of La Salette and Their Importance: Final Revelations about Coming Events." In this brochure, Girard printed a text that, according to him, constituted at least a part of Maximin's secret, which he had acquired by a rather circuitous route. When Maximin wrote down his secret on 2 July 1851, it will be recalled, his first draft was considered too poorly written to be sent to the pope, and he had been forced to recopy it neatly. According to Girard, Maximin gave the first copy to Dausse, who conserved it faithfully and who made two copies several years later at the requests of Ginoulhiac, the new bishop of Grenoble, and Taxis, his fellow witness. According to the brochure, Taxis had spoken to Girard and others about this text and had sent a copy to Father Pierre-Julien Emyard, a Marist and founder of the Congregation of the Holy Sacrament. Emyard had sent a copy to M. Houzelot, who had long been involved in the cause of La Salette, and Houzelot had in turn sent a copy to Girard. The brochure also noted that Emyard had sent a copy of the same text to a vicar of Lyon, identified only by the initials "F.M.G.," who had sent it to the author of "The Future Unveiled," who then published it in a supplement to his work.[60]

A somewhat different version of the origin of this text appears in Dausse's biography of his friend, Abbé Gerin, curé of the cathedral of Grenoble. Dausse said that on 11 August 1851, he told Maximin the story of how Mélanie forgot to include something when she first wrote her secret and then asked him if he were not afraid that he too had omitted something. Maximin replied that he knew his secret well, and to prove this he sat down, wrote out the text again, and gave this copy to Dausse. At their request, Dausse then gave copies of this text to Ginoulhaic and Taxis.[61]

The first seven paragraphs of this text, which are contained in Girard's brochure, are terse statements concerning the final events of world history: Three-fourths of France will lose the faith, and the rest will be lukewarm in its practice. Peace will be granted to the world only when people are converted. A Protestant nation in the North will be converted to the faith, and through this nation others will return to the Holy Catholic Church. The next pope will not be a Roman. When people are converted, God will give peace to the world, but this peace will be disturbed by the monster which will arrive at the end of the nineteenth century or the beginning of the twentieth. A longer version of the text found in some later publications adds to this a description of the birth of the antichrist and his subsequent activity, the passage of the Church into an age of darkness, and the arrival of Enoch and Elias and their role in the final events.[62] Thus, in these versions, the secret of Maximin contains a brief scenario of the world's last days, but it is not the scenario of "mercy and the rehabilitation of things" envisioned by earlier commentators like Gerin.[63]

Maximin responded to the publication of "The Secrets of La Salette and their Importance" in two letters to Girard written in mid-September 1871 and in a communication of 2 February 1872, printed by Xavier Drevet. He denied that he had given the first, sloppily written copy of his secret to Dausse, claiming rather, that he had burned this in the presence of Dausse, Taxis, and Bruillard. Moreover, he had the assurance of Rousselot and Gerin that the seal on the more carefully written secret had been broken only by the pope himself. Thus, Maximin argued, the pope alone knew the secret, and the pope alone could communicate it. He himself would continue to be silent on the subject. He refused to respond to the question of whether the text printed by Girard was his secret. Printed with Maximin's response was a letter from Dausse to Girard dated 31 October 1871, in which Dausse accused Girard of distorting information that he had conveyed in confidential conversations. Dausse, like Maximin, argued that the prerogative of divulging the secrets belonged only to the pope and not to Girard, who, he said, was "only possessed of the envy of knowing them."[64]

Because of the criticism leveled at him by Maximin and Dausse, Girard was forced to make a retraction.[65] But the text which he printed was already in circulation, and its authenticity has remained a matter of controversy. Both Le Hidec and A. Parent (a nineteenth-century devotee of La Salette who wrote a biography of Maximin, from which Le Hidec quotes) agree that this transmission of the text began with Dausse, who believed that it was Maximin's secret. Le Hidec points out that Dausse, in his letter of protest to Girard, did not deny that he knew or had received the secret from Maximin. Both Le Hidec and Parent, however, dispute the story that Dausse was given the first, sloppily written copy of the secret; they believe, rather, that Maximin wrote out a text specifically for Dausse.[66] Parent, however, argued against this text actually being Maximin's secret. He speculated that Dausse had pestered Maximin for the secret and that to rid himself of this annoyance the child wrote out a kind of prophetic revelation, as he had done in letters to others who had harassed him for information about the future. On the basis of Maximin's reaction to contemporary political events and of statements made by Pius IX, who had read the secret, Parent went on to speculate that Maximin's secret concerned primarily the Great Monarch, a frequent figure in Christian apocalyptic prophecy and literature, who would come to the rescue of the pope and facilitate the triumph of the Church.[67] While Le Hidec is inclined to believe Maximin's avowal that he did not reveal his secret to anyone, he admits that the issue has not been put to rest. The controversial text, both in its shorter and longer versions, continues to be reproduced in prophetic anthologies, where it is usually identified simply as the secret of Maximin.[68]

While the authorship of the text alleged to be the secret of Maximin is thus a matter of dispute, there is no question that Mélanie herself wrote a brochure containing an account of the apparition and her secret, entitled "The Secret of La Salette and the Apparition of the Very Holy Virgin on the Holy Mountain, 19 September 1846." This brochure, which received the imprimatur from Monseigneur Zola, bishop of Lecce (Italy), was first published in 1879.[69]

Parts of this text had been in circulation, however, at least since August 1853.[70] Handwritten copies of a text of Mélanie's secret, with omitted sections indicated by ellipses or summarized by et ceteras, were being circulated in religious communities and among the clergy by 1860. (This was the year when Mélanie left the Carmelite Convent in Darlington, England, where she had stayed for six years, and went to Marseille where her mother was living.) Then, in January of 1870, Mélanie sent to Abbé Bliard a text that she identified as a part of the secret that she had received from Mary during the apparition and that "should no longer be secret," telling Bliard that he could do with this text "what seems good before God and man." Bliard communicated this text to Girard, who published it in his brochure.

This text was also published by Abbé Curicque in 1872 in his anthology "Prophetic Voices," and Bliard himself published it a year later in a brochure entitled "Letters to a Friend on the Secret of La Salette," which bore the imprimatur of Cardinal Xyote Riario Sforza, archbishop of Naples.[71] In fact, at around this time, a number of versions of Mélanie's secret were in circulation, differing in length and in the order in which the contents were arranged.[72] A critical edition of Mélanie's secret which would compare the texts of these versions and sort out their histories has yet to be published.

Mélanie's secret attracted considerable public attention for many years, and her brochure was reprinted numerous times.[73] The secret as disclosed in this lengthy text is an unrelenting account of the evils that will beset the world in the last times, two features of which are particularly striking.[74] The first is an anticlericalism that begins in the opening paragraphs: a denunciation of priests who through their evil lives, their irreverence, their disrespect in celebrating the holy mysteries, their love of money, glory, and pleasure have become "cesspools of iniquity." The second is the announcement of the vindication of the righteous, which will accompany the brief period of peace initiated when Jesus Christ, by an act of his justice and mercy, commands his angels to put to death the persecutors of his Church and all men addicted to sin. Evils follow this period of peace, but a call is issued to "the true imitators of Christ made man," the "apostles of the last times," to come forth and strengthen the world. The text ends on a note of triumph. With the defeat of the beast by the archangel Michael, the earth will be purified, the works of people's pride will be consumed, all will be renewed, and "God will be served and glorified."

Mélanie also said that the Virgin conveyed to her a rule of life for the "Order of the Mother of God." An eschatological note is sounded in the mission which Mélanie said would be given to the male branch of this order: those who joined it would be "apostles of the last times," preaching "the Gospel of Jesus Christ in all its purity throughout the world." The themes of their preaching would be the reform of hearts, penitence, obedience to the law of God, the necessity of prayer, contempt for earthly things, death, judgment, paradise and hell, and the life, death and resurrection of Jesus. Their purpose, in short, would be to fortify people in faith so that when the demon would come "a great number would not be deceived." While Mélanie seems to have been reluctant to put this rule as such into writing and give it wide circulation, she spent much of her life trying to establish the "Order of the Mother of God."[75]

Mélanie's brochure and the secret contained therein immediately provoked controversy. Its opponents denied that the secret had any value or authority, characterizing it as crude and full of folly, and within a year of the brochure's publication, Mgr. Cortet, the bishop of Troyes, worried that it would cause trouble in France and sought to have it condemned.[76] Cardinal Caterini, secretary of the Congregation of the Holy Office, responding to Cortet in a letter of 14 August 1880, noted that he and the other cardinals commended Cortet for his zeal in denouncing this brochure and said that the Holy See viewed its publication with displeasure and wanted the copies to be withdrawn from the hands of the faithful.[77] Cortet passed this letter on to Mgr. Besson, the bishop of Nîmes, and in the fall of 1880 an excerpt from it appeared in the publications of several French dioceses. It was not clear, however, whether Caterini's letter was merely a private communication or carried the authority of an official condemnation.[78]

Proponents of Mélanie's secret claimed that it had been received positively by prominent clergy, including several bishops.[79] And Amédée Nicolas, a lawyer at Marseille, claimed in an 1880 publication that Cardinal Ledochowski, archbishop of Pozlau in exile at the Vatican, had commissioned him to defend the secret so that people would better understand it and would see that it was not so "black as those who rise against it make it."[80] Nicolas and Mgr. Zola, who gave Mélanie's brochure the imprimatur, believed that Pope Leo XIII himself had read the entire text of Mélanie's secret and had responded to it favorably.[81] Zola also pointed out that similar criticisms of the clergy were to be found in the books of the biblical prophets and had been offered by many others as well throughout the history of the Church.[82]

Commentaries on Mélanie's secret, written by partisans who were derisively called Melanists, did finally bring it into general disrepute. Two of these commentaries, written around the turn of the century by the Abbé Gilbert-Joseph-Emile Combe, curé of Diou (Allier), were placed on the Index.[83] Since these commentaries contained the so-called secret of Mélanie, however, there was confusion about whether the secret itself had been placed on the Index, and the Marquis de la Vauzelle, a partisan of the secret, put this question to Cardinal Luçon of Reims in a letter of 6 November 1912. Luçon submitted the question to Lepidi, an officer of the Sacred Congregation of the Holy Office who also bore the title Master of the Holy Palace, and Lepidi replied that while Combe's two commentaries had been formally and directly condemned, Mélanie's secret itself had not been.[84]

Official Church decrees that directly pertained to Mélanie's secret were issued in 1915 and 1923. The first, issued by the Congregation of the Holy Office on 21 December 1915, noted that despite the responses and decisions of the Sacred Congregation, people had in various forms continued "to treat and to discuss the question called 'the secret of La Salette', its different texts and its adaptations to the present times and the times to come." This decree ordered the faithful to refrain from treating and discussing the matter under any pretext and in any form, and detailed the sanctions that would be imposed on laity and clergy who transgressed the decree.[85]

The decree of 1923 came in response to the reprint of the 1879 edition of Mélanie's brochure in 1922 by the Societé Saint-Augustin, a number of copies of which had been altered by an anticlerical partisan of the secret. Lepidi, whose several offices suggested he was a person of some importance, gave this brochure the imprimatur, which appeared first, followed by the text of the "secret" and supporting materials (six letters from Zola, a letter of Petagna, an historical account of the letter of Caterini, two letters from Mélanie, and diverse commentaries).[86] Dr. Grémillion of Montpellier, who had written commentaries on the secret under the pseudonym of Dr. Henry Mariavé, had purchased a thousand copies of this reprint and in the back of each had pasted a "Letter to Abbot Z" that drew on and expanded the reproaches to the clergy found in the secret's opening paragraphs. According to Le Hidec, readers assumed that the imprimatur applied to everything that followed it, including Grémillion's addition, and on 9 March 1923, the Sacred Congregation of the Holy Office considered the problem raised by these expanded copies. Lepidi, reportedly, was not in attendance due to illness, and the Congregation's decision was to condemn the brochure as such and to order that all copies be withdrawn from the hands of the faithful. Pope Pius XI approved this resolution, and the decree was published in the *Acta Apostolica Sedis* on 1 June 1923.[87]

With Mélanie's brochure now officially discredited, many wondered if the lengthy text which appeared in this brochure was in fact identical to the text of her secret that she wrote and sent to Pope Pius IX in 1851. It was noted, for example, that the text in the 1879 brochure seemed longer than what Mélanie could have written on the three sheets of paper which had been sent many years earlier to the pope.

The so-called Melanists argued that the secret conveyed to Mélanie during the apparition in 1846 was identical with that which she later published. They accounted for the apparent differences in the length, and thus presumably the content, of the 1851 text sent to the pope as compared with later texts by maintaining that Mélanie had a "mission" to divulge the secret to the public only insofar as the Virgin inspired her to do so. Mgr. Zola, for example, in an 1880 letter to Abbé Isidore Roubaud, suggested that Mélanie had not sent Pius IX the whole secret but only "that which at that hour the Holy Virgin had inspired her to write of this important document," as well as things which might concern the pope personally. Zola went on to say that based on very precise information he knew that the reproaches addressed to the clergy and religious communities—the parts of the secret that were provoking the most controversy—were contained word for word in the text given to Pius IX. Mélanie had, he said, revealed portions of the secret to various people, as the occasion required.[88]

Others were apparently suggesting that Mélanie had added to the "authentic secret" some of her own imaginative ideas, a charge that she herself vehemently denied.[89] Nonetheless, at least two modern scholars who are supporters of the cause of La Salette have opted for this view. Jean Stern, archivist for the Missionaries of La Salette, after carefully comparing Mélanie's published secret with the writings of her supporters such as Amédée Nicolas, has suggested that she may have absorbed some of the ideas of these people prior to writing down the "complete" text of her secret.[90] Le Hidec believes that Mélanie began to elaborate on her secret as early as 1847, when she went to live with the Sisters of Providence at Corenc. The text that she sent to the pope in 1851 would then presumably be an expanded version of the original secret conveyed by the Virgin at the time of the apparition. Le Hidec has called on the Roman Church to release the text sent to Pius IX in 1851 and has also attempted on his own, without the aid of this text, to reconstruct the original and "authentic" secret.[91]

Many who believed in the La Salette apparition but who were skeptical about the texts of the La Salette secrets welcomed the conclusions set forth by Bishop Ginoulhiac on the ninth anniversary of the apparition in 1855. Ginoulhiac argued that the mission of the children as witnesses to the apparition had ended with the decree of 19 September 1851, issued by his predecessor Bruillard, which gave approval to the apparition, and that at this point the mission of disseminating the Virgin's message was assumed by the Church. Ginoulhiac probably summarized the thinking, and certainly he summarized the hopes, of many Church officials when he noted that no matter what the children did subsequent to this decree, it could not "react on the miracle of the Apparition, which is certain, canonically proven, and will never be seriously shaken."[92]

Others, however, have maintained that the children's mission, or at least the mission of Mélanie, did not end at that time. Henri Dion, for example, has called attention to the directive with which Mélanie said the Virgin prefaced the secret: "Mélanie, that which I am going to tell *you* now will not always be secret; *you* can make it public in 1858" (italics Dion's).[93] If these words are authentic, Dion argues, then they constitute an order directed to Mélanie herself. Dion has been careful to distinguish between Mélanie's role with respect to her secret and that of Lucia dos Santos with respect to the secret of Fatima. The secret of Fatima, he has noted, exists in only one version, of which only two parts were destined to be made public, and it does not appear that Lucia was given the mission to publicize the third part. The Virgin's words to Mélanie make it clear, however, according to Dion, that the publication of her secret was indeed an essential part of Mélanie's mission.[94]

Most of those who, like Dion, believe that Mélanie's mission did not end in 1851 also believe that it did not end with her death in 1904, and since then several groups have taken up what they understand as Mélanie's mission and cause.[95] Since, however, these groups make up only a rather small constituency, they have directed many of their efforts toward encouraging a greater appreciation of Mélanie in religious orders such as the Missionaries of La Salette, which has supported the position that Mélanie's secret was assumed by the Church in 1851 and which is today the largest of the orders promoting devotion to the Virgin of La Salette. These latter-day Melanists have, for example, attempted to gain the support of this order in the dissemination of Mélanie's secret and in their promotion of the cause of Mélanie's canonization.

The controversies about the La Salette secrets and the seers' missions which they presumably represent show clearly how a diversity of views may arise and be tolerated in the Roman Catholic Church with respect to the significance of an apparition which has been recognized by the Church, which was widely perceived as having prophetic import, and whose seers became public figures and lived as such for many years after their initial visionary experiences. These controversies also show the types and configurations of authority in the framework of which the more enthusiastic devotees of such an apparition arrive at and promulgate their views, the energy and ingenuity with which they may do this, and the importance for the processing and dissemination of these views of both the handwritten and the printed word, especially personal letters and inexpensive pamphlets and paperback books.

Particularly interesting in these struggles, and indeed in the saga of La Salette as a whole, are the efforts of the two seers to maintain some control over their apparition experiences. These efforts might be said to have seriously begun with their realization that they had been given secrets, and they evolved, for each seer, into rather different strategies for maintaining these secrets. While Maximin eventually established considerable distance between himself and the persons who were intent upon learning his secret, Mélanie was more inclined toward cooperation, at least with a handful of people who were sympathetic to her peculiar religious mentality. Thus interest in Melanie's secret, while sometimes tied to particular political concerns, developed into a kind of spirituality which looked to her as a model and which appears to be surviving if not flourishing in some Roman Catholic circles to the present day.

CHAPTER 5

A Secret in Three Parts

FATIMA

NO APPARITION reported in the twentieth century has attracted as much attention with regard to secret revelations as that at Fatima in Portugal. While this apparition occurred between May and October of 1917, it was not well known outside of Portugal until the 1940s, when devotional accounts based on Lucia's memoirs began to be published in various languages. It was these memoirs, in which Lucia related the first two parts of a three-part secret that she and her cousins had received from the Virgin on 13 July 1917, which gave rise to a flood of interest in and speculation about "the secret of Fatima" in the years just after the Second World War.

Much of the behavior of the seers, of their interrogators, and of the public with respect to this secret has followed the pattern of La Salette. The drama of bribes, threats, and prolonged questioning aimed at eliciting the secret; the gradual release, with the Virgin's acquiescence, of material previously understood by the children as confidential; and the notion, especially on the part of the clergy and laity, that the pope was the appropriate final recipient of the secrets—these characteristics of the Fatima scenario all appear to be borrowed from La Salette. There were, however, at least two aspects of the situation at Fatima that gave it a distinct advantage over La Salette as a bearer of apocalyptic meaning for twentieth-century Roman Catholics. The first of these was the ongoing presence of the reticent but ever-obedient Lucia and her propensity to continue to explore, and to share with a selected fraternity of spiritual advisors, her memory of her many years of unusual experiences.[1] The second was the seeming coincidence of "the secret," as gradually set forth by Lucia, with some of the tumultuous and clearly epoch-making events of the first decades of the new century.

Secrets in 1917

Lucia herself set the tone of reticence and secrecy surrounding the initial appearances of the Virgin that she and her two cousins reported in 1917. As indicated in Chapter 1, Lucia had suffered embarrassment at the time of her First Communion when she had related her sins in a loud voice and then refused to divulge the one thing that had not been overheard, which her mother had termed "the secret" of her confession. She had been keenly hurt and humiliated by the scorn with which her family, in 1915, had greeted her reports that she and her three companions had seen a mysterious unidentified figure, and while she showed no inclination thereafter to deny any of her unusual experiences, she was clearly ambivalent about discussing them. When Jacinta, on 13 May 1917, in spite of Lucia's warnings to remain silent, described to her family what they had seen and heard earlier that day, the consequences of not being silent suddenly became apparent to all three of the children. Word of the apparition quickly spread through the village, and the children were all subjected to the ridicule of family and neighbors. Lucia made it clear that she was displeased with Jacinta for talking about the experience. Moreover, Lucia was treated harshly by her family on account of the apparition story, and this compounded the guilt felt by Jacinta for her betrayal of her cousin's wishes. By June 13, the date of the second episode of the apparition, Jacinta and Francisco had joined Lucia in the conviction that they should say little about their experiences.

On June 13, the three children went to the Cova da Iria, where about fifty people had gathered. Of their encounter that afternoon, they would only say that the lady told them that they must say the Rosary every day, that they must return on the thirteenth of the next month, and that later she would tell them what she wanted. Lucia also reported that the lady had said that she was to learn to read, a statement that her mother greeted with sarcasm.[2] According to Lucia, whenever someone asked whether the lady had said anything else, she and her cousins began to say that she had, but that it was a secret.[3]

As interest in the apparition spread, the secret that some people believed the children had received from the Virgin soon became, as at La Salette, a focal point of the public's interest and questioning. Jacinta and

Francisco's father described the ordeal his daughter endured at the hands of those determined to learn this secret. Although he said that he himself never questioned Jacinta about the supposed secret, the womenfolk were curious and tried to bribe her with offers of jewelry. He described Jacinta at first as being very upset and declaring that she would not tell the secret even if she were given the whole world. Later, however, while she still refused to divulge anything, she reportedly adopted a more teasing attitude.[4]

On July 13, the children again went to the Cova da Iria. On this occasion some two to three thousand people were on hand to observe them, and according to some, Lucia, who appeared to be in conversation with an unseen person, suddenly took a deep breath, turned pale, and cried out in terror. The apparition ended shortly thereafter. When asked what the lady said that was so unpleasant, Lucia replied that it was a secret, and when asked if it was a nice secret, she said, "For some people it's good and for others, bad."[5] Lucia recalled in her *Fourth Memoir* that it was at this time that they began to say that the lady had forbidden them to tell this secret to anyone. What they meant by this, Lucia said, was a specific part of the message of July 13.[6]

At about this time Arturo Santos, the mayor of the county to which Fatima belonged and a man known for antireligious sentiments, became concerned about the events at Fatima. He sent a summons to the children's parents, ordering them to bring their children to him for questioning on August 11 at Vila Nova de Ourém. Lucia's father obeyed and took her on the nine-mile journey, but her uncle went without his children, avowing that they were not old enough to be responsible for their actions and to make such a long journey. Both Lucia and her uncle reported that the mayor was determined to have her reveal the secret. Lucia added that he also wanted her to promise that she would not return to the Cova da Iria and that he spared neither promises nor threats to get what he wanted. When he saw that his attempts were futile, he dismissed the group, but he warned Lucia that he would gain his end, even if he had to take her life.[7]

Two days later, on August 13, when the next episode of the apparition was expected, the mayor renewed his efforts to learn the secret and to have the children promise not to return to the Cova da Iria. He questioned them at the home of Jacinta and Francisco, and failing to achieve his purposes, took them then to the parish priest, Fr. Manuel Marques Ferreira.[8] Ferreira later affirmed that the children had been brought to him for questioning under the pretext of obtaining more accurate information about the secret, but he denied having any knowledge of or involvement in the mayor's plans and actions. Lucia alone was taken into Ferreira's house for questioning, and there she maintained that she had not been lying or deceiving people and affirmed that the lady had told her a secret. If Ferreira wanted to know the secret, she said, she would ask the lady for permission to tell it to him. At this point, the mayor brought the interview to a close.[9] But instead of taking the children to the Cova da Iria as he had promised their parents, he took them to Ourém for further questioning.

At Ourém the children, who by now felt quite abandoned by their families, were subjected to further attempts to obtain the secret. On August 14, when questioning and bribes failed to wrest it from them, they were placed in the public jail and told they would remain there until a cauldron of boiling oil was prepared, into which they would be thrown alive. After about two hours they were taken back to the mayor, who again questioned them about the secret. He issued an order for the cauldron to be prepared and then shut the children in another room. They were led out individually and asked again to tell the secret. This ruse also failed, however, and on the next day (August 15) the mayor returned the children to their parents.[10] Twice during the month that passed between the apparitions of September 13 and October 13, again on the evening of October 13, and yet again on October 19, the three children were questioned extensively about their experiences by Dr. Formigão.[11] In the first of these interviews Lucia affirmed that she had been told a secret that she was to tell no one. When asked whether this secret concerned her alone or her cousins also, she replied that it concerned all three of them. Referring to the children's brief imprisonment at Ourém, Formigão asked Lucia whether she had told the mayor something that he would mistake for the secret in order to be freed from him and had then boasted of this deceit afterwards. She affirmed that the mayor had tried all means to make her reveal the secret. She had told him everything the lady had said except the secret, and she speculated to Formigão that perhaps because of this the mayor had mistakenly thought she had told him the secret also. But she denied that she had ever tried to deceive the mayor.[12]

Formigão questioned Jacinta about the secret during his second interview with her. Asked whether she had heard the secret as well as Lucia, Jacinta replied that she had heard the secret also, during the second apparition on St. Anthony's Day (June 13). She denied that the secret was that she would be rich or go to heaven but affirmed that it was for the good of all three children. She could not tell the secret, she said, because the lady had said they were to tell it to no one, but she did agree with Formigão's suggestion that if people knew the secret they would be sad.[13]

Formigão questioned Francisco extensively about the secret during the third interview, on the evening of October 13. Francisco conceded that he had been told the secret not by "the lady" herself but by Lucia. While he insisted that he could not reveal the secret, he denied Formigão's suggestion that this was because he was afraid Lucia would beat him if he did. To the suggestion that he did not tell the secret because the secret was a sin, Francisco replied that to tell the secret might be a sin. The secret, on the other hand, was for the good of his soul, and the souls of Jacinta and Lucia, but he did not know if it was for the good of the soul of the parish priest. Francisco agreed that people would be sad if they knew the secret.[14]

Francisco and Jacinta said nothing about the secret apart from what they said in these interviews in response to Formigão's suggestions: that the lady had forbidden them to tell it, that it was for the good of all three seers, and that people would be sad if they knew it. Both Francisco and Jacinta, as has already been noted, fell victim to the flu epidemic that swept through Portugal in the fall of 1918, and died in 1919 and 1920, respectively. Lucia, who in 1987, at eighty years of age, was residing in a convent of the Discalced Carmelites in Coimbra, thus became the primary source of information about the secret and about the experiences she had shared with her cousins.

Lucia's Experiences, 1925–1927

On 17 June 1921, Lucia entered the College of the Sisters of St. Dorothy at Vilar do Porto. Impressed by her teachers, she joined their order, the Institute of St. Dorothy, on 24 October 1925, spending her first months as a postulant in Pontevedra. It was here, in her cell, that Lucia had the first of three experiences that led her to speak and write about some matters that she had at first apparently intended to keep to herself.

Lucia wrote an account of these experiences in late December 1927, at the request of Fr. P. Aparicio, then her spiritual director.[15] She recorded that on 25 December 1925 the Virgin appeared to her, accompanied by a child, who was elevated on a luminous cloud. While the Virgin showed her a heart encircled by thorns, the child told her to have compassion on the heart of her Most Holy Mother. This heart, he said, was pierced with thorns by ungrateful people, and there was no one to make an act of reparation to remove them. The Virgin then called her attention to the heart and said: "You at least try to console me and say that I promise to assist at the hour of death, with the graces necessary for salvation, all those who, on the first Saturday of five consecutive months, shall confess, receive Holy Communion, recite five decades of the Rosary, and keep me company for fifteen minutes while meditating on the fifteen mysteries of the Rosary, with the intention of making reparation to me."[16]

Lucia understood this to be a request that she encourage the practice described here as a special form of devotion to Mary. It is difficult, however, to establish just what happened between this experience and her second one, on 15 February 1926, in which this devotion became a special object of concern. She apparently reported the initial vision and the request for the devotion to her superior, Mother Magalhaes, and to her confessor at Pontevedra, Dom Lino Garcia, and wrote about it in a letter to her former confessor at Vilar, Mgr. Pereira Lopes. Lucia's 1927 account of this experience and a letter that she wrote to Lopes suggest that Magalhaes was inclined to encourage the devotion, but that the two men were skeptical.[17] It appears that Garcia told her not to speak about her experience to anyone, and Lopes, responding to her in a letter, expressed some reservations, raised some questions, and advised her to wait for further developments.[18]

After her second experience, Lucia wrote a letter to Lopes which reveals her struggle at this time to reconcile obedience to him with the task that she felt the Virgin had entrusted to her, and which describes her state of mind just prior to this experience. When she had received his cautionary letter and realized, therefore, that she could not yet respond to the Virgin's request, she was sad but comforted herself with the thought that it was the Virgin's wish that she obey her former confessor. She wrote then that the next day, after she had received Jesus in Communion, she read Jesus the letter she had received from Lopes, telling Jesus that she would do "all that obedience allowed" and that he inspired her to do, but that the rest he would have to do himself. She described herself in the following days as suffering a continual internal mortification, wondering if her first experience had been merely a dream and if not, why Jesus would deign to appear a second time to one so poorly suited to receive his graces.[19]

This letter to Lopes continues then, with a longer, more complete description of Lucia's second experience than the one that appears in the 1927 account written at the request of Aparicio. On February 15, she told Lopes, she was occupied with her regular duties when the child Jesus appeared to her in the convent garden and asked her if she had spread through the world what the Virgin had asked of her. Lucia reminded him that he knew very well what her confessor (that is, her former confessor, Lopes) had said to her in the letter: that it was necessary for the first experience to be repeated, that further events must establish its credibility, and that with respect to the propagation of the special devotion her superior could do nothing on her own. Jesus replied that while it was true that her superior could do nothing alone, with his graces she could do all. "It is enough," he said, "that your confessor gives you permission and that your superior speak of it [the devotion] for it to be believed, even without people knowing to whom it has been revealed." Lucia then asked Jesus about Lopes's objection that this devotion was already to be found in the world and that many people took Communion on the First Saturdays in honor of the Virgin and the Fifteen Mysteries of the Rosary. Jesus replied that while it was true that many began the cycle of First Saturdays, few finished them, and those who did, did so merely to obtain the promised graces. It would please him more, he said, if they did five mysteries with fervor and with the intention of making reparation to the heart of their Heavenly Mother, than if they did fifteen "in a tepid and indifferent manner."[20]

Lucia did not, in this letter, suggest any connection between the request for a special devotion of reparation to Mary and the apparition of 1917. Aparicio, who succeeded Garcia as Lucia's spiritual director when she was transferred in July 1926 to the convent of the Sisters of St. Dorothy in Tuy, Spain, did see such a connection. In a visit to the convent during the first week of December 1927, he asked her to provide a written account of her recent experiences and to say whether the origin of devotion to the Immaculate Heart of Mary (as the request was now identified) was included in the secret that the Virgin had confided to her. Troubled over just how she should comply with Aparicio's directives, Lucia went before the tabernacle on 17 December 1927 to place the matter before Jesus. There, in an interior locution, she said, Jesus told her that she should write what Aparicio had asked her to write. She should also, while continuing to maintain silence about the rest of the secret, write "all that had been revealed to her in the apparition in which the Virgin spoke of this devotion."[21]

Shortly thereafter, Lucia acceded to Aparicio's request, writing an account which sketched and brought together this latest experience, an episode of the 1917 apparition, and her two visionary encounters of 1925 and 1926. She now revealed that in the course of the 1917 apparition—she does not specify the date—the Virgin said that she would soon take Jacinta and Francisco to heaven. Lucia, however, was to stay on earth longer, because Jesus wanted to make use of her to make the Virgin known and loved. Jesus, the Virgin said, wished to establish in the world devotion to her Immaculate Heart, and she promised salvation to those who embraced it. To Lucia's question "Am I to stay here all alone?" the Virgin replied, "No!" and promised that her Immaculate Heart would be her refuge and the way that would lead her to God. According to this account, then, devotion to the Immaculate Heart of Mary, in the promotion of which Lucia was to have a special role, was an important but previously undisclosed element of the 1917 apparition.[22]

The Request for the Consecration of Russia, 1929

A year and a half later, in the convent chapel in Tuy, Lucia had a fourth experience, the earliest published account of which is a transcription of Lucia's notes, made in 1941, by Fr. José Bernardo Gonçalves, who shortly before this experience had succeeded Aparicio as her spiritual director.[23] According to this account, Lucia had obtained permission from her superiors to make a holy hour each week on Thursday night from eleven o'clock until midnight. It was during this holy hour, on 13 June 1929, that she had a vision of the Trinity and of the Virgin, the latter appearing as "Our Lady of Fatima," holding in her left hand her Immaculate Heart. The Virgin told her: "The moment has come in which God asks the Holy Father in union with all the bishops of the world to make the consecration of Russia to my Immaculate Heart, promising to save it by this means." The Virgin added that she had come to ask for reparation because so many souls were condemned by the justice of God for sins committed against her, and she told Lucia to sacrifice herself for this intention.[24] Lucia reported this experience to

Gonçalves, who in turn reported it to the bishop of Leiria, Mgr. José Correia da Silva. The bishop reportedly replied that he was already aware of the matter and needed to think about it.[25] References in later letters of Lucia suggest that Gonçalves also attempted to communicate this vision and the accompanying request to Pope Pius XI. There is no clear evidence, however, that Pius XI ever received such a communication.[26]

Lucia's Memoirs, 1935–1941

Lucia wrote four memoirs between 1935 and 1941, each of which was composed as a response to a specific request from her superiors, and the texts of which were made available, beginning in 1942, to persons who were preparing historical accounts of the apparition for publication. In the *First Memoir*, written in December 1935, on the occasion of the transfer of Jacinta's remains from Ourém to Fatima, Lucia's primary concern was to provide a portrait of her cousin.[27] While this memoir added little or nothing to the understanding of the apparition as such that had developed out of the earlier materials, it did add significantly to how Jacinta was understood to have responded to the apparition. Jacinta was described here as having been preoccupied with the suffering of sinners in hell and thus as having developed a penchant for making sacrifices for the conversion of sinners. This memoir also led Lucia's superiors to believe that she was still guarding information that she would probably reveal only under obedience to a direct order.

Lucia made a significant new claim in her *Second Memoir*, written in November 1937, at the prompting of Bishop da Silva, with the support of the mother provincial of the Dorothean Sisters.[28] She said that in 1916 she and her cousin had received three visits from an angel.

On the first visit this angel identified himself as the Angel of Peace, taught the children a special prayer, and told them that the hearts of Jesus and Mary were attentive to their supplications. On the second visit he enjoined them to offer prayers and sacrifices constantly to God and said that the hearts of Jesus and Mary had "designs of mercy" on them. "Make of everything you can a sacrifice," he said, "and offer it to God as an act of reparation for the sins by which he is offended, and in supplication for the conversion of sinners." If they did this, he said, they would draw down peace on their country, and he then identified himself as their country's guardian angel, the Angel of Portugal. He concluded by exhorting them to accept and bear with submission the suffering that

God would send them. On the third visit, according to Lucia, the angel served them Communion, giving her the host and allowing Jacinta and Francisco to share the chalice. Lucia recalled that after the first appearance of the angel she warned her cousins that this encounter had to be kept secret, and this secret, she noted, was one which they were able to keep.[29]

Lucia wrote her *Third Memoir* in August 1941, as planning was under way for the publication of a third edition of the book *Jacinta*, by Fr. José Galamba da Oliveira.[30] Da Silva had written to Lucia at the end of July asking that she recall and write down everything she could about her cousin, and Lucia took this request as a sign from God that she should reveal the first two parts of the secret that the Virgin had conveyed to them on 13 July 1917.[31] In the *Third Memoir*, therefore, Lucia gave an account of these two parts of the secret and of how she understood Jacinta to have been affected by them.

The first part of the secret, as Lucia related it here, was a vision of hell. The Virgin showed them a great sea of fire. In it were demons, who resembled frightful and unknown animals, and souls in human form which were raised up by the flames and then fell back, all amid shrieks and groans of pain and despair. The vision lasted only an instant, but she and her cousins were left horrified and trembling with fear. The Virgin told them that they had seen "hell where the souls of poor sinners go."[32]

The second part of the secret, according to Lucia, concerned devotion to the Immaculate Heart of Mary. The Virgin had told them that to save those poor sinners

> God wishes to establish in the world devotion to my Immaculate Heart. If what I say to you is done, many souls will be saved and there will be peace. The war is going to end; but if people do not cease offending God, a worse one will break out during the pontificate of Pius XI. When you see a night illumined by an unknown light, know that this is the great sign given you by God that He is about to punish the world for its crimes, by means of war, famine, and persecutions of the Church and of the Holy Father.
>
> To prevent this, I shall come to ask for the consecration of Russia to my Immaculate Heart, and the Communion of reparation on the First Saturdays. If my requests are heeded, Russia will be converted, and there will be peace; if not, she will spread her errors throughout the world, causing wars and persecutions of the Church. The good will be martyred; the Holy Father will have much to suffer; various nations will be annihilated. In the end, my Im-

maculate Heart will triumph. The Holy Father will consecrate Russia to me, and she will be converted, and a period of peace will be granted to the world.[33]

Satisfied now that she had revealed the first and second parts of the secret, Lucia went on in her *Third Memoir* to complete her recollections of Jacinta. Sometime after 13 July 1917, she remembered, while she and her cousins were spending their siesta by her parents' well, Jacinta had a vision of the pope, which she immediately communicated to Lucia. She had seen the pope in a house, kneeling by a table, burying his head in his hands and weeping. Outside the house was a crowd of people, some of whom threw stones at him and some of whom cursed him. Jacinta concluded her account by stating that they must pray a great deal for him. Sometime later Jacinta had another vision of the pope, which again she immediately reported to Lucia. "Can't you see all those highways and roads and fields full of people," Jacinta asked Lucia, "who are crying with hunger and have nothing to eat? And the Holy Father in a church praying before the Immaculate Heart of Mary? And so many people praying with him?" A few days later Jacinta asked Lucia if she could tell people that she had seen the Holy Father, and Lucia replied negatively, saying that this was a part of the secret, and that if she did tell, the entire secret would quickly be discovered. Jacinta then agreed, according to Lucia, that she would say nothing at all.[34]

In this memoir Lucia also commented on the spectacular lights that had illumined the skies on the night of 25–26 January 1938. She reminded da Silva (to whom all the memoirs were addressed) that astronomers had identified these lights as the aurora borealis. She believed that if the matter were properly investigated, the form in which these lights appeared would not support this identification. Whatever these lights were, however, she understood them to be the sign referred to in the July 13 secret. God had made use of the lights, she said, to make her understand that the "guilty nations" were about to be punished, and thereafter she began to plead insistently for the Communion of Reparation on the First Saturdays and for the consecration of Russia to Mary's Immaculate Heart. Her intention, she said, was to obtain mercy and pardon for the whole world and especially for Europe, and she reminded the bishop that when God had made her feel that the terrible moment of punishment was drawing near, she had taken every opportunity to make this known.[35]

In her *Fourth Memoir*, written in December 1941, Lucia added a sentence to that part of the secret which concerned devotion to the Immaculate Heart of Mary, as related in her *Third Memoir*. She now recalled that the Virgin had also said, "In Portugal, the dogma of the faith will always be preserved." She also noted that the Virgin had told her that they (Lucia and Jacinta) were to tell all this to no one except Francisco, who, although he could see the Virgin, did not hear her speak.[36] Lucia drew here a more complete portrait of Francisco than she had done previously.[37] She also gave a more systematic account of her earlier experiences, beginning with the ambiguous vision she had shared with three companions in 1915, through the apparitions of the angel in 1916 and of the Virgin in 1917, shared with her cousins.[38] Much of what she had said previously about these experiences, in scattered statements, has been assembled here into a strict chronological sequence.

According to her memoirs, the vision of hell, the admonition concerning devotion to Mary's Immaculate Heart, and the third part of the secret (that Lucia said she would not reveal) were all that the Virgin explicitly forbade the children to make known. Lucia said that she had kept confidential other aspects of the apparitions and the events associated with them for fear that these would lead to the disclosure of the essential secret. For Lucia, then, the meaning of the apparitions eventually came to focus on the now partly revealed secret of July 13. This secret brought together the perhaps otherwise disparate themes of the apparitions, of her cousin's experiences, and of her own later experiences (hell, devotion to Mary's Immaculate Heart, the consecration of Russia, the Communion of Reparation, sacrifices for sinners, war, the suffering of the pope) in a way that seemed to her and to a growing number of believers in the Fatima apparitions to provide a key to the course of twentieth-century history. When, therefore, accounts of the apparitions based on Lucia's memoirs began to appear in print during the years in which the outcome of the Second World War was being decided, many Roman Catholics became very concerned about the third part of the secret—which became known simply as the "third secret of Fatima"—and about the question of when or if it would be publicly disclosed.

Unpublished "Third Secret" Sent to Rome

No sooner had Lucia written in her *Third Memoir* that the July 13 secret had three parts, one of which she would not reveal, than a clamor for the revelation of this material arose among those who knew of or who had access to this memoir. On 7 October 1941, for example, da Silva, and Galamba da Oliveira arranged to meet Lucia at Valencia do Minho for further questioning. Galamba da Oliveira had asked the bishop to order Lucia to write a full account of the apparitions and to hide nothing, but he refused, avowing that he did not want "to interfere in that which is secret."[39] In her *Fourth Memoir* Lucia expressed her relief and her conviction that in this refusal the bishop must have been moved by the Holy Spirit. Such an order, she said, would have been a source of perplexities and scruples to her, and she would have asked herself a thousand times whether she should obey God or his representative.[40] The situation began to change, however, in 1943, when Lucia became seriously ill and the bishop became concerned about the fate of the undisclosed portion of the secret.

While for years Lucia had generally been in good health, suffering from no more than occasional bouts of bronchitis, in June of 1943 she developed a severe case of pleurisy. In a letter to da Silva she speculated that her illness might be "the beginning of the end" and noted that she was content. It was well, she mused, that to the extent that her mission on earth was finished, God was preparing for her the paths of heaven. In July, however, she began to recover, only to fall ill again from a poorly administered injection. On August 2, apparently once again on the way toward recovering, she wrote to Aparicio that she had placed herself in the hands of God and was striving to do everything according to the divine will, as this was made known to her both directly and indirectly, through those who were God's representatives. The publication of the things that she had carefully "tried to hide" pained her, she said, but if her sacrifice meant something for God's glory and for the good of souls, she would be content.[41]

It is not clear just what Lucia meant by this reference to the things that she had tried to hide. Da Silva had directed her to make new notes for yet another edition of Galamba da Oliveira's book, perhaps shortly before she wrote this letter, and this may partly explain the remark. Brother Michel de la Sainte Trinité, who has done a detailed study of the events surrounding the Fatima secret, has suggested that the bishop, concerned over Lucia's health, may also have asked her to record the third part of the secret.[42] But he admits that there is no clear evidence of this, and in fact a conversation that he reports between Lucia, Galamba da Oliveira and the bishop late that summer would seem to preclude it.

This conversation, which Michel de la Sainte Trinité says he learned about in speaking personally with Galamba da Oliveira, evidently took place in August 1943, as Lucia was experiencing some respite from her illness. Galamba da Oliveira had arranged an interview with Lucia in the presence of her mother superior and da Silva. In the course of this interview Galamba da Oliveira reportedly asked Lucia why she did not reveal the third part of the secret and suggested that she tell it to them then. Lucia, nodding her head in the direction of the bishop, who was conversing with the mother superior, replied that she could tell it "if the Monseigneur wished." Galamba da Oliveira reported then that he said to the bishop, when they had stood up and were preparing to leave, "Monseigneur, Lucia says that if you wish it she could now reveal the third part of the secret!" The bishop replied, however, that he wanted nothing to do with the matter and repeated his earlier statement that he did not want to intervene. Galamba da Oliveira's response was that this was a pity, and he suggested that the bishop at least tell Lucia to write the third part on a piece of paper and send it to him in a sealed envelope.[43] If accurately reported, this conversation indicates that as of August 1943, da Silva was still reluctant, in spite of Lucia's periods of serious illness, to tell her to reveal the third part of the secret, even though she was ready to do so if ordered by her superiors.

Whatever da Silva may have thought in August, it seems that he made a rather concrete proposal when he went to Tuy to converse with Lucia on September 15. Lucia was again bedridden, and her conversation with the bishop took place in the infirmary. As Lucia reported it, the bishop asked her then to write down the remainder of the secret if she wished, not for publication at that time but simply to assure that it would be recorded.[44]

Shortly after this Lucia's pleurisy abated, but she developed a problem with her leg that called for surgery. She was transferred to Pontevedra where she was hospitalized September 22–26, and where she spent some time recuperating at the Dorothean convent. At the beginning of October she returned to Tuy. What transpired in these days and in the days following with respect to the recording of the secret has been pieced together by Fr. Joaquin Maria Alonso and Michel de la Sainte Trinité from circumstantial evidence, primarily a series of letters which Lucia wrote to her spiritual directors. While da Silva had given her permission, it would seem, to record the remainder of the secret, Lucia was hesitant. In a letter to one of her spiritual directors, Dom Antonio Garcia, apostolic administrator of Tuy, Lucia reiterated her belief that the will of God was expressed through her superiors. The bishop, however, in the conversation of September 15, had not ordered her to record the remainder of the secret; he had merely said, "If the sister wishes." This, Lucia said, left her perplexed. She was not yet convinced that God had clearly authorized her to act.[45]

In a letter of mid-October 1943, da Silva finally gave Lucia a direct order to record the secret. Lucia said that he asked her to write it down in one of the notebooks in which she had been told to keep a spiritual journal, or on a sheet of paper that she should then place in an envelope and seal with wax. Here, then, was the sort of directive that in the past Lucia had interpreted as a direct expression of God's will. There was, however, still something which troubled her. In the past she had had experiences which confirmed these mandates—such as the interior locution of 17 December 1927, in which Jesus told her that she could indeed do what her superiors had asked—but on this occasion she had had no such experience. In letters from this period she described herself as beset with doubts and unable to act. She felt that heaven was maintaining silence and that her obedience was being tested. But several times, she said, she had tried to obey the bishop's order, had taken up her pen, and had been unable to write.[46]

In several letters dating from the first half of December 1943, Garcia tried to speak to Lucia's spiritual dilemma, advising her to be prudent and patient. These letters, however, apparently did not reach Lucia until late January 1944, by which time she had overcome her doubts and had in fact recorded the remainder of the secret.[47] On January 9, she wrote to da Silva that she had done what he had asked. God, she said, had wished to test her a little. But the text of the secret had now at last been written down, sealed in an envelope, and put in one of her notebooks.

It is not clear just how Lucia finally overcame her reluctance to commit to writing the remainder of the secret. The editor of two major collections of documents concerning Fatima, Fr. Antonio Maria Martins, reported that Lucia's superior at Tuy, Mother Cunhe Mattos, stated in some written testimonies that the Virgin Mary had appeared to Lucia on 2 January 1944 and had authorized her then to record the remainder of the secret.[48] Lucia herself, however, has never publicly acknowledged such an apparition.

In June of 1944 arrangements were made to deliver the written secret to da Silva. On June 17 the bishop of Gurza met Lucia at Valencia do

Minho and obtained from her a sealed envelope, which he then immediately delivered to da Silva. Lucia also wrote a letter to da Silva (as yet unpublished) in which she apparently suggested that he retain the document in his possession until his death, when it should be given to the cardinal patriarch of Lisbon. According to Alonso, who has studied and written about the events surrounding the secret, da Silva, while inclined to do as Lucia suggested, did not really want to have the document in his possession and tried, without success, to get the cardinal patriarch to take it immediately. Alonso quotes Cardinal Ottaviani as surmising that the bishop then tried, also without success, to transfer responsibility for the safekeeping of the document to the Vatican.[49] On 8 December 1944, da Silva, frustrated in his efforts to entrust the text to a higher authority, placed the envelope containing the text in a larger envelope, sealed this envelope, and wrote on it: "This envelope with its contents is to be given to His Eminence, Cardinal Dom Manuel, Patriarch of Lisbon, after my death." He then dated and signed it and deposited it in the safe of the chancery where it remained until 1957.[50]

For the thirteen years that the alleged text of Lucia's secret was in his possession, da Silva apparently maintained the same privately encouraging and protective but publicly very cautious stance toward the secret that had helped bring about its recording. He evidently removed the envelope from the safe only on rare occasions, as in 1948, when he was photographed with it by a reporter from *Life* magazine (see figure 3). Ottaviani maintained that while Lucia had given the bishop permission to read the secret, he did not wish to do so, which is consonant with various conversations during these years in which the bishop reportedly indicated that "the secrets of heaven" were not his cup of tea and that he did not want the responsibility of being apprised of them.[51]

Early in 1957, the apostolic nuncio to Portugal, Mgr. Fernando Cento, informed da Silva that the Sacred Congregation for the Doctrine of the Faith at Rome was requesting of the curia of Leiria photocopies of all of Lucia's writings. The bishop apparently saw this as an invitation, or at least a suitable occasion, for the transmission to Rome of the text which he had sought for so long to dispose of. According to Michel de la Sainte Trinité, Mgr. Venancio, the auxiliary bishop of Leiria, reported that after photocopies of everything but this text had been made, the bishop asked Cento if he was also to send the third secret and was told, "Naturally! the secret also! Above all the secret!" Da Silva then reportedly instructed his aide to give the Nuncio the sealed envelope containing Lucia's handwritten document along with the photocopies of her other writings. These were then delivered to Rome, an acknowledgment of their receipt apparently being sent on 16 April 1957 to the bishop of Leiria.[52]

Cold War Anxieties, the Third Secret, and 1960

The publication of devotional accounts of the apparitions at Fatima containing the texts of the first and second parts of Lucia's secret accompanied and strengthened the growing conviction of many Roman Catholics that the messages the Virgin had conveyed at Fatima directly concerned twentieth-century events. Believers understood the Virgin's statement in the second part of the secret that "the war is going to end soon" as a prophecy of the end of World War I, and they saw a clear prophecy of the Second World War in her statement that if people did not stop offending God another war would break out during the pontificate of Pius XI. Because these aspects of the secret were seen as having recently been fulfilled, the Virgin's statements concerning Russia were taken very seriously and were understood in the context of the then-unfolding "Cold War." In the 1950s articles began to appear in Catholic magazines that argued that the devotional practices recommended at Fatima, especially the recitation of the Rosary, were powerful weapons against the growing menace of Russia to world peace.

In 1952, for example, L. M. Dooley wrote an article entitled "Mary and the Atom" for the devotional magazine *Ave Maria*. Dooley had seen in a post office window a civil defense poster that gave detailed recommendations for what to do in case of atomic attack, and this led him to reflect that as the nations of the world ignored Mary's warning and actually prepared for atomic destruction, her "ultimatum" at Fatima was coming to fulfillment. Citing statistics indicating that thirty-seven out of every hundred people were "languishing under communism," he observed that Mary's warnings concerning the spread of communism were in the process of being realized.[53] He understood the Virgin's words at Fatima to mean that "wars come because of sin," and he argued that personal, family, and national sins had so weakened people's minds and wills that they were more inclined to follow the "demon of darkness" than the Mother of God. The key to the elimination of war was a forsaking of sin and a change of heart through prayer and penance. The Virgin at Fatima had emphasized devotional means to achieve that change, and Dooley called on people to " 'fatimise', to christianize individual lives."

European Roman Catholic authorities found in the Virgin of Fatima an important resource for curbing the spread of communism. In the early 1940s the clergy began to promote missions that aimed at reviving religious faith and bringing people to confession and Communion. A particular goal of these missions was to bring back to the Church the males who had joined or had strong sympathies for the communist movements. At the end of the decade, this missionary activity came to focus on the "traveling statue" of the Virgin of Fatima. From May 1947 to March 1948, for example, this statue was carried "on pilgrimage" from Portugal through Spain and France to a Congress of Marian Congregations at Maastricht (Netherlands); conversions and miracles were reported at each of its stops. Replicas of this statue were made and displayed in cities and dioceses throughout Europe and some were dispatched on international missions.[54]

The hope that many Church authorities placed in the Virgin of Fatima for a victory over communism was well summarized by remarks made at Fatima on 31 October 1951 by the popular American bishop Fulton J. Sheen. The occasion was the end of the "Holy Year," and about 100,000 people had assembled at the Cova da Iria, waving white handkerchiefs and, according to Sheen, turning the Cova da Iria into a "White Square." The Bolshevik Revolution and the apparitions at Fatima had both begun in 1917, the bishop noted. Thirty-four years had passed since then, and in another thirty-four years, he predicted, one of the two phenomena would cease to exist. "What will disappear," he said, "will be a dictator reviewing his troops in the Red Square; what will survive will be a Lady reviewing her children in the White Square." He foresaw a time when, as a result of the sacrifices and prayers of the "millions in the White Square," the symbol of the hammer on the Red Flag would look like a cross, and the sickle would look like the moon under Mary's feet.[55]

With the second part of the secret understood by virtually all devotees of Fatima in these years as pertaining to the events of the present and the immediate future, it is not surprising that the third, unrevealed part of the secret came to be seen in the same light. This conviction was heightened by the expectation that this part of the secret would be made public in 1960 and by the publication of two accounts of interviews with Lucia in the 1950s.

The expectation that the third part of the secret would be made public in the year 1960 began in the mid-1940s with a series of statements that led people to believe that Lucia and da Silva had agreed on this date for the opening of the envelope. On February 3 and 4, 1946, Lucia was interviewed by Fr. Jongen, who reminded her that she had made public two parts of the secret and asked her when the time would come for revealing the third part. She replied that she had already communicated the third part in a letter to da Silva, and that it could not be made known before 1960.[56] The vagueness of this reply, however, soon gave way, reportedly, to much clearer statements that the envelope would be opened and the secret made public in 1960. Canon Barthas, for example, after interviewing Lucia on October 17 and 18, 1946, said that when he asked when the third part of the secret would be publicized, both Lucia and da Silva replied without hesitation or qualification "in 1960."[57] Soon the devotional literature that centered on the apparitions and Lucia's subsequent experiences began to mention 1960 as the year when the remainder of the secret would be revealed. William Thomas Walsh, for example, in *Our Lady of Fatima* (1947), reported that when Lucia had been ill and in danger of death, she had obtained (at the prompting of the Bishop of Leiria) permission from the Virgin to write down the secret, and having done so she sealed it in an envelope marked "not to be opened until 1960." While Walsh admitted that this could not now be verified, he said that he had heard it in Portugal from "a man of the highest credibility."[58]

In 1953, one of the persons involved in the study and propagation of the apparitions at Fatima, Fr. Sebastiao Martins dos Reis, sounded a cautionary note with respect to the 1960 date. He granted that if the secret had been written down this was no doubt so that it could eventually be read, but he believed there were strong reasons (which he does not enumerate) for doubting that this reading would take place in 1960.[59] Throughout the 1950s, however, this expectation was apparently widespread among Roman Catholic authorities: Cardinal Tisserant, secretary of the Sacred Congregation for the Eastern Church, Cardinal Piazza, secretary for the Consistorial Congregation, and Mgr. Venancio, auxiliary bishop of Leiria, all, for example, made statements affirming, or at least implying, that the secret would be made public in 1960.[60]

Canon Barthas had said in 1946 that Lucia had told him that it was necessary to wait until 1960 "because the Virgin wishes it so."[61] At a conference in 1967, Cardinal Ottaviani reported that when he had interviewed Lucia in Coimbra in 1955 and had asked her then why 1960 had been specified as the date before which the secret could not be opened, she had replied, "Because then it will appear clearer." This made him think, the cardinal recalled, that the message of the secret was prophetic, manifesting the characteristics of scriptural prophecies, which are "surrounded by a veil of mystery and often expressed in a language not open, clear, or comprehensible to everyone."[62]

As early as 1956, according to J. M. Alonso, reports were circulating that the third secret involved prophecies of particular tragedies, and texts describing or hinting at such tragedies and purporting to represent the third part of the secret were circulated on mimeographed sheets and published in popular magazines.[63] According to one account, da Silva was said to have opened the envelope; according to another, Lucia was said to have gone to Rome herself to tell the secret to Pius XII. Several versions of the secret focused on the pope. According to one of these, Adolph Hitler was to have taken the pope prisoner and made him a Nazi puppet. According to another, the pope would be captured, tortured, and finally killed by Italian communists. According to yet another, the pope would abandon Rome and transfer the see of Peter to a new location across the ocean.[64]

Two interviews with Lucia that were widely publicized at the end of the 1950s reinforced the growing idea that the secret was a prophecy of dire events soon to come. The first of these interviews took place in 1954 when Father Riccardo Lombardi, the founder of the Better World Movement, met with Lucia in the Carmelite Convent in Coimbra. When he asked her if his organization was the Church's response to Mary's message to her, she answered, according to him, that the need for renewal was so great that, given the present condition of humanity, only a limited portion would be saved. Saying that he himself hoped that God would save a greater number, as he had written in his book *The Salvation of Those Who Have No Faith*, Lombardi then asked her if she really believed that many would go to hell. Lucia's reply to this, reportedly, was that, indeed, many were condemned. When he observed that while the world was "an abyss of vice" there was still hope of salvation, she responded, "No, Father, many, many are lost."[65]

The second interview with Lucia which contributed to the idea of widespread apostasy and impending judgment was one held late in 1957 by a Mexican priest, Fr. Augustine Fuentes, who had been ap-

pointed postulator for the causes of the beatification of Francisco and
Jacinta. Reporting on the interview about six months later at a conference in Mexico, Fuentes said that Lucia told him that the Virgin was
sad because no one, good or bad, had heeded her message. The good
were continuing in virtue but without paying attention to the message
of Fatima, while sinners were "following on the road of evil" because
they did not see the threatening chastisement. In less than two years
1960 would arrive and what, Lucia asked, would happen then? If people did not pray and do penance, it would be very grievous for everyone.
Lucia recalled that the Virgin had said repeatedly that many nations
would be annihilated and that Russia, if it were not converted, would
be the instrument of God's chastisement for the entire world. She also
said that the Virgin was now engaged in a decisive battle with the devil.
He saw that his time was growing short, and he was making every effort
to gain as many souls as possible. While the Virgin had not told her that
they were living in the last epoch of the world, she had made Lucia
understand that a decisive battle was being waged, at the end of which
people would be "either of God or the evil one." Lucia said that "the
last means" God would give the world for its salvation were the Rosary
and devotion to the Immaculate Heart of Mary. When God was about
to chastise the world, Lucia reportedly told Fuentes, he first offered every means to save it, and when he had seen that these means were not
being used, he gave his Mother as "the last anchor of salvation."[66]

When it was published in periodicals of popular piety, according to
Alonso, this statement of Fuentes was glossed with detailed descriptions
of apocalyptic cataclysms.[67] On 2 July 1959, the bishop's office in
Coimbra reacted to the publication of Fuentes's statement in *A Voz* and
took issue with the fact that this priest had been allowed to make some
"sensational declarations, of a prophetic, eschatological, and apocalyptic
character" that he said he had received from the very mouth of Lucia.
Given the seriousness of such declarations, which people who were "too
enthusiastic about the marvelous" had now spread to Mexico, the
United States, Spain, and finally, Portugal, the diocesan curia had ordered a rigorous investigation into their authenticity. Lucia had been
questioned about her statements to Fuentes, apparently by an official of
the diocese, and had denied that she knew anything about the coming
punishments that she had reportedly described to Fuentes. She had spoken with him, she said, only because he was the person charged to promote the beatification of her cousins, and their conversations had fo-

cused solely on that subject. The diocesan curia of Coimbra was authorized to say that Lucia had already disclosed what she believed she was free to disclose on the subject of Fatima, that this had already been published in books on that subject, that Lucia had in the meantime revealed nothing new, and that since at least February 1955, no one had been authorized to publish the "novelties" that had been attributed to her.[68] Several authorities defended Fuentes, Cardinal José Garibi y Rivera, archbishop of Guadalajara, for example, stating that Fuentes had "announced nothing terrible" in his statement.[69] Most recently, Alonso has argued that Fuentes's "genuine statement" was in accord with other things Lucia has said, and that the curia of Coimbra failed to distinguish this statement in its original form from the "distorted" versions of it and rumors about it published by various magazines.[70] In any case, in March 1961, Fuentes was replaced as postulator for the causes of Jacinta and Francisco by Fr. Luis Kondor.[71]

In the wake of such rumors, it is understandable that Roman Catholic theologians would remind the faithful in these years that the Church did not give a stamp of approval or a guarantee of veracity to the prophetic content of private revelations, and that they should urge them also to recall and respect the Church's teaching authority. Pascal Boland, a student of mystical and ascetic theology at Catholic University of America, for example, writing in 1958, noted several reasons why these private revelations could be liable to error or misinterpretation. While admitting that prophecies of impending doom could have the beneficial result of bringing people to repentance, he noted that they might also arouse fears, and could thus never be taken or understood by the Church as matters of faith. Only the passage of time, he observed, would reveal whether the particular predictions of even the most saintly people would be fulfilled. In considering what the third secret of Fatima might concern, he opted for a much brighter possibility than was being entertained in most of the popular literature. The response of millions of people to the message of Fatima, he argued, should incline believers toward the "optimistic opinion that the remaining secret of Fatima concerns an era of peace."[72]

Fr. Francis L. Filas, a Jesuit and assistant professor of theology at Loyola University (Chicago), was somewhat more critical than Boland of the widespread interest in Lucia's pronouncements. He suggested, in an article published in 1959, that some writers and magazine editors who had helped promulgate the message of Fatima had not kept in mind "the approved teaching of Catholic theologians concerning private revelations."[73] The Church, he admitted, had given approval in a general sense to the revelation of Mary at Fatima, but he expressed concern about Lucia's continuing statements and the importance people were attributing to them. "What happens to belief in the infallible *magisterium* of the Catholic Church," he asked, "if the claims of an individual, even of a woman as sincere and as holy as Sister Lucy, are treated as the word of God?" Any revelation that pretended to solve a problem considered a mystery by theologians and the Church should certainly be regarded as suspect, and such matters as the nearness of the end of the world and the proportion of human race that would be "lost" were mysteries so far as the "official and public deposit of the faith was concerned." The teaching authority of the Church had not emphasized divine chastisements but had encouraged "trust in the love and care of an all-loving God, whose punishments are indeed manifestations of his love, but who, nonetheless, does not work by means of dire, vague predictions that tend to stifle all initiative and planning for the future." He reminded his readers that Catholic biblical scholars who worked with the permission and encouragement of the official *magisterium* taught that even in the Scriptures God did not give prophecies that contained full details of time and place. Why, then, he wondered, should one expect such information from a private revelation?

In spite of such warnings, speculations about the date of the opening of the secret and its content continued to appear in both the public and the Catholic press in the waning months of 1959 and the early months of 1960. A reporter for a Portuguese periodical, for example, wondered whether in 1960 there might be an "unforeseen and miraculous solution to the basic problems which divide the world into two blocs, east and west," and whether the period of peace promised to humanity might in fact be brought about by devotion to Mary's Immaculate Heart.[74] Some people speculated that the secret would be opened and made public on the anniversary of the first apparition (May 13), but others worried that the secret might not be made public at all, and rumors circulated that Lucia had said that a failure to reveal the secret would signify the imminence of the end of the world at the hands of Russia.[75]

The Portuguese news agency ANI reported on 9 February 1960 that Vatican sources had told representatives of the United Press International that it was likely that Lucia's letter containing the text of the third secret would never be opened. The Vatican, according to the news release, faced with pressure from both those who wanted the secret to be disclosed and those who did not, had decided to keep the text rigorously sealed. Three reasons for this were cited: (1) that Lucia was still living; (2) that the Vatican already knew the content of the letter; and (3) that although the Roman Catholic Church had recognized the Fatima apparitions, it could not guarantee the truth of any particular communication that the seers claimed to have received.[76]

The decision of the Vatican in 1960 not to release Lucia's text of the third part of the secret did not, however, stop the rumors about it, the calls for its publication, or indeed the appearance of texts purported to be Lucia's secret. Of the texts purported to be all or part of the third secret of Fatima, the most famous was probably that which appeared in the German weekly *Neues Europa* on 15 October 1963. According to the article accompanying this text, Pope Paul VI had arranged for the secret to be read and studied by President Kennedy, Prime Minister MacMillan, and Party Chairman Khrushchev. So impressed were these three world leaders by the content of the secret, according to the story, that they drew up and promoted the treaty, signed by more than ninety nations on 6 August 1963, that banned atomic experiments in the air, on land, and under the water. Journalist Louis Emrich of *Neues Europa* had allegedly tried to obtain the full text of the third secret but had failed because the Vatican had taken steps to insure that this text would not be released to anyone. Emrich had, however, according to the article, been able to obtain the extracts of the secret that had been presented to the diplomats of Washington, London, and Moscow. The text printed in *Neues Europa*, then, did not purport to be the "exact original text" but only the "essential points of the original."[77]

According to the *Neues Europa* text, it was just after the "great miracle of the sun" at Fatima on 19 October 1917, that Mary conveyed this special secret to Lucia. She prefaced this secret by telling Lucia that she was to convey it to the world, warning her that she would.be met with hostility but promising that if she were steadfast in the faith she would overcome that hostility. People needed to amend their lives and to seek remission of the sins that they had committed and would continue to commit. Lucia, the Virgin said, had asked her for a miraculous sign so that people might understand the words that she was addressing to them, and the miracle that had just transpired, "the great miracle of the sun" that had been seen by "believers and unbelievers, country and city dwellers, scholars and journalists, laymen and priests," was that sign.

Then followed the message that Lucia was to proclaim. In the second half of the twentieth century a great punishment would come to all humankind, Mary said. This was the same message that she had already given at La Salette through Mélanie and Maximin. People had not developed as God expected but had been sacrilegious and had trampled underfoot the gifts that they had been given.

Order was lacking, Mary further warned, and even in the highest positions Satan was the one deciding how affairs were conducted. He would know how to find his way to the highest positions in the Church. He would succeed in planting confusion in the minds of those great scholars who invented weapons that could destroy humankind in a few minutes. He would bring the mighty ones under his power and make them manufacture armaments in great numbers. If people did not refrain from such endeavors, Mary would be forced to let her Son's arm fall. If world and Church leaders did not oppose such acts, she warned, she would herself oppose them and would pray to God her Father "to visit his justice on men." Then God would punish people more severely than he had during the flood; both the great and powerful and the small and weak would perish. A time of severe trials for the Church would come, cardinals opposing cardinals and bishops opposing bishops. Great changes would take place in Rome. What was rotten in the Church would fall, and what fell should not be maintained. The Church would be darkened and the world plunged into confusion.

There would be a "big, big war," the Virgin said, in the second half of the twentieth century. She described fire and smoke falling from the sky, the oceans turning to steam, and the deaths of "millions and millions" of people. After a period in which Satan's henchmen would rule the earth, however, there would come a time when God and his glory would again be invoked and served. Mary then specifically addressed all true imitators of her Son, all true Christians and latter-day Apostles: "The time of times is coming and the end of all ends, if people are not converted and if this conversion does not come from the directors of the world and church." She then told Lucia to proclaim this message, promising that she would be by her side to help her.

The *Neues Europa* text, then, explicitly connected the apparition at Fatima with that of La Salette and addressed an issue of growing concern—why repeated apparitions were necessary. It is important to remember here that there had been a proliferation of apparitions in the postwar years, with a peak between 1947 and 1954 when, according to one estimate, approximately fourteen cases per year were reported to Roman Catholic authorities.[78] The message at Fatima was the same as at La Salette, according to the *Neues Europa* version of the secret, but repetition was necessary because the earliest warnings had been ignored and people had not responded as God had expected. The language of the text echoed the secret published by Mélanie in 1879, especially in its final appeal to "all true Christians and latter day Apostles." Perhaps most importantly, the text addressed the issue of the arms race, and the context in which the article placed it—as a motivation for the test ban treaty—suggested that world leaders could be moved by a directive from heaven. Despite what appear to be discrepancies in historical details, many people have accepted the *Neues Europa* text as a genuine extract from the third secret, and it continues to be circulated and identified as such.[79]

The Third Secret and the Popes

A great deal of interest in and speculation about the third secret on the part of Fatima devotees has revolved around the pope. Since da Silva sent the controversial text to the Vatican in April 1957, it has been widely assumed that this text has been accessible to the occupant of the papal see, and that he might read it. It is not clear from the evidence currently available just who took possession of the envelope when it arrived in Rome. Ottaviani has stated that the papal nuncio delivered the envelope to the Sacred Congregation for the Doctrine of the Faith as had been requested, and that—sometime later—it was given, still sealed, to Pope John XXIII.[80] According to Mgr. Loris Capovilla, a papal secretary and advisor, the new pope received the document at Castelgandolfo on 17 August 1959, the envelope being delivered by Fr. Paul Philippe, commissioner to the Sacred Congregation.[81] Based on these statements, Alonso has suggested that the envelope was kept in the archives of the Sacred Congregation during the final years of the pontificate of Pius XII.[82]

Michel de la Sainte Trinité, however, has argued that the envelope had been given to Pius XII and was in his personal possession until his death. He bases this view on the testimony of a journalist, Robert Serrou, who reportedly visited the private apartments of Pius XII on 14 May 1957 for the purpose of preparing a photographic essay for *Paris-Match*. Serrou described this visit many years later in a letter to Michel de la Sainte Trinité. Sister Pascalina, head housekeeper and confidant of the pope, accompanied Serrou on this visit, and when Serrou saw on a table a little wooden chest bearing the inscription "Secretum Sancti Officii" (Secret of the Holy Office), he asked Sister Pascalina what the chest contained. She allegedly replied, "There is in there the third secret of Fatima."[83] Serrou's essay was published in mid-October 1958, just after the death of Pius XII, and one of the photographs in the essay was of the table on which this chest was sitting, along with some personal belongings of the recently deceased pope. Printed with the photograph was this caption: "In breaking the seals of the private apartments, the Pope discovers the instruments of the work that awaits him, those of Pius XII, and the chest of the secrets of the Church."[84]

The implication of this caption—i.e., that the photograph was made after the death of Pius XII—was, as Michel de la Sainte Trinité has suggested, probably just a journalistic device by which the essay was adapted to the situation prevailing at the Vatican at the time of its publication.[85] The result illustrates very well, however, the structure in terms of which many Fatima devotees saw the pope's guardianship of the third secret and the critical event of its transfer from one pope to another. While Fatima, the secret, and Sister Pascalina were specifically mentioned nowhere in this essay, it is likely that what Serrou was told by Sister Pascalina about the content of the chest, as reported by Michel de la Sainte Trinité, mirrored what a great many Roman Catholics at this crucial time would have thought when they saw this photograph or heard about the mysterious chest through other channels.

For Roman Catholics who attributed some importance to the alleged secret, whether any of the popes actually read this secret and what their response may have been were matters of some concern. Reports had begun to circulate soon after the envelope containing the secret arrived in Rome that Pius XII had opened the envelope, read the secret, and (according to one report) wept,[86] or (according to another) fainted and remained unconscious for three days.[87] A close friend of Pius XII, however, publicly denounced these reports, and they seem to have gained little credence, at least among the better-known partisans and historians of the Fatima secrets.[88] Both Alonso and Michel de la Sainte Trinité have assumed that the statements of Ottaviani and Capovilla are true: that the secret was delivered to the new pope, John XXIII, still sealed.[89]

It has generally been accepted, however, that John XXIII read the secret. Capovilla reported that when the new pope received the envelope on 17 August 1959 at Castelgandolfo, he said that he would wait to read it with his confessor, Mgr. Alfredo Cavagne. The reading, to judge from Capovilla's account, took place a few days later, and Mgr. Paulo Tavares, a translator of Portuguese for the Vatican's secretary of state, reportedly was called on to help the pope with a few difficult phrases. Capovilla also said that the pope made known the content of the secret to the heads of the Sacred Congregation for the Doctrine of the Faith and to the secretary of state, but he did not say whether the pope gave them the text or merely spoke with them about it.[90] Ottaviani has claimed to have read the text, but he did not specify when or under what circumstances. John XXIII himself made no public statement concerning the secret.[91] Alonso has reported that he stated explicitly that the text did not pertain to his times and that he preferred to leave an assessment of it to his successors.[92] Capovilla has reported that he himself transcribed a personal note written by the pope and added it to the envelope containing the secret, which was then taken to the Vatican and put in a desk in the pope's chamber.[93]

John XXIII's successors have followed a policy of reserve with regard to the so-called secret. Paul VI succeeded John XXIII in 1963, and, according to Capovilla, either in July of that year, just after his coronation, or a few months later, he requested information about the controversial document. "One could assume," said Capovilla, "that he read it."[94] He did not, however, reveal its contents to the public.

Michel de la Sainte Trinité has noted that in 1977, the year before his brief occupation of the Holy See, John Paul I had visited Fatima and had spoken at length with Lucia. He has admitted, though, that there is little evidence with which to determine whether John Paul I did or did not read the secret during the several weeks of his papacy.[95] The same author has said, however, that he learned from a very sure source that John Paul II, before his visit to Fatima on 13 May 1982 (which Fatima devotees note was the anniversary of the attempt on his life), did read the secret, and indeed, that he consulted with a Portuguese member of the Curia in order to catch "all the nuances of the language." During this visit, however, he is said to have ignored the secret "purely and simply." Michel de la Sainte Trinité has also called attention to an interview conducted by a journalist on 15 August 1984 with Cardinal Ratzinger, Ottaviani's successor as Prefect of the Sacred Congregation for the Doctrine of the Faith, in which Ratzinger said that John Paul II had read the secret but had no intention of making it public.[96] An account of an informal question and answer session with John Paul II was published in the German review *Stimme des Glaubens*, in which the pope allegedly gave a glimpse into the content of the third secret.[97] This was in the course of a 1980 trip to West Germany, in front of the cathedral at Fulda, where he is said to have answered several questions asked by a group of pilgrims, one of which concerned the third secret and whether it should have been made public in 1960. The pope said, according to the article, that because of the gravity of the secret and in order not to encourage the spread of communism, his predecessors had delayed publication. He noted that many wanted to know about the secret from mere curiosity and a taste for sensationalism. He then reportedly seized his rosary and exclaimed, "There is the remedy against evil. Pray! Pray! and ask nothing else. Entrust all the rest to God." When then asked what lay ahead for the Church, he is said to have replied that people ought to begin to prepare themselves for great trials and for sacrifice, perhaps even the sacrifice of one's life in total submission to Christ and for Christ. This trial could be alleviated, the pope reportedly said, by prayer, but it could not be avoided, because it was only by such a trial that the Church could be renewed. People should be strong, prepare themselves, entrust themselves to Christ and his Mother, and devote themselves to praying the Rosary.

Conclusion

It is clear that the prophetic character of the second part of the secret of Fatima contributed to its popularity in the postwar years and to the fact that its third, unrevealed part has continued to be an object of curiosity and concern for many Roman Catholics. It appeared to them that here the Virgin had predicted three major events of the twentieth century—a swift end to the First World War, the beginning of the Second, and the rise of communist Russia as a world power—and had provided as an explanation for the latter two catastrophes the failure of people to amend their sinful lives and to heed her requests for special acts of devotion to her Immaculate Heart. It appeared that here, as in the public message at La Salette, the Virgin had predicted important events that had in fact come to be realized.

The two parts of the secret revealed by Lucia carried the drama associated with apparitions in general and with secrets in particular much further than this drama had been carried in connection with La Salette. Unlike La Salette, which was a single apparition experienced by Mélanie and Maximin when they were alone, Fatima was a serial apparition, and the three children were in the presence of others beginning with the apparition on June 13. Material that Lucia revealed later could be connected with events remembered to have happened during the apparition. Thus, although Lucia did not say on 13 July 1917 that she and her cousins had seen a vision of hell, when she did write of having seen this in her *Second Memoir*, people remembered that she had cried out on that occasion, apparently in fright, and they connected this cry with the vision of hell. This vision underlined the importance both for individual and social salvation of the scenarios that followed in the second part of the secret.

The Virgin was understood to have made a specific request of the pope in the second part of the secret. She said she would return to ask the pope to consecrate Russia to her Immaculate Heart. Two scenarios were then laid out: what would happen if the request were met, and what would happen if it were not. This promised return was understood by Lucia to have occurred in her vision of 6 June 1929. Whether this request has been fulfilled by Pope Pius XII's dedication of the world to Mary's Immaculate Heart and his letter to the Russian people is a matter of dispute among Fatima devotees. But these events had implications for the role of the pope in the unfolding of the eschatological drama in the second part of the secret, for here the pope is not simply a passive sufferer (although this aspect is certainly present in the visions attributed to Jacinta by Lucia) or the recipient of information so that he can prepare the faithful to endure coming trials. Rather, he is given an active role, in the sense that his response to Mary's request would in itself determine the course of world history.

Finally, although Lucia has lived within the cloister since 1925 and the access of persons to her has been restricted, her continuing presence has had an important impact on the perception of the seer as a source of information about the apparition she or he has experienced and as an interpreter of that apparition. Important here are not only a seer's opinions about the meaning of the Virgin's statements and about whether her requests have been fulfilled but also a seer's proclamations about public events which are assumed to have some connection with the apparition. Lucia's identification of the aurora borealis as a sign that the Virgin had told her would signal God's punishment of the world helped reestablish the belief, discouraged by the Church in the aftermath of La Salette, in the ongoing prophetic vocation of the apparition seer.

CHAPTER 6

The Drama of Secrets
in Post–World War II
Marian Apparitions

The Development of Dramatic Scenarios around Secrets

THE ABBÉ HENRI SOUILLET was a priest in charge of a parish near l'Île Bouchard, France, where four children reported an apparition of the Virgin in December 1947. Shortly after these reports, in a letter to a Belgian priest whom he considered somewhat of an authority on apparitions, Souillet probably expressed the thoughts of a good many Roman Catholic authorities in the years after the Second World War with respect to the phenomenon of apparition "secrets." He noted here, first of all, that he shared his colleague's general skepticism about such secrets. The phenomenon had begun, he recalled, at La Salette, and almost every apparition since then, it seemed, had had its secrets. It remained a mystery to him why God, who would surely not speak without good reason, would choose to reveal something to seers which they then would refuse to divulge, and he suggested that there was something bizarre here which called for the greatest caution.[1] Somewhat later and in a somewhat more positive vein, Souillet suggested that although this was a subject "surrounded by the supernatural" it nonetheless deserved a serious study, conducted "with all science, all piety [and] all desirable prudence."[2]

While Souillet may have erred in suggesting that all apparitions since La Salette had involved secrets, it was clear, certainly, that after La Salette secrets had become an important aspect of Marian apparitions and attended them with ever-increasing frequency, and that a very considerable impetus was given to this trend by Fatima. As noted earlier, however, Fatima was initially not widely publicized, its so-called secrets were scarcely publicized at all until the 1940s, and in the post-Fatima apparitions which predate this publicity, secrets were important in a way more characteristic of some nineteenth-century apparitions than of the apparitions of a decade or two later.

There were two apparitions in this period which are worth noting because they have both been recognized by Roman Catholic authorities: the apparitions at Beauraing (1932) and Banneux (1933), both in Belgium. At Beauraing, three of the five seers claimed to have received secrets during the Virgin's final appearance on 3 January 1933. These three children, Gilberte Degeimbre, Gilberte Voisin, and her brother Albert, each said that before the Virgin bid them goodbye, she told them a secret that they were to tell no one. They were then subjected to the same sort of interrogations as had their predecessors at La Salette and Fatima, and when asked if they would be willing to tell the secrets to the archbishop or to the pope, they insisted that they would not. In January and February of 1933, just after the events at Beauraing, Mariette Beco of Banneux also claimed to have received two secrets during a series of appearances of the Virgin. She too was reportedly both interrogated and threatened in attempts to force her to disclose her secrets, and in the course of one of these interrogations she is alleged to have said to her father, while pointing to her breast, "Papa, even if you would place your gun there, I would not tell."[3]

Stories such as these about the seers' secrets at Beauraing and Banneux apparently served, as in most of the earlier apparitions, to remind and to assure those who believed in the apparitions of the integrity and credibility of the seers and their messages. The children at Beauraing are reported to have said, for example, "If the Holy Virgin did not help us, we would have told it [that is, their secret] already a hundred times."[4] The Beauraing and Banneux secrets do not seem, however, to have given rise to any excitement in their own right, as had the secrets of La Salette and, especially, Fatima. It does not seem, in other words, that they were understood by anyone as prophecies awaiting fulfillment. The paradigm that came to expression here, rather, was that of Lourdes, where the public messages were understood as devotional admonitions addressed to particular individuals and where the secrets were understood as relevant only to the seer. A more intensive study of the Beauraing and Banneux apparitions would be needed before one could judge why this was the case and why the prophetic legacy of La Salette and Fatima (or what was then known of Fatima) bore so little fruit in these apparitions.

It was after the tumultuous years of the Second World War that this prophetic legacy, now more accessible and apparently speaking directly to the times in the literature circulating about the third secret of Fatima, began to come into its own, for these years witnessed a great surge of apparition reports of a decidedly apocalyptic nature, reports in which the motif of secrets began to give dramatic structure to the apparitions themselves.

In the apparition with which the Abbé Souillet had been concerned at l'Île Bouchard, for example, which occurred 8–14 December 1947, the four young seers reported that on the second day of the apparition the Virgin suddenly became very sad and said that she would tell them a secret that they could make known in three days. She then said that many prayers were needed for France, which was in grave danger in these times. The next day, the children said they were given another secret, which they said the Virgin had forbidden them to tell anyone. Souillet, who followed the events as they unfolded, does not make it clear just when the children made these claims and if and when the secrets were actually made public.[5]

The concern with Russia which had permeated the literature about the secret of Fatima became a major theme in a number of these postwar apparitions and their secrets. A particularly good example of this, which shows how actively and vividly this theme could be expressed during this period, was at Heroldsbach-Thurn, West Germany, where from 1949 to 1952 a group of children reported apparitions of the Virgin and of other religious and not-so-religious figures on an almost daily basis. The seers of Heroldsbach-Thurn spoke of a number of secrets which the Virgin had communicated to them, some of which they said concerned themselves (these they confided to the several adults who accompanied them), some of which concerned the meaning of symbols or requests made during the apparitions (these were communicated to local priests), and some of which were written down and taken to a notary, with the intention that they would be opened and revealed when the events of which they spoke should begin to unfold.[6]

It is these recorded and notarized secrets that are of particular interest, since they both expressed the children's experiences and helped to shape the way these experiences were subsequently dramatized. On 10 February 1950, in the aftermath of a vision in which the Virgin announced that she would cease appearing to them on February 18, two eleven-year-old girls, Gretl Guegel and her friend Erika, reported that the Virgin had given them two secrets. The girls wrote these down, and when the Virgin appeared to them the next day, she reportedly told Erika that the secrets were not to be made public until the events which they concerned should take place. Several months later, several different seers began to report "Russian Visions," that is, scenes in which they saw battles with Russians or themselves encountered Russians, and apparently described these aloud to the people gathered around them. On May 15, for example, Antonie Saam (age eleven), looked into the sky over some birch woods and reported seeing there a battle with Russians, but she also saw a village over which the Virgin had spread her cloak for protection. The next day, Marian Heilmann (age ten) and Gretl also saw battle scenes, and all four girls reported walking through ruins where they said they encountered Russians, some of whom hit and kicked them, and some of whom were converted when the girls told them they had seen the Virgin. Similar visions were reported the following day, and it seems that at this point the adults, who had been anxiously following the children's visions, determined that something needed to be done. On the following day, May 18, the secrets of Gretl and Erika were opened, apparently ahead of schedule, and were found to contain a measure of comfort. Gretl's secret, reportedly, was a special promise from the Virgin "When the Russians come I will protect Heroldsbach and Thurn. Even the houses will shake when the bombs fall. But I will protect Heroldsbach and Thurn." Erika's secrets, it is said, conveyed the same message in similar words.[7]

Secrets concerning Russia came to expression in a form less vivid but more prolonged, and more directly in accord with the literature concerning the secret of Fatima, in an apparition of the Virgin to Caterina Richero, at Balestrino, Italy, which began in 1949 and continued until 1971. Caterina, like many of the more recent seers who claim to have received secrets from the Virgin, understood herself to have a mission to reveal these gradually to the public, as the Virgin gave her permission. On 5 November 1958, for example, she said that the Virgin had told her when she could reveal four secrets that had previously been conveyed to her. On 5 March 1960, in connection with two more secrets she had received, Caterina reported that the Virgin told her: "At this moment I see before me so many afflicted, weak, and sinful souls. My children, know that I am the mediatrix of all graces. Whoever has recourse to me with great faith, nothing will be refused that one. Dear children, today, pray! Because I come to convert and bring Russia to Jesus."[8]

Albert Marty, who collected the messages reported by Caterina and wrote an account of the apparition through 1971, has understood Caterina's secrets as part of a tradition of more or less orthodox Roman Catholic prophecy stemming from La Salette and Fatima. He suggested, for example, that a secret conveyed to Caterina on 5 October 1961 (to which the other secrets she received were presumably similar) was really identical with the secrets conveyed by the Virgin at La Salette and Fatima, and also in other more recent Marian apparitions. This secret, he thought, pertained to a variety of chastisements that would strike the world if it did not heed the Virgin's warnings and turn from its evil ways.[9]

While there were few postwar apparitions which met with much favor from Roman Catholic authorities, the seers and their followers typically saw these apparitions as thoroughly consistent with Catholic teaching, and at least several seers reportedly made efforts to communicate their secrets directly to the pope. Bruno Cornachiola, for example, who had converted to Roman Catholicism after experiencing an apparition of the Virgin at Tre Fontane (Rome, Italy) in 1947, was said to have been following the Virgin's own strict orders when he took to the pope a secret message from her. At Espis, France, where several seers reported an apparition of the Virgin from 1946 to 1949, five-year-old Gilles Bourhous was said to have been given a secret message by the Virgin on 13 November 1949. He was then apparently taken to Rome, where on December 5 he was reportedly given an audience with Mgr. Montini (the future Paul VI) and delivered this message to him.[10] Whether or not such encounters between the seers and high-ranking Church officials actually took place, the idea that they had taken place was clearly important for the many devotees of these apparitions who considered themselves faithful Roman Catholics, and this in turn demonstrates the unusual importance for the devotees of the secrets with which they believed these seers had been entrusted.

Dramatic scenarios developed around secrets in most of the post–World War II apparitions, and while those associated with the apparitions of the late 1940s and 1950s are certainly interesting, they have, in fact, had little lasting impact. The apparition at Garabandal, however, which took place in the 1960s, had a very considerable impact on most recent apparitions and the piety that developed around them in international Roman Catholic circles. To understand developments in the past several decades concerning the role of secret revelations in Marian apparitions, it is important to examine in some detail the drama that has evolved at Garabandal, and then to examine the more elaborate drama of secrets in the ongoing apparition at Medjugorje, Yugoslavia.

The Great Miracle of Garabandal

The apparition of Mary to four children at Garabandal (1961–1965) is not usually seen as involving secrets. In the devotional literature that has grown up around this apparition, there are no references either to secrets that concern the seers personally or to secrets of wider scope that are to be revealed at some future time. Conchita González did, however, say that during some of the apparitions she and the other three girls received confidential information from the Virgin about persons who were present in the crowd and that they communicated this information to those persons. Devotees have understood this as evidence of special abilities bestowed upon the girls during the apparitions and thus as an argument for the divine origin of the apparitions themselves. But the seers have also claimed that the Virgin revealed to them three future events that have come to be known as a "great miracle," a "warning," and a "chastisement." Conchita has claimed to know the nature and date of the miracle and the nature of the warning and chastisement, but she has said that she can only describe these events in a general way.[11] The anticipated unfolding of these events, the extraordinary phenomena associated with them, and the role of Conchita in their revelation to the public function for the devotees of Garabandal much as the secrets associated with other Marian apparitions function for their respective devotees.

The great miracle, or simply "the miracle," which has become part of the end-time scenario envisioned by devotees of Garabandal appears to have had its beginning in the prayers of the visionaries for a public proof of the divine origin of their experiences. On 30 June 1961, four weeks after they first reported seeing the Virgin and six weeks after they first reported the appearance of an angel, the four girls are said to have asked the Virgin for a miracle so that people would believe them. During subsequent apparitions they continued their requests for a miracle and claimed that the Virgin looked grave each time they made these requests. Observers said that on 8 August 1961 the girls were particularly insistent in their pleas, and that during an apparition at noon in front of the altar of the parish church, Conchita supported their petitions by reminding the Virgin that "at Lourdes and Fatima you gave them proof."[12]

It was during the evening apparition of that same day that a sequence of events began that would determine how believers in the Garabandal apparition would come to understand this miracle. Fr. Luis María Andréu, a Jesuit, had come to Garabandal on July 29 to observe the visionaries, along with his brother, Fr. Ramón María Andréu, also a Jesuit. Conchita noted in her diary that when they arrived neither priest believed in the apparitions. Fr. Luis was present, however, on the evening of August 8 when the girls fell into an ecstasy and walked towards the pines. It was reported that he followed them closely and that when they arrived at the pines he stood near them, looked upward, and exclaimed four times, "Miracle!" Conchita has said that during their ecstasies she and the other three visionaries could normally never see anyone but the Virgin. On this occasion, however, they reported that they could also see Fr. Luis and that the Virgin told them that he was seeing both her and "the great miracle."[13]

After the apparition, at about ten o'clock that evening, Fr. Luis left Garabandal and traveled by jeep to Cosio, a neighboring town, where, at about one o'clock, he met with the pastor of Cosio and Garabandal, Valentín Marichalar. According to Marichalar, Fr. Luis told him that he believed that what the children said was true, but cautioned that he should not repeat this, because the Church could not be too prudent in such matters.[14] Fr. Luis then left in a caravan of four cars traveling to Reinosa. According to the driver of the car in which Fr. Luis was riding, the Jesuit "radiated happiness" and, after sleeping for about an hour, awoke feeling refreshed and fit. At about four o'clock in the morning the travelers made a brief stop in Reinosa and then resumed their journey, and at this time Fr. Luis again spoke of his happiness and of his confidence in the events at Garabandal and expressed gratitude for the favor the Virgin had bestowed on him. He said that they were fortunate to have such a mother in heaven and that there was no reason to fear the afterlife, and he concluded by declaring, "This is the happiest day of my life." At this point, according to the driver, Fr. Luis then raised his head and was silent, and when asked if anything was wrong, he responded that he was sleepy. Then lowering his head, he coughed slightly, his eyes rolled upwards, and he died.[15]

Fr. Luis's death made a profound impression on those associated with the apparition at Garabandal. The priest was only thirty-six years old, was apparently physically fit, and had no previous history of ill health, and there was no family history of heart trouble. Believers in Garabandal have associated his death with the events of the preceding evening, maintaining that Fr. Luis died of "excessive joy resulting from the sharing in the vision and the preview of the great miracle," and that he was one of two people who had such a preview.[16]

The adjective "great" has commonly been used to distinguish the miracle anticipated by the visionaries and supposedly previewed by Fr. Luis from the "little miracle" (*milagrucu*) of the visible Communion host which has been discussed in some detail in Chapter 3.[17]

While Conchita has not said that she herself has seen the great miracle, she has said that the Virgin has revealed to her its nature and date and has entrusted her with the task of announcing it to the public. These claims were first made, apparently, in an undated entry in her diary which probably stems from the summer of 1963, two years after Fr. Luis's death. Conchita wrote here that the Virgin told her that through her intercession God would work a very great miracle. She was informed, she said, of what this miracle would be and when it would happen, and instructed to announce it publicly eight days before it was to occur, so that people could come to Garabandal. She was told, moreover, that the pope would see the miracle "from wherever he is," as would the Italian stigmatic Padre Pio. All sick people present for the great miracle would be healed, and sinners would be converted.[18]

Conchita added some details to this portrayal of the great miracle in a personal letter, apparently written that same summer. She wrote that although the Virgin forbade her to reveal the nature and date of the miracle, she was permitted to reveal that it would take place on a Thursday at eight-thirty in the evening, on the feast of a martyr dedicated to the Holy Eucharist, and would coincide with an event in the Church. It would be visible to everyone in Garabandal and the surrounding mountains, and it could be photographed and televised. A permanent sign of the miracle would be left in the pine grove, where many of the apparitions to the four girls had occurred.[19]

On 20 July 1963, Conchita reported a locution of Jesus in which there was some clarification of the purpose of the miracle and her own role in its unfolding. When she asked Jesus the purpose of the miracle, asking if it was "to convert many people," Jesus reportedly replied that it was "to convert the whole world." When she asked specifically if Russia would be converted, Jesus replied affirmatively and added that "thus everybody will love Our Hearts." Conchita then expressed her concern that when the miracle took place people would think that she alone had seen the Virgin. Jesus' response to this was that he was allowing her to play a part in bringing about the miracle by her prayers and sacrifices. When she asked Jesus if it would not be better if she were joined by the others (i.e., the three other seers) in the role of intercession, or else that none of them should assume this role, Jesus answered simply "No."[20]

In the summer of 1964, Conchita made statements which gave rise to some additional expectations with respect to the great miracle. The first of these concerned Joey Lomangino, an American who had been blinded by an accident in 1947 at the age of sixteen. Lomangino had made two visits to Garabandal, the first in the spring of 1963, following a visit to Padre Pio at San Giovanni Rotondo, and the second because he had been quite impressed with Conchita on the first in the spring of 1964.[21] Just after this second visit, Conchita wrote to Lomangino that she had received a locution from the Virgin concerning him. The Virgin had asked her to tell him that on the day of the great miracle he would receive "new eyes," and the miracle would be the first thing he would see. His sight would be permanently restored.[22] In an interview in 1972, Conchita specified that what was meant here was not spiritual vision but physical sight.[23]

The second statement concerned the body of Fr. Luis. On 18 July 1964, Conchita reported that the Blessed Virgin had told her that on the day after the great miracle the Jesuit priest's body would be removed intact from his grave. This information was conveyed to Fr. Luis's brother, Fr. Ramon, in a letter dated 2 August 1964.[24]

Believers in Garabandal, following Conchita's lead and taking her statements in 1963 and 1964 as prophetic, have come to understand the great miracle as a future event that would be accompanied by these signs: the healing of the sick and the conversion of sinners present at Garabandal, the restoration of Lomangino's sight, the establishment of a permanent sign at the pines, a vision of the miracle seen by the pope and Padre Pio, and the discovery of Fr. Luis's incorrupt body.[25] Since those years, however, two things have happened which have forced believers to make some changes in their understanding of two of these expected signs.

On 23 September 1968, Padre Pio, who Conchita said was to see the great miracle, died. Conchita herself was apparently surprised and initially disturbed by the death of the famous stigmatic. In an interview on

9 February 1975, she told of a trip which she had made to Lourdes in October, 1968, with Fr. Alfred Combe. There, she said, she met Fr. Bernardino Cennamo, a monk at San Pascual Monastery (Benevento, Italy) who was Padre Pio's personal friend. She asked Cennamo why the Virgin had told her that Padre Pio would see the miracle, when, as it turned out, he was to die before it occurred. Cennamo reportedly replied, "Padre Pio saw the miracle before he died. He told me so, himself."[26] Devotees of Garabandal have understandably been very receptive to this idea and have helped to publicize it. Fr. Joseph Pelletier, for example, who has provided a commentary on Conchita's diary in *Our Lady Comes to Garabandal*, has assured the reader that he has it from a reliable source, whom he does not name, that Padre Pio did indeed see the miracle before he died. Believers in the apparition, therefore, now understand Padre Pio and Fr. Luis as having been granted, prior to death, personal visions of the great miracle.[27]

At the beginning of 1976, the Jesuit seminary at Oña (province of Burgos), where Fr. Luis had been a professor of theology and where he was buried, was converted into an asylum, and the bodies of all those buried there were exhumed. It was found at that time that Fr. Luis's body had been reduced to a skeleton, which was then transferred to the ossuary of the Society of Jesus in Loyola. The discovery that Fr. Luis's body had decayed has, for devotees of Garabandal, apparently not greatly affected belief in the great miracle. Combe, who reported the transfer of the bones, has himself suggested how this discovery should be understood. Pointing out that the Virgin told Conchita that the body would be found intact on the day after the great miracle, Combe has argued that Conchita's locution did not concern the state of Fr. Luis's body in the interim.[28]

Some supporters of the Garabandal apparition also hold that Conchita revealed the date of the miracle to Pope Paul VI and to Cardinal Ottaviani during a trip to Rome in January 1966. There are differing accounts of this trip. It is generally agreed that Conchita, her mother, and Fr. Luna, a priest of Zaragosa who had been present during some of the apparitions, spent about a week in Rome.[29] According to Pelletier, Ottaviani wrote directly to Conchita asking her to come to Rome. Luna worked out the details of the trip, and Francisco Sanchez-Ventura y Pascuel, who had written about Garabandal, covered expenses with proceeds from the sale of his book.[30] According to Ramon Pérez, Ottaviani had written to Luna, asking him to bring the seers to Rome, "with or without the permission of the bishop." He attributed the organization of the trip to Princess Cecile de Bourbon-Parme.[31]

It is also generally agreed that Conchita participated in a public audience with the pope toward the end of her visit, probably on January 19. But whether she had an earlier, private interview with him is a matter of dispute. According to Pérez, Conchita was interviewed by Cardinal Ottaviani, Cardinal Marella, and two other members of the Roman Curia. Cardinal Ottaviani, who was then prefect of the Congregation for the Doctrine of the Faith, reportedly told Luna afterwards that among the many alleged apparitions which were being studied by the Holy See, those at Garabandal seemed "very interesting." Pérez said that Conchita was then interviewed by Paul VI in a private audience, and that he gave her a special blessing, saying, "I bless you and, with me, the whole Church blesses you." Pérez noted that the reality of this private audience has been disputed by opponents of the Garabandal cult and that when Luna, Conchita, and Aniceta have been questioned about it, they have merely smiled. But there is no doubt in Pérez's mind that the meeting occurred and that during the meeting Conchita told the pope the date of the miracle.[32]

Pelletier has given a more complicated account of the events in Rome, noting that the whole affair smacked of palace intrigue. He said that Conchita asked for and was given an appointment with Paul VI but that it was subsequently cancelled. Instead, arrangements were made for her to meet with a high-ranking personal representative of the pope. This person told Conchita that the pope gave her "his blessing and with it that of all the Church." The following day, in an unexpected turn of events, Paul VI did meet with Conchita and repeated in person what his representative had told her. Pelletier differentiated this interview from other private audiences granted by the pope. The latter, he said, are in reality only semiprivate in nature; other people are present, and the meetings are listed in the Vatican's daily newspaper, *Osservatore Romano*. Paul VI's interview with Conchita, on the other hand, was private "in the true sense of the word" (implying that it was not listed in this newspaper and that apparently no one else was present).[33]

The Chastisement and the Warning

The idea that the miracle would be part of a call to conversion that would mitigate a "divine chastisement" developed out of two public messages delivered in 1961 and 1965 and an apparition of 1 January 1965 in which Conchita was told about a "warning" from God.

Conchita reported in her diary that on 6 July 1961 the Virgin appeared to the girls for the third time and gave them a message that they were to announce publicly on October 18. Conchita said that she did not understand this message but that the Virgin told the girls the following day that she would explain the message and tell them just how it was to be disclosed. Soon it was announced that the four visionaries were to read the message publicly on October 18 at the entrance to the village church and also communicate it to Marichalar, who would then read it at ten-thirty that evening at the pines. It is unclear from Conchita's diary and from devotional accounts of the events just how far in advance of October 18 the girls made known this anticipated scenario. In any case, the ecclesiastical commission that had been established to investigate the apparitions objected to having the four visionaries read the message from the church steps. Conchita then reportedly wrote the message on a piece of paper which she and the other three girls signed.[34]

It was raining in Garabandal on October 18, which apparently led the visionaries and the crowd, estimated to be about five thousand strong, to go to the pines early. At about ten o'clock, Marichalar read to the assembled crowd this message: "We must make many sacrifices, perform much penance, and visit the Blessed Sacrament frequently. But first we must lead good lives. If we do not, a chastisement will befall us. The cup is already filling up and if we do not change, a very great chastisement will come upon us." The girls themselves then read the message in unison, but because they could not be clearly heard by the crowd, an unidentified man read the message yet a third time.[35]

The following spring, on June 19 and 20, 1962, before the Feast of Corpus Christi, the girls experienced two frightening visions. On the first of these days, according to observers, Mari Loli and Jacinta, who were at the pines in a state of ecstasy, suddenly began to cry out in terror. On the next day, Conchita, Mari Loli, and Jacinta reportedly had a similar experience. Observers said that they held their hands out as if to push something formidable away and cried out, "Oh! Let the little children die before that happens! . . . Give the people time to go to confession beforehand!" While the girls have publicly said very little about their experiences on these two nights, their behavior and what people heard them say led many to believe that they were given a preview of the chastisement spoken of in the message of the preceding October.[36]

About two and a half years later, on 1 January 1965, Conchita experienced an ecstasy at the pines that lasted approximately two hours, during which the Virgin told her of a forthcoming "warning." People had ignored the message of 18 October 1961, the Virgin said, and so she would give the world yet another message, which would be the last. About a month before this, Conchita had reported that the Virgin had told her in a locution that the archangel Michael would appear to her on 18 June 1965 (the anniversary of his first appearance to the girls). The Virgin now made it clear to her that the purpose of the forthcoming apparition would be to deliver her new and final message.[37] A large crowd gathered at Garabandal on June 18 in anticipation of the announced event. At about midnight that night, Conchita experienced an ecstasy lasting about twenty minutes. Afterward, she reported that the archangel had appeared to her and had conveyed the promised message. She wrote it out and made it public the next day. It reiterated that the earlier message had been neither obeyed nor publicized, and that this new message was to be the Virgin's last. The cup that had been filling up was now overflowing. Some criticism of the clergy, absent from the first message, was then introduced. Many cardinals, bishops and priests were on the road to perdition and were taking many souls with them. Too little importance was being attached to the Eucharist. Everyone would have to exert great effort to turn away the wrath of God. If people asked God for forgiveness with sincere hearts, he would pardon them. It was Mary, their Mother, through the intercession of the archangel Michael, who was asking them now to amend their lives. The last warnings were now being issued, but Mary loved them very much and did not want their condemnation; if people prayed with sincerity, their requests would be granted. The message concluded by exhorting people to make more sacrifices and to think about the passion of Jesus.[38]

A few months later, in the fall of 1965, Conchita made it clear that while the June 18 message had indeed been a warning, the warning about which the Virgin had spoken on January 1 was not this message but an event which had not yet come to pass. She described it as something like a chastisement intended both to warn the wicked and to bring good people closer to God. Although she said she expected this warning to last only a short time, she believed it would be very formidable and that it would be visible from every part of the world. While it would not cause physical injury, it would involve suffering, and if some were to die, it would be not from the warning itself but from the emotion they experienced as the warning was taking place. Conchita said that for both believers and unbelievers the warning would be an interior realization of one's sins, and that from the nature of the warning itself it would be clear that it had come directly from God.[39]

While the great miracle, the chastisement, and the warning have thus come to be seen by the seers and their followers as separate events, they are nonetheless understood to be closely related. Conchita has said that the warning will precede the miracle, but she has said she cannot be more specific about dates and periods of time.[40] Mari Loli has claimed that the Virgin revealed to her the nature of the warning and told her that it would occur about a year before the great miracle.[41] The girls have agreed, however, that if people do not convert after the warning and the miracle, God will send a chastisement proportional in its severity to the severity of the sins of the world. The warning, the great miracle, and the chastisement are, therefore, for believers in the Garabandal apparitions, the basic terms of an impending end-time scenario which they will know to be imminent or already in progress when Conchita announces that the great miracle is at hand.[42]

The Ten Secrets of Medjugorje

The most complex of modern Marian apparitions, with respect to the confidential information that the visionaries claim to have received, is the continuing apparition at Medjugorje, Yugoslavia. As already noted, this apparition began in June 1981, when six children began reporting almost daily appearances of the Virgin. While the number of the seers still residing in the village and reporting the apparition has now declined, the apparition has continued for eight years and has become, under the guidance of the Franciscan clergy who lead the parish, a part of an elaborate program of daily confessions, Masses, and other events designed to accommodate the hundreds of pilgrims from all over the world who arrive at the village almost every day.

This confidential information claimed by the six seers of Medjugorje is of three types. First, there are personal secrets which concern the seers individually and which do not appear destined ever to be revealed to the public.[43] Second, there are matters of interest to the public but not necessarily considered particularly important for public well-being. Vicka

Ivanković, for example, reports that she has received new information concerning Mary's earthly life which may be revealed later when the Virgin gives permission.[44] Finally, there are crucial public secrets that allegedly concern the Roman Catholic Church and the whole world and that will be revealed gradually.[45] The transmission of this confidential material to the children and the eventual revelation of much of it to the public is understood by the faithful as an integral part of the gradual unfolding of this serial apparition.

The conveying of confidential material to the seers of Medjugorje is understood both by the seers and by Medjugorje devotees as linked to the important matter of the duration of the apparition, both for the individual seers and for the seers as a group. According to the visionaries, Mary has promised to confide to each of them ten secrets. This specific number is important, for when a seer has received a tenth secret, it is understood that the frequent appearances of Mary to that seer will cease. Mirjana Dragicević, for example, received a tenth secret on 25 December 1982, at which time the Virgin told her that henceforth she would only appear to her annually on her birthday and in times of crisis, and Mirjana has indicated that this is indeed what has come to pass.[46] Ivanka Ivanković received a tenth secret on 7 May 1985 and was told that she would receive annual visits from Mary on the anniversary of the apparition (June 25); the appearances to Ivanka have accordingly decreased.[47] Many devotees believe that when each of the seers has received ten secrets, the Medjugorje apparition per se will cease and that the events that they understand as the fulfillment of the public secrets will begin to occur.[48]

On the basis of the information available to the general public, the specific content of each seer's secrets—that is, those which they now claim to have received up to this time—cannot now be determined. Reports about these secrets often convey the idea that the ten secrets are identical for all the seers and that there is variation only in the rate at which they are revealed to each seer.[49] The children's responses to close questioning, however, suggest that this might not be the case and that each set of secrets might be distinctive.

At the beginning of December 1982, Fr. Ljudevit Rupčić asked each of the children, "Did Our Lady confide any secrets to you?" Marija Pavlović replied that she had received six secrets that concern "us, the Church, people in general." Ivanka responded that she had seven and added, "Some concern us personally, others, the Church and the world."[50] Such responses suggest that for at least some of the children both personal and public secrets are included in their set of ten.[51]

Mirjana, the first of the visionaries to receive ten secrets, however, has maintained that all of her secrets are of public relevance. Her response in December 1982, to Rupčić's question was much like the responses of the others. Her secrets, she said then, "have to do with us ourselves, the [final] sign, the whole world, and Medjugorje."[52] When questioned more closely about her secrets, however, by Fr. Tomislav Vlašić on 10 January 1983, after she had received her tenth secret, Mirjana was more specific. Vlašić asked her directly whether she had received any personal secrets, and she replied that none of her secrets concerned herself alone. To Vlašić's remark that Ivan Dragicević had received personal secrets, she replied, "My secrets are for all mankind generally, for the world, Medjugorje, some other areas, and about the sign."[53]

The seers' responses to one of Rupčić's questions illustrate the problem of precisely categorizing the material that they regard as confided to them by the Virgin. Rupčić asked each seer if Mary had a message for the pope. Mirjana (who at that time had received nine secrets) and Ivan replied simply, "No." Marija said she did not know, while Jakov Čolo reported that Mary had conveyed such a message to Vicka. Ivanka said that she could only say "that he should extend the faith to all the people because we are now more or less equal and that he persevere on his path." Vicka's reply was much like that of Ivanka, but she added that "this is found among the secrets that she gave us, but we shouldn't speak about it now, only when she permits us to say it."[54] The message for the pope, then, could be understood as contained in the ten secrets to be entrusted to Ivanka and Vicka, or it could be understood as contained in other less important material that has presumably been confided to them. If it were understood as contained in their ten secrets, one would probably have to say that the seers each received in a different order the secrets that are of public relevance, or that they each received among their ten secrets some which were unique and not shared by the others.[55]

Mirjana provided quite a bit of information about some of her secrets in the interview with Vlašić after the reception of her tenth secret. Vlašić, perhaps having in mind the secrets reported at La Salette and Fatima, asked her whether those confided to her had been revealed to anyone in previous generations. Mirjana replied that she was unable to answer this question but that while Vlašić knew all the secrets that "have been told before," he did not know all of her secrets. Vlašić then asked if she had received the last of the secrets and if she could tell what it related to. Mirjana said that she had received the tenth secret but that she could not say anything about it. She could, however, say that the eighth secret was worse than the other seven. After hearing it she prayed for a long time and asked the Virgin during each daily appearance that the chastisements described in this secret might be mitigated. When the Virgin told her that everyone should pray for such a mitigation, she convinced many people in Sarajevo, she says, to join her in this prayer, and later the Virgin told her that she (the Virgin) had been able to ease the appointed chastisements. But then, Mirjana reported, the Virgin told her the ninth secret, which was worse, and the tenth, which was "totally bad" and could not be mitigated in any degree.[56] Mirjana has since corrected this report to note that it was the chastisements described in the seventh secret, and not the eighth, which had been mitigated through prayer.[57]

Mirjana told Vlašić that she also knew the dates on which the events described in the secrets would happen and outlined for him the process by which she would make these secrets known. She said that before each event was to happen she would have the right, perhaps two or three days in advance, to reveal the secret to a priest of her choice. That priest would then decide how to handle the information and whether to make it public before or after the event that the secret announced.[58]

Mirjana's plans, apparently, have since been modified. On 4 September 1985, Fr. Petar (Pero) Ljubičić issued a public statement about Mirjana's religious experiences, her secrets, and his own role in their eventual revelation. He reported that for some time Mirjana had been hearing interiorly the same voice that she had heard during the apparitions. This voice had been speaking to her in particular about her secrets. Mirjana had told Ljubičić sometime before that she had decided he would be the one to whom she would reveal her secrets, a decision confirmed by her inner voice on 1 June [1985]. She told him that ten days before an event revealed to her in one of her secrets was about to occur, she would communicate it to him on a paper similar to a parchment. He would then disclose the secret to the public three days before the event. After the event occurred, he would give the paper back to Mirjana and wait for the next prophecy.[59]

In the eyes of believers, the Virgin's secret revelations to the children at Medjugorje have been accompanied by phenomena of a miraculous character, and similar phenomena are expected when these secrets are made known to the world. These perceptions and expectations of miraculous events may be suggested by what the seers have said but may also rest on interpretations of what they have said. On 5 March 1986, for example, Wayne Weible, a newspaper columnist who had come to believe in the apparitions, reported that Mirjana and Ivanka each received from the Virgin a "parchment" made of a special, indestructible material on which the ten secrets were written along with the dates of their fulfillment. Each parchment could be read only by the seer to whom it was given, and it is this document, according to Weible, that will be given to a priest of the seer's choice ten days before one of the events inscribed upon it is about to transpire. The priest will be able at that time to read the relevant secret, but not any of the others. Weible has also noted that when Mirjana told Vlašić the name of the priest she had chosen to receive the secrets, he advised her that this priest was situated too far from Medjugorje and that she should choose someone closer. Mirjana reportedly replied that the Virgin would arrange things, and Vlašić was eventually replaced in the St. James parish by the priest in question.[60]

In his update on Medjugorje, *The Apparitions at Medjugorje Prolonged*, René Laurentin offers a somewhat different interpretation from Weible's of the means by which the secrets were transmitted to Ivanka and Mirjana. Laurentin reports that Ivanka told him she had not been given a piece of material such as Weible describes. Rather, long before her apparitions ended, she received a special code and began to record her secrets using this code, thus preserving their confidentiality.[61] Laurentin reports that Mirjana, on the other hand, does claim to have received a special piece of material on which her secrets are written. She claims that the writing is not presently visible but will become so when the time comes for each secret to be revealed, and that she has shown this material to a cousin, a Swiss engineer, who was not able to identify its composition. She also says that she has shown it to her mother and to another cousin, but not to any priest. Laurentin cautions against placing too much credence in this unusual object, which he believes may have more in common with magic than with "the habitual manner of God, according to the tradition of the Church." The seers, he warns, are "not exactly infallible."[62]

In her interview with Vlašić, Mirjana quite clearly placed her secrets in the context of a scenario of the end-time reminiscent of the book of Revelation. After Satan had appeared to her, she said, the Virgin revealed that the twentieth century had been given over to the devil. Asked to clarify whether the Virgin meant the twentieth century literally or "generally speaking," Mirjana replied rather cryptically, "Generally, part of which is in the twentieth century, until the first secret is unfolded." She thought that a few secrets would be revealed so that people would believe that Mary had actually appeared at Medjugorje; then they would understand the promised sign.[63]

The Sign of Medjugorje

The visionaries all claim that Mary confided to them information about a sign that she has promised will be manifest on the hill Podbrdo, the site of her first appearance. This information was reportedly conveyed on 4 September 1981 and apparently forms one of the seers' ten secrets.[64] Each seer has said that the sign will be visible and permanent but that its precise nature and the date of its appearance cannot now be revealed.[65] Mary told them that the sign is for atheists, because "you faithful already have signs and you must become the signs for atheists."[66] In several public messages the sign is connected with conversion and with a sense of apocalyptic urgency. In the spring of 1983, for example, Mary is reported to have urged the faithful not to wait for the sign before converting and warned that "when the sign comes it will be too late for many."[67]

The end-time scenario within which many devotees of Medjugorje understand this sign is made clear in a report sent by Vlašić to John Paul II on 2 December 1983.[68] The report was drafted and sent because Marija had told Vlašić that during the apparition on 30 November 1983 the Virgin had told her that the pope and the bishops should be immediately advised "of the urgency and great importance of the message of Medjugorje." In the introduction to this report, Vlašić observed that Mary's appearances at Medjugorje had been frequent and had continued over a long period of time because "these apparitions are the last apparitions of the Blessed Virgin on earth."[69] Vlašić based the body of his report on a conversation with Mirjana that took place on 5 November 1983. Mirjana had told him that she would be a witness to three warnings, in the form of earthly events which would precede the promised sign. She would tell a priest of her choice about each of these events three days beforehand. The visible sign would appear at the site of the apparition after all three of the "warnings" had been realized. The function of the sign here would be twofold: it would stand as a witness to the authenticity of the apparitions, and it would be a call to conversion. The urgency of this call to conversion is highlighted in Vlašić's report by Mirjana's ninth and tenth secrets, which are understood as concerning chastisements for the sins of the world. Vlašić argues that these chastisements are inevitable. Although their severity might be lessened through prayer and penance, one cannot expect them to be eliminated entirely, since one cannot expect the whole world to be converted. The time between the warnings and the sign is thus a time "of grace and conversion," he concludes, but after the sign, "those who are still alive will have little time for conversion."[70]

Although many supporters of the apparition at Medjugorje believe that the events prophesied in the public secrets and the promised sign on the hill Podbrdo will occur, as the seers themselves obviously believe, during the seers' own lifetimes, others think that this is unlikely. They argue that the children's words should be understood as prophetic messages and stress that the children themselves are not necessarily the best interpreters of the prophecies they are mediating. Such an approach to understanding the children's messages is usually accompanied by a deemphasis of their apocalyptic urgency and a reaffirmation of the teaching office of the Roman Catholic Church. Dr. Frane Franić, archbishop metropolitan of Split, Yugoslavia, for example, has said that the children do not understand many of the things they say because they have not studied theology and have no grasp of exegesis or hermeneutics. He has compared their statements to those of the biblical prophets, who, he notes, spoke about many things that they incompletely understood. The children's prediction that the special sign was near at hand might be best understood in relationship to St. Paul's language suggesting the imminence of the Second Coming (parousia) of Christ. Franić argues that "near" could mean five thousand years and that down through the centuries many have been mistaken about the "nearness" of the Second Coming. Apparently referring to trained theologians, those to whom the teaching authority of the Church has been entrusted, he stresses that "we are here to explain all their expressions about the words, messages, signs and so on" and calls for a special method of interpretation that would avoid both fanaticism and rationalization.[71]

The continuation of the Medjugorje apparition into its eighth year combined with what might seem to be a delay in the revelation of the secrets concerning world history, has led some persons who were once swept up in a sense of eschatological urgency to adopt more moderate views in which the apocalyptic emphasis has given way to an emphasis on one or more elements of traditional Catholic teaching. Vlašić, for example, has now said that it is a mistake to understand the messages only in terms of dramatic apocalyptic upheavals; that these messages are rather an invitation for people "to gather together in love, with humility, joy and hope."[72] This suggests that Vlašić's position is now essentially in accord with the position of Laurentin, who with Rupčić had showed some sympathy with Vlašić's earlier, more apocalyptic ideas, and also with that of Fr. Slavko Barbarić. Barbarić, a psychologist who has worked closely with the visionaries, has recently compared Mary's role in the apparitions to that of a mother crying "Fire!" when she sees a burning house. Neither, he notes, comes simply to announce a catastrophe but rather to help avoid one.[73] Without denying that the apparitions are genuine and that they address a crisis of global proportions, these persons have now come to emphasize what Laurentin calls "an evangelical message," a call to prayer and penance.[74]

Secrets and the Negotiation of Authority

The study of secrets, only parts of which, presumably, have been made public and the full contents of which, presumably, are known only to the apparition seers, brings into rather sharp focus the various interests that are represented in modern Marian apparitions and the various authorities that compete to define their meaning. This study suggests that the seer or (assuming a believer's perspective) the Virgin often has considerably less influence in defining an apparition's meaning than one might suppose. It also suggests that the authority to interpret the seer's secrets—which is to say, the Virgin's revelations—is to a considerable extent the authority to determine the meaning of the apparition as a whole and that this authority is essentially a matter of negotiation between the major parties or figures associated with the apparition. The seers, Church officials, the devotees, and of course the Virgin herself as understood by these persons, all take part in the negotiation, which in recent apparitions has moved increasingly into the public arena and has begun to become an important aspect of the apparition itself. A brief review of how the drama of the modern public serial apparition has developed, as sketched in this and in the two preceding chapters, with the phenomenon of secrets moving from the wings onto center stage, will demonstrate this interesting development in the negotiation of authority.

La Salette is important for an understanding of modern Marian apparitions involving secrets insofar as here a single private experience of the seers has set the stage for the understanding of secrets and the expectations attached to them in virtually all of the apparitions which followed. It was here that two types of apparition secrets were clearly defined: (1) personal secrets, which were understood to concern matters of importance for the seers themselves and for no one else; and (2) public secrets, which were understood to concern matters of importance for the future of the Church and of the world. In the public apparitions which followed La Salette, the first of these meanings took hold when the public messages came to be understood as devotional and as lacking in prophetic content. The second of these meanings came into play, however, when the public messages of an apparition were understood as prophetic; devotees came to see the apparition as a source of privileged knowledge; and the apparition began to assume an apocalyptic character. This paradigm, which was clearly expressed at Fatima and which was emphasized and widely publicized in the Fatima literature of the 1940s, has been repeated in the majority of the public serial apparitions of recent decades.

The secrets of the children at La Salette were "discovered" as the children were being questioned by members of the clergy investigating their claims, and stories of the children's ability to withstand attempts to pry these secrets from them were soon in circulation, apparently serving to reinforce belief in the supernatural origin of the children's experiences and in the apparition as such. Similar stories grew up around later apparitions and probably served the same function. With the advent, however, of the public serial apparitions, and especially in the wake of Fatima, the supernatural drama which believers found in stories such as these became something in which they themselves could participate. People present at such an apparition and even those who followed it by word of mouth or in the newspapers could speculate on the meaning of messages or the content of secrets announced early in the course of the apparition, and then, as the apparition progressed, look for signs of their fulfillment. For devotees of many of the post-Fatima apparitions, an announcement in the course of an apparition that confidential material had been conveyed to the seers by the Virgin was made all the more meaningful by the attendant drama of the apparition itself, constructed around such things as the seers' expressive movements or gestures, cries of fear (presumably at visions of hell or coming chastisements), and proclamations suggesting a rhythm of danger and salvation (e.g., involving Russia). It is unlikely that persons caught up in such compelling spectacles would understand an announced secret as anything other than a prophecy.

The devotees, the seers, and the Virgin (represented especially by her secrets) were not, however, the only participants in these post-Fatima apparition dramas. Various well known, or at least recognizable, persons often played rather visible parts and sometimes even came to figure in the prophecies, and it is noteworthy that in the more recent apparitions, especially those at Garabandal and Medjugorje, these eminent participants have generally been representatives of the Church. At Garabandal, while no Church officials were publicly involved in the apparition as such, priests and members of religious orders figured prominently in the apparition's conversion and miracle stories, and in the case of Fr. Luis, a Jesuit became the central figure of a prophetic sign which was of great importance for many devotees. Even more significant here, however, is the fact that in the prophetic scenario of the "great sign" described by Conchita, presumably speaking for the Virgin, it was said that the pope would be among the sign's privileged viewers. Many believed that Conchita, in a visit to Rome, had shared with Pope Paul VI her privileged knowledge (or secret) of the date of "the great miracle."

At Medjugorje, the schema of secrets and prophecies has grown more complex than at Garabandal, and it has also, certainly, been amenable to apocalyptic interpretation. In most of the literature on Medjugorje, however, this schema has been softened and spiritualized in such a way as now to cause few problems for either governmental or ecclesiastical authorities, reflecting the remarkable extent to which theologians and other Church officials have both accepted the phenomenon and taken over the task of interpreting it. Indeed, they have now become a part of the apparition event itself.

At Medjugorje, the ten secrets that the seers say they are in the course of receiving from the Virgin have clearly given a structure to the apparition as such. As the years have passed, more and more of the seers have come close to receiving their quota of secrets, and it is commonly believed that when the last secret has been given to the seer, the apparition will end. Many devotees have understood this structure of gradual revelation in an apocalyptic light. Important in this connection are Mirjana's dramatic pronouncements that, according to the Virgin, the twenti-eth century is a period of testing, that chastisements are coming, and that the Virgin's prolonged appearances at Medjugorje will be her last appearances on earth. These devotees believe that when the last of the seers has received the last of his or her secrets, a sequence of dire events, presumably described in these secret revelations, will begin to unfold. The Virgin did, however, according to Mirjana, arrange for a priest to supervise the announcement of the secrets entrusted to her. One might even say that the Franciscan supporters of the children have kept a mea-sure of control over the apocalypticism of Medjugorje by confining all announcements and messages to well-ordered devotional settings. The apocalyptic potential of the end of the apparition and of the events that will presumably follow it has been tempered, moreover, by the Virgin's directive, delivered through Marija, that the pope and the bishops be advised of the most important of the messages.

The extent to which even some well known Catholic theologians have been willing to accede to a mellowed apocalypticism built around the messages and secrets at Medjugorje is remarkable. For the most part, however, these persons have become less and less sure that the forth-coming trials presumably described in the secrets can or should be un-derstood literally, their initial eschatological enthusiasm giving way to a more general sense of urgency or intensity, channelled especially into pastoral admonitions to pray and do penance. Certainly Roman Cath-olic authorities have not yet reached a consensus about what ought to be said and done about Medjugorje; there were, for example, some spir-ited disagreements on the subject in the more informal moments of the International Mariological Congress at Kevelaer, West Germany, in September 1987. The ability of theologians such as René Laurentin and Michael O'Carroll, however, to live with, and indeed to find positive pastoral meaning in, the seers' presumably apocalyptic secrets appears to have had an effect on Catholic leaders who were originally skeptical of Medjugorje. This may also be an indication that in the negotiations of authority with respect to this apparition—negotiations that have been, for the most part, quite public—persons who are reasonably com-fortable with existing Roman Catholic structures and who have become a part of the apparition event, in the sense that they direct and support its pilgrimages and associated retreats and circulate the messages that issue from it, may be taking control and may eventually succeed in hav-ing the apparition officially recognized.

Whatever the officials at the Vatican may eventually decide about Medjugorje, it can be predicted that many people will continue for many years through various kinds of efforts to reconcile and integrate the messages and secrets of the Medjugorje seers with the doctrine of the Roman Catholic Church. If, as seems likely, a decision is made before all of the seers have died, and if this decision is positive, some persons, no doubt, will follow the lead of the nineteenth-century prelates who argued with respect to La Salette that with the recognition of the apparition by the Church, the mission of the seers was ended. Others, however, particularly if any of the seers should continue to have visions or auditions, will undoubtedly follow the lead of the Melanists and will regard the seers as still retaining the mission entrusted to them by the Virgin, along with the authority this seems to entail. Efforts may be made by these persons to arrange meetings between the seers and the pope so that the latter may be instructed concerning the Virgin's will. It is likely that the discussion and debate over the importance and content of the secrets conveyed in Marian apparitions will continue as well, since these secrets have in the past proved so important, both for the simple believers who understand apparitions as sources of privileged knowledge and for the persons involved in the negotiations of authority which seem to be necessary whenever and wherever such an understanding arises.

CHAPTER 7

The Fundamentals of Modern Apparition Worldviews

Messages from the Heavenly Mother: The Popular Apocalyptic Ideology of Apparitions

THE APPARITIONS of the Virgin Mary reported in the last two centuries have been focal points of significant religious experiences like some of those described in the first part of this study for vast numbers of modern Roman Catholics who have made pilgrimages to the sites of these apparitions. It is as if these persons have been able to transcend time and to enter into the experiences and meanings which first drew attention to these sites, encountering Mary for themselves in ways which reflect and build on these earlier experiences and meanings. As the second part of this study has shown, however, the immediacy of the initial religious experiences and the personal meanings attached to these experiences by the seers and by other early participants in these apparition dramas have usually been understood in terms of some much more comprehensive structures of meaning. The worldviews that have grown up around modern Marian apparitions, a few of which have already been sketched in the second part of this study, are in themselves phenomena of considerable importance, and it is appropriate that this study conclude with a brief discussion of the basic elements of these worldviews and some of the typical forms in which they appear.

Before beginning this discussion, it should perhaps be reemphasized that the Roman Catholic Church allows for a considerable variety of views with respect to apparitions. Because belief in even the most credible of apparitions is considered in Roman Catholicism a matter of human faith, and the revelation that may be involved, a nonbinding private revelation, some Roman Catholics might hold that the Virgin, since her death and Assumption, has never appeared on earth or given messages to anyone. Others would carefully restrict the scope of their belief and interest in her appearances and revelations to apparitions recognized by Church authorities. And still others, aware that the Church has made no judgment on most apparitions and believing that some negative judgments that have been issued are not necessarily irreversible, hold that in the more recent and as yet unrecognized apparitions the Virgin has delivered messages which have reaffirmed and expanded on messages delivered in the earlier recognized apparitions. It is with the views of persons in the third of these categories that this discussion will be primarily concerned.

Most apparition devotees have understood recent Marian apparitions as part of a pattern of divine activity in the "last days" immediately preceding the Second Coming of Christ. They have seen connections between various apparitions and between these apparitions and other religious and secular events of recent times, and they have found keys to an understanding of the contemporary world situation and of history in general in these visitations of Mary and in the messages and secrets associated with them. History as they see it is an all-encompassing divine plan in which the Virgin, appearing on earth in the last days, has been assigned a very special role.

The simplest versions of this divine plan appear in the writings of Roman Catholic authors concerned only with the Marian apparitions recognized by the Church, many of whom have organized their thinking around the image of the woman "clothed with the sun" in the twelfth chapter of the book of Revelation. Typical here is John Beevers's book, *The Sun Her Mantle*. While Beevers, whose worldview has been constructed chiefly out of biblical materials and the messages of La Salette and Fatima, does not think we can be certain that these are literally the last days of the world, he portrays the present age as in great trouble and suggests that unimaginable horror may lie only a short time ahead. For more than a century now, he says, the Virgin has been intervening with weeping, exhortation, pleading, threatening, and miracles, to turn people away from their folly and wickedness and to urge them to pray and do penance. Especially crucial for Beevers is what he understands as the choice presently confronting people between that which will bring joy now and forever and that which will merit punishment now and forever.[1]

Most supporters of the nonrecognized apparitions would have little to argue with here. They would, however, put more emphasis than

Beevers on the crisis that they see as threatening the world in our time, and they would not be satisfied with Beevers's portrayal of this crisis only in terms drawn from the Bible and from the apparitions recognized by the Church. The messages of other later apparitions, such as Garabandal, San Damiano, and Medjugorje, would for them be an indispensable explication of the messages of La Salette and Fatima, and the apocalyptic worldviews to which most of these persons are committed usually lay out the divine plan for the final age of the world in considerable detail. These worldviews, however, typically retain some elements of Catholic sacramentalism, and do not, as a rule, lead to the kinds of inflexible literalism and sectarianism that characterize some forms of Protestant apocalypticism.

In fact, something like a single, transcultural, apocalyptic ideology based on apparition messages has grown up in recent years around the edges of mainline Roman Catholic institutions which incorporates the messages of various apparitions and to which the majority of supporters of the more recent unrecognized apparitions could be said to subscribe. This ideology is a sort of popular, free-floating apocalyptic worldview, built out of images and themes prominent in the messages of the more recent apparitions and can be seen as anchored in almost any one, or any combination of, these apparitions. To judge from the immense amount of apparition literature published in recent years in various languages which propagates one form or another of this popular apocalyptic ideology or worldview, the themes and images which define this phenomenon merit some attention.

Fundamental to this worldview are the images of intercession and intervention. It is assumed here that a divinely appointed figure may, on the heavenly plane, intercede with God or Christ, and on the earthly plane, intervene in history to change an otherwise predetermined course of events. Most modern apparition devotees assume that the Virgin Mary has been appointed by God as the chief executor of both of these tasks, although she may, on occasion, enlist other heavenly or human figures to assist with her interventions in earthly life. Intercession, as it is understood here, usually involves a dramatic interaction between God, who in the persons of the Father and the Son represents the divine law, and the Virgin, who represents divine mercy.

In this schema, God is portrayed as angry with the world because the sins of humanity have overturned or disrupted the established order, and indeed, he is portrayed as so angry that his justice demands immediate chastisement. At La Salette, according to Mélanie and Maximin, the Virgin told them that the arm of her son was "so heavy and pressing" that she could no longer restrain it, that only her unceasing entreaties had thus far held back the chastisement, and that people would never be able to repay her for this. In the Fatima messages, the image of an offended God is especially marked in the second part of the so-called secret. Mary told the young seers in 1917, Lucia reported many years later, that if people did not stop offending God, another war greater than the current one would begin in the reign of Pius XI. "When you see a night illumined by an unknown light, know that this is the great sign given you by God that he is about to punish the world for its crimes by means of war, famine, and persecutions of the Church and of the Holy Father."[2] Of the messages reported in the major post–World War II apparitions, it is those of San Damiano in which the image of an offended God is most striking. The Heavenly Mama told her in 1969, Rosa said, that the "Eternal Father" was "tired of my children down here" and wanted to show his power in the world. The following year, the Heavenly Mama warned her, "The Eternal Father wants to do Justice! I repeat it: Why do you not reflect? Why do you not examine your conscience?"[3]

In this worldview and in the apparition messages on which it is based, God is portrayed as most offended by sins of a particular kind. In the La Salette messages, the sins which were said to be particularly offensive to Mary's son were working on Sunday, swearing in her son's name, neglecting to attend Mass, mocking religion, and eating meat during Lent—all transgressions against a ritually defined sacred order. In the Fatima messages too, the epitome of sin and evil is a kind of violation of such a sacred order. In the warning about Russia in the second part of the secret, the great calamity threatening the world is seen as the spread of atheism, i.e., the collapse of the ritual of confession of faith in God. There is also offered here, however, a prescribed ritual which would restore something of the sacred order. According to Lucia, the Virgin told her that she had come to ask for the consecration of Russia to her Immaculate Heart and the Communion of Reparation on the First Saturdays. If her requests were heeded, Russia would be converted and there would be peace.

Russia and the sin of atheism also figure prominently in the messages associated with the current series of apparitions at Medjugorje. Speaking of the visible sign that she promised to leave at Medjugorje, the

Virgin is reported to have said, "This sign will be given for the atheists. You faithful already have signs, and you have to become the signs for the atheists."[4] In the Medjugorje messages, however, in contrast to those at Fatima, atheism is understood more in a practical than in a purely theoretical sense, and the converted Russia of the future is portrayed as spiritually superior to the nations of the West. Mary is reported to have told Marija Pavlović in October 1981 that "Russia is the people where God will be most glorified. The West has advanced civilization but without God, as though it were its own creator."[5]

War, famine, persecution, catastrophic illness, and other calamities are in this worldview understood as both chastisements for sin and admonitions to reform or conversion. At La Salette Mary reportedly told the seers that the failure of the potato crop had been a warning about their sins; because they had not heeded her warning, however, they faced famine and disease. At Fatima, the Virgin warned in the second part of Lucia's secret of the imminent threat of war, hunger, and persecution of the Church. At Garabandal, according to the seers, the Virgin warned that people needed to lead good lives, and that if they did not, a chastisement would be forthcoming.

Future chastisements are not, however, seen in this worldview as inevitable. Indeed, the major purpose of the Virgin's latter-day appearances is to give the world a last opportunity to restore the disrupted sacred order and the divine-human relationship which this order represents—through repentance or conversion, a return to appropriate devotional practices, and submission to the ordinances of the Church. At La Salette the Virgin reportedly urged the seers to say their prayers at night and in the morning, saying at least an "Our Father" and a "Hail Mary," and told them that a general conversion would bring general abundance: the rocks would become piles of wheat, and the potatoes would appear to have sown themselves. In the messages of Garabandal, Mary exhorted people to take part in the Eucharist, and at San Damiano, according to Rosa, she particularly emphasized the Rosary. "Take the rosary in your hands," the Virgin told Rosa, "and you will win every battle."[6] And at Medjugorje, according to the young seers, Mary said explicitly that war could be averted by fasting and prayer. She identified herself as the Queen of Peace and stressed that people could be reconciled to God and to each other through faith, prayer, fasting, and confession.[7]

In the messages of the more recent apparitions, particularly in the context of the devotee's question of why she has been appearing so often in recent times, Mary's motherly qualities have been especially emphasized. In most of these apparitions, there have been messages suggesting that it is a mother who is best able to rescue her children from impending disaster. At Garabandal the Virgin was pictured by the young seers basically as a mother concerned to educate her children in moral and spiritual matters. In the four years of their visions she reportedly taught the girls how to pray and told them to add the phrase "and our Mother" to the petition "Holy Mary, Mother of God, pray for us. . . ."[8] Conchita, then, reported on 18 June 1965 that the Virgin had said that the last warnings were being given, that she loved them very much, and that it was as a mother that she had come to ask people to amend their lives.

In the messages of San Damiano, Mary's motherhood and the theme of mother as savior are emphasized even more than in the Garabandal messages. "The Father, the Son, and the Holy Spirit," the Virgin told Rosa, "will lead the Mother of all people across the earth, because she wishes to save her children, those she loves so much with such a great love."[9] Indeed, in these messages Mary's motherly love is understood as so special that those who reject it are seen as beyond hope. "I will come in triumph. I will come to give light to all souls," Mary told Rosa. "But it will be too late for those who do not understand the love of a mother! They will be in the midst of a terrible trial! Heaven and earth will be unleashed, and they will not be able to lift up their eyes to Heaven and plead for pity."[10]

These themes, so prominent in the messages of the later apparitions, of Mary as mother and mother as savior in the last days are the central and unifying themes of the free-floating apocalyptic worldview that comes to expression in the more popular apparition literature. While the basic concepts and images of this worldview have now been sketched, there are some less popular, more formal, and more sophisticated constructions built around apparitions and apparition messages that also deserve our attention. It is interesting to note that these more elaborate and self-conscious constructions are grounded in some of the same themes and images as their more popular counterparts.

History as Divine Plan: Modern Conceptions of a Marian Age

Most of the more formal and sophisticated attempts of recent years to build comprehensive structures of meaning around apparitions and apparition messages rely, often quite explicitly, on the theories of a seventeenth-century Marian devotee, St. Louis-Marie Grignion de Montfort (1673–1716), who founded two strongly Marian religious orders, the Montfort Fathers and the Daughters of Wisdom. In his work *The True Devotion to Mary*, which was only discovered in the nineteenth century, Montfort reasoned that because Mary had hardly appeared in public at all in the first coming of Christ, in the Second Coming "Mary has to be made known and revealed by the Holy Ghost in order that, through her, Jesus Christ may be known, loved and served."[11] Montfort, who understood Mary as the most formidable of all the figures which God had appointed to oppose the Devil, suggested, therefore, that the power of Mary will especially shine forth in the latter times, when Satan will lay his snares for "her heel," the latter being "her humble slaves and poor children" whom she will raise up to make war against him.[12] Montfort's idea of the last period or age of the world as an age of Mary, which would be peculiarly characterized by Mary's interventions in history, has been the basis in recent years for a number of interpretations of recent events as evidence of the dawning of a Marian age. The three modern conceptions of a Marian age which will be sketched here will illustrate the range and the more significant types of these interpretations.

Johannes Maria Höcht, whose book *Fatima und Pius XII* appeared in 1952, believed that the age of Mary had begun with the Rue du Bac apparition in 1830 and was moving toward its culmination. While he was not sure that the times in which he was writing were literally the last days, he did believe that a catastrophe of immense proportions was pending. The world was confronted, he believed, with a choice between a third world war and peace, and it was only by a wholehearted trust in the Virgin Mary that the disaster of war could be averted. Mary, who in a very special way had shared in her son's victory over sin and death, had been active, according to Höcht, in the course of history as a "victorious helper" and a "bringer of peace."[13] He believed, moreover, that historical events had a symbolic quality through which the divine plan could be perceived, and he was convinced that a person's search through history for events that exhibited Mary's victories would give rise to faith in Mary and so give birth to the victory of Christ in the depths of the soul.

Höcht found the basis for his study of the Marian dimension of history in Engelbert Zeitler's *Die Herz-Maria-Weltweihe*, an exhaustive explication of the symbolism of Pius XII's consecration of the world on 31 October 1942 to Mary's Immaculate Heart. Höcht cited Zeitler throughout his own book in support of his ideas, but he was particularly indebted to Zeitler on two specific counts.

Zeitler believed that the most decisive victories in the history of the Church had been achieved on Marian festivals through personal appeals for Mary's assistance, and Höcht made this idea into a principle for the interpretation of history. For Höcht, the liturgical feast on or near which an important event took place usually suggested the quality of the divine intervention which that event manifested. Höcht, however, was most concerned with events in and around the Second World War, and the way he interpreted these events made it clear that, for him, divine intervention usually meant the intervention of Mary.

In the years just before the tide of the war turned in favor of the Allies, Höcht perceived several important Marian interventions. The bombing of Pearl Harbor, he noted, took place on 6 December 1941, and the United States entered the war in the Pacific two days later, on December 8. In Europe, at almost the same time, Hitler had been defeated on the Russian front and had to retreat—on December 7. As Höcht saw it, both of these events took place on the eve of December 8, the Feast of the Immaculate Conception, which celebrated Mary's victory over sin and Satan. Höcht saw even more significance in the date of the entry of the United States into the Pacific war, for about a hundred years before then, he observed, on 8 December 1846, the United States had been "consecrated to the Mother of God."[14]

The turning point of the war in Europe was, according to Höcht, Pius XII's consecration of the world to Mary's Immaculate Heart on 31 October 1942. He noted that the Allied fleet had set sail on the previous evening, and that almost all major Allied victories after this took place on Marian festivals. Sicily had been liberated on 15 August 1943, the Feast of the Assumption, and Italy had surrendered on 8 September 1943, the Feast of Mary's Birth. Höcht also saw these festivals as significant in the Pacific theater, for the Japanese surrendered, he observed, on 15 August 1945 and signed a formal pact pertaining to their surrender in San Francisco six years later on 8 September 1951.[15]

Zeitler's work was also important for Höcht for its mediation and interpretation of Montfort's idea of the eschatological character of Mary's participation in salvation history. Zeitler held that the progressive revelation of the Mystery of Christ in the Church was accompanied by a progressive revelation of the Marian modality of redemption and it was this revelation, according to Höcht, which reached its climax in Pius XII's consecration of the world to Mary's Immaculate Heart. This act, as Höcht saw it, was universal in a very special sense, the pope exercising here the full power of his office in such a way as to bring the whole of humanity into his consecration. Both Höcht and Zeitler saw this act of the pope as a climactic victory for redemption in an accelerating dialectical struggle: the more the world was menaced by the powers of hell, they believed, the more clearly Jesus and Mary would manifest their loving and redeeming will, symbolized by the heart. They both saw Pius XII's act of consecration as a completion of Leo XIII's earlier dedication of the world to the Sacred Heart of Jesus, bringing to a humanity on the brink of disaster a new revelation of God's saving and loving will.[16]

Höcht understood Pius XII's several Marian pronouncements, including this act of consecration, to be "in the spirit of Fatima," and he agreed with those who were calling Pius XII "the Pope of Fatima." He believed, moreover, that an "epoch of Fatima" had been inaugurated by the four visions of the Virgin which, accompanied by sun miracles, were said to have been experienced by Pius XII in late October and early November of 1950.[17]

The Virgin's warning, through Lucia, about Russia, was important, Höcht thought, but he held to the hope that Bolshevism would fail. The first great heresy of the century, he believed, had been the national dictatorship and racial hatred that was manifested especially in Germany under National Socialism. That heresy had been defeated under the sign of Mary, however, and he expected Bolshevism to meet the same fate. Höcht applauded the unprecedented expression of concern represented by Pius XII's message to the Russian people, published on 7 July 1952 and transmitted in Russian on Vatican Radio on July 25, and he was gratified by the enthusiastic response to the European tour of the Pilgrim Statue of Fatima. But while Höcht certainly saw these external acts as important, just as important, he insisted, were the Virgin's call for inner conversion and her promise that her Immaculate Heart would triumph, for here, he thought, was the means through which the victory of the West could finally be achieved.[18]

Höcht was not interested in laying out in detail a schedule of final events, and he was not concerned with Marian apparitions and their messages in the sort of detailed, analytic way that has often been characteristic of apparition devotees. He was, rather, concerned with the religious character of the present age, which he understood, particularly through the Fatima messages, as an age of spiritual transformation and renewal, symbolized the Immaculate Heart of Mary and the Sacred Heart of Jesus. Höcht believed that the present age of Mary would be followed by an age of Jesus. What was needed in a world facing dire crisis was the victory of Christ through Mary, a victory that could be achieved, he thought, through a "mountain-moving faith in Mary" such as could be seen at Fatima and in the Pope of Fatima, Pius XII.[19]

Albert Marty, like Höcht, was convinced that the world of the late 1950s was in a perilous state, but unlike Höcht, he put considerable emphasis on prophecy as a means provided by God for understanding the course of human events. In *Le monde de demain vu par les prophètes d'aujourd'hui* (1957), Marty collected prophecies from a number of nineteenth- and twentieth-century seers, most but not all of whom were associated with Marian apparitions, e.g. Mélanie Calvat, Maximin Giraud, Martin Drexler, Sister Josefa Mendenes, Barbara Reuss, Berte Petit, Padre Pio, and Pope Pius XI. He organized these prophecies chronologically and commented on the symbols or sequences of events reported in the various messages. In *Alerte au monde* (1959), Marty focused especially on the figures of the Great Monarch and Great Pope and on a conflict between East and West which he believed these prophecies foretold.

As can be seen especially in his book *Balestrino* (1971), which was an apology for the apparition of the Virgin reported at that Italian site by Catherine Richero beginning in 1949, Marty saw Marian apparitions not only as particularly important forms of prophecy but also as "interventions" of the Virgin in history. He argued in this book that Mary was playing a special role in bringing about her Son's earthly kingdom, and that her many appearances in the past two centuries were signs that these were indeed the last times.

Marty saw the world of the twentieth century as denying the supernatural to an unprecedented extent. All human attempts to heal this sick world had failed, he observed, and unbelief and infidelity were more widespread than ever. It was necessary in this desperate situation, of course, for people to seek God, but God himself, Marty noted, had for centuries been sending his prophets to revive people's flagging faith, and Jesus and Mary were not to be understood apart from these prophets. Jesus was the Good Shepherd who sought his lost sheep, and Mary, "his most ardent, most loving, most effective collaborator."[20] The apparitions of the last two centuries had been warnings, according to Marty, that divine justice had to be satisfied, and at Fatima the Virgin had made it clear what would happen if these warnings were ignored. But these apparitions were also a last call to eternal salvation, through prayer, penitence, and reparation.

It was Mary's motherhood that for Marty particularly dictated her efforts to restore straying humanity to God. Some of the things which spiritual writers of earlier centuries had said about the Virgin's motherhood were used by Marty as a basis for explaining the many reported apparitions of Mary in the past two centuries. Particularly important is his citation of the three reasons given by St. Alphonsus Ligouri (1696–1787) for the immensity of Mary's love for humanity. First: the commandment that whoever loves God must also love the neighbor, in effect, brings together the two loves, so that as the one increases, so does the other—with the implication that Mary's surpassing love for God is necessarily matched by a surpassing love for humanity. Second: mothers love most tenderly those children whose well-being has cost them dearly, and thus human beings are exceedingly dear children to Mary because they have cost her exceedingly great suffering. And third: the blood of Mary's son was poured out for the salvation of humanity, and thus for Mary to love humanity is part of the esteem in which she holds the sacrifice of Jesus. Marty insisted that a mother who thus loves her children would not ignore them in so perilous a time as this. He agreed with Fathers Pel and Jean Curtet (and Rosa Quattrini) that if Mary were not involved with her children in such dangerous times, she would not properly be a mother or a "mama," and he believed that it was the extraordinary situation of the world of the present day which had made necessary the extraordinary number of recent visits from the "heavenly Mama."[21]

These numerous appearances were a sign to Marty that the end-time had indeed come. In explaining this conclusion, Marty cited Grignion de Montfort's conviction that "it is by the Very Holy Virgin Mary that Jesus has come to the world and it is also by her that he ought to reign in the world," and he then quoted the section from *The True Devotion to Mary* where Montfort gave seven reasons why, in the Second Coming of Jesus, "Mary has to be made known and revealed by the Holy Ghost so that through her Jesus Christ may be known, loved, and served."[22]

Especially important to Marty was Montfort's conviction (the last of the seven reasons) that in the last days, the devil, knowing his time was short, would increase his efforts to destroy souls by instigating persecutions and placing snares before the true children of Mary, and that she would appear "as terrible as an army ranged in battle" against him and his crew. Marty found confirmation of his belief that this was indeed a portrayal of the present age in the messages of some recent apparitions. He noted, for example, Rosa Quattrini's reported communication from the Virgin on 10 November 1967 that "the devil is ravaging souls . . . this is a most terrible moment, for the devil wants to make carnage." Nonetheless, Marty believed, the outcome of the battle between Mary and Satan was not in doubt, for centuries of prophecies had maintained that Mary would be victorious.[23]

If, as Marty believed, the recent apparitions were a final call to salvation and an important part of Mary's struggle with Satan, it was crucial to disseminate the messages received by the seers of these apparitions. Marty was convinced, however, that Mary's many recent interventions added nothing to Catholic doctrine. These interventions were, for Marty, of the order of reminders; they evinced her concern "that the sacrifice of her Son not be rendered useless by the negligence or bad will of men."[24] They were to remind people that God was their most efficacious helper and only hope for peace, and that there was an urgent need for prayer, penitence, and love of neighbor.

Because Mary was issuing what Marty considered an orthodox and necessary call to salvation, he was particularly bitter that Roman Catholic authorities had forbidden the publication of the messages of some of the more recent apparitions. While many laity had heard these messages and thousands were making pilgrimages to the apparition sites, Marty lamented that a majority of the clergy were ignoring or trying to discredit these apparitions, and he suggested that the Church was being imprudent in attempting to suppress these "messages from heaven." The opponents of these apparitions would bear a great burden of responsibility, he believed, if indeed this was the age of Marian intervention which would immediately precede Christ's Second Coming.[25]

One of the few authors of recent years to understand apparitions as placing the Second Vatican Council in a positive light is Raoul Auclair. In his defense of the apparitions of the Virgin reported at Amsterdam from 1945 through 1959 by Ida Peederman (who was about forty at the time of her first experience), Auclair argues that the messages reported at Amsterdam continue and develop the eschatological "landmarks" of La Salette, Pontmain, Fatima, and Beauraing.[26] These messages reported by Ida contain warnings of chastisements, but they also speak of a "new era" that will bring the Holy Spirit on earth to all peoples. Auclair associates this new era with the Second Vatican Council, seeing in the Council the first sign that the divine plan described in Ida's visions is about to be accomplished. On 11 February 1951, for example, Ida said she saw the pope on the portico of a cathedral, with cardinals and bishops filling the nave. She said she was told by the Virgin, "These are the bishops of all countries. The doctrine is good, but the laws could and should be changed."[27] It was necessary, the Virgin continued, to walk with the times. New structures needed to be introduced among religious, seminarians, and laity. There might be a shortage of priests, she said, but there was still the laity, and an effort should be made to mobilize them. Rome was being offered an opportunity to save the whole world. Auclair understood John XXIII's unexpected decision in the first year of his pontificate to call an ecumenical council as the seizing of this opportunity to "usher in the new era."[28]

Writing not long after the Council had ended, Auclair tried to walk a middle course in the struggle over change. He saw the Roman Catholic Church being menaced both by those who were frenetic for reform, whom he described as motivated by a "bad spirit," and by the overly narrow traditionalists who were unwilling to allow the Holy Spirit to change the structures of the Church. The pope, he said, who should be above and beyond these quarrels, should be reassured by the messages of the Virgin, who had promised to help both the pope and the Church.[29]

Auclair understood the Council's definition of Mary as Mother of the Church as its most important action. He saw the "new era" announced in the messages as one in which all people would be gathered into one flock, and he understood Mary as the only one who could give birth to such a unified "Mystical Body." This idea too he saw reflected in one of the messages reported by Ida: "The Lord and Master wants to carry spiritual unity to the people of this world. This is why he sends Myriam, or Mary, and he sends her as the 'Lady of all Peoples.' "[30]

But Auclair thought the Church needed to go further than it had yet gone. In these last days, with the forces of Satan gathering to do battle with Mary and her followers, it was time, Auclair said (basically only repeating what Ida said the Virgin had told her), for the Church to proclaim her, as she had asked, "Co-redemptrix, Mediatrix, and Advocate." When Ida had been asked why this was necessary, she had said it was because the Lord and Creator had sent Mary as the Lady of All Peoples, along with a special prayer, "to preserve the world from a universal disaster."[31] Auclair understood this as a basic "condition of salvation" found in the Scriptures: the victorious woman promised in Genesis would appear and be crowned in the days spoken of in the Apocalypse. In his comments on this biblical and historical symmetry, Auclair built on the theme of the contrast between Eve and Mary that had been a favorite of many early Christian writers. As Eve had led Adam into sin, so the New Eve (Mary) had opened the way for redemption by the New Adam. And since it was by Mary, the Virgin Mother, that Jesus had come at Christmas, so it would be by Mary, Mother of the Church, that Christ the King would come at the final Epiphany in order to reign over all the people.[32]

Like the messages of many other apparitions, those reported at Amsterdam emphasized the sacraments, and especially the Eucharist, as the means for maintaining order in the face of threatening calamity. Ida said that in 1957 the Virgin had told her that Jesus had given people a great mystery, "the great miracle each day, each hour, each minute: He had given himself."[33] It was not simply "an idea," but Christ himself under the form of bread and wine. Two years later, Ida said, the Virgin told her that the clergy should be placed on guard against false ideas, especially about the Eucharist.[34] Auclair saw in both of these messages a warning about the "theological innovations" emanating from the Netherlands at that time that saw in the Eucharist only a sign or a symbol and denied the mystery of transubstantiation. He was thinking, apparently, of the works of Edward Schillebeeckx, some of whose writings were intensely criticized by Dutch traditionalists and were eventually censured by Rome as well. Auclair applauded what he saw as the lifting of restrictions limiting access to the Eucharist. He approved, for example, the 1951 decision of Pius XII to mitigate the eucharistic fast. Such steps were essential, he believed, not simply for individual welfare but for the corporate welfare of the Church. The few who would remain faithful at the time of the great Apostasy, he thought, should be encouraged to receive all the spiritual nourishment necessary for the survival of the Mystical Body.[35]

For Auclair, the message of the "Lady of All Peoples" was an urgent one, but he did not want it to be used as an excuse for impulsive or ill-considered actions. History was sealed, he believed, and the seals would be opened one by one. The first seal to be opened was the Council, and the rest would be opened in time. Auclair understood all that had happened in and around the Second Vatican Council as a confirmation of what had been revealed in the messages reported by Ida Peederman at Amsterdam. While Mary had indeed warned in those messages about the perils of the journey that lay ahead and about the "artifices of seduction," the main point of her communications, Auclair concluded, was the "great embracing of the Universal Pentecost" that Mary said she was charged to announce.[36]

History as Conspiracy: Necedah and Its Later Development

While devotees of most recent Marian apparitions have seen history as a divine plan in which the Virgin appears on earth in the last times to warn of coming chastisements, the Virgin's return has not always been interpreted as a triumph over the enemies of God, nor the last days as a Marian age in which this triumph is realized. Indeed, the evils that apocalyptic thinkers anticipate in the last times have sometimes assumed such a dominant role in the worldview of apparition devotees that the divine forces at work in the world are pictured in a defensive posture, and history is viewed not so much as a divine plan as an evil conspiracy, with the Virgin engaged in a sort of holding action to ward off the threatening destruction.

A movement from simple messages urging a return to traditional lines of devotion in order to forestall impending punishments to a fully developed theory of a worldwide demonically inspired conspiracy against God and God's people can be seen in the history of the apparition reported by Mary Ann Van Hoof at Necedah, Wisconsin. Mary Ann, a forty-one-year old farm wife, announced in the spring of 1950 that the Virgin Mary had appeared to her, had recommended a specific set of devotions for her, her family, and the community, and had told her she would appear to her again on several forthcoming religious festivals. Public interest in her experiences grew, and on the Feast of the Assumption, 15 August 1950, an estimated 100,000 people gathered around the seer in Necedah in what a state trooper called "the largest gathering in rural Wisconsin history."[37] While Mary Ann quickly attracted a tightly knit group of lay supporters who understood her continuing visions as divine revelations, Roman Catholic authorities became increasingly convinced, as the apparition progressed, that it was not of divine origin. The local bishop, after an investigation, formally condemned the apparition in 1955, and his successor issued interdicts against Mary Ann and her followers in 1970 and 1975. Mary Ann's visions, however, apparently continued until her death in 1984, and there are a number of people today, many with ties to the "For My God and My Country" organization at Necedah, who remain convinced of the apparition's authenticity.[38]

During the first year of her experiences, the messages that Mary Ann said the Virgin had given her to convey to the American people, and particularly to American Catholics, were basically a repetition and an application of the messages of Fatima. On 29 May 1950, for example, Mary Ann said the Virgin instructed her to "tell the children of God to pray the Rosary, to live clean lives, and to make a sacrifice for sinners to show God that they love Him." The Virgin gave her messages for nuns (teaching in parochial schools) and for archbishops, bishops, and priests, and warned her that the enemy of God was creeping all over America and that it was necessary for America to "wake up." "I am warning you people again," the Virgin reportedly said, "as I warned you at Fatima, Lipa [Philippines], and La Salette, of what did happen and will happen. Still, you believe me not and you have no faith in me. You turn your back on me."[39] In this and in other episodes of the apparition in the year 1950, Mary Ann said that the Virgin urged people to pray for the conversion of Russia and to become acquainted with the three apparitions just mentioned, and she remarked that it should not take thirty years for this [Necedah] apparition to be recognized as it had at Fatima.[40]

The message that Mary Ann delivered in her not very polished and not very well organized speech to the thousands of people who had come to Necedah that year on the Feast of the Assumption set forth these same themes. It put more emphasis, however, on the warnings and made these somewhat more specific. The time had come, the Virgin reportedly told her, for people to "pray and pray hard and devotedly." They must remember the Commandments, the Rosary, and the Way of the Cross, for "the Enemy of God is all over America." Mary Ann said the Virgin told her that Catholics could not carry on alone, and that all religions "must work together, not in jealousy and hatred but in love." She warned, however, that "a more horrible time" was coming for America, because the "Enemy behind your so-called Iron Curtain is mighty powerful," indeed, more powerful than America. The Virgin, Mary Ann said, told the laity to pray, do penance, participate in the sacraments, practice special devotions such as the First Saturdays, and obey their priests and bishops; she exhorted priests and bishops to remember and to remind their people of her warnings at Fatima, Lipa, and La Salette. Priests and bishops who neglected this, she said, would be hurting themselves as well as their congregations. Finally, Mary Ann said, the Virgin warned that black clouds were gathering over both North and South America, that Alaska was the first stepping-stone, and that people should "remember the Pacific coast."[41]

Soon, the Virgin's messages reported by Mary Ann from her home at Necedah began to be laced through with the America-under-threat motif that was being articulated in these same years by Wisconsin Senator Joseph McCarthy. In these messages, in fact, McCarthy appears as a sort of American saint, and later, as a martyr.[42] On various occasions, Mary Ann reported that she had been shown the "Brown Bear [i.e., Russian] submarines" along both of America's coasts, and on 20 April 1962, she warned that "baby subs" were coming up the St. Lawrence Seaway.[43] The "Madonna Maria" had also warned her, she said, about food poisoning, water poisoning, chemicals in clothing, food, feed for livestock, soil, and air. These chemicals, she thought, weakened the minds and wills of the American people and made them amenable to the work of evil forces.[44] Among the places which Mary Ann identified as centers for these gathering forces of evil were the United Nations in New York and the Baha'i Temple in Wilmette, Illinois.[45]

It was apparently Henry Swan, one of Mary Ann's early followers and the compiler and editor of her reports of the Virgin's messages, who was responsible for gradually leading the seer and her disciples into a conspiratorial view of history. Swan was particularly concerned about "the destructive forces of Satan" at work in the world, whose leaders he spoke of as "Satan's chain of command." At the top of this chain, according to Swan, were the "Grand Masters," and under them, the "Learned Elders of Zion," a select group of about four hundred people spread throughout the world. These people, he said, were known to each other but not to anyone else, not even to "their own people, the Jews or Yids." These "Learned Elders" were leaders in every field—bankers, industrialists, doctors, lawyers, politicians—who had carefully been brought to positions of great power and influence in every nation, including the United States. Communism and Freemasonry were some of the tools, according to Swan, that these Zionists used to gain their objectives, the most important of which was the creation of a single world-government which they would control. Swan said that the ignorance of American Catholics with respect to Leo XIII's condemnation of Freemasonry and with respect to apparitions of the Virgin had contributed to the power already amassed in the United States by the forces of evil.[46]

Swan denied that his views were anti-Semitic. Just because the forces of Satan were primarily made up of Jews, he said, was no reason to blame all Jews, many of whom had thrown off the yoke of Satan's leadership and were "good, patriotic Americans," some even giving their lives in defense of the United States. These "true Jews," he said, had maintained a strong sense of ethnic identity and had not "mongrelized" their bloodlines by intermarriage, as the "Yids" had done.[47]

It is not clear from Swan's introductions to, and annotations of, Mary Ann's messages just when he first promulgated his theories, and a study of the relationship of Mary Ann and Swan is beyond the scope of this book. It is clear, however, that by the mid-1950s, the revelations of the Virgin which the seer was continuing to report began to reflect some of the theories which Swan himself had more systematically set forth. On 12 April 1957, for example, Mary Ann claimed to know that the "Grand Master" was in the United States and that "something was up among the Yids." There would be a big banquet at 6:00 P.M. that day at the Waldorf Astoria in New York, she said, where the "Grand Master" would be meeting with the "Masters" of other countries.[48] Several years later, on 4 March 1960, she said that the "Grand Masters" had been able to sink their roots in the New World because people had ignored the encyclicals of Pope Leo XIII.[49]

One of the most interesting expressions of Mary Ann's later understanding of the American crisis and how it had developed was her description of the Virgin's alleged appearances and revelations to George Washington. The "Madonna Maria," Mary Ann said, had warned Washington about the future of the nation he had founded and had told him that this nation would have to withstand five great sieges. The first, apparently, was the American Revolution; the second, the Civil War; the third, World War I; and the fourth, World War II. After this, the Virgin reportedly told Washington, there would be a long period of corruption and bloodshed, because people would continue to offend God through the blackest of sin. This would lead to the fifth and most terrible period of all, in which blood would flow all over the globe. There would be "man-powered flying machines" dropping great destruction from the sky, and all nations on earth would be involved. The Virgin also told Washington, according to Mary Ann, about coming racial conflicts, saying that white Christians would battle black and yellow races, whom evil forces had roused against them. This final phase was upon us, Mary

Ann said, and only if people followed the mandates of God and God's Mother could they be saved. It is important to note, however, that Mary Ann said the Virgin had also told Washington that she would help protect his country through each of these five great sieges.[50]

Something of what may lie behind the paranoia that bloomed in Mary Ann's later messages may be detected in one of the earliest which the seer reported. On 30 May 1950, Mary Ann said that the Virgin told her: "You took punishment for others to protect them. You received no love which you longed for in your home. You always worked hard and were honest to your family. Yes, you committed sins, but you have been forgiven for them long ago. At the time of your sins, your surroundings were more to blame than you."[51] This seems to describe an unhappy child who was constantly misunderstood and abused.

In her own descriptions of her childhood in her published writings, Mary Ann said only that she came from a poor family and had to work hard. The ecclesiastical commission which investigated her experiences, however, found evidence of more specific problems, to which the May 30 message may be a reference. In his report of the findings of the commission to an audience at Marquette University on 14 July 1955, Fr. Claude Heithaus said that Mary Ann and her mother, Elizabeth Bieber, had been united in fear of Mary Ann's abusive father. Mary Ann had told the commission, he said, that she had been repeatedly beaten by her father when she was a child, and that her dislike for him bordered on hatred.[52] Mary Ann's view of America as a threatened and vulnerable nation, whose every lapse could invite the intrusion of powerful evil forces, corresponded, it seems, to memories of a childhood in a dysfunctional family in which her own lapses, and probably those of other members of her family as well, brought upon her the violent anger of an abusive father. Mary Ann's mother was probably able to offer her no more protection at these crucial times than, in the worldview of her later revelations and messages, the "Madonna Maria" was able to offer a faltering America.

Suffering, Knowledge, and Exploitation: Apparitions as Apocalyptic Experience

Mary Ann Van Hoof was in some respects an atypical apparition seer. She was American and proud to be such; she had not always been a practicing Catholic, and in reporting her experiences she used her own idioms as well as some traditional Catholic ones; and finally, after some initial shyness, she made full use of the opportunities for verbal self-expression which her apparition brought to her. While she had only an eighth grade education, she was able, in *Mary Ann Van Hoof's Own Story of the Apparitions of the Blessed Virgin*, to give a lengthy, candid, and remarkably unguarded account of her struggle to make sense out of her long series of experiences and of her complex relationships with her followers.

Mary Ann was typical, however, in the way she interpreted her apparition and in the kinds of experiences that framed it—so typical, in fact, that her case may serve as a good starting point for the conclusion of this study.

If there is any one thing, other than their perception of the Virgin's intervention in human affairs, which the seers and devotees of the apparitions discussed in these chapters have in common, it would seem to be an acute awareness of suffering, and Mary Ann, to judge both from her own writings and from the testimonies of others, knew a great deal about suffering. We have seen that her childhood, according to Heithaus, was marked by beatings from her father, and that she recalled her married life as a constant struggle against poverty. She had also been afflicted with a series of physical complaints, and it was these, more than anything else, which set the stage for her apparition experience.

Prior to her apparitions, Mary Ann was hospitalized on several occasions for serious illnesses and injuries, and these hospitalizations were apparently times in which she felt what it was like to receive real care and affection. In the message on 30 May 1950, the Virgin reminded her that she had faced death four times and reassured her that the nurse, a Catholic sister, who had cared for her during those crises, was now in heaven. "You felt very close to her during her devotion and her tireless effort and vigils to keep you alive," the Virgin reportedly said to her, and Mary Ann herself observed that she received from this sister "such kindness as [she] had never experienced before."[53]

It was in the context of physical suffering that Mary Ann reported her first unusual experiences. She said she was lying awake in bed on the evening of 12 November 1949, suffering from heart pain and a kidney ailment (which she connected to an injury sustained when she was thirteen), when she saw a tall female figure enter her bedroom and stand by her bed. This experience was followed by another in the spring of 1950 on Good Friday (April 7) when, again lying awake suffering from heart pain, she saw the crucifix on her bedroom wall begin to glow and heard a voice tell her that while her cross was heavy to bear, the world faced a greater burden of sorrow, unless she would pray. The voice, which Mary Ann understood to be that of the Virgin, commissioned her to go to the parish priest with a request that everyone be directed to recite the Rosary each evening at eight o'clock. When Mary Ann had done this, the Virgin said, she would appear to her again, "where and when the flowers bloom, trees and grass are green."[54] When the Virgin did appear to her, on 28 May 1950, she told Mary Ann that she must fast and go to Mass for fifteen days as a penance for the members of the community who had not responded to this request.[55] This experience thus marked the point at which Mary Ann's personal suffering began to be transformed into a kind of penance for the sins of others.

Mary Ann's illnesses did not cease; they became more acute and more ritualized. Beginning in November 1950, she said she witnessed on every weekend in Advent scenes from Christ's passion and could herself feel the wounds of Christ. According to those who gathered around her and who recorded what they saw, she would become oblivious to her surroundings, and her body would convulse and assume the shape of a cross.[56] These sufferings were repeated the following year during Lent, and Mary Ann now said she could feel (and some said they could see) on her face the wounds of the crown of thorns. During Advent in 1951, Mary Ann said she vomited constantly, and since she was unable to retain any food, she undertook a liquid diet for twenty-four consecutive days with no ill effects, a regime she then followed in subsequent years during Lent and Advent.[57]

Mary Ann's claims to have manifested the stigmata were challenged by Bishop Treacy in the spring of 1952. He asked her to report during Holy Week (April 7–12) for a week of tests at the Marquette University Medical School. In his lecture on the results of the investigating commission, Fr. Heithaus revealed some part of what apparently took place during this hospitalization. He said that tests made when Mary Ann entered the hospital had shown a normal level of salt in her system, proving, he said, that she had been eating solids (and not following a liquid diet as she had claimed). Moreover, at her insistence she maintained a liquid diet in the hospital, with the result that she lost weight and her salt content declined. Her head, arms, and hands had reportedly been bandaged, and all sharp objects taken away from her. Under those conditions, Heithaus said, she had not manifested the stigmata. The investigating committee took this as evidence that there was nothing supernatural about her physical symptoms or, for that matter, her visions.[58]

Mary Ann's followers, however, felt she had not been treated fairly and criticized the procedures followed by the bishop and the investigating committee.[59] They saw Mary Ann as a "Victim Soul" who participated in the suffering of Christ. The girl who had taken "punishment to protect others" was now, in their eyes and in her own, a woman doing penance on behalf of a sinful community, nation, and world. And the Church which denied Mary Ann and her followers this understanding of her suffering could not be, in their eyes, the Church of the kindly supernatural figure who had been appearing and speaking to her.

The ideology of suffering as reparation, built around the theologically orthodox Anselmian atonement theory of the vicarious suffering of Christ, and the personalization of this ideology in the image of the Victim Soul have played various roles in modern Roman Catholic piety, not all of which have been associated with apparitions.[60] The frequency and intensity, however, with which this ideology and image have come to expression in the messages of modern Marian apparitions and in the piety of their devotees is very striking. Moreover, while the claim that the seer of such an apparition has manifested the stigmata is a bit unusual, we have seen enough evidence of a link between recent Marian apparition cults and the cult of Padre Pio, that most famous of recent stigmatics and Victim Souls, that the possibility of a corresponding link between the primary symbols of these cults has to be taken very seriously.

The motif of suffering is pervasive in most modern Marian apparitions. Its manifestations range from the suffering of the mother who appears and voices her laments, sometimes with tears, to the suffering both before and after her appearances of those who bear her messages, to the suffering of the many people, finally, who are drawn to these appearances and messages. While these people may come with many different interests and concerns, it is the sense of suffering in and around an apparition which brings them together and creates a community, where they feel that even their most personal afflictions are shared with others. This community, then, often begins to think of itself as suffering on behalf of a larger community or the world. The experiences of those who join such a community recapitulate the experience of the apparition seer, which is a passage from a meaningless to a meaningful suffering, through an encounter with a maternal figure whose own suffering is meaningful in the sense that it is accepted as part of an all-encompassing divine plan. For the Catholic Christian, such a passage is a kind of spiritual journey to Calvary, where, according to a long-established tradition, the mother of Jesus, at the foot of the cross, was cut to the heart by the suffering and death of her son, her own suffering being joined with his so as to take part, in some way, in the work of reparation that was accomplished there.

The experience of a typical seer or devotee of a modern Marian apparition is, as the case of Mary Ann very well illustrates, an experience framed and defined by crisis. The subject is not merely a sufferer in a general sense but a person with vivid memories of past suffering, who faces, or at least desperately fears, an imminent danger, which is symbolically if not literally life-threatening (e.g., serious illness, family violence, rejection by loved ones, poverty, or war). It is in the context of this fear that the maternal figure is suddenly encountered, and, while she may bring an immediate message of consolation, she also usually confirms, and brings an explanation for, the perceived crisis and a prescription for its alleviation. It is usually explained as the result of ritual transgressions, which can be overcome by the performance of some presumably more fundamental ritual. This schema of explanation and prescription defines a door, so to speak, through which the subject may pass into a new or restored order, where crisis is assuaged and where his or her suffering acquires meaning as part of a preordained cosmic plan. The symbolic kernel of this experience seems to be the sense of return to and realignment with the mother, who represents a pure and pristine order from which the world as such has turned away but which, for those who know themselves to be her children, is still present and accessible. The sense of crisis which frames and defines this experience, the considerable psychic energy which comes to focus here, and finally the subject's sudden perception of a new order and sense of entry into that order, suggest that this experience of the apparition seer or devotee might legitimately be called "apocalyptic experience."

The peculiar experience of apparition seers and devotees is certainly subject to exploitation. In their recent book *Under the Heel of Mary*, Nicholas Perry and Loreto Echeverría have described how, from the middle ages up to the present day, various political interests have appropriated and profited from the energies of Marian devotions and cults, including those surrounding several of the apparitions that have been discussed here. While Perry and Echeverría admit that Marian devotion has sometimes been allied with progressive or liberal agendas, they treat few if any of these alliances in their book, the tone of which is set by discussions of the manipulation of Marian devotion by repressive political regimes such as that of Franco's Spain, which exploited the cult of Fatima.[61] Perry and Echeverría suggest that Marian apparitions are the focal point of the oppressive Marianism which is the main theme of their book.[62] It is chiefly in a brief epilogue that they mention the progressive forces at work today in Roman Catholicism to counteract, in Mary's own name, this oppressive Marianism, and indeed, they suggest finally that in the Church today "Our Lady is going through the acutest identity crisis," with conservatives and progressives entering into an ideological tug-of-war in which each will attempt "to deploy her cult to their advantage."[63]

While there is as yet no scholarly study of the progressive channeling of the energies surrounding Marian apparitions that is comparable to Perry and Echeverría's study of their regressive channeling, it is not difficult to find examples in modern Roman Catholic devotional and theological literature of reflection on Marian apparitions that can, by various criteria, be called progressive. It may be noted here, first of all, that a number of recent Roman Catholic thinkers have defended some of the more recent apparitions on the grounds that their messages are in accord with those of the Second Vatican Council or with papal statements and activities since Vatican II. François Turner, for example, has argued that a number of concerns expressed in the past ten years by John Paul II—for prayer, the Eucharist, the family, the sanctity and authority of the Church and its priesthood—are concerns expressed directly or by implication at Garabandal.[64] While few liberal American Catholics would find much that is progressive in this particular list of concerns, they would perhaps find more to sympathize with in the argument of Mark Miravalle that there are fourteen "developmental themes" in the Medjugorje messages which are also found in the documents of the Second Vatican Council and in postconciliar papal statements. Miravalle, for example, notes that the eschatological urgency that comes through so clearly at Medjugorje echoes statements issued by John Paul II which speak of the present age as one critical for the future of humanity.[65]

In a recent work, *Mary: Mother of God, Mother of the Poor*, which is certainly progressive by the standards of most modern liberal American Catholics, the Brazilian theologians Ivone Gebara and Maria Bingemer, building on the more theoretical work of liberation theologians such as

Leonardo Boff, have used Latin American Marian devotion as the basis for sketching a liberation Mariology. Working from the premise that Marian devotion "retains an anthropological and ideological substrate common to all adherents, which is expressed in pursuit of their needs and in defense of their interests,"[66] the authors observe that while the early conquistadors could understand their American conquests on behalf of the Spanish and Portuguese monarchs as proceeding under Mary's protection,[67] the leaders of the later independence struggles could, conversely, understand their Marian devotion as "one of the most powerful weapons for winning autonomy for their countries."[68] Gebara and Bingemer maintain that in her appearances and in the miracles attributed to her, Mary has identified with and assisted those who are in the most dire of straits, evidence for which they find especially in the apparition to Juan Diego at Guadalupe, near Mexico City, in 1531. By appearing here to an Indian, speaking to him in his own language, and calling for a place of worship on Indian soil, they argue, the Virgin shows that she has adopted these native folk and has become their mother.[69] This apparition, according to the authors, has helped these exploited people achieve a religious and, finally, a national identity.

The work of Gebara and Bingemer and of other Roman Catholics who have recently argued for the presence of progressive elements in some Marian movements may give some pause to those who have been inclined to see Marian devotion as little more than a seedbed of conservative religious and political ideologies. It is unlikely, however, to persuade very many that the exploitation documented by Perry and Echeverría has not been a serious problem with which both Marian devotees and critics of the cult of Mary must come to terms. A fundamental question here, which neither Gebara and Bingemer nor Perry and Echeverría have addressed, is *why* devotion to Mary and especially that which takes shape around Marian apparitions has lent itself to so much exploitation. The answer would seem to lie in the experiential and quasi-cognitive dimensions of Marian apparitions which have been sketched in this study and in the nature of the apocalyptic experience that has just been described.

It is the fact that the experiences of apparition seers and devotees are quasi-cognitive experiences of the unveiling of another realm (such unveiling being the fundamental meaning of the word "apocalyptic") that underlies these persons' passionate concern for messages, secrets, and hidden meanings; their remarkable efforts to ascertain and disseminate particular constellations of apparition facts; and their inclination, finally, to think of those who cannot share their perception as children of darkness, dispatched in the last days of the world to persecute the Virgin's children of light. And the fact that these quasi-cognitive experiences are preceded by suffering and a sense of crisis and come to focus in a vision or an awareness of a maternal presence (perhaps a symbol of the sufferer's lost paradise) may explain the immense psychic energy with which representations of these experiences are cathected and defended. Even very simple images of these experiences are very highly treasured by their subjects, and this is probably why this energy and these people are so easily exploited.

It may not be easy to say at what point the presumably sincere acknowledgment of the experiences of apparition seers and devotees by persons in positions of authority or social power becomes a form of exploitation. Moreover, there may be something even more insidious than exploitation coming into play when persons who have had particularly intense experiences of this sort are encouraged by some, and led by the rejection of others, to remember and to project into their post-experience environment the negative aspects of what they have experienced, for example, paranoia leading to racism, anti-Semitism, hyper-nationalism. This is what seems to have happened at Necedah.

One cannot envy the officials of a church who are charged with making decisions about the authenticity of the symbols which have enabled a group of sufferers to find meaning in their suffering. One would hope, however, that they and everyone else who is called upon to make judgments about such a symbol as an encounter with the Virgin Mary, because of their concern for those who believe they have had such encounters, might find ways to take the experiences that have coalesced into this symbol more seriously, even when they cannot accept the encounter itself as a religious or theological truth.

Suggestions for Further Reading and Study

THERE IS a vast body of literature about Marian apparitions, most of which is apologetic and devotional; that is, its authors are interested in defending and publicizing what they believe to be the Virgin's appearances in particular apparitions. While this literature gives much insight into the worldview of apparition devotees, it may prove disappointing to those who wish to understand the nature of an apparition event and the process by which devotees draw meaning from it. Scholarly approaches to apparitions are rather scarce, and some of the most helpful of them treat apparitions only as aspects of other phenomena, such as visions or pilgrimages. It may be difficult, therefore, to find one's way into the serious study of apparitions without some assistance. The following suggestions for reading, which focus primarily but not exclusively on works written in English, are meant to be starting points for readers who are sufficiently intrigued by this subject to wish to investigate it further.

In recent decades scholarship in this area has been aided by the publication of important collections of documents recording the early history of some of the apparitions recognized by the Roman Catholic Church. Students of Lourdes have the two multivolume sets of documents compiled by René Laurentin (*Lourdes: Documents authentiques*, [1957–]); (*Lourdes: Histoire authentique*, [1962–]). Laurentin and Albert Durand have published a similar collection for Pontmain (*Pontmain: Histoire authentique*, [1970, 1977]); Jean Stern has done the same for La Salette (*La Salette: Documents authentiques*, [1980, 1984]); and A. Martins for Fatima (*Novos Documentos*, [1984]). The only comparable collection of documents for an apparition not recognized by the Roman Catholic Church is that published for San Damiano by Maisonneuve and De Belsunce (*San Damiano, histoire et documents*, [1983]). The reader should be warned, however, that not everything relevant to these apparitions can be found in the documents cited and that the critical apparatus that accompanies these collections generally reveals an apologetic bias.

To understand Marian apparitions one must have some understanding of the religious contexts in which they occur. Perhaps the most helpful introduction to these contexts is Ann Taves's *The Household of Faith: Roman Catholic Devotions in Mid-Nineteenth Century America* (1986). In this study, after surveying some samples of nineteenth-century devotional materials, Taves sketches the sources, the character, the rationale, and the major expressions of recent Roman Catholic devotionalism. Most of the religious contexts described here are transcultural but with European roots, and while Taves does not say a great deal about apparitions, it is clear that the major nineteenth- and even twentieth-century Marian apparitions fit very well into the patterns of devotionalism which she describes. Of particular relevance for the student of these apparitions are Taves's observations that the images that characterize this type of piety are mostly images of the family, with the relationship of devotees to their supernatural patrons (i.e., the saints and Mary) being cast in terms of the relationship of dependent children to their parents.

It is also important for an understanding of Marian apparitions to understand the thinking about Mary that has been going on in the more intellectual sectors of Western culture in recent years. Three major works in English published in the mid-1970s will serve as a good introduction to this aspect of the question. The first of these, Marina Warner's *Alone of All Her Sex: The Myth and Cult of the Virgin Mary* (1976), is probably the best nonapologetic introduction to Marian doctrine and imagery now available. Warner's chief concern is Marian imagery, its history and significance, and while not everyone would agree with her conclusions, no one seriously interested in Marian matters can afford to be unfamiliar with this study. The second book, Andrew M. Greeley's *The Mary Myth: On the Femininity of God* (1977), unlike Warner's book, is an explicitly apologetic work which is basically a series of intellectual and poetic meditations building a case for a "return to Mary" on the part of better-educated American Catholics. While Greeley apparently has little sympathy for Marian apparitions, students of apparitions who want to understand the modern American Catholic intellectual's fascination with Mary would do well to start with this book. The third book, Geoffrey Ashe's *The Virgin* (1976), is, to a much greater degree than Greeley's, the work of a Marian romantic and enthusiast. While this sketch of the history and significance of Marian devotion has generally been seen as much inferior to Warner's, Ashe is perhaps more sensitive than Warner to the importance of the Marian piety of the masses, and for this reason his study is worth reading.

The most important scholarly work on Marian apparitions as such has been done by anthropologist William A. Christian, Jr. In his book *Apparitions in Late Medieval and Renaissance Spain* (1981), Christian has traced the origin and history of a number of late-medieval and early-modern apparition sites in Castile and Catalonia, most of them Marian, and has shown very clearly the importance of these sites and the associated narratives for the religious life of these regions. Christian argues here that apparitions have functioned as focal points of "local religion," bringing shrines to villages where shrines had been lacking and thus filling in gaps in the religious landscape—a thesis which he has also illustrated and defended, though with less specific concern for apparitions, in *Local Religion in Sixteenth Century Spain* (1981) and *Person and God in a Spanish Valley* (1972; revised 1989).

Students of Marian apparitions should be particularly interested in two later articles by Christian. In the first of these, "Religious Apparitions and the Cold War in Southern Europe" (1984), Christian has traced the influence of Fatima on post–World War II apparitions and has shown how Fatima was used by the Church as a weapon in its struggle against postwar communism. More recently, in "Tapping and Defining New Power: The First Month of Visions at Ezquioga, July 1931" (1987), he has shown how public interest in and support for this Spanish apparition was largely determined by a complex of local conditions, and how the mass media, in response to various public concerns and beliefs, publicized some of the unusual phenomena reported at Ezquioga and suppressed others, thus contributing significantly to how this apparition came to be understood.

There are several other important studies of apparitions and related phenomena by anthropologists, which, while not as nuanced as Christian's, present significant theses and are well worth reading. Victor and Edith Turner, in their article "Post-Industrial Marian Pilgrimage" (1982), have suggested that in recent Marian apparitions the Virgin seems to come to intervene in the economic and political crises that characterize modern industrial society. Her message is identified, generally, with lower-middle class interests, and both big business and international socialism are singled out as leading to grievous sins from which humanity is called to turn away. In a similiar vein, the Irish scholar D. ó'hÓgáin, in "A Manifestation of Popular Religion" (1985), has argued that since an objective evaluation of consumerist culture demands more education than most people have had, a majority will turn, in economic and political crisis, to phenomena that appeal to the emotions and that seem to reinforce traditional ideologies. A much more interesting thesis, which involves a more subtle use of the tools of the social scientist, is that of Dutch scholar Mart Bax, who has argued in "Religious Regimes and State Formation: Toward a Research Perspective" (1987) that the eighty apparitions reported in Catholic Dutch Brabant between 1830 and 1950, which all gave rise to important pilgrimage sites and local devotions, served to uphold and augment the power of the monastic clergy in an area and in a period when other social processes were reinforcing the power of the diocesan clergy. Bax has analyzed Medjugorje in similiar terms in his article "Maria-verschijningen in Medjugorje: Rivaliserende religieuze regimes en staatsvorming" (1987).

Turning from the studies of anthropologists to those of persons trained in the historical disciplines, one work stands out as an indispensable introduction to the sociohistorical contexts of the most important Marian apparitions of the nineteenth century: Thomas Kselman's *Miracles and Prophecies in Nineteenth-Century France* (1983). Here Kselman examines the process by which, in the midst of religious, political, and social anxieties, popular interest in miracles and prophecies grew and eventually put pressure on ecclesiastical authorities, as arbiters of the supernatural, to integrate these phenomena into the life of the Church. This study contains a great deal of information about the apparitions at La Salette and Lourdes, presented in such a way as to show how and why these apparitions (along with Rue du Bac) came to attract so much attention and gained the Church's stamp of approval. More recently Kselman, along with Steven Avella, has turned his attention, in the article "Marian Piety and the Cold War in the United States" (1986), to the sociohistorical context of the Necedah apparition, showing how this apparition, like its European counterparts examined by Christian, reflected the conservative politics and Cold War anxieties of Catholics in the 1950s.

Kselman's study of the contexts from which nineteenth-century French apparitions emerged should perhaps be supplemented by two later studies which call particular attention to some of the feminine imagery that came to the fore in these same contexts. The focus and major themes of Stéphane Michaud's *Muse et Madone: Visages de la femme de la*

Révolution française aux apparitions de Lourdes (1985) are expressed quite well in its title (*Muse and Madonna: Faces of Woman from the French Revolution to the Apparitions of Lourdes*). Students of Marian apparitions will want to look particularly at Chapter 1 and Chapter 2 of this work, which focus on the cult of Mary Immaculate in nineteenth-century France. Barbara Corrado Pope, in her article "Immaculate and Powerful: The Marian Revival in the Nineteenth Century" (1985), ventures farther than Michaud into some of the politics of these images. Pope argues that what is most striking in the Rue du Bac and Lourdes apparitions are images of Mary's purity and power, and that the embattled nineteenth-century Roman Catholic hierarchy, identifying itself closely with Mary, used this imagery very effectively to defend and promote its own interests.

The studies by Michaud and Pope represent a growing body of feminist scholarly literature which is of considerable importance today for those concerned with Marian symbolism. For more than three decades now, the women's movement has been challenging traditional institutions to recognize, support, and encourage the full participation of women in all areas of human life. With regard to religion, feminists have been especially concerned to examine the images of women or of the "feminine" found in each religious tradition and to examine how these images either inhibit or promote women's expression of their spiritual lives. Those interested in what feminists have had to say about the Marian tradition, particularly persons who are Roman Catholic, would do well to begin with two articles by Elizabeth Johnson.

In the first of these articles, "The Marian Tradition and the Reality of Women" (1985), Johnson examines three basic criticisms of Marian imagery that have been made by feminist theologians: (1) that the cult of Mary has been associated with the denigration of women; (2) that it has led to a perception that the being and roles of men and women in the church are different and mutually exclusive; and (3) that the image of Mary has had an inhibiting effect on women, preventing them from leading full, whole lives. After surveying these critiques of Marian doctrine and devotion, Johnson explores three possible avenues for re-presenting the image of Mary so as to yield a more viable image and model for contemporary women: (1) recovering the little that is known about the historical Mary and viewing her as an individual who had much in common with contemporary women; (2) seeing Mary as a type of the Church and thus as representative of both women and men; and (3) reinterpreting Mary's virginity and motherhood in a way that emphasizes her autonomy and creativity and thus proclaims liberation.

In the second of these articles, "Mary and the Female Face of God" (1989), Johnson develops the positive contribution she believes the Marian tradition has to make to contemporary theology. She surveys ten contemporary approaches to religious symbolism in general and to Mary in particular—including several theological, psychological, and anthropological studies—and argues that the Marian tradition provides a rich source of imagery which may be justifiably used "to image" God in a more inclusive way. Although limited in scope and decidedly theological in orientation, these two articles provide an overview of the reflections of many moderate and liberal Roman Catholic theologians today on Marian matters, and they are a useful starting point from which to examine the works of the liberation theologians.

Two important studies of religious festivals and pilgrimages have recently appeared which are of considerable value for students of Marian apparitions. The first of these, Robert A. Orsi's *The Madonna of 115th Street: Faith and Community in Italian Harlem, 1880–1950* (1985), focuses on the celebration of the annual festival of the Madonna of Mount Carmel in an Italian immigrant community as a means for tracing the most deeply held values of these persons from the time of their arrival in the New World through their assimilation into American society. Orsi holds, not unlike Christian, that the figure of the Virgin is intimately linked with the lives of the people who venerate her, and that to understand the rituals that focus on her one must understand the daily lives of her devotees. Orsi's detailed study of the social history of a Marian symbol in one particular community over a period of seventy years gives much insight into the importance of social context for Marian devotion, though it does not, of course, address the peculiarities of the type of community created by the typical Marian apparition.

The second of these studies is Mary Lee Nolan and Sidney Nolan's *Christian Pilgrimage in Modern Western Europe* (1989). There is a wealth of important information here on Marian shrines and pilgrimages, and while its "geographical" approach to Marian devotion is much different than that employed by Ann Taves, this work serves very well, along with Taves's work, as a general introduction to Marian devotion and its varied manifestations. It offers a number of maps, statistics, and photographs, which assist the reader to grasp the continuing importance in modern Western Europe of places sacred to Mary and the pilgrimages associated with them.

There are three major German works on religious visions and visionary experience of which the student of Marian apparitions ought to be aware. The first of these, Ernst Benz's *Die Vision: Erfahrungsformen und Bilderwelt* (1969), is a lengthy phenomenology of religious visionary experience, based mostly on published accounts of such experiences in the Christian tradition from the first centuries of Christianity up to the present day. The material Benz has collected is invaluable, but the schema in terms of which he presents this material reflects a certain individualistic, Protestant bias, and it is not surprising, given the categories of this schema, that he includes practically no discussion of Marian apparitions. The student of these apparitions may, however, profit from many parts of this work; for example, from the discussions of factors which seem to induce or encourage visions (Chapter 2), the main types of visions and the phenomena which often accompany them (Chapter 3), the behavior of visionaries during their visions (Chapter 4), and visions of the Heavenly Wisdom and of the Church (Chapter 8).

A later work which is more successful as a phenomenology, because it is more limited in its time frame and because its focus is not so much visionary experience per se as the literature which has recorded it, is Peter Dinzelbacher's *Vision und Visionsliteratur im Mittelalter* (1981). There is more material here on visions of Mary than in Benz's study, in part because, with a focus on the middle ages, such material can scarcely be avoided, and in part because of Dinzelbacher's greater sensitivity to the social and religious contexts of medieval visions and his unwillingness to stray from the language used in these contexts. Students of modern Marian apparitions who turn to this work will find a great deal of continuity in some of the contexts of Marian visions from the middle ages up to the present day, and they can profit from many of the discussions here—for example, of the visionary's relations with inhabitants of the other world (Chapter 12), of the role the vision plays in the life of the visionary (Chapter 14), and of the functions of visions (Chapter 15)—even though there is no particular attention given in this work to Marian apparitions.

Of these three German works, the only one which directly deals with modern Marian apparitions is Gerd Schallenberg's *Visionäre Erlebnisse: Erscheinungen im 20. Jahrhundert. Eine psychopathologische Untersuchung* (1979). In spite of what might be suggested in the subtitle by the phrase "a psychopathological investigation," this is basically a phenomenological and psychological study of thirteen modern cases of religious visionary experience, and it is only in the final chapters that the author makes some rather modest judgments, from a liberal Roman Catholic perspective, about the psychopathology of some of the visionaries. Six of the visions discussed in this work are Marian apparitions, and several others have much in common with Marian apparitions in terms of the religious contexts in which they take place and the phenomena associated with them (e.g., stigmata). Schallenberg's study is important as an introduction to several recent Marian apparitions which are not very well known today (e.g., those at Amsterdam, Heroldsbach and Pfaffenhofen), and it is virtually the only published study of such recent apparitions that is free from any significant positive or negative bias.

Finally, in a recent book that has attracted a considerable amount of attention, *The Cult of the Virgin Mary. Psychological Origins* (1986), Michael P. Carroll has written a sustained analysis of the cult of the Virgin from the perspective of psychoanalytic theory. While Carroll's attempts to explain Marian devotion in terms of classical Freudianism have not been very convincing to most reviewers, this book should be high-priority reading for persons interested in Marian apparitions. Carroll makes at least two important contributions to the study of these phenomena. First, in attempting to show why each seer "hallucinates" a particular image of the Virgin, he has begun to explore the important but, until now, much-neglected area of the meaning of apparitions for the visionaries themselves. Second, in his careful analysis of the interaction between the young visionaries at Pontmain and the crowd which gathered around them, he has shown clearly how the people that flock to the site of a serial apparition can impinge on and affect the content of the seers' experiences and thus the content and course of the apparition itself.

Those interested in the politics of Marian apparitions should not overlook the important book of Nicholas Perry and Loreto Echeverría, *Under the Heel of Mary*, mentioned in Chapter 7.

Most of the works that have been mentioned here contain bibliographies that will assist the reader in finding other interesting and relevant materials. For additional bibliography, including references to recent works on particular apparitions, see René Laurentin's "Bulletin Marial," which appears about every four years in the *Revue des sciences philosophiques et théologiques*.

NOTES

INTRODUCTION

1. Some useful but not very critical discussions of apparitions understood as psychic phenomena are H. Evans, *Visions, Apparitions, Alien Visitors* (Wellingborough, U.K.: Aquarian Press, 1984); C. Green and C. McCreery, *Apparitions* (London: Hamish Hamilton, 1975); H. Hart, "Six Theories about Apparitions," *Society for Psychical Research* 50 (1956): 153–181. The first of these works includes a chapter on religious apparitions. A work which focuses specifically on Marian apparitions in the context of a general interest and belief in psychic phenomena is K. McClure, *The Evidence for Visions of the Virgin Mary* (Wellingborough, U.K.: Aquarian Press, 1983).

2. For discussions of some of the characteristics of religious apparitions, see R. Laurentin, "Apparitions," in *Année Sainte 1983–1984*, R. Laurentin and B. Billet (Paris: Office d'Édition, 1983), 108–118; and S. Zimdars-Swartz, "Religious Experience and Public Cult: The Case of Mary Ann Van Hoof," *Journal of Religion and Health* 28/4 (Spring 1989): 36–57.

3. Caesarius of Heisterbach, *The Dialogue on Miracles*, trans. H. von E. Scott and C. C. Swinton Bland (New York: Harcourt, Brace and Company, 1929), vol. 1, 453–546; the lay brother's vision, Book 7, Chapter 12, 469–470.

4. William A. Christian, Jr., *Apparitions in Late Medieval and Renaissance Spain* (Princeton: Princeton University Press, 1981).

5. Caesarius of Heisterbach, *The Dialogue on Miracles*, vol. 1, Book 7, Chapter 4, 458–459.

6. Ibid., Book 7, Chapter 34, 502–503.

7. Ibid., Book 7, Chapter 2, 455.

8. Jacobus de Varagine, *The Golden Legend*, trans. G. Ryan and H. Ripperger (London: Longmans, Green and Co., 1941), 417–418.

9. Caesarius of Heisterbach, *The Dialogue on Miracles*, vol. 1, Book 7, Chapter 3, 456–458.

10. W. A. Christian, Jr., "Holy People in Peasant Europe," *Comparative Studies in Society and History* 15 (1973): 106–114.

11. R. Laurentin, "Apparitions," 130–131. It should be noted that private revelation refers to the fact that its content can add nothing to "public revelation," which is understood by Roman Catholics to have ended with the death of the Apostles. See also K. Rahner, *Visions and Prophecies*, trans. C. Henkey and R. Strachan (London: Burns and Oates, 1963), 18–30.

12. One of the best succinct statements of the status of apparitions within Roman Catholic doctrine and the formal and informal means of giving ap-

proval to them is to be found in Michael O'Carroll, *Theotokos: A Theological Encyclopedia of the Blessed Virgin Mary* (Wilmington, DE: Michael Glazier, 1982), 47–48.

13. Only very brief information on the apparition at Fehrbach is found in the listing of B. Billet, "Le fait des apparitions non reconnues par l'Église," in *Vraies et fausses apparitions dans l'Église*, B. Billet et al. (Paris: Lethielleux, 1973), 13. The current status of the apparition site was ascertained by a visit to the parish in September 1987 and a discussion with the present parish priest.

14. Information on the apparition at Melleray was gathered during two trips to Ireland, in October 1985, and in June 1986. Both Cait Cliffe and William Deevey generously shared the information they had gathered, and Mary Murphy kindly granted the use of her living room for two days of interviews with the members of the Melleray grotto committee. For a more complete account of this apparition, see S. Zimdars-Swartz, "Popular Devotion to the Virgin: The Marian Phenomena at Melleray, Republic of Ireland," *Archives de sciences sociales des religions*, 67/1 (January–March 1989), 125–144.

15. For information and analysis of the phenomena of moving statues in the Republic of Ireland, see *Seeing is Believing: Moving Statues in Ireland*, ed. C. Toibin (Dublin: Pilgrim Press, 1985). For a map showing the location of the shrines and a brief discussion of the events at each site, see *The Sunday Tribune* [Dublin] (7 September 1985), 8–9.

16. See, for example, M. McCafferty, "Virgin on the Rocks," *New Statesman*, 13 September 1985, 24–26, reprinted in Toibin, *Seeing is Believing*, 53–58; and M. Holland, "Ballinspittle and the Bishops' Dilemma," *Irish Times*, 21 August 1985, reprinted in *Seeing is Believing*, 45–48; and D. ó'hÓgáin, "A Manifestation of Popular Religion," in *Seeing is Believing*, 67–74.

17. I wish to thank Robert L. Lineberry for calling my attention to the anticipated events at St. John Neumann parish in Lubbock, Texas. For accounts of the crowd reaction, see B. Pratt, "Many Profess to Feel Holy Presence," *Lubbock Avalanche-Journal*, 16 August 1988, 6A; S. Kaye, "Believers Feel Miracle Occur through Visions, Reassurances," *Lubbock Avalanche-Journal*, 16 August 1988, 6A; "Worshippers Report They Saw a Miracle," *Kansas City Times*, 16 August 1988, 1A, 10A; "Statement on 'Rosary Messages' in Lubbock," *Origins: NC Documentary Service* 18 (3 November 1988): 333, 335–336; B. Berak, "Miracle in Lubbock: Did Many Come?" *Kansas City Times*, 8 April 1989, 9E.

18. For a discussion of this militant Marian ideology and its use by conservative political regimes, see N. Perry and L. Echeverría, *Under the Heel of Mary* (London: Routledge, 1988).

19. J. B. Torelló notes that of the more recent apparitions, these three have become especially well known because of the publicity accorded them in the international press. "Echte und falsche Erscheinungen: Besonnenheit und Offenheit vor der Marienerscheinungen," in *Der Widerschein des Ewigen Lichtes: Marienerscheinungen und Gnadenbilder als Zeichen der Gotteskraft*, ed. G. Rovira (Kevelaer: Verlag Butzon & Bercker, 1984), 90.

CHAPTER ONE

1. On the process and the meaning of this recognition, see T. Kselman, *Miracles and Prophecies in Nineteenth-Century France* (New Brunswick: Rutgers University Press, 1983), 153–154.

2. J. Stern, "Introduction," in *La Salette, Documents authentiques: dossier chronologique intégral*, vol. 1, *Septembre 1846–début mars 1847* (Paris: Desclée de Brouwer, 1980), p. 21.

3. J. Stern, *La Salette, Documents authentiques: dossier chronologique intégral*, vol. 2, *Le procès de l'apparition fin mars 1847–avril 1849* (Paris: Cerf, 1984), Doc. 340, p. 202.

4. M. Calvat, *Vie de Mélanie, bergère de la Salette* (Paris, 1919), 3–50.

5. Stern, vol. 1, "Introduction," pp. 17–19.

6. Ibid., p. 34.

7. Ibid., p. 41 and note 6. See also Stern, vol. 2, Doc. 296, pp. 149–151; and Doc. 297, pp. 151–153; for an English translation of these documents, see W. B. Ullathorne, *The Holy Mountain of La Salette*, 9th ed. (Altamont, NY: La Salette Press, 1942), 30–33. Selme said that he had seen the two children playing together on Friday (the eighteenth). He did not know when they might have met, but he had never seen them together before.

8. Stern, vol. 1, Doc. 96, pp. 284–294; for an English translation, see Abbé Lagier, *The Abbé Jots It Down*, ed. and trans. E. La Douceur (Altamont, NY: La Salette Press, 1946), 8–34. In the following account, I have given the circumstances of the encounter which Mélanie described to Lagier in her first interview with him sometime before 26 February 1847. It is unclear, however, precisely how many times and for how long Lagier interviewed Mélanie. Lagier himself said that he held three interviews with the seer, each about four hours in length. One of the sisters of the convent, however, said he held only two interviews with Mélanie, one of which lasted between four and nine hours and was cut off only because it was time for the sisters to retire for the night. According to Rousselot, Lagier interviewed both seers even more frequently, sometimes together and sometimes separately (Stern, vol. 1, 277–278).

The English translation of Lagier's notes is considerably longer than the French text edited by Stern. What La Douceur translates as the first interview (*The Abbé Jots It Down*, 8–34), Stern breaks into three interviews (vol. 1, Doc. 96, pp. 281–294; Doc. 99, pp. 306–314; Doc. 107, pp. 330–332). Stern gives no text equivalent to the second and third interviews of the English translation.

9. Stern, vol. 1, Doc. 1, p. 47–48. I have translated the message from this earliest account.

10. Stern, vol. 1, Doc. 96, p. 290; Lagier, *The Abbé Jots It Down*, 16.

11. Stern, vol. 1, Doc. 96, p. 294; Lagier, *The Abbé Jots It Down*, 20.

12. Lagier, *The Abbé Jots It Down*, 49.

13. Ibid., 57–58.

14. Stern, vol. 1, Doc. 105, pp. 324–325; Lagier, *The Abbé Jots It Down*, 75.

15. Michael Carroll takes the extreme position here. He sees Maximin as the

originator of this Marian "hallucination" and takes the comments attributed to him as the desire that he, as an abused child, could have beaten his abusive stepmother. Carroll argues that the hallucination then was shaped as the fulfillment of Maximin's wish for revenge against his stepmother. *The Cult of the Virgin Mary: Psychological Origins* (Princeton: Princeton University Press, 1986), 149–156.

16. Stern, vol. 1, Doc. 121, p. 353; see also "Introduction," p. 41 and note 6.

17. Two weeks later the curé was replaced for this action by the Abbé Louis Perrin (no relation). Stern, vol. 1, p. 45.

18. Michael Carroll has described this process in *The Cult of the Virgin Mary*, pp. 148–194.

19. Stern, vol. 1, pp. 49–50, 54.

20. Ibid., Doc. 2, p. 55.

21. Ibid., Doc. 125, p. 368.

22. Ibid., Doc. 5, pp. 60–61.

23. Kselman, *Miracles and Prophecies in Nineteenth-Century France*, 174–175.

24. According to contemporary reports, the names of the lieutenants were Angelini and Bornedave, and the event took place at the Café Magnon. Stern, vol. 1, Doc. 13, pp. 89–80; Doc 16 bis, p. 109; Doc. 22, p. 124; Doc. 23, p. 126; Doc 28 bis, pp. 136–137; Doc. 36, p. 151; Doc. 48, pp. 194–195; Doc. 64, p. 225; Doc. 125, pp. 369–370.

25. Lagier, *The Abbé Jots It Down*, 61–64.

26. Stern, vol. 1, pp. 62–63; Doc. 17, p. 111.

27. Ibid., p. 251.

28. Lagier, *The Abbé Jots It Down*, 61–64.

29. Stern, vol. 1, Doc. 109, p. 336; see also Stern, vol. 2, Doc. 296, p. 150.

30. Stern, vol. 1, Doc. 56, p. 211.

31. Ibid., pp. 49–50. Maximin's cousin's name was Mélanie Carnal.

32. Ibid., Doc. 36, pp. 150–151.

33. Ibid., p. 160.

34. Ibid., pp. 147–148; Doc. 41, p. 175; Doc. 43 bis, pp. 184–185; Doc. 125, p. 369.

35. Ibid., p. 160; Doc. 43 bis, pp. 185–186.

36. Ibid., p. 154; Doc. 43, p. 183; Doc. 43 bis, p. 185; Doc. 47, p. 193. The child's name was Mélanie Dournon and her parents, Joseph Dournon and Marie Pellissier.

37. Ibid., Doc. 17, pp. 111–112.

38. Stern, vol. 2, Doc. 427, p. 275; see also Stern vol. 1, Doc. 71, p. 235.

39. Stern, vol. 1, Doc. 25, p. 127.

40. Ibid., Doc. 37 bis (*Le Censeur*, 26 November 1846), pp. 153–154.

41. Ibid., Doc. 59 (*Le Censeur*, 27 January 1847), pp. 214–215.

42. Ibid., Doc. 74 (*Siècle*, 16 February 1847), pp. 242–244.

43. Ibid., Doc. 59 bis (*Lyons Gazette*, 9 January 1847), pp. 216–217.

44. Ibid., Doc. 60 bis (*Journal de Rennes*, 16 January 1847; *L'Ami de la religion*, 23 January 1847; *Écho de l'Aveyron*, 30 January 1847), p. 218.

45. On the significance of La Salette and its prophecies in the general context of nineteenth-century French history and prophecy, see the important work of T. Kselman, *Miracles and Prophecies in Nineteenth-Century France*, especially 62–68.

46. Stern, vol. 1, Doc. 49, pp. 201–202.

47. Kselman, *Miracles and Prophecies in Nineteenth-Century France*, 65–66.

48. Ibid., 174–179. Kselman provides a good description of this opposition, which continued for many years after 1851.

49. Ibid., 154–155. Kselman observes that this was at the urging of the local clergy and understands it as a defensive measure on the part of a Church, which was then already preparing for the likelihood of the apparition's recognition.

50. Stern, vol. 1, "Introduction," pp. 19–20. For a recent study of Maximin, see H. Dion, *Maximin Giraud, berger de La Salette, ou la fidélité dans l'épreuve* (Montsûrs: Résiac, 1988).

51. Stern, vol. 1, "Introduction," pp. 21–33. For recent studies of Mélanie, see H. Guilhot, *La vraie Mélanie de la Salette* (Saint-Céneré: Éditions Saint-Michel, 1973); P. Gouin, *Sister Mary of the Cross: The Shepherdess of La Salette* (London: Billings and Sons, 1981); and H. Dion, *Mélanie Calvat, bergére de la Salette, étapes humaines et mystiques* (Paris: Téqui, 1984).

52. Mélanie did begin to recount miraculous incidents about her childhood which were believed by her followers. For a critical discussion, see J. Jaouen, *La Grâce de la Salette 1846–1946* (Paris: Cerf, 1946), 230–263; and Mélanie's autobiography, *Vie de Mélanie, bergère de la Salette*, 3–50.

53. Kselman, *Miracles and Prophecies in Nineteenth-Century France*, 178–179.

54. R. Laurentin, *Lourdes, histoire authentique*, vol. 2, *L'enfance de Bernadette et les trois premières apparitions, 7 janvier 1844–18 février 1858* (Paris: Lethielleux, 1962), 16, note 27, no. 1. Louise's sister, Bernarde, told an investigator that Louise could no longer nurse Bernadette because she was six months pregnant (17, note 27, no. 3); see also Jeanne Védère (no. 4).

55. This is the account accepted by Laurentin (*Lourdes, histoire authentique* 2: 16–17), despite the fact that he cites only one rather late testimony in support of it (note 27, no. 5). Most sources say that Bernadette was about six months old when she was taken to Marie Laguës. However, as Laurentin has pointed out, Marie's son was born on November 4 and died on November 14, thus making it likely that Bernadette was taken to the Laguës home at the end of November or the beginning of December 1844 (p. 17, note 28).

56. Ibid., 17–21, 28–33, 51–64.

57. Ibid., 34–36.

58. Ibid., 45.

59. Ibid., 45–46, note 129.

60. Ibid., 36–37, note 102.

61. According to Laurentin, the wooden plank was confiscated by the police and kept at the town hall for its owner, but as it was never claimed, it was later used as the post to which town officials affixed a notice forbidding people access to the grotto. R. Laurentin, *Bernadette of Lourdes* (Minneapolis: Winston Press, 1979), 14.

62. Laurentin, *Lourdes, histoire authentique* 2: 41–43.

63. R. Laurentin, *Lourdes, dossier des documents authentiques*, vol. 1, *Au temps des seize premières apparitions, 11 février–3 avril 1858*, 2d ed. (Paris: Lethielleux, 1962), Doc. 11, pp. 175–178; see also Doc. 22, pp. 188–190. The Lourdes prosecutor was V. Dutour.

It is interesting that while practically everyone who knew them has agreed that the Soubirous were in great financial distress in the years before the apparition, opinions have been sharply divided over the causes of this distress. Some have suggested that it was the result of a lack of business sense. Both François and Louise, it was said, lavishly entertained their customers, did not collect on overdue bills, and did not charge friends for grinding their wheat (Laurentin, *Lourdes, histoire authentique*, 2: 22, notes 46 and 47). Their financial problems were, as these persons saw it, really brought on by their generosity. Others, however, including some of their relatives, painted a picture of Bernadette's parents as irresponsible. François, they said, had always been given to laziness (20, note 38) and Louise had taken to drinking too much (78–79). Modern interpreters have generally perpetuated one or the other of these views. Curiously, few seem to have associated the family's plight at the time of the apparition with the poor harvest of 1856 and the threat of famine reported in the area at that time, or even with the more general difficulties of the French populace in the first decade of the Second Republic.

Laurentin attributes the early criticism of Bernadette's parents to family partisanship. The Soubirous' friends and relatives blamed Louise and called her a drunk, while the Casterots blamed François and called him indolent. He notes also that at that time wine was believed to impart strength, attributes Louise's apparent fondness for it to her belief that it would help her health, and characterizes the testimonies of some eighteen people (who attest to this fondness on Louise's part) as "ambiguous." Laurentin opts for the view that the Soubirous declined financially because of their generosity. See Laurentin, *Bernadette of Lourdes*, 15.

64. Laurentin, *Lourdes, histoire authentique* 2: 51–68.

65. Laurentin, *Lourdes, documents authentiques*, vol. 1, Doc. 3, pp. 161–163.

66. Ibid., Doc. 3, p. 163. Later accounts of Bernadette's experience on February 14 described a more complex series of events. According to these accounts, when Bernadette saw *aquerò*, she pointed to her, but her companions could see nothing. Then she took the bottle of holy water, stepped forward a little, and asking the figure "to remain if she came from God and to go away if not," she threw the water in the figure's direction. It was at this point, according to these accounts, that the stone which Jeanne had thrown fell into the grotto. Bernadette reportedly did not run but remained immobile and was unresponsive to the attempts of her companions to arouse her. Some of them went to seek help and summoned a miller, Antoine Nicolau, to the grotto. Nicolau reportedly said he found the young seer quite heavy, and it was with difficulty that he carried her to his mill. Bernadette became aware of her surroundings and of what was happening, it was said, only as the miller was carrying her away from

the grotto. See also Laurentin, *Lourdes, histoire authentique* 2: 253–277 and *Bernadette of Lourdes*, 32–35.

67. Laurentin, *Lourdes, documents authentiques*, vol. 1, Doc. 3, p. 163.

68. Ibid., Doc. 3, p. 164. In another early account of her experiences on February 18, Bernadette recalled the sequence of events in her conversation with *aquerò* somewhat differently and noted an additional element in that conversation. According to this account, she asked *aquerò* about Millet's presence before offering *aquerò* the paper and pen and before being asked to come to the grotto for fifteen days. After all of this, *aquerò* reportedly told her that she would make her happy, if not in this world then at least in the next (Doc. 4, pp. 167–168). See also Laurentin, *Lourdes, histoire authentique* 2: 354–371; and *Bernadette of Lourdes*, 36–38.

69. Laurentin, *Lourdes, histoire authentique* 2: 368–369 and note 94.

70. The issue of the Lourdes weekly newspaper, *Le Lavedan*, carries the date of February 18, but Laurentin points out that several details in the article suggest that it could not have been written much before February 21 (*Lourdes, documents authentiques*, vol. 1, Doc. 5, p. 168). The information in this article was included in two reports sent to important government officials (Doc. 6, p. 171; Doc. 7, p. 172).

71. Ibid., Doc. 12, p. 179. For a summary of accounts of Bernadette's demeanor and actions during her experiences, see R. Laurentin, *Lourdes, histoire authentique*, vol. 3, *La quinzaine des apparitions* (Paris: Lethielleux, 1962), 81–136. Edith Saunders points out that many compared Bernadette's complexion to white wax, a substance that was much admired at the time, but argues that it is difficult to see from the descriptions why people were so moved watching her (*Lourdes* [New York: Oxford, 1940], 55–56).

72. Laurentin, *Lourdes, documents authentiques*, vol. 1, Doc. 12, p. 179.

73. Ibid., Doc. 13, p. 181. According to this account by police commissioner Jacomet, Bernadette also announced that the Virgin had washed herself in the water as she (Bernadette) had done. For a complete dossier of accounts of this apparition, see R. Laurentin, *Lourdes, histoire authentique des apparitions*, vol. 4, *La quinzaine au jour le jour, première semaine, 19 au 25 février 1858* (Paris: Lethielleux, 1963), 317–364.

74. Clarens wrote that while this water's curative powers "should not be surprising," it was thought to contain a considerable amount of calcium or lime and that persons who drank it regularly might be exposed to considerable danger (Laurentin, *Lourdes, documents authentiques*, vol. 1, Doc. 23, pp. 203–204). This, apparently, had been the view of a local pharmacist, who admitted that he wanted to discourage people from going to the grotto (p. 204, note 31; Doc. 65, p. 249; Doc. 67, p. 250).

75. Ibid., Doc. 23, p. 201.

76. L.-J.-M. Cros, *Histoire de Notre-Dame de Lourdes d'après les documents et les témoins*, vol. 1, *Les apparitions (11 février–7 avril 1858)* (Paris: Beauchesne, 1925), 348–349.

77. Ibid., 352–353. As Dominiquette recalled it, Peyramale's request that Bernadette ask *aquerò* her name and his request that *aquerò* make the rose bush

bloom were both made on March 2. Laurentin, however, concluded that the first of these requests was made on the evening of March 2 and the second on the next evening, March 3 (*Bernadette of Lourdes*, 62–66).

78. Cros, 1: 352–353. Reported by Dominiquette Cazenave as Peyramale's reaction on March 2. Laurentin places this comment on March 3 (*Bernadette of Lourdes*, 65–66).

79. Cros, 1: 364–365. Reported by Jeanne Védère, Bernadette's cousin. Cros places this on March 3, Laurentin places it on March 4 (*Bernadette of Lourdes*, 69).

80. Laurentin, *Lourdes, documents authentiques*, vol. 1, Doc. 19, p. 187; see also Doc. 36, p. 216.

81. Ibid., Doc. 36, pp. 216–217. The newspaper was *L'ère impériale*. For an overview of the social composition of the crowd that came to observe Bernadette during her experiences, see Laurentin, *Lourdes, histoire authentique* 3: 63–70.

82. Laurentin, *Lourdes, documents authentiques*, vol. 1, Doc. 36, p. 219.

83. Ibid., Doc. 57, p. 237.

84. Ibid., Doc. 44 bis, p. 231.

85. Ibid., Doc. 75, p. 267; Doc. 76, p. 275.

86. Ibid., Doc. 25, p. 207.

87. Ibid., Doc. 69, pp. 259–260.

88. Cros, 1: 386.

89. Laurentin, *Lourdes, documents authentiques*, vol. 1, Doc. 71, pp. 261–262.

90. Ibid., Doc. 76, p. 275.

91. Ibid., Doc. 81, pp. 282–283.

92. A. Ravier, *Les écrits de sainte Bernadette et sa voie spirituelle* (Paris: Lethielleux, 1980), 59, 65, 71, 75, 93, 97.

93. Cros, 1: 462.

94. Kselman, *Miracles and Prophecies in Nineteenth-Century France*, 92.

95. Laurentin, *Lourdes, documents authentiques*, vol. 1, Doc. 81, p. 282. The letter that Peyramale wrote to Bishop Laurence giving Bernadette's report of *aquerò*'s words is lost. See also *Bernadette of Lourdes*, 87.

96. Laurentin, *Lourdes, documents authentiques*, vol. 1, Doc. 85, p. 285.

97. R. Laurentin, *Lourdes, dossier des documents authentiques*, vol. 2, *Dix-septième apparition, gnoses, faux miracles, fausses visions, la grotto interdite, 4 avril–14 juin 1858* (Paris: Lethielleux, 1957), Doc. 126, p. 149.

98. Kselman, *Miracles and Prophecies in Nineteenth-Century France*, 92–94.

99. R. Laurentin, *Lourdes, documents authentiques*, vol. 2, Doc. 138, p. 161; see also the report of the Lourdes prosecutor, Dutour, Doc. 150, pp. 179–180.

100. On local pilgrimages (that is, those drawing pilgrims from a limited geographical area) see W. A. Christian, Jr., *Person and God in a Spanish Valley*, 2nd ed. (Princeton: Princeton University Press, 1989) and *Local Religion in Sixteenth-Century Spain* (Princeton: Princeton University Press, 1981).

101. Laurentin, *Lourdes, documents authentiques*, vol. 1, Doc. 90, p. 290.

102. Laurentin, *Lourdes, documents authentiques*, vol. 2, Doc. 137, pp. 159–160.

103. Ibid., Doc. 127, pp. 149–150; see also Laurentin, *Lourdes, documents authentiques*, vol. 1, Doc. 36, p. 219; and Doc. 58, p. 239.

104. Laurentin, *Lourdes, documents authentiques*, vol. 2, Doc. 158, pp. 195–198.

105. For a discussion of some later "miraculous cures" at Lourdes and at other French shrines as social drama, see Kselman, *Miracles and Prophecies in Nineteenth-Century France*, 40–49.

106. L.-J.-M. Cros, *Histoire de Notre-Dame de Lourdes d'après les documents et les témoins*, vol. 2, *Les luttes (avril 1858–février 1859)* (Paris: Beauchesne, 1926), 158–195, 415–454. See also, Laurentin, *Bernadette of Lourdes*, 82.

107. Cros, 2: 215.

108. Laurentin, *Lourdes, documents authentiques*, vol. 2, Doc. 155, pp. 187–189; Doc. 156, pp. 191–192.

109. Ibid., Doc. 155, pp. 185–187; Doc. 156, pp. 193–194.

110. Ibid., Doc. 162, pp. 200–201; Doc. 164, pp. 202–204; see also Laurentin, *Bernadette of Lourdes*, 81–82.

111. Laurentin, *Lourdes, documents authentiques*, vol. 2, Doc. 164, pp. 204–205. Laurentin, however, describes these women as church members of good reputation and says that Peyramale gave them a better reception than he had given Bernadette (*Bernadette of Lourdes*, 82).

112. Laurentin, *Lourdes, documents authentiques*, vol. 2, Doc. 149, p. 171 and note 4.

113. Ibid., Doc. 164, pp. 202–203.

114. Ibid., Doc. 209, p. 258.

115. Ibid., p. 63.

116. Ibid., p. 65.

117. Ibid., pp. 63–65. Dominiquette, who had observed both Bernadette and Marie in their ecstasies, said that Marie looked much like Bernadette at these times but seemed to be more joyful and to have a paler complexion. Marie, she said, like Bernadette, would kiss the ground, which the Virgin had reportedly commanded her to do "for sinners." According to Dominiquette, the Virgin had also said to Marie, "I am Mary, conceived without sin," and told her that she wanted a chapel built there (pp. 65–66).

118. Cros, 2: 248–252.

119. Ibid., 246.

120. Ibid., 253.

121. Ibid., 246.

122. Ibid., 248, 288–291.

123. Laurentin, *Bernadette of Lourdes*, 83.

124. Laurentin, *Lourdes, documents authentiques*, vol. 2, p. 62.

125. Laurentin, *Bernadette of Lourdes*, 79–82, 87.

126. Kselman has excellent discussions of the various factors which led the commission during these years to a positive assessment of Bernadette's experiences (*Miracles and Prophecies in Nineteenth-Century France*, 143–144, 153, 156–159, and *passim*).

127. For recent biographies of Bernadette, see Laurentin, *Bernadette of*

Lourdes; A. Ravier, *Bernadette*, trans. B. Wall (London: Collins, 1979); and F. Trochu, *Saint Bernadette Soubirous, 1844–1879*, trans. J. Joyce (Rockford, IL: TAN Books and Publishers, 1957).

128. A. M. Martins, ed., *Novos Documentos de Fatima* (São Paolo, Brazil: Edições Loyola, 1984), 97–102.

129. Martins, *Novos Documentos*, 179–180; L. Kondor, ed., *Fatima in Lucia's Own Words*, trans. Dominican Nuns of the Perpetual Rosary (Fatima, Portugal: Postulation Centre, 1976), 52. Quotations from Lucia's memoirs are taken from Kondor's English edition.

130. Martins, *Novos Documentos*, 180–182, 229; Kondor, *Fatima in Lucia's Own Words*, 52–54, 99; see also the recollections of Maria dos Anjos, Lucia's older sister, in J. de Marchi, *Fatima: The Facts*, trans. I. M. Kingsbury (Cork: Mercier Press, 1950), 20; and in J. de Marchi, *The Immaculate Heart*, ed. W. Ray (New York, Farrar, Straus and Young, 1952), 22.

131. Martins, *Novos Documentos*, 145–148; Kondor, *Fatima in Lucia's Own Words*, 22–24. See also de Marchi, *Fatima: The Facts*, 20, 32; and *The Immaculate Heart*, 23, 36–37.

132. Martins, *Novos Documentos*, 181; Kondor, *Fatima in Lucia's Own Words*, 53.

133. Martins, *Novos Documentos*, 146; Kondor, *Fatima in Lucia's Own Words*, 22–23. See also, De Marchi, *Fatima: The Facts*, 21–22; and *The Immaculate Heart*, 24–25.

134. Martins, *Novos Documentos*, 182; Kondor, *Fatima in Lucia's Own Words*, 54.

135. Lucia discusses her First Communion in some detail in her *Second Memoir*; see Martins, *Novos Documentos*, 182–187; Kondor, *Fatima in Lucia's Own Words*, 54–59. I have followed Lucia's account here.

136. The visiting priest was Fr. Francisco da Cruz, national director of the Apostleship of Prayer. See N. Perry and L. Echeverría, *Under the Heel of Mary*, 184.

137. Martins, *Novos Documentos*, 187–188; Kondor, *Fatima in Lucia's Own Words*, 59–60. Lucia's three companions were Teresa and Maria Rosa Matias and Maria Justino.

138. Martins, *Novos Documentos*, 188–190; Kondor, *Fatima in Lucia's Own Words*, 60–61.

139. In her first two memoirs, Lucia suggested that both her cousins were anxious to accompany her (Martins, *Novos Documentos*, 150–151, 189; Kondor, *Fatima in Lucia's Own Words*, 27, 61). However, in her *Fourth Memoir*, she suggested that it was primarily Jacinta who wanted to be with her, and that Francisco followed more or less out of devotion to his sister (Martins, *Novos Documentos*, 279–280; Kondor, *Fatima in Lucia's Own Words*, 120).

140. Martins, *Novos Documentos*, 190; Kondor, *Fatima in Lucia's Own Words*, 62.

141. Martins, *Novos Documentos*, 310; Kondor, *Fatima in Lucia's Own Words*, 151.

142. For a discussion of the importance of Fatima in reinforcing popular re-

sistance to this religious persecution, see Perry and Echeverría, *Under the Heel of Mary*, 181–193.

143. W. T. Walsh, *Our Lady of Fatima* (Garden City, New York: Image, 1954), 11–14.

144. Martins, *Novos Documentos*, 193; Kondor, *Fatima in Lucia's Own Words*, 64.

145. Walsh, *Our Lady of Fatima*, 17–18. Neighbors such as Manuel Gonçalves, while careful to assert that Lucia's father was not "a bad man," admit that he had problems with drinking and attribute the poverty of the family to his "fecklessness" (De Marchi, *Fatima: The Facts*, 110; and *The Immaculate Heart*, 124–125).

146. Martins, *Novos Documentos*, 193; Kondor, *Fatima in Lucia's Own Words*, 64. I have followed Lucia's account here.

147. Martins, *Novos Documentos*, 192; Kondor, *Fatima in Lucia's Own Words*, 64.

148. Martins, *Novos Documentos*, 193; Kondor, *Fatima in Lucia's Own Words*, 65.

149. Martins, *Novos Documentos*, 153; Kondor, *Fatima in Lucia's Own Words*, 29.

150. De Marchi, *Fatima: The Facts*, 43–44; and *The Immaculate Heart*, 50–51. De Marchi's interviews with the inhabitants of Fatima began in 1943.

151. De Marchi, *Fatima: The Facts*, 45–46; and *The Immaculate Heart*, 52–53.

152. Martins, *Novos Documentos*, 153; Kondor, *Fatima: The Facts*, 29–30.

153. Martins, *Novos Documentos*, 195–196; Kondor, *Fatima in Lucia's Own Words*, 66–67. See also the account of Maria dos Anjos, in De Marchi, *Fatima: The Facts*, 50; and *The Immaculate Heart*, 58.

154. Martins, *Novos Documentos*, 195–196; Kondor, *Fatima in Lucia's Own Words*, 67.

155. De Marchi, *Fatima: The Facts*, 53, 54; and *The Immaculate Heart*, 60.

156. De Marchi, *Fatima: The Facts*, 54, 56; and *The Immaculate Heart*, 60–62, 63–64.

157. De Marchi, *Fatima: The Facts*, 64, 67; and *The Immaculate Heart*, 72–73, 77.

158. De Marchi, *Fatima: The Facts*, 81–82; and *The Immaculate Heart*, 93–94.

159. Martins, *Novos Documentos*, 164–165, 302–303, 319–320; Kondor, *Fatima in Lucia's Own Words*, 39–40, 142–143, 167.

160. Martins, *Novos Documentos*, 313–322; Kondor, *Fatima in Lucia's Own Words*, 156–170. Although Lucia places the apparition on the day the children returned from Ourém (August 15), most scholars place it on the following Sunday (August 19).

161. De Marchi, *Fatima: The Facts*, 120–121; and *The Immaculate Heart*, 138.

162. De Marchi, *Fatima: The Facts*, 123–130; and *The Immaculate Heart*, 139–150.

163. Martins, *Novos Documentos*, 321–322; Kondor, *Fatima in Lucia's Own Words*, 168–170.

164. De Marchi, *Fatima: The Facts*, 130–136, 138–145; and *The Immaculate Heart*, 151–157, 159–166.

165. De Marchi, *Fatima: The Facts*, 56, note 4; and *The Immaculate Heart*, 63, note 4.

166. Martins, *Novos Documentos*, 157; Kondor, *Fatima in Lucia's Own Words*, 33.

167. Martins, *Novos Documentos*, 196–198; Kondor, *Fatima in Lucia's Own Words*, 68–69.

168. Martins, *Novos Documentos*, 198–199; Kondor, *Fatima in Lucia's Own Words*, 70–71.

169. Martins, *Novos Documentos*, 200–201, 210–211, 213–217; Kondor, *Fatima in Lucia's Own Words*, 72, 81, 84–87.

170. De Marchi, *Fatima: The Facts*, 81; and *The Immaculate Heart*, 93.

171. Martins, *Novos Documentos*, 199–200; Kondor, *Fatima in Lucia's Own Words*, 71.

172. Martins, *Novos Documentos*, 202, 206–207; Kondor, *Fatima in Lucia's Own Words*, 73, 77–78.

173. Martins, *Novos Documentos*, 207; Kondor, *Fatima in Lucia's Own Words*, 78.

174. De Marchi, *Fatima: The Facts*, 75; and *The Immaculate Heart*, 85–86.

175. De Marchi, *Fatima: The Facts*, 110; and *The Immaculate Heart*, 125.

176. Martins, *Novos Documentos*, 201–202; Kondor, *Fatima in Lucia's Own Words*, 72–73.

177. Martins, *Novos Documentos*, 159; Kondor, *Fatima in Lucia's Own Words*, 35.

178. De Marchi, *Fatima: The Facts*, 137; and *The Immaculate Heart*, 158–159.

179. De Marchi, *Fatima: The Facts*, 137–138, note 1; and *The Immaculate Heart*, 159, note 1.

180. Martins, *Novos Documentos*, 168–169; Kondor, *Fatima in Lucia's Own Words*, 44.

181. De Marchi, *Fatima: The Facts*, 138; and *The Immaculate Heart*, 159.

182. Martins, *Novos Documentos*, 215; Kondor, *Fatima in Lucia's Own Words*, 85–86.

183. Martins, *Novos Documentos*, 219–220; Kondor, *Fatima in Lucia's Own Words*, 89–90.

184. Martins, *Novos Documentos*, 199–200; Kondor, *Fatima in Lucia's Own Words*, 71.

185. Martins, *Novos Documentos*, 202–203; Kondor, *Fatima in Lucia's Own Words*, 74.

186. Pierina Gilli said that on 7 December 1947, at the parish church in Montichiari, Italy, Mary appeared to her as "Rosa Mystica" and was accompanied by Jacinta and Francisco. Mary told Pierina that the two children would be companions for her in her affliction, noting that "they too have suffered, though

they were much younger than you," and admonishing Pierina to be as simple and good as the two children had been. (A. M. Weigl, *Mary—Rosa Mystica*, trans. N. C. Reeves and I. Muske [Essen: J. Bürger, 1975], 22–23.)

187. According to an early brochure recounting the apparition of the Virgin at San Damiano, Italy (see Chapter 2), on 19 October 1964, three days after the Virgin had appeared to Rosa Quattrini and had made a plum and a pear tree burst into unseasonable bloom, three cousins of Lucia arrived in San Damiano with a message for Rosa from Lucia herself. S. Di Maria, who reports this visit, implies that Lucia learned of the apparition of the Virgin to Rosa by miraculous means. (S. Di Maria, *Our Lady of San Damiano* [Bulle, Switzerland: Éditions du Parvis, n.d.], 19–20.)

CHAPTER TWO

1. Probably the best known stigmatic of the twentieth century and certainly the best known of Italy's recent living saints, the Capuchin Padre Pio (1887–1968) lived for more than fifty years at San Giovanni Rotondo near Foggia, where his renown led to the building of a large church and a famous hospital. Thousands of pilgrims came to this town every year to see and hear him and to receive his spiritual counsel. Rosa Quattrini was apparently not the only modern seer to have had some contact with this much-revered man. Conchita Gonzàlez is reported to have met with him as well, and there are few modern apparition devotees who are not familiar with his life and work. On Padre Pio's involvement in the end-time scenario associated with Garabandal, see Chapter 6. On Padre Pio as a typical twentieth-century European holy person, see W. A. Christian, Jr., "Holy People in Peasant Europe."

2. R. Maisonneuve and M. de Belsunce, *San Damiano: histoire et documents* (Paris: Téqui, 1984), 15–17. This collection of texts translated into French by Maisonneuve and De Belsunce is the most important source for the history of the apparition at San Damiano. The translations into English from these texts are my own.

3. Ibid., 18. Pierina, the eldest, became a sister of the Sacred Heart and was sent as a missionary to Brazil; Anna, the second child, became a Franciscan and was sent as a missionary to Sri Lanka; Giuseppina, the youngest, became a Carmelite at San Colombano di Lucca, Italy.

4. Ibid., 18–19, 23–25, 320–323.

5. "Cartella clinica établie à la Casa di Cura Policlinica S. Giacomo di Ponte dell'Olio. Reparto Chirurgia. No ordine 66." Quoted in Maisonneuve and De Belsunce, *San Damiano*, 322.

6. "Attestation de séjour à l'Ospedale Civile di Piacenza, délivrée par les services administratifs de l'hôpital, signée par le directeur sanitaire, en date du 29 decembre 1976." Quoted in Maisonneuve and Belsunce, *San Damiano*, 322.

7. Maisonneuve and De Belsunce, *San Damiano*, 19, 24, 27.

8. D. Buzzati, *I misteri d'Italia* (Milan: Arnoldo Mondadori Editore, 1978), 120–122; for a French translation, see Maisonneuve and De Belsunce, *San*

Damiano, 20–23; for an English account, see J. Osee, *Call of the Virgin at San Damiano* (North Quincy, MA: Christopher Publishing House, 1977), 45–47.

9. Maisonneuve and De Belsunce, *San Damiano*, 22, note 12. The dating of the documents cited in the footnotes is given on p. 20, note 5.

10. Ibid., 22, note 13.

11. Ibid., 22, note 12.

12. Transcript of interview, 5 August 1974, quoted in Maisonneuve and De Belsunce, *San Damiano*, 19, note 4; for the date of this interview, see p. 20, note 5.

13. Transcript of an interview, 18 September 1968, quoted in Maisonneuve and De Belsunce, *San Damiano*, 23, note 16; for the dating of this interview, see p. 20, note 5.

14. Interview with Fr.-X. Brodard, 13 April 1968, quoted in Maisonneuve and De Belsunce, *San Damiano*, 23, notes 17 and 18; for the dating of this interview, see p. 20, note 5; for an English translation of some of this interview, see S. di Maria, *The Most Holy Virgin at San Damiano* (Hauteville, Switzerland: Éditions du Parvis, 1983), 24–24. Di Maria mistakenly translates the phrase *ta malade* as "your illness" rather than "your sick one" or perhaps more properly in this context, "your sick niece."

15. Maisonneuve and De Belsunce, *San Damiano*, 25.

16. Ibid., 24.

17. Pellacani was accused not just of having staged Rosa's healing but of having written the messages Rosa attributed to the Virgin, of having profited from the offerings of the faithful at the expense of the parish, of influencing by his attitude the influx of pilgrims to San Damiano, and of connecting the name of Padre Pio to the events there (Maisonneuve and De Belsunce, *San Damiano*, 315).

18. Maisonneuve and De Belsunce, *San Damiano*, 316.

19. Rosa told Buzzati that she thought it was "our priest" (apparently Pellacani) who had sent her the money (*I misteri d'Italia*, 122). In responding to the questions of Maisonneuve and De Belsunce, Pellacani, however, said simply that he thought someone had given her the money for the pilgrimage since she did not have it herself (*San Damiano*, 317). Maisonneuve and De Belsunce, in their French translation of Rosa's interview with Buzzati, include a statement by Rosa, which is not in Buzzati's published Italian text, that two hours before her departure she received clothing for the trip. She thought this must have come from someone who knew her well, for the clothes fit perfectly (*San Damiano*, 23).

20. Maisonneuve and De Belsunce, *San Damiano*, 28. The authors do not give a date for this account.

21. Ibid., 28, and note 20.

22. Ibid., 28; Rosa gave Buzzati a short account of her encounter with the woman on the square (*I misteri d'Italia*, 122; Osee, *Call of the Virgin*, 49).

23. Maisonneuve and De Belsunce, *San Damiano*, 28, notes 22 and 23. This account is not dated (20 note 5).

24. Ibid., 317.

25. Ibid., 29.

26. Ibid., 30. Summaries of Rosa's activities during her "service to the sick" are found in Di Maria, *San Damiano*, 27, and Osee, *Call of the Virgin*, 49. However, the encounters described by Di Maria appear to have been conflated and made to appear more miraculous than Rosa's own descriptions would warrant. This summary, therefore, should be compared with the documents found in Maisonneuve and De Belsunce.

27. Maisonneuve and De Belsunce, *San Damiano*, 31.

28. Ibid., 34 and note 26. The text of Pellacani's manuscript is found on pp. 35–38.

29. Ibid., 35 and note 28. The woman, "I. B.," who was about twenty-four years of age, confirmed that she visited Rosa that morning and also wrote an account of the apparition Rosa had seen.

30. Ibid., 35 and note 32.

31. Ibid., 35–36; see also the account given to Buzzati, *I misteri d'Italia*, 123; for an English translation, see Osee, *Call of the Virgin*, 53–54.

32. Maisonneuve and De Belsunce, *San Damiano*, 37.

33. This message should be compared to that which Rosa related to Buzzati in 1966. Rosa said then that Mary told her, "My daughter, I come from far away. Announce to the world that everyone should pray because Jesus can no longer carry the cross. I want everyone, everyone to be saved, the good as well as the evil. I am the mother of love, the mother of all; all are my children. I want all to be saved. Therefore I have come to warn the world to pray, because chastisements are near. I will return each Friday, and I will give you messages that you must announce to the world" (*I misteri d'Italia*, 123). Here Rosa has apparently condensed what was reported to Pellacani as separate parts of her conversation into one long message. It is this version of the message which was published in devotional works (e.g., Osee, *Call of the Virgin*, 53–54; Di Maria, *San Damiano*, 29). Maisonneuve and De Belsunce provide a compendium of the versions of this message that Rosa gave in interviews (*San Damiano*, 43–45) and some reflections on the problems presented by these different versions (*San Damiano*, 46–47)

34. Maisonneuve and De Belsunce, *San Damiano*, 37, note 41.

35. Ibid., 38.

36. Ibid., 38, note 44, version R.V.1.

37. Ibid., 38, note 44, version M.C.

38. Ibid., 41–42; see also G. de Lutiis, "Novi Casi esemplari," in *Studi sulla produzione sociale de sacro* (Naples: Liguori Editore, 1978), 127. The little crossroads of San Damiano is quite overshadowed by this air base, and indeed, to reach the town from the north one must drive around much of the base.

39. Maisonneuve and De Belsunce, *San Damiano*, 39; an excerpt from the article in this paper, *Libertà*, translated into French, is found on pp. 39–40.

40. Ibid., 40, where an excerpt from this paper, *Piacenza Oggi*, has been translated into French.

41. Ibid., 40–41, where an excerpt from this paper, *Libertà*, has been translated into French.

42. Ibid., 42.

43. Ibid., 42–43.

44. Ibid., 42.

45. Ibid., 315, n. 5.

46. Ibid., 41. Pellacani's remarks here are quoted by Maisonneuve and De Belsunce from an interview with Pier Capello ("Mama Rosa," *Gente*, 2/44 [30 October 1981]: 47).

47. Ibid., 32, 317; Di Maria, *San Damiano*, 34–35.

48. Buzzati, *I misteri d'Italia*, 123; Maisonneuve and De Belsunce, *San Damiano*, 43; Osee, *Call of the Virgin*, 54.

49. Maisonneuve and De Belsunce, *San Damiano*, 44, version R.V.1.

50. For a description of the public rituals held at the pear tree during the first years of the cult, see Osee, *Call of the Virgin*, 58–59.

51. Ibid., 62–63. Di Maria has garbled this information in his translation (*San Damiano*, 50).

52. Maisonneuve and De Belsunce, *San Damiano*, 110.

53. Ibid., 110–111; Di Maria, *San Damiano*, 50, 52–53.

54. Maisonneuve and De Belsunce, *San Damiano*, 111; Di Maria, *San Damiano*, 50–51. There is some discrepancy in the sources about whether this message was delivered on November 16 or November 18.

55. Maisonneuve and De Belsunce, *San Damiano*, 111–112; Di Maria, *San Damiano*, 51–55.

56. Maisonneuve and De Belsunce, *San Damiano*, 113. For a long time, Giuseppe, Rosa's husband, was designated to draw water from the well with a bucket; later an electric pump and taps were installed (Di Maria, *San Damiano*, 55).

57. Maisonneuve and De Belsunce, *San Damiano*, 113.

58. Ibid., 116–121.

59. Ibid., 122.

60. Ibid., 122–123. Rosa turned over some three million lire to this association according to some reports (122, note 107).

61. De Lutiis, "Novi casi esemplari," 126–129.

62. De Lutiis, "Novi casi esemplari," 130–131. Maisonneuve and De Belsunce note the decisive break between Rosa and Pro San Damiano in the fall of 1976 but do not make any reference to the relationship between the Swiss and Lefebvre (*San Damiano*, 125).

63. Legal recognition of the Ospizio Madonna della Rose as a nonprofit organization was apparently hindered at this point by Italian laws which required that any group planning this sort of development be chartered as a commercial corporation (Maisonneuve and De Belsunce, *San Damiano*, 123, 125).

64. Ibid., 123–124.

65. Ibid., 125–126.

66. Ibid., 129–130.

67. Ibid., 353–354.

68. *Libertà* (11 February 1983), quoted in Maisonneuve and De Belsunce, *San Damiano*, 355–356.

69. Ibid., 354.

70. Program of the International Youth Meeting, 7–8 May 1988, at San Damiano. The program and updating of the activities of the Associazione Ospizio delle Rose were provided by Paul Cunane, National Center for the Society of Madonna delle Rose in the United Kingdom (1 De Montfort Grove, Hungerford, Berkshire, England).

71. For a listing of the dates of the statements issued by the bishops of Piacenza and an overview of their content, see Maisonneuve and De Belsunce, *San Damiano*, 48–49.

72. *La documentation catholique*, 66/1531 (5 January 1969): 47–48.

73. *La documentation catholique*, 67/1559 (15 March 1970): 295.

74. *La documentation catholique*, 66/1532 (19 January 1969): 91 and editor's note. It should be noted in this connection that all of the Swiss dioceses as well as some of the dioceses of Italy such as Piacenza are not parts of any archdiocese and are said to stand directly under the jurisdiction of the Holy See.

75. *La documentation catholique*, 67/1559 (15 March 1970): 295.

76. *La documentation catholique*, 68/1577 (3 January 1971): 34.

77. *La documentation catholique*, 68/1577 (3 January 1971): 32–34.

78. The letter (66/890) was addressed to the secretary of state (of the Vatican) and a copy was sent to Manfredi.

79. Manfredi cites here *Lumen Gentium*, 23.

80. *La documentation catholique*, 70/1629 (1 April 1973): 348.

81. *La documentation catholique*, 81/1869 (4 March 1984): 271.

82. San Damiano is not mentioned, for example, in P. Bartolotti and P. Mantero, *Guida alle Apparizioni Mariani in Italia* (Milan: Sugar Co. Edizioni, 1988).

CHAPTER THREE

1. The primary publisher and distributor of information about Garabandal for the United States is The Workers of Our Lady of Mount Carmel, Inc., P. O. Box 606, Lindenhurst, NY, 11757.

2. J. A. Pelletier, *Our Lady Comes to Garabandal, Including Conchita's Diary* (Worcester, MA: Assumption Publications, 1971), 13–14. In addition to a translation of Conchita's *Diary*, this work contains translations of several of her letters as well as an introduction and commentary by Pelletier. For the sake of clarity, references to Conchita's *Diary* will be cited as González, *Diary*, in *OLCG*; references to commentary by Pelletier will be cited as Pelletier, *Our Lady Comes to Garabandal*.

3. R. Pérez, *Garabandal: The Village Speaks*, ed. A. Orhelein, trans. A.I.C. Mathews (Lindenhurst, NY: The Workers of Our Lady of Mount Carmel, 1981), 94–102.

4. Father François Turner, whom I spoke with in Paris on 16 October 1989, has collected a number of other firsthand accounts of the apparitions and knows

of several other collections of similar materials. No judgment about the importance of this material can be made until it is published.

Among the important apologetic studies of Garabandal are F. Sanchez-Ventura y Pascual, *The Apparitions of Garabandal* (Detroit: San Miguel, 1966); F. Sanchez-Ventura y Pascual, *Stigmatisés et Apparitions* (Paris: Nouvelles éditions latines, 1967), 250–272; M. Laffineur and M. T. le Pelletier, *Star on the Mountain*, trans. S. L. Lacoutre (Newtonville, NY: Our Lady of Mount Carmel of Garabandal, 1968); G. Le Rumeur, *Notre-Dame du Carmel à Garabandal* (Argenton l'Eglise: G. Le Rumeur, 1975); H. Daley, *Miracle at Garabandal* (Dublin: Ward River Press, 1985); and Pérez, *Garabandal: The Village Speaks*.

The religious beliefs and rituals of the people of Garabandal and its vicinity have been the object of a study by W. A. Christian, Jr., entitled *Person and God in a Spanish Valley*, recently issued in a second edition by Princeton University Press (1989). While it was some years after the Garabandal apparition that Christian lived in these villages and gathered the data for this remarkable study, Christian has not been concerned here with the apparition as such, and indeed he says very little about it. His concern here, rather, has been with the more traditional structures of local religious belief and activity which could be considered its setting and with how these have been threatened, or have been perceived to be threatened, by some of the changes associated with the Second Vatican Council. Christian sees the apparitions at Garabandal as a rather striking reaction to those changes.

5. González, *Diary*, in *OLCG*, 15–16.

6. Ibid., 16–17.

7. Ibid., 17–18. Conchita's mother, Aniceta, said that she thought Conchita was simply telling her a story to avoid a scolding (Pérez, *Garabandal*, 183).

8. González, *Diary*, in *OLCG*, 23–24. Pelletier notes that although Conchita used the first person plural pronoun at this place in her *Diary* ("We had started our prayers when we heard a voice that said . . . we continued to pray with great fervor"), she is referring to herself with a grammatical construction permissible in Spanish. In a conversation with Pelletier in 1970, Conchita confirmed that she was the only one of the four girls to have heard this voice.

9. Ibid., 26.

10. Ibid., 28.

11. Pérez, *Garabandal*, 287–289. Clementina told Pérez that she trusted the girls and that they knew it, which is why they sought her out to go with them to the calleja as a witness.

12. Pérez lists only seven appearances of the angel after the first: June 22, 23, 24, 25, 27, 28, and July 1 (*Garabandal*, 16–18). I have preferred here to follow Conchita's account, in which she reports appearances of the angel on Thursday (June 22), Friday (June 23), Saturday (June 24), Sunday (June 25), Wednesday (June 28), Thursday (June 29), Friday (June 30), and Saturday (July 1); see González, *Diary*, in *OLCG*, 28–35.

13. González, *Diary*, in *OLCG*, 29.

14. Ibid., 34.

15. Ibid., 21.

16. Ibid., 30.

17. Ibid., 30–31.

18. Ibid., 35–36.

19. Ibid., 37–38. Conchita does not say in her *Diary* how she knew that one of the angels was St. Michael; the angel had not spoken until the last appearance, and in that conversation she does not report that he identified himself.

20. Ibid., 38. This characterization of the relationship between the seers and the Virgin was mentioned by Simon González, Jacinta's father, to Pérez (*Garabandal*, 263).

21. González, *Diary*, in *OLCG*, 55–56. Conchita's mother gave an account of Conchita's one apparition in Santander to Pérez (*Garabandal*, 191–193).

22. González, *Diary*, in *OLCG*, 56; Pérez, *Garabandal*, 191, 194.

23. Pérez, *Garabandal*, 133–134.

24. González, *Diary*, in *OLCG*, 56.

25. See, for example, ibid., 61, 64, 88; and Pérez, *Garabandal*, 25.

26. González, *Diary*, in *OLCG*, 41–42.

27. Ibid., 42.

28. Pérez, *Garabandal*, 217, 247, 316–317.

29. Ibid., 235, 291.

30. Ibid., 168, 204, 256–257, 303–304.

31. Ibid., 161.

32. Pérez, *Garabandal*, 113, 115, 123, 125, 139, 164, 186, 203, 215–216, 273.

33. Ibid., 148–149, 165–166, 171, 198–199, 203–204, 216, 245–246, 309–310.

34. Ibid., 131, 165, 179, 203–204, 232–233, 238, 262–263, 274–275, 283, 299–300, 316.

35. Ibid., 179, 262–263, 305.

36. González, *Diary*, in *OLCG*, 32–33.

37. Pérez, *Garabandal*, 146–147.

38. Ibid., 129–130; see also, 187–188.

39. Ibid., 149–150; see similar testimonies on 165–166, 171, 198–199, 203–204, 216, 309–310.

40. Ibid., 147.

41. For testimonies to the girls' lack of signs of physical exertion, see ibid., 148, 164, 213, 216, 245, 254, 258, 296, 304, 309.

42. Ibid., 140. The inability of observers to release themselves or objects from the seers' grasp once their experiences began is mentioned in several testimonies: 179, 213, 232–233, 274–275, 316. Especially interesting are the stories of Conchita falling into ecstasy while clinging to a pet sheep (262–263) and Mari Loli falling into ecstasy while changing a light bulb (179).

43. Ibid., 120–121; see also, 164–165, 254, 313.

44. González, *Diary*, in *OLCG*, 42.

45. Pelletier, *Our Lady Comes to Garabandal*, 43–45.

46. Pérez, *Garabandal*, 141.

47. Ibid., 159–161; see similar testimonies on pp. 115, 129–130, 230, 291, 294–295, 317.

48. Ibid., 128–129.

49. Ibid., 238–239.

50. Ibid., 125–126.

51. Ibid., 231–232.

52. Ibid., 126–127. Fr. José Ramón Garcia de la Riva gives a full account of this episode in his pamphlet, *Memories of My Visits to Garabandal*, trans. Mary of Jesus (Tacoma, WA: Northwest Garabandal Center, 1969), 36–38. Garcia de la Riva says that before going to bed he had asked for a sign that the Virgin was not displeased with him for not following the apparition that evening after the Rosary. He was, he said, very tired and he felt a bit sad because he was not following the seers in ecstasy as other visitors to Garabandal were doing. In her account of this incident, Maximina has apparently generalized the priest's motive into a request for proof of the authenticity of the apparition (and not simply a desire to know that the Virgin was not displeased with him).

53. Priests were discouraged by the bishop of Santander from going to Garabandal, which may be one reason why some priests who went to the village chose to dress in secular garb.

54. Pérez, *Garabandal*, 128.

55. Ibid., 188–189; see Maximina's description of the same event, 130–131. In an interview in 1973, Conchita recalled that one priest tried to trick her by arriving with a girl who said she was his fiancée, but she didn't recall how she found out he was a priest; see also H. Daley, *Miracle at Garabandal*, 174.

56. Indeed, it has been suggested that the popularity of many modern apparition shrines reflects a return to power of the monastic—over against the secular—clergy in recent centuries. See M. Bax, "Religious Regimes and State Formation: Towards a Research Perspective," *Anthropological Quarterly* 60 (1987): 1–11; and "Maria-verschijningen in Medjugorje: Rivaliserende religieuze regimes en staatsvorming," *Sociologisch Tijdschrift* 14/2 (October 1987): 95–223.

57. Pérez, *Garabandal*, 26.

58. González, *Diary*, in *OLCG*, 93.

59. Pérez, *Garabandal*, 252–253. Pelletier includes a photograph of Conchita receiving invisible Communion in *Our Lady Comes to Garabandal*, 138.

60. González, *Diary*, in *OLCG*, 100.

61. Ibid., 101–103. According to Pérez, Conchita and her fellow seers told Garcia de la Riva about the nature of the miracle on July 2 but it was only on the following day, July 3, that Conchita received an interior locution about the date of the miracle and announced it publically and in some letters (*Garabandal*, 27–28).

62. Garcia de la Riva, *Memories of My Visits to Garabandal*, 27–28; see also Garcia de la Riva's recollection of these events in Perez, *Garabandal*, 107–108. Garcia de la Riva said that he learned about the nature of the miracle on July 2, but that the girls had not yet learned the date when the miracle would take place and that he returned to his parish on July 5 without that information.

63. González, *Diary*, in *OLCG*, 103–105. The girls received their calls only

in anticipation of the appearances of the Virgin, not of the angel. The calls on this occasion were appropriate, however, since the Virgin did unexpectedly "appear" to Conchita after the appearance of the angel (Pelletier, *Our Lady Comes to Garabandal*, 106).

64. González, *Diary*, in *OLCG*, 105.

65. Pérez, *Garabandal*, 151–154.

66. Ibid., 153.

67. Ibid., 221.

68. Ibid., 247.

69. Ibid., 169.

70. Ibid., 154.

71. Ibid., 28.

72. González, *Diary*, in *OLCG*, 104–105. See also the testimony of Lucia Fernandez, Conchita's cousin, who told Perez that she spent the afternoon and evening of July 18 with her. Contrary to the rumors, Fernandez said, they had not prepared the host prior to Conchita's ecstasy but had only sat in a room looking out the window at the festival (211–212).

73. Pérez, *Garabandal*, 197.

74. There are so many photographs that believers claim have captured a variety of miraculous phenomena at Marian apparitions that these might in themselves merit a special study. Only a few interesting and readily accessible examples are cited here. For a picture of Mary Ann Van Hoof, the seer at Necedah, Wisconsin, purporting to show a profile of Jesus, see H. Swan, ed., *My Work with Necedah*, vol. 1, *Mary Ann Van Hoof's Own Story of the Apparitions of the Blessed Virgin Mary* (Necedah, WI: For My God and My Country, 1959), opposite p. 43. For a picture taken at San Damiano, Italy, in which the image of the Virgin is supposed to have miraculously appeared above a tree, see the cover of J. Osee, *Call of the Virgin at San Damiano* (North Quincy, MA: Christopher Publishing House, 1977). For a series of photographs purporting to capture a variety of phenomena (for example, crosses in the sun, an image of the crucified Jesus on the breast of a statue of Mary, images of the Virgin in the sun) at Medjugorje, Yugoslavia, see R. Laurentin and H. Joyeux, *Scientific and Medical Studies on the Apparitions at Medjugorje*, trans. L. Griffin (Dublin: Veritas, 1987), inserted between pp. 90 and 91.

75. Pelletier, *Our Lady Comes to Garabandal*, 106–107. Pelletier has pointed out that there was a similar discrepancy between official time and sun time in connection with the final apparition reported by the three children at Fatima on 13 October 1917. This appearance had been announced for noon, he noted, and it was in fact noon according to sun time, although the clock stood at 1:30 when the children reported the Virgin's appearance and the miracle of the sun. See also Sanchez-Ventura y Pascual, *The Apparitions of Garabandal*, 129.

76. González, *Diary*, in *OLCG*, 115.

77. Pérez, *Garabandal*, 194.

78. Ibid., 135.

79. Ibid., 135–136. At other times Maximina has said, less specifically, that

it was sometime during July 1961 that Conchita first made this statement (Pelletier, *Our Lady Comes to Garabandal*, 116, note 9).

80. Pérez, *Garabandal*, 218.

81. Ibid., 181.

82. González, *Diary*, in *OLCG*, 115.

83. Ibid., 119. When Pérez gathered his testimonies from villagers in 1971, Mari Cruz's parents declined to be interviewed. Pérez said he did speak with Mari Cruz's mother for an hour. He characterized her apparently passionate denunciation of the apparition as "an outward expression of a great internal suffering." Her arguments, he said, were the same as those of the young priests who had been sent by the bishopric of Santander to "eradicate all ideas of the supernatural from the minds of the Garabandal inhabitants." Pérez did not find these arguments convincing (*Garabandal*, 95).

84. Pérez, *Garabandal*, 194–195.

85. Pelletier, *Our Lady Comes to Garabandal*, 203–205.

86. According to believers, Bishop Puchol Montis of Santander replaced Marichalar, who had been supportive of the apparition, first with Fr. Amador Fernandez Gonzalez, and then with Fr. José Olano, with the express purpose of undermining faith in the apparition. See, for example, Sanchez-Ventura y Pascual, *The Apparitions of Garabandal*, 144; Pérez, *Garabandal*, 77; Le Rumeur, *Notre-Dame du Carmel à Garabandal*, 118.

87. Pérez, *Garabandal*, 76–77. Le Rumeur adds to this the suggestion that Conchita wanted to live a normal life like everyone else (*Notre-Dame du Carmel à Garabandal*, 119). On this point, see Aniceta's report of a conversation between Conchita and the chaplain of the clinic in Bilbao in 1971. According to Aniceta, who had gone to consult the chaplain about her daughter, he talked with Conchita after her visit, and Conchita reportedly told him that she had never tried to deceive anyone and that she had only one desire, namely "to be a good girl, but like the others" (Pérez, *Garabandal*, 198).

88. Pérez, *Garabandal*, 195–196.

89. The dates of the interviews were August 30, September 2, 7, 27 and October 11, 1966. See "Note officielle de l'évêque de Santander" (17 March 1967), in *La documentation catholique*, 64/1491 (2 April 1967): 671. For an English translation of this document, see Pérez, *Garabandal*, 64–65.

90. Pérez, *Garabandal*, 78.

91. Ibid., 194–197.

92. Quoted in Le Rumeur, *Notre-Dame du Carmel à Garabandal*, 122–123.

93. See note 89.

94. Pérez, *Garabandal*, 62–63.

95. "Note officielle de l'évêque de Santander" (7 October 1962), in *La documentation catholique*, 62/1452 (18 July 1965): 1344–1345. For an English translation of this text, see Pérez, *Garabandal*, 63–64.

96. "Note officielle de l'évêque de Santander" (8 July 1965), in *La documentation catholique*, 62/1457 (17 October 1965): 1823–1824. For an English translation, see Pérez, *Garabandal*, 64.

97. "Communiqué de l'évêque de Santander" (9 October 1968), in *La docu-*

mentation catholique, 66/1531 (5 January 1969): 47. Pérez provides only a short summary of this statement in *Garabandal*, 65.

98. "Lettre de l'évêque de Santander aux évêques du monde entière" (June 1970), in *La documentation catholique*, 68/1577 (3 January 1971): 30–32. Pérez provides a translation of sections of this text along with some lengthy commentary (*Garabandal*, 65–69). He incorrectly gives the date of the issue of *La documentation catholique* as 1 March 1971.

99. Conchita made a trip to Rome at the beginning of 1966 in which she was said to have had both a private audience with the Pope and to have received his special blessing. For a full discussion of this trip, see Chapter 6.

100. "Lettre de l'évêque de Santander aux évêques du monde entière" (June 1970), 32; Pérez, *Garabandal*, 69.

101. Garcia de la Riva, *Memories of My Visits to Garabandal*, 11–13.

102. Pérez, *Garabandal*, 70–71. Laffineur provides an account of this interview with the clerk in *Star on the Mountain*, 87–90.

103. Quoted in Pérez, *Garabandal*, 69, note 9; see also, José Maria de Dios, *Dios en la Sombra* (Editorial Círculo, 1967), 241–242. For another response to the Commission, see R. Paco, *Contributions à l'étude des faits négatifs par la Commission de Santander contre le surnaturalisme des faits de Garabandal* (Blois, France: privately printed, 1968).

104. Three of the four seers—Conchita, Jacinta, and Mari Loli—came to reaffirm their faith in the apparition. All three married and moved to the United States, where, to differing degrees, they have remained accessible to Garabandal devotees. Mari Cruz, who has maintained her denial of the apparition, has also married but remained in Spain.

105. See, for example, W. Proudfoot, *Religious Experience* (Berkeley: University of California Press, 1985).

CHAPTER FOUR

1. A. Ravier, *Les écrits de sainte Bernadette et sa voie spirituelle*, 47–48, 81, 109, 239.

2. M. Le Hidec, *Les secrets de la Salette* (Paris: Nouvelles éditions latines, 1969), 47–67, 69–129.

3. Stern, *La Salette, Documents authentiques*, vols. 1 and 2.

4. Stern, vol. 1, Doc. 1, pp. 47–48; Stern, vol. 2, Doc. 297, pp. 151–153. See also Ullathorne, *The Holy Mountain of La Salette*, 30–33.

5. Stern, vol. 1, p. 49.

6. Maximin's statement was originally published in November 1881, in the *Annales de N.-D. de la Salette* as part of "Le récit de Maximin," quoted in Le Hidec, *Les secrets*, 16 and note 6. See also Stern, vol. 1, p. 26 and note 4.

7. Stern, vol. 1, Doc. 6, pp. 61–62.

8. Ibid., Doc. 7: description and dating, pp. 64–64; text, pp. 70–78.

9. Ibid., Doc. 7, p. 75.

10. Ibid., pp. 64, 90; see, for example, Doc. 40 bis, pp. 170–173, and its

derivative, Doc. 64, pp. 221–226. Documents in which the secrets are referred to as personal are: Doc. 7 bis, p. 67; Doc. 11, p. 80; Doc. 16, p. 105; Doc. 20, p. 118; Doc. 22, p. 123; Doc. 27, p. 130; Doc. 64, p. 225; Doc. 71, p. 238.

11. Le Hidec, *Les secrets*, 15–16.

12. Stern, vol. 1, Doc. 13 bis, critical notes, p. 90; text, pp. 90–93.

13. Ibid., Doc. 7 bis, p. 67; see also Doc. 64, p. 225; Doc. 71, p. 239; and Stern, vol. 2, Doc. 184, p. 84.

14. Stern, vol. 2, Doc. 135, pp. 33–34; Doc. 184, pp. 84–85.

15. Stern, vol. 1, Doc. 16, p. 105; Doc. 20, p. 118; Doc. 28 bis, p. 135; Doc. 42, p. 179; Doc. 57, p. 213; Doc. 64, p. 225; Doc. 66, p.229; Doc. 71, p. 239. Stern, vol. 2, Doc. 135, pp. 31–34; Doc. 163, pp. 54–55, 57; Doc. 169, p. 62; Doc. 182, p. 80; Doc. 184, pp. 84–85; Doc. 310, pp. 173–174; Doc. 343, p. 207. For an English translation of excerpts from some of these investigations, see Ullathorne, *Holy Mountain*, 59–69.

16. Stern, vol. 1, Doc. 20, p. 118.

17. Stern, vol. 1, Doc. 71, p. 239; see also, Doc. 64, p. 225.

18. Stern, vol. 1, Doc. 43, p. 181; Doc. 57, p. 213. Stern, vol. 2, Doc. 135, p. 30; Doc. 343. p. 207. See also Ullathorne, *Holy Mountain*, 73–77.

19. Stern, vol. 1, Doc. 99, pp. 310–311; for an English translation, see Abbé Lagier, *The Abbé Jots It Down*, 25–28. Concerning the problem of dating the interviews of Lagier with the two seers, see Chapter 1, note 8, above.

20. Stern, vol. 1, Doc. 64, p. 225; see also Doc. 71, p. 239.

21. Stern, vol. 2, Doc. 182, p. 80.

22. Stern, vol. 1, Doc. 124, p. 360.

23. Stern, vol. 2, Doc. 213, pp. 103–105.

24. Ibid., Doc. 310, p. 174.

25. Stern, vol. 1, Doc. 99, p. 309; Lagier, *The Abbé Jots It Down*, 23.

26. Stern, vol. 2, Doc. 163, p. 57.

27. Mlle. M. des Brulais, *L'Écho de la sainte montagne*, 3d ed. (Nantes: Charpentier, 1854), 65; Stern, vol. 2, Doc. 264 bis, p. 131.

28. Stern, vol. 2, Doc. 411, p. 266.

29. Ibid., Doc. 501, p. 313.

30. Ibid., Doc. 523, p. 321.

31. This account is given in Mgr. Ginoulhiac's mandement of 4 November 1854, quoted in Le Hidec, *Les secrets*, 47–49; see also L. Carlier, *Histoire de l'Apparition de la Mère de Dieu sur la montagne de la Salette* (Tournai: Les Missionaires de la Salette, 1912), 129–143.

32. Stern, vol. 2, Doc. 518, p. 320.

33. Le Hidec, *Les secrets*, 48.

34. Vianney and Maximin held two conversations on that morning, the first at about nine o'clock lasting about twelve minutes and the second at eleven o'clock, lasting just a few minutes. J. Jaouen, *La Grâce de la Salette 1846–1946*, 171–172.

35. Ibid., 174–177.

36. Des Brulais, *L'Écho*, 265–268.

37. Jaouen gives a thorough analysis of the conflict in *La Grâce de la Salette*, 172–196.

38. Ibid., 198–199; Le Hidec, *Les secrets*, 51; Carlier, *Histoire de l'Apparition*, 143.

39. Quoted in Le Hidec, *Les secrets*, 51; Carlier, *Histoire de l'Apparition*, 143; and L. Bassette, *Le fait de la Salette: 1846–1854* (Paris: Cerf, 1965), 204.

40. Le Hidec, *Les secrets*, 52–53; Carlier, *Histoire de l'Apparition*, 144; Bassette, *Le fait de la Salette*, 205; Des Brulais, *L'Écho*, 228–230; for an English translation of the conversation see Ullathorne, *Holy Mountain*, 90–91.

41. Le Hidec, *Les secrets*, 54–55; Carlier, *Histoire de l'Apparition*, 144–145; Bassette, *Le fait de la Salette*, 205–206; Des Brulais, *L'Écho*, 230–232; Ullathorne, *Holy Mountain*, 93. Jean Stern believes that Maximin's first demur (that he would decide when he was in the presence of the pope) indicates that he too understood something of the politics of the request for his secret.

42. Le Hidec, *Les secrets*, 55; Des Brulais, *L'Écho*, 233; Ullathorne, *Holy Mountain*, 93.

43. Le Hidec, *Les secrets*, 57; Carlier, *Histoire de l'Apparition*, 146; Des Brulais, *L'Écho*, 235; Ullathorne, *Holy Mountain*, 95.

44. Le Hidec, *Les secrets*, 58; Carlier, *Histoire de l'Apparition*, 147; Bassette, *Le fait de la Salette*, 208.

45. Le Hidec, *Les secrets*, 58–59; Bassette, *Le fait de la Salette*, 208–209.

46. The account of the transcription of the children's secrets that has been accepted as standard was compiled by Father Bossan, a historian of La Salette, with the assistance of three of the witnesses (F. Benjamin Dausse, Canon de Taxis, and the Abbé Gerente). See Le Hidec, *Les secrets*, 59–61 and Bassette, *Le fait de la Salette,* 209, note 84; account, 209–211. For a discussion of Benjamin Dausse, see Stern, vol. 1, 278–279.

47. Carlier states that when Mélanie rewrote her secret on July 6, Auvergne and Sister Saint-Louis, superior of the convent, were the witnesses rather than Auvergne and Dausse. His source for this information is not clear (*Histoire de l'Apparition*, 149–150).

48. Des Brulais, *L'Écho*, 244, 259, 271.

49. Ibid., 259–260.

50. Ibid., 271.

51. This account is cited in *Maximin peint par lui-même* (1881), attributed to the Abbé Le Bailiff; quoted in Le Hidec, *Les secrets*, 65.

52. Le Hidec, *Les secrets*, 66–67; Des Brulais, *L'Écho*, 236–243. Although the letter is listed in the archives of Pius IX, the copies are no longer there.

53. Le Hidec, *Les secrets*, 59–61; Carlier, *Histoire de l'Apparition*, 150; Bassette, *Le fait de la Salette*, 211; Des Brulais, *L'Écho*, 236–238; Ullathorne, *Holy Mountain*, 97; see also Mlle. Marie des Brulais, *Suite de l'écho de la sainte montagne* (Nantes: Charpentier, 1855), 29–30. According to Des Brulais, Mélanie asked the meaning of the word "infallibly" and the meaning and spelling of the word "antichrist." The word "soiled" (*souillée*) is not mentioned in this account (Des Brulais, *L'Écho*, 236, note 1; see also Ullathorne, *Holy Mountain*, 97).

54. Des Brulais, *L'Écho*, 237, 239–240; Ullathorne, *Holy Mountain*, 100–101. The translation is my own.

55. Des Brulais, *L'Écho*, 239–243; Ullathorne, *Holy Mountain*, 100–101. The translations are my own. Stern points out that Lambruscini and Fornari are both Italian and believes that by "secret" these men may simply have meant the public message in the sense of a "new revelation."

56. Des Brulais, *L'Écho*, 255; Ullathorne, *Holy Mountain*, 101–102.

57. Le Hidec, *Les secrets*, 67; Carlier, *Histoire de l'Apparition*, 153.

58. Des Brulais, *L'Écho*, 236; Ullathorne, *Holy Mountain*, 99.

59. For an edition of this text, see Dion, *Maximin Giraud, berger de la Salette ou la fidélité dans l'épreuve*, 148.

60. C.-R. Girard, *Les secrets de la Salette et leur importance: derniers révélations sur de prochains évènements*, 4th ed. (Grenoble: F. Allier, 1872), 111–112; see also Le Hidec, *Les secrets*, 70–71.

61. M. Dausse, *L'homme d'oraison: l'abbé J.-B. Gerin, curé de la cathédrale de Grenoble* (Grenoble: Baratier et Dardelet, 1880), note 1, pp. 226–227; see also Le Hidec, *Les secrets*, 73–74.

62. For a summary of the variations of the short text of the secret, see H. Dion, *Maximin Giraud*, 146–147. Dion does not deal with the longer version, although he does note that letters from Mme. Jourdain, Maximin's "adopted" mother, refer to a secret eleven paragraphs in length (146). For the text of the secret, see J. Curicque, *Voix prophétiques; ou, signes, apparitions et prédictions modernes* (Paris: V. Palme, 1872), 120–121. E. Culligan provides an English translation of the longer text in *The Last World War and the End of Time* (Rockford, IL: TAN Books and Publishers, 1981), 168–169; see also R. G. Culleton, *The Reign of Antichrist* (Rockford, IL: TAN Books and Publishers, 1974), 170–171.

63. Some commentators apparently saw the description ("mercy and the rehabilitation of things") as referring to the first phase of the scenario (universal conversion and peace) and ignored the ending (the arrival of the monster) and the events of the longer version.

64. Le Hidec, *Les secrets*, 74–80.

65. A. Parent, *Vie de Maximin*, 27, quoted in Le Hidec, *Les secrets*, 81.

66. Ibid., 80–81.

67. Ibid., 82–87. For a history of the figure of the Great Monarch, see M. Reeves, *The Influence of Prophecy in the Later Middle Ages: A Study in Joachism* (Oxford: Clarendon Press, 1969), 293–392; B. McGinn, *Visions of the End: Apocalyptic Traditions in the Middle Ages* (New York: Columbia University Press, 1979), 43–45, 246–248. Concerning the role of the Great Monarch in nineteenth-century French prophecy, see Kselman, *Miracles and Prophecies in Nineteenth-Century France*, 68–83, 121–140.

68. See, for example, Culligan, *The Last World War*, 168–169; Culleton, *The Reign of Antichrist*, 170–171; and E. Culligan, *The 1960 Fatima Secret and the Secret of La Salette* (San Bernardino, CA: Culligan Book Co., 1967), 22–23.

69. Le Hidec, *Les Secrets*, 92–93. For an edition of this brochure, see M. Calvat, *L'Apparition de la T. S. Vierge sur la montagne de la Salette*, in *Pour*

servir à l'histoire réelle de la Salette (Paris: Nouvelles éditions latines, 1963), 1:74.

70. J. Stern, "La Salette vue par Léon Bloy," in *Léon Bloy*, ed. M. Arveiller et P. Glaudes (Paris: Les Cahiers de L. Herne, 1988), 166; 169, note 41. Jean Stern's forthcoming third volume of *Documents authentiques* contains a thorough discussion of the early history of Mélanie's secret.

71. Le Hidec, *Les secrets*, 133 and note 4, 145–146; text, 146–151. See also Curicque, *Voix prophétiques*, 107–111; and F. Bliard, *Lettres à un ami sur le secret de la bergère de la Salette* (Naples, Ancora, 1873).

72. See E. Appolis, "En Marge du catholicisme contemporain: Millenaristes, cordiphores, et naundorffistes autour du 'secret' de La Salette," *Archives de sociologie des religions* 14 (July–December 1964): 104.

73. On the popularity of this secret, see T. Kselman, *Miracles and Prophecies in Nineteenth-Century France*, 136.

74. The text of Mélanie's secret is found in *Pour servir à l'histoire réelle de la Salette* 1: 74–80; for an English translation, see Gouin, *Sister Mary of the Cross: The Shepherdess of La Salette*, 64–69; see also Culligan, *The 1960 Fatima Secret and the Secret of La Salette*, 24–29.

75. *Pour servir à l'histoire réelle de la Salette* 1: 80; for a text of this rule, see *La Règle de l'Ordre de la Mère de Dieu* (brochure n.d.; nihil obstat, 22 August 1952, Dom D. Huerre; imprimatur, 26 October 1952, Archbishop F. Lamy). The mission of the apostles of the last times is dealt with in paragraphs 22–23. Mélanie wrote a short version of the rule before she went to Darlington, perhaps in 1853 or early in 1854, and a longer version in 1878–1879, which she submitted to the Holy See.

76. Le Hidec, *Les secrets*, 109.

77. Printed in F. Corteville, *La Bergère de Notre-Dame de la Salette et le Serviteur de Dieu, Mgr Zola, Évêque de Lecce* (Paris: Nouvelles éditions latines, 1981), 198–200. See also Le Hidec, *Les secrets*, 110; and Jaouen, *La grâce de la Salette*, 211.

78. This matter was not clarified and corrected until May 1913, when a photocopy of the letter was published in the *Annales de N.-D. de la Salette*. Le Hidec, *Les secrets*, 111–113.

79. Zola, who had given Mélanie's 1879 brochure the imprimatur, included in this list Mgr. Petagna, bishop of Castellamare di Studi, Mgr. Mariano Riccardi, bishop of Sorrento, Cardinal Guidi, and Cardinal Xyste Riario Sforza. Extracts of this letter from Mgr. Zola to Abbé Roubaud (24 May 1880) are printed in F. Corteville, *Pie IX, le Père Pierre Semenenko, et les défenseurs du message de Notre-Dame de la Salette* (Paris: Téqui, 1987), 94. Portions of the letter omitted here are found in F. Corteville, *La Bergère de Notre-Dame*, 115–117. See also Le Hidec, *Les secrets*, 132.

80. H. Dion, *Mélanie Calvat, bergère de la Salette, étapes humaines et mystiques* (Paris: Téqui, 1984), 262; and Le Hidec, *Les secrets*, 133.

81. Letter from Mgr. Zola to Abbé Roubaud (24 May 1880), printed in F. Corteville, *Pie IX*, 94; and Le Hidec, *Les secrets*, 132–133.

82. Letter from Mgr. Zola to Abbé Roubaud (24 May 1880), printed in F. Corteville, *La Bergère de Notre-Dame*, 115–116.

83. Abbé Combe's *Le Grand Coup avec sa date probable* was published in 1894, raised a great deal of controversy, and was placed on the Index in 1901. *Le secret de Mélanie et la crise actuelle* was published in 1906 and placed on the Index in 1907. See Le Hidec, *Les secrets*, 114.

84. Extracts from the Marquise de la Vauzelle's letter and Lepidi's reply are printed in Le Hidec, *Les secrets*, 116–117; and also H. Dion, *Mélanie Calvat, étapes humaines et mystiques*, 266.

85. The decree is printed in Le Hidec, *Les secrets*, 123–124.

86. Ibid., 126–129; 217–218.

87. The decree is reproduced in Le Hidec, *Les secrets*, 128–129.

88. Letter from Mgr. Zola to Abbé Isidore Roubaud (24 May 1880), printed in F. Corteville, *Pie IX*, 93.

89. Le Hidec, *Les secrets*, 140–141.

90. J. Stern, "Mélanie Calvat," *Catholicisme*, vol. 7 (Paris: Letouzey et Ane, 1979), cols. 1110–1111; and "La Salette vue par Léon Bloy," 66.

91. Le Hidec, *Les secrets*, 143, 145, 151–152, 215–216.

92. A. Nicholas, *La Salette devant la raison et le devoir d'un catholique*, 2d ed. (Lyon: J.-B. Pélagaud, 1857), 155; Le Hidec, *Les secrets*, 185–186; see also, Des Brulais, *Suite de l'écho*, 277–278 and note 1.

93. H. Dion, *Mélanie Calvat, bergère de la Salette*, 272.

94. Ibid., 272–274. Dion raises the question of whether there were two versions of the secret, one sent to Pius IX in 1851, the other published by Mélanie in 1879 (270–272).

95. The most important association which understands itself to be carrying on the mission of Mélanie is the Association des Enfants de N. D. de la Salette et de Saint Louis-Marie Grignion de Montfort (F. Corteville, President, 12 Avenue du Grain d'Or, 49600 Beaupreau, France).

CHAPTER FIVE

1. It should be noted here that not everyone who has had contact with Lucia has been convinced of the trustworthiness of her recollections. Apparently, however, her recording of these recollections has continued, and it was rumored in 1987 that she had begun to use a word processor so that these could not be read and circulated without her consent.

2. Walsh, *Our Lady of Fatima*, 72.

3. Martins, *Novos Documentos de Fátima*, 286, 316; Kondor, *Fatima in Lucia's Own Words*, 126, 161.

4. Walsh, *Our Lady of Fatima*, 72; De Marchi, *Fatima: The Facts*, 58, 73; De Marchi, *The Immaculate Heart*, 66.

5. De Marchi, *Fatima: The Facts*, 67–68; De Marchi, *The Immaculate Heart*, 77; Walsh, *Our Lady of Fatima*, 83; V. Montes de Oca, *More about Fatima and*

the Immaculate Heart of Mary, trans. J. da Cruz (n.p.: L. Owen Traynor, 1979), 24–25.

6. Martins, *Novos Documentos*, 286; Kondor, *Fatima in Lucia's Own Words*, 126.

7. Martins, *Novos Documentos*, 201–202; Kondor, *Fatima in Lucia's Own Words*, 72–73; De Marchi, *Fatima: The Facts*, 77–78; De Marchi, *The Immaculate Heart*, 88–89; Walsh, *Our Lady of Fatima*, 98–101; Montes de Oca, *More about Fatima*, 27–28.

8. Martins, *Novos Documentos*, 203–204; see also the testimony of Lucia before Drs. Formigão, Manuel Marques dos Santos, and Manuel Pereira Lopes on 8 July 1924, 110–111. Kondor, *Fatima in Lucia's Own Words*, 74–75; De Marchi, *Fatima: The Facts*, 79–80; De Marchi, *The Immaculate Heart*, 90–91; Walsh, *Our Lady of Fatima*, 102–104.

9. De Marchi, *Fatima: The Facts*, 80, note 1; De Marchi quotes here from Lucia's testimony before the Canonical Inquiry. Fr. Ferreira was sufficiently upset by this episode—and the apparent hostility of partisans of the children toward him—that he wrote a letter to the newspapers of Lisbon and Ourém disclaiming any knowledge of the mayor's intentions (82–83, note 2). See also De Marchi, *The Immaculate Heart*, 91, note 1, and 94–95, note 2.

10. Martins, *Novos Documentos*, 159–160, 203–204; Kondor, *Fatima in Lucia's Own Words*, 35–37, 74–75; De Marchi, *Fatima: The Facts*, 83–87; De Marchi, *The Immaculate Heart*, 96–100; Walsh, *Our Lady of Fatima*, 110–114.

11. On Dr. Formigão, see Chapter 1 above.

12. Martins, *Novos Documentos*, 34. For an English translation see De Marchi, *Fatima: The Facts*, 107–108; and *The Immaculate Heart*, 122–123.

13. Martins, *Novos Documentos*, 37–38. De Marchi, *Fatima: The Facts*, 113–114; idem, *The Immaculate Heart*, 128–129.

14. Martins, *Novos Documentos*, 43–44; De Marchi, *Fatima: The Facts*, 136; idem, *The Immaculate Heart*, 156–157.

15. Kondor, *Fatima in Lucia's Own Words*, 189. According to Kondor, Lucia wrote an account of her experience shortly after it occurred but later destroyed this first text. The account written for Aparicio is thus a second account. See also Michel de la Sainte Trinité, *Toute la vérité sur Fatima*, vol. 2, *Le secret et l'Église (1917–1942)* (Saint-Parres-les-Vaudes: La Contre-Réforme Catholique, 1984), 154 and note 2.

16. Martins, *Novos Documentos*, 120–121; Kondor, *Fatima in Lucia's Own Words*, 195–196.

17. Michel de la Sainte Trinité, *Toute la vérité sur Fatima* 2: 155, with notes 1 and 2.

18. Ibid., 155–156, and 156, note 2.

19. Martins, *Novos Documentos*, 114–116. For a French translation, see Michel de la Sainte Trinité, *Toute la vérité sur Fatima* 2: 156–158.

20. Martins, *Novos Documentos*, 115–116; Michel de la Sainte Trinité, *Toute la vérité sur Fatima* 2: 157–158. An English translation of part of this text is found in Kondor, *Fatima in Lucia's Own Words*, 196–197.

21. Martins, *Novos Documentos*, 120–121; Kondor, *Fatima in Lucia's Own*

Words, 189, 195–196. See also J. M. Alonso, *The Secret of Fatima: Fact and Legend*, trans. Dominican Nuns of the Perpetual Rosary (Cambridge, MA: Ravengate Press, 1979), 29–30.

22. Martins, *Novos Documentos*, 120–121; Kondor, *Fatima in Lucia's Own Words*, 189, 195–196.

23. Martins, *Novos Documentos*, 252–253. Lucia wrote her account of this experience in 1936 as part of some biographical notes she had made at the request of Fr. Gonçalves. See also Michel de la Sainte Trinité, *Toute la vérité sur Fatima* 2: 292, notes 3 and 4.

24. Martins, *Novos Documentos*, 257–258; for an English translation, see Kondor, *Fatima in Lucia's Own Words*, 199–200. See also Michel de la Sainte Trinité, *Toute la vérité sur Fatima* 2: 292–294.

25. Michel de la Sainte Trinité, *Toute la vérité sur Fatima* 2: 335. For some correspondence between Lucia and Gonçalves on details of this experience, see Martins, *Novos Documentos*, 121–125; for a French translation, see Michel de la Sainte Trinité, *Toute la vérité sur Fatima* 2: 331–335.

26. Michel de la Sainte Trinité, *Toute la vérité sur Fatima* 2: 335–336. See also letters of Lucia to Pope Pius XII, 24 October 1940 (Martins, *Novos Documentos*, 241–243) and 2 December 1940 (Martins, *Novos Documentos*, 247–248).

27. Michel de la Sainte Trinité, *Toute la vérité sur Fatima* 2: 396; Martins, *Novos Documentos*, 143–171; Kondor, *Fatima in Lucia's Own Words*, 15. An English translation of the text is found in Kondor, 16–46.

28. It should be noted that Lucia had revealed the apparitions of the angel and several other experiences in an account written on 13 May 1936 to Fr. Gonçalves, who did not transcribe this text until April 24, 1941. For this text, see Martins, *Novos Documentos*, 252–259. Michel de la Sainte Trinité notes that while this account is important for understanding the development of the themes of the apparitions, it was not utilized by the early historians of Fatima, who learned of Lucia's new revelations through the last three *Memoirs* (*Toute la vérité sur Fatima* 2: 418). Concerning the writing of the *Second Memoir*, see Martins, *Novos Documentos*, 178 (text, 179–229); and Kondor, *Fatima in Lucia's Own Words*, 49 (English translation, 50–99).

29. Martins, *Novos Documentos*, 190–192; Kondor, *Fatima in Lucia's Own Words*, 61–63.

30. Michel de la Sainte Trinité, *Toute la vérité sur Fatima* 2:483–484; Kondor, *Fatima in Lucia's Own Words*, 101; Alonso, *The Secret of Fatima*, 31–32.

31. Martins, *Novos Documentos*, 265 (text, 265–275); Kondor, *Fatima in Lucia's Own Words*, 102 (English translation, 102–113). See also Michel de la Sainte Trinité, *Toute la vérité sur Fatima* vol. 3, *Le troisième secret* (Saint-Parres-les-Vaudes, France: La Contre-Réforme Catholique, 1985), 31.

32. Martins, *Novos Documentos*, 266; Kondor, *Fatima in Lucia's Own Words*, 104.

33. Martins, *Novos Documentos*, 266–267; Kondor, *Fatima in Lucia's Own Words*, 104–105. The quotation is taken from Kondor's translation.

34. Martins, *Novos Documentos*, 270–271; Kondor, *Fatima in Lucia's Own Words*, 108–109.

35. Martins, *Novos Documentos*, 272; Kondor, *Fatima in Lucia's Own Words*, 109–110.

36. Martins, *Novos Documentos*, 318; Kondor, *Fatima in Lucia's Own Words*, 162.

37. Martins, *Novos Documentos*, 278–307; Kondor, *Fatima in Lucia's Own Words*, 119–148.

38. Martins, *Novos Documentos*, 308–322; Kondor, *Fatima in Lucia's Own Words*, 149–170.

39. Michel de la Sainte Trinité, *Toute la vérité sur Fatima* 3: 31; Kondor, *Fatima in Lucia's Own Words*, 115.

40. Martins, *Novos Documentos*, 308–309; Kondor, *Fatima in Lucia's Own Words*, 149–150.

41. Michel de la Sainte Trinité, *Toute la vérité sur Fatima* 3:32–33; Alonso, *The Secret of Fatima*, 35–36.

42. Michel de la Sainte Trinité, *Toute la vérité sur Fatima* 3:33.

43. Ibid., 34.

44. Ibid., 35; Alonso, *The Secret of Fatima*, 37.

45. Quoted in Michel de la Sainte Trinité, *Toute la vérité sur Fatima* 3: 36 and in Alonso, *The Secret of Fatima*, 37–38.

46. Michel de la Sainte Trinité, *Toute la vérité sur Fatima* 3: 36–37; Alonso, *The Secret of Fatima*, 38.

47. Michel de la Sainte Trinité, *Toute la vérité sur Fatima* 3: 37–38; Alonso, *The Secret of Fatima*, 39–41. Michel de la Sainte Trinité believes that these letters, despite the good intentions of Garcia, went against the formal order of the bishop and would have increased Lucia's inner conflict. He sees it as fortunate that they did not reach Lucia until mid-January and did not delay the recording of the secret. Alonso, on the other hand, sees these letters as conveying wise and prudent counsel to a soul in distress. He speculates that the mother superior, acting with questionable discretion, intervened to keep the letters from Lucia. Although Alonso agrees that Lucia might have delayed writing the secret had she received the letters, he thinks they would have guaranteed her an atmosphere of inner peace and calm.

48. Martins, *Novos Documentos*, xxv–xxvi, note 5; see also Michel de la Sainte Trinité, *Toute la vérité sur Fatima* 3: 38.

49. Alonso, *The Secret of Fatima*, 44.

50. Michel de la Sainte Trinité, *Toute la vérité sur Fatima* 3: 42–43.

51. Michel de la Sainte Trinité, *Toute la vérité sur Fatima* 3: 310–311; Alonso, *The Secret of Fatima*, 45–47.

52. Michel de la Sainte Trinité, *Toute la vérité sur Fatima* 3: 320–321; Alonso, *The Secret of Fatima*, 48–49.

53. L. M. Dooley, "Mary and the Atom," *Ave Maria* 75 (22 March 1952): 359–362.

54. W. A. Christian, Jr., "Religious Apparitions and the Cold War in

Southern Europe," in *Religion, Power and Protest in Local Communities*, ed. E. Wolf (Berlin: Mouton, 1984), 239–266.

55. Quoted in Dooley, "Mary and the Atom," 361–362. For a more complete statement of this popular American bishop's views on Fatima in relation to communism, see F. J. Sheen, *Communism and the Conscience of the West* (Indianapolis: Bobbs Merrill Company, 1948), 199–247.

56. *Médiatrice et Reine* (October 1946): 110–112, quoted in Michel de la Sainte Trinité, *Toute la vérité sur Fatima* 3: 313 and in Alonso, *The Secret of Fatima*, 44–45.

57. C. Barthas, *Fatima, merveille du XXe siècle* (Fatima-éditions, 1952), 83; quoted in Michel de la Sainte Trinité, *Toute la vérité sur Fatima* 3: 314, and in Alonso, *The Secret of Fatima*, 45.

58. Walsh, *Our Lady of Fatima*, 207.

59. S. Martins dos Reis, *Fatima, as suas provas e os seus problemas* (Lisbon, 1953), 323–325. Michel de la Sainte Trinité criticizes Martins dos Reis for not citing any evidence or authorities to support his position and for ignoring the statements of Bishop da Silva and other church officials who expected the secret to be opened in 1960 (*Toute la vérité sur Fatima* 3: 315).

60. Michel de la Sainte Trinité, *Toute la vérité sur Fatima* 3: 316–317; Alonso, *The Secret of Fatima*, 45–47.

61. C. Barthas, *Fatima, merveille du XXe siècle*, 83, quoted in Michel de la Sainte Trinité, *Toute la vérité sur Fatima* 3: 314.

62. Cardinal Ottaviani, "A propos du secret de Fatima," *La documentation catholique* 64/1490 (19 March 1967): 542. For an English translation of this part of Ottaviani's speech for the fiftieth anniversary of the apparitions, celebrated in Rome on 11 February 1967, see Alonso, *The Secret of Fatima*, 47. Cardinal Ottaviani, it should be noted, was the leader of the conservative faction of the Roman Curia, which was adamantly opposed to the changes that began to be unleashed in 1959, when the newly elected Pope John XXIII announced the convening of the Second Vatican Council.

63. Alonso, *The Secret of Fatima*, 52–53.

64. P. Boland, "Fatima's Third Secret," *The Christian Democrat* 9 (October 1958): 484. See also J. A. Pelletier, "The Fatima Secret in 1960?" *The Messenger of the Sacred Heart* 95 (January 1960): 20.

65. Quoted in Alonso, *The Secret of Fatima*, 106.

66. Quoted in Michel de la Sainte Trinité, *Toute la vérité sur Fatima* 3: 336–338 and in Alonso, *The Secret of Fatima*, 109–110.

67. Alonso, *The Secret of Fatima*, 111.

68. Michel de la Sainte Trinité has given the full statement of the curia of Coimbra in *Toute la vérité sur Fatima* 3: 367–368. For an English translation of part of this text, see Alonso, *The Secret of Fatima*, 111–112.

69. Michel de la Sainte Trinité, *Toute la vérité sur Fatima* 3: 368–369.

70. Alonso, *The Secret of Fatima*, 112–113.

71. Michel de la Sainte Trinité, *Toute la vérité sur Fatima* 3: 368–369.

72. Boland, "Fatima's Third Secret," 488.

73. F. L. Filas, "What of Lucy's Claims?" *America* 101 (4 July 1959): 490–491.

74. Quoted in Alonso, *The Secret of Fatima*, 53.

75. Quoted in Alonso, *The Secret of Fatima*, 54.

76. Quoted in Michel de la Sainte Trinité,*Toute la vérité sur Fatima* 3: 386–387 and in Alonso, *The Secret of Fatima*, 55–56.

77. Michel de la Sainte Trinité, *Toute la vérité sur Fatima* 3: 431–432 (text, 431–434); Alonso, *The Secret of Fatima* 113 (text, 113–116). The translations in the summary that follows are my own.

78. Christian, "Religious Apparitions and the Cold War in Southern Europe," 241.

79. See, for example, E. J. Culligan, *The 1960 Fatima Secret and the Secret of La Salette* (San Bernardino, California: The Culligan Book Company, 1967).

80. Cardinal Ottaviani, "À propos du secret de Fatima," 543.

81. See letters of Loris Capovilla to P. Freire (20 June 1977) and to P. Alonso (24 July 1977), printed in Michel de la Sainte Trinité, *Toute la vérité sur Fatima* 3: 380–382.

82. Alonso, *The Secret of Fatima*, 49–51.

83. Michel de la Sainte Trinité, *Toute la vérité sur Fatima* 3: 324.

84. Ibid., facing 330.

85. Ibid., 324–325.

86. Alonso, *The Secret of Fatima*, 49.

87. G. J. Gustavson, "Private Revelations and Prudence," *The Priest* 15/9 (September 1959): 714.

88. Michel de la Sainte Trinité, *Toute la vérité sur Fatima* 3: 326; Alonso, *The Secret of Fatima*, 49.

89. Michel de la Sainte Trinité, *Toute la vérité sur Fatima* 3: 326; Alonso, *The Secret of Fatima*, 49–50.

90. See letters of Loris Capovilla to P. Freire (20 June 1977) and to P. Alonso (24 July 1977), printed in Michel de la Sainte Trinité, *Toute la vérité sur Fatima* 3: 380–382.

91. Ottaviani, "A propos du Secret de Fatima," 544; see also Alonso, *The Secret of Fatima*, 50.

92. Alonso, *The Secret of Fatima*, 51.

93. See letters of Loris Capovilla to P. Freire (20 June 1977) and to P. Alonso (24 July 1977) printed in Michel de la Sainte Trinité, *Toute la vérité sur Fatima* 3: 380–382

94. Ibid. Alonso believes that Pope Paul VI read the secret and that this lay behind his sudden decision to go to Fatima for the fiftieth anniversary of the apparitions (13 May 1967). Alonso further believes that the contents of the secret were reflected in the homily he delivered at the Pontifical Mass there (*The Secret of Fatima*, 51). Michel de la Sainte Trinité also believes that Paul VI read the secret but he argues that from 1967 until the pope's death on 6 August 1978, he maintained a public silence about its contents (*Toute la vérité sur Fatima* 3: 426).

95. Michel de la Sainte Trinité, *Toute la vérité sur Fatima* 3: 426–427.

96. Ibid., 427.

97. Quoted in Michel de la Sainte Trinité, *Toute la vérité sur Fatima* 3: 442–443. Both he and Alonso doubt that this interview is authentic.

CHAPTER SIX

1. H. Souillet, *Les apparitions de Notre-Dame à l'Île Bouchard* (Saint-Cénéré: Éditions Saint-Michel, 1972), 133.

2. Ibid., 93–94. Regarding the secrets conveyed to three of the children at Beauraing, see also E. de Greef, "Notes sur les faits de Beauraing," in *Les faits mystérieux de Beauraing*, Bruno de Jesus-Marie, et al. (Paris: Declée de Brouwer, 1933), 82–23.

3. E. Tizané, *Les apparitions de la Vierge: Un enquêteur laïc s'interroge* (Paris: Tchou, 1977), 124–125.

4. Ibid., 124.

5. H. Souillet, *Les apparitions de Notre-Dame à l'Île Bouchard*, 47–48, 53, 91–93.

6. G. Schallenberg, *Visionäre Erlebnisse*, (Aschaffenburg: Paul Pattloch Verlag, 1979), 181–233, 357–361.

7. Ibid., 194, 202–203.

8. A. Marty, *Balestrino* (Paris: Nouvelles éditions latines, 1971), 88, 97. See also P. Bartolotti and P. Mantero, *Guida alle Apparizioni Mariani in Italia* (Milan: Sugar Co Edizioni, 1988), 45–49, where Caterina discusses the apparitions and claims to have received ten secrets, some of which concern the future and others of which are personal. Caterina's last apparition was 5 October 1971. She was absent from the village for a while but returned to live there in 1986 with her husband and daughter. Rumors of sun miracles began in 1983, and since Caterina's return she has reported some other apparitions.

9. Ibid., 92.

10. E. Tizané, *Les apparitions de la Vierge*, 125. W. A. Christian, Jr. mentions the dramaturgy of secrets in the post–World War II apparitions in "Religious Apparitions and the Cold War in Southern Europe," 251.

11. Pérez, *Garabandal: The Village Speaks*, 50, 53, 56–58; González, *Diary*, in *OLCG*, 113; Daley, *Miracle at Garabandal*, 181ff.

12. Pelletier, *Our Lady Comes to Garabandal*, 67.

13. González, *Diary*, in *OLCG*, 63–65, and discussion by Pelletier, 69–73; Pérez, *Garabandal*, 24; Daley, *Miracle at Garabandal*, 123–126, 153–154.

14. Pelletier, *Our Lady Comes to Garabandal*, 74.

15. Ibid., 75; Pérez, *Garabandal*, 43–44.

16. Pelletier, *Our Lady Comes to Garabandal*, 75.

17. For a full discussion, see Chapter 3; in the spring of 1962, it will be recalled, the four girls began to claim that during some of their ecstasies the archangel Michael had been administering Communion to them. Conchita said that Michael had told her the preceding summer that he would soon perform a miracle, namely, that the host would become visible on her tongue. She said she expressed surprise to him, because she had thought that the host must already

have been seen by those gathered around her during her experiences, and she told him that this promised miracle of the visible host was only "a little miracle," which reportedly made the archangel laugh. Persons who gathered at Garabandal on July 15, the date Conchita had announced for this little miracle, claimed that the host was indeed visible on Conchita's tongue during her ecstasy that day.

18. González, *Diary*, in *OLCG*, 113, and commentary by Pelletier, *Our Lady Comes to Garabandal*, 113–115; Daley, *Miracle at Garabandal*, 160–161.

19. Sanchez-Ventura y Pascual, *The Apparitions of Garabandal*, 179; Pelletier, *Our Lady Comes to Garabandal*, 151–161; Pérez, *Garabandal*, 53–54; Daley, *Miracle at Garabandal*, 180–185.

20. Pelletier, *Our Lady Comes to Garabandal*, 143–145. Pelletier quotes here the account that Conchita wrote soon after her experience.

21. Pelletier, *Our Lady Comes to Garabandal*, 155, which differs in certain respects from other documents in dating the visits; Pérez, *Garabandal*, 47–50; Daley, *Miracle at Garabandal*, 106–110.

22. Quoted in Pelletier, *Our Lady Comes to Garabandal*, 155–156; and in Daley, *Miracle at Garabandal*, 110. See also Pérez, *Garabandal*, 49.

23. Pérez, *Garabandal*, 49–50.

24. Ibid., 46; Pelletier, *Our Lady Comes to Garabandal*, 157.

25. Pérez (*Garabandal*, 53–54) and Pelletier (*Our Lady Comes to Garabandal*, 146–154), for example, discuss these events as "Garabandal prophecies" that are awaiting fulfillment.

26. Pérez, *Garabandal*, 54, note 10.

27. Pelletier, *Our Lady Comes to Garabandal*, 114–115 and note 3.

28. Pérez, *Garabandal*, 46 and note 5. These remarks concerning the exhumation and relocation of the body of Luis Andréu were published in Fr. Combe's bulletin of 8 December 1976. I thank Fr. François Turner for sending me a copy of the original bulletin of Fr. Combe. See also Conchita's comments during an interview in Daley, *Miracle at Garabandal*, 184–185.

29. According to Pérez, Conchita and her party were in Rome 12–19 January 1966 (*Garabandal*, 32). According to Pelletier, Conchita left Spain on January 12 and returned on January 21 (*Our Lady Comes to Garabandal*, 201–203).

30. Pelletier, *Our Lady Comes to Garabandal*, 200 and note 1.

31. Pérez, *Garabandal*, 32.

32. Ibid., 32 and note 12.

33. Pelletier, *Our Lady Comes to Garabandal*, 200–203; Daley, *Miracle at Garabandal*, 111–112, 119–120.

34. González, *Diary*, in *OLCG*, 49–50, 52–53, and commentary by Pelletier, 51–52, 53; Pérez, *Garabandal*, 21, 26.

35. González, *Diary*, in *OLCG*, 52. The message read by Marichalar differs slightly from that recorded by Conchita in her *Diary*. There she omits the word "frequently" from the first sentence and adds the word "very" to "good lives" in the second sentence (50–51).

36. Pérez, *Garabandal*, 26–27; see witnesses testimonies on 132–133, 157–159, 179–180, 217, 233–234, 246–247, 284–285, 310–311. Pérez says that

Mari Cruz was present on the first night, but according to villagers, she was not. Conchita does not write about this night in her *Diary*.

37. Pelletier, *Our Lady Comes to Garabandal*, 167–170; Pérez, *Garabandal*, 29–31.

38. Pelletier, *Our Lady Comes to Garabandal*, 170–176; Pérez, *Garabandal*, 36–37.

39. Pelletier, *Our Lady Comes to Garabandal*, 147–150; Pérez, *Garabandal*, 50–51; Daley, *Miracle at Garabandal*, 185–187.

40. Pelletier, *Our Lady Comes to Garabandal*, 148; Daley, *Miracle at Garabandal*, 187.

41. Pérez, *Garabandal*, 51–52.

42. The warnings in the June 18 message about the erring clergy and the neglect of the Eucharist bring to mind what William A. Christian, Jr., has written of the Garabandal apparition in *Person and God in a Spanish Valley*, 182. Christian has suggested that the apparition was an "incredible reaction of the village and its [traditional] gods" to the changes introduced in the wake of Vatican II by young humanistically oriented priests who, unlike the older priests, were intolerant of the villagers' semipantheism and need for heavenly intermediaries.

43. R. Laurentin and L. Rupčić, *Is the Virgin Mary Appearing at Medjugorje?* trans. F. Martin (Washington, DC: The Word Among Us Press, 1984), 33.

44. M. Miravalle, *The Message of Medjugorje: The Marian Message to the Modern World* (Lanham, MD: University Press of America, 1986), 2.

45. Ibid., 1–2; Laurentin and Rupčić, *Is the Virgin Mary Appearing at Medjugorje?* 33.

46. Miravalle, *The Message of Medjugorje*, 1; for a description of several recent apparitions, not on her birthday, claimed by Mirjana, see R. Laurentin, *The Apparitions at Medjugorje Prolonged*, trans. J. Lohre Stiens (Milford, OH: The Riehle Foundation, 1987), 24–35.

47. Ibid., 145; Laurentin, *The Apparitions at Medjugorje Prolonged*, 20–24.

48. See, for example, Laurentin and Rupčić, *Is the Virgin Mary Appearing at Medjugorje?* 3, where the authors cite this as a reason for believing that the apparitions will soon end.

49. Miravalle, *The Message of Medjugorje*, 1–2; Laurentin and Rupčić, *Is the Virgin Mary Appearing at Medjugorje?* 33; Tomislav Vlašić, "The Message of Medjugorje," *Our Lady Queen of Peace* (November 1985): 2.

50. Laurentin and Rupčić, *Is the Virgin Mary Appearing at Medjugorje?* 54.

51. M. O'Carroll, in *Medjugorje: Facts, Documents, Theology* (Dublin: Veritas Publications, 1986), 40, is careful to allow for this possibility in his statements, as is S. Kraljević, *The Apparitions of Our Lady at Medjugorje 1981–1983* (Chicago: Franciscan Herald Press, 1984), 56–57.

52. Laurentin and Rupčić, *Is the Virgin Mary Appearing at Medjugorje?* 54.

53. Kraljević, *The Apparitions of Our Lady at Medjugorje 1981–1983*, 127; the interview is found on 121–140. An abridged version is found in Miravalle, *The Message of Medjugorje*, 10–21.

54. Laurentin and Rupčić, *Is the Virgin Mary Appearing at Medjugorje?* 55. See also Mirjana's interview with Vlašić (10 January 1983), where she states

that she did not receive a message for the pope (Kraljević, *The Apparitions of Our Lady at Medjugorje 1981–1983*, 133).

55. Kraljević limits the number of secrets known by all the children to three. At that time Mirjana had received her full ten secrets; the others, from seven to nine (*The Apparitions of Our Lady at Medjugorje 1981–1983*, 57). Laurentin now admits that it is not evident that the ten secrets are exactly the same for each of the children (*The Apparitions at Medjugorje Prolonged*, 97).

56. Ibid., 126–128; Miravalle, *The Message of Medjugorje*, 14–16.

57. Laurentin, *The Apparitions at Medjugorje Prolonged*, 25.

58. Kraljević, *The Apparitions of Our Lady at Medjugorje 1981–1983*, 126; Miravalle, *The Message of Medjugorje*, 14.

59. O'Carroll, *Medjugorje: Facts, Documents, Theology*, 44; see also Laurentin, *Apparitions at Medjugorje Prolonged*, 27–30.

60. W. Weible, "Miracle at Medjugorje" (privately printed, March 1987), 6.

61. Laurentin, *The Apparitions at Medjugorje Prolonged*, 22–23.

62. Ibid., 27.

63. Kraljević, *The Apparitions of Our Lady at Medjugorje 1981–1983*, 126–127; Miravalle, *The Message of Medjugorje*, 14–15.

64. P. Blatty, "Collected Words of Our Lady, Queen of Peace," in *Our Lady Queen of Peace* (November 1985): 16.

65. Laurentin and Rupčić, *Is the Virgin Mary Appearing at Medjugorje?* 56–57.

66. T. Vlašić, "The Message of Medjugorje," *Our Lady Queen of Peace* (November 1985): 2; see also Miravalle, *The Message of Medjugorje*, 2, where "atheists" is translated "unbelievers."

67. Blatty, "Collected Words," 11.

68. Vlašić's report is printed in Miravalle, *The Message of Medjugorje*, 22–24; Laurentin and Rupčić, *Is the Virgin Mary Appearing at Medjugorje?* 142–144; and O'Carroll, *Medjugorje: Facts, Documents, Theology*, 209–212.

69. See Vlašić's interview with Mirjana (10 January 1983), in Kraljević, *The Apparitions of Our Lady at Medjugorje 1981–1983*, 133–134, and Miravalle, *The Message of Medjugorje*, 19.

70. Miravalle, *The Message of Medjugorje*, 23; Laurentin and Rupčić, *Is the Virgin Mary Appearing at Medjugorje?* 143; O'Carroll, *Medjugorje: Facts, Documents, Theology*, 211.

71. "An Interview with Dr. Frane Franić, Archbishop Metropolitan of Split, Yugoslavia, After His Two-Day Stay in Medjugorje, December 16–17, 1984," in *Our Lady Queen of Peace* (November 1985), 50–51.

72. Laurentin, *The Apparitions at Medjugorje Prolonged*, 35.

73. Ibid., 31.

74. Ibid., 97.

CHAPTER SEVEN

1. J. Beevers, *The Sun Her Mantle* (Dublin: Browne and Nolan, 1953), 196–225.

2. Martins, *Novos Documentos de Fatima*, 266–267; Kondor, *Fatima in Lucia's Own Words*, 104–105. The quotation is taken from this English translation.

3. Di Maria, *The Most Holy Virgin at San Damiano*, 64.

4. Vlašić, "The Message of Medjugorje," 2; see also Miravalle, *The Message of Medjugorje: The Marian Message to the Modern World*, 2, where the word "unbelievers" replaces the word "atheists."

5. Laurentin and Rupčić, *Is the Virgin Mary Appearing at Medjugorje?* 80.

6. Di Maria, *The Most Holy Virgin at San Damiano*, 91.

7. Laurentin and Rupčić, *Is the Virgin Mary Appearing at Medjugorje?* 79–80.

8. Le Rumeur, *Notre-Dame du Carmel à Garabandal*, 54–57.

9. Di Maria, *The Most Holy Virgin at San Damiano*, 81.

10. Ibid., 80.

11. L.-M. Grignion de Montfort, *True Devotion to Mary*, ed. The Fathers of the Company of Mary, trans. F. W. Faber (Rockford, IL: TAN Publishers, 1941), 28.

12. Ibid., 30–35.

13. J. M. Höcht, *Fatima und Pius XII* (Wiesbaden: Credo-Verlag, 1959), 11. This work combines two previously published studies, *Maria rettet das Abendland* (Wiesbaden: Credo-Verlag, 1953) and *Fatima und Pius XII* (Wiesbaden: Credo-Verlag, 1952). An earlier version of this discussion of Höcht was presented at the Tenth International Mariological Congress, Kevelaer, West Germany, September 1987.

14. Ibid., 233–234.

15. Ibid., 241–250, 256–263.

16. Ibid., 264–270.

17. Ibid., 286–287.

18. Ibid., 11–12, 333–349.

19. Ibid., 12.

20. A. Marty, *Balestrino*, 105–106, 128; see also *Le monde de demain vu par les prophètes d'aujourd'hui* (Paris: Nouvelles éditions latines, 1962).

21. A. Marty, *Balestrino*, 113–117.

22. Ibid., 134–136.

23. Ibid., 136–137, 148.

24. Ibid., 118.

25. Ibid., 182.

26. R. Auclair, *La Dame de tous les peuples* (Paris: Nouvelles éditions latines, 1967), 10. Auclair does not mention the seer of the "Lady of All Peoples" by name. Concerning her identity, see Billet, "Le fait des apparitions non reconnues par l'Église," 28–33.

27. Ibid., 108–111.

28. Ibid., 18–22.

29. Ibid., 19–20.

30. Ibid., 21, 135–137.

31. Ibid., 166.

32. Ibid., 34.

33. Ibid., 197.

34. Ibid., 199.

35. Ibid., 23–24.

36. Ibid., 38–39.

37. J. Kanady, "Woman Prays, Claims to See Vision Again," *Chicago Daily Tribune*, 16 August 1950, 1.

38. For a discussion of the recent history of Van Hoof's followers, see M. Winiarski, "Where Mother Cabrini Warns against Speeding," *National Catholic Reporter*, 12 September 1975, 1–2; R. I. McClory, "TV Report Says 'Fanatics' Run Shrine at Necedah," *National Catholic Reporter*, 21 December 1979, 3, 19; and J. G. Melton, ed., *The Encyclopedia of American Religion*, 3d ed. (Detroit: Gale Research, Inc., 1989), 195–196.

39. Swan, *My Work with Necedah* 1: 8–9.

40. Ibid., 9–10.

41. Ibid., 31–36.

42. M. A. Van Hoof, *Revelations and Messages*, ed. M. Sommers (Necedah, WI: For My God and My Country, 1971), 146–147, 238, 245–246. For a discussion of the Necedah phenomenon in the specific context of the anticommunist politics of American Catholics in these years, see T. Kselman and S. Avella, "Marian Piety and the Cold War in the United States," *Catholic Historical Review* 72 (July 1986): 403–424.

43. Van Hoof, *Revelations and Messages*, 303; see also, H. Swan, ed., *My Work with Necedah* vol. 4 (Necedah, WI: For My God and My Country, 1959), 210–218.

44. Van Hoof, *Revelations and Messages*, 27–28, 67, 76–77, 84.

45. Ibid., 171, 222.

46. Ibid., "Introduction," xlviii-lxiii.

47. Ibid., "Introduction," lvi-lvii, lxi-lxii.

48. Van Hoof, *Revelations and Messages*, 65–66.

49. Ibid., 158.

50. Ibid., 155–156; see also Swan, *My Work with Necedah* 4: 68–69.

51. Swan, *My Work with Necedah* 1: 11–12; *Revelations and Messages*, xxxix, 5.

52. "Jesuit Investigator Explains Rejection of Necedah Visions," *Madison Capital Times*, 15 July 1955, 2.

53. Swan, *My Work with Necedah* 1: 12; Van Hoof, *Revelations and Messages*, 5.

54. Swan, *My Work with Necedah* 1: 2–3.

55. Ibid., 5.

56. Descriptions of Mary Ann's sufferings are found in H. Swan, *My Work with Necedah* vol. 2, *The Narrative of the Passion from the Sufferings on the Fridays of Advent and Lent* (Necedah, WI: For My God and My Country, 1959), 164–179.

57. Ibid., 21–28; a photograph purporting to show Mary Ann manifesting the stigmata is found opposite p. 164. See also Swan, *My Work with Necedah* 1: 185.

58. See note 52.

59. Swan, *My Work with Necedah* 2: 29, 79–80; see also, Van Hoof, *Revelations and Messages*, xx-xxv.

60. For a discussion of this ideology in nineteenth-century France, see Kselman, *Miracles and Prophecies in Nineteenth-Century France* (New Brunswick, NJ: Rutgers, 1983), 102–106.

61. N. Perry and L. Echeverría, *Under the Heel of Mary* (London: Routledge, 1988), 219–227.

62. Ibid., 1.

63. Ibid., 313.

64. F. Turner, "Part I: John Paul II and Garabandal," *Garabandal* (July–September 1980), 10–13; "Part II: John Paul II and Garabandal," *Garabandal* (October–December 1980), 15–19.

65. Miravalle, *The Message of Medjugorje*, 79–100. The fourteen developmental themes are: Jesus Christ, the one Redeemer and Mediator; renewal in the Holy Spirit; Mary as universal mother and intercessor; Mass and eucharistic adoration; sacramental Confession; the Rosary; renewal of sacred scripture; devotion to the Sacred Heart of Jesus and Immaculate Heart of Mary; heaven, hell, purgatory, and Satan; ecumenism; family and community prayer; and eschatological urgency.

66. I. Gebara and M. Bingemer, *Mary: Mother of God, Mother of the Poor*, trans. P. Berryman (Maryknoll, NY: Orbis Books, 1989), 135.

67. Ibid., 129.

68. Ibid., 133.

69. Ibid., 144–154.

BIBLIOGRAPHY

Adler, M. *Zeichen der Zeit, Lourdes und Fatima in endzeitlicher Sicht.* Leutesdorf: Johannes-Verlag, 1968.

Alacoque, M.-M. *The Autobiography of Saint Margaret Mary.* Trans. V. Kerns. Westminster, MD: Newman Press, 1961.

Albano, T. O. *The Apparitions of Cabra Islet Philippines.* Ed. E. C. de Vera. Cabre Islet, Philippines: Alver Tied Charities and Cultural Circle, 1978.

Alonso, J. M. "Histoire 'ancienne' et histoire 'nouvelle' de Fatima." In *Vraies et fausses apparitions dans l'Église*, B. Billet et al., 55–95. Paris: Lethielleux, 1973.

———. *The Secret of Fatima: Fact and Legend.* Trans. Dominican Nuns of the Perpetual Rosary. Cambridge, MA: Ravengate Press, 1979.

Appolis, E. "En Marge du catholicisme contemporain: Millenaristes, cordiphores et naundorffistes autour du 'secret' de La Salette." *Archives de sociologie des religions* 14 (1962): 103–121.

Armstrong A. O., and M. F. Armstrong. "The Third Secret of Fatima." *Catholic Digest* 18 (October 1954): 1–4.

Aradi, Z. *Shrines to Our Lady around the World.* New York: Farrar, Straus and Young, 1954.

Ashe, G. *The Virgin.* London: Routledge and Kegan Paul, 1976.

Auclair, R. *La Dame de tous les peuples.* Paris: Nouvelles éditions latines, 1967.

———. *Les épiphanies de Marie, Paris, la Salette, Pontmain, Fatima, Beauraing, Banneux.* Paris: Beauchesne, 1976.

———. *La fin des temps, le nouveau livre des cycles.* Paris: Fayard, 1973.

———. *Histoire et prophétie.* Paris: Nouvelles éditions latines, 1973.

———. *Kerizinen: Apparitions en Bretagne?* Paris: Nouvelles éditions latines, 1968.

Barbier, J. *Pour vous qu'est-ce que Lourdes?* Paris: Lethielleux, 1976.

Barthas, C. *Three Children: Our Lady's Three Messengers of Fatima.* Dublin: Clonmore and Reynolds, 1953.

Barthas, C., and G. da Fonseca. *Fatima, merveille inouie.* Toulouse: Fatima-éditions, 1962.

———. *Our Lady of Light.* Milwaukee: Bruce Publishing Company, 1947.

Bartolotti, P. and P. Mantero. *Guida alle Apparizioni Mariani in Italia.* Milan: Sugar Co. Edizioni, 1988.

Bassette, L. *Le fait de la Salette: 1846–1854.* Paris: Cerf, 1965.

Bax, M. "Maria-verschijningen in Medjugorje: Rivaliserende religieuze regimes en staatsvorming." *Sociologisch Tijdschrift* 14/2 (October 1987): 95–223.

———. "Religious Regimes and State Formation: Towards a Research Perspective." *Anthropological Quarterly* 60/1 (1987): 1–11.

Bearsley, P. "Mary, The Perfect Disciple." *Theological Studies* 41 (1980): 461–504.

Beevers, J. *The Sun Her Mantle*. Dublin: Browne and Nolan, 1953.

———. *Virgin of the Poor*. St. Meinrad, IN: Abbey Press, 1972.

Begg, E. *The Cult of the Black Virgin*. London: Arkana, 1985.

Beinert, W., and H. Petri, eds. *Handbuch der Marienkunde*. Regensburg: Verlag F. Pustat, 1984.

Benz, E. Die Vision: Erfahrungsformen und Bilderwelt. Stuttgart: E. Klett, 1969.

Bergin, R. *This Apocalyptic Age*. Manchester, England: Voice of Fatima International, 1970.

Billet, B. "Le fait des apparitions non reconnues par l'église." In *Vraies et fausses apparitions dans l'église*, B. Billet et al., 5–54. Paris: Lethielleux, 1973.

Billet, B., L. Bohler, G. Cholvy, M.-L. Guillot, and G. Laurans. *Notre-Dame du Dimanche: Les apparitions à Saint-Bauzille-de-la-Sylve*. Paris, Beauchesne, 1973.

Blatty, P. "Collected Words of Our Lady, Queen of Peace." *Our Lady Queen of Peace* (November 1985): 7–37.

Bliard, F. *Lettres à un ami sur le secret de la bergère de la Salette*. Naples: Ancora, 1873.

Bobrinskoy, B. "Les apparitions de la Mère de Dieu dans l'orthodoxie." In *Vraies et fausses apparitions dans l'Église*, B. Billet et al., 97–122. Paris: Lethielleux, 1973.

Boff, L. *The Maternal Face of God: The Feminine and Its Religious Expressions*. Trans. R. R. Barr and J. W. Diercksmeier. New York: Harper and Row, 1987.

Boissarie, P. G. *Les grandes guérisons de Lourdes*. Paris: Téqui, 1900.

———. *Histoire médicale de Lourdes*. Paris: Petithenay, 1891.

———. *Lourdes depuis 1858 jusqu'à nos jours*. Paris: Sanard et Derangeon, 1894.

Boland, P. "Fatima's Third Secret." *The Christian Democrat* 9 (October 1958): 484–488.

Borelli, A., and J. Spann. *Our Lady at Fatima: Prophecies of Tragedy or Hope for America and the World?* N.p.: The American Society for the Defense of Tradition, Family, and Property, 1985.

Borresen, K. "Mary in Catholic Theology." *Mary in the Churches*. Ed. H. Küng and J. Moltmann. New York: Seabury, 1983. (Concilium 168)

Branick, V., ed. *Mary, the Spirit and the Church*. Ramsey, NJ: Paulist Press, 1980.

Branz, F. *Ich komme vom Himmel: Prophetie auch heute?* Wiesbaden: Credo-Verlag, 1960.

Brochado, C. *Fatima in the Light of History*. Milwaukee: Bruce Publishing Company, 1955.

Bruno de Jésus-Marie, E. de Greef, A. Janssens and P. van Gehuchten. *Les faits mystérieux de Beauraing*. Paris: Desclée de Brouwer, 1933.

Bukowczyk, J. J. "Mary the Messiah: Polish Immigrant Heresy and the Malleable Ideology of the Roman Catholic Church, 1880–1930." *Journal of American Ethnic History* 4/2 (Spring 1985): 5–32.

Bullivant, R. "The Visions of the Mother of God at Zeitun." *Eastern Churches Review* 3 (Spring 1970): 74–76.

Buzzati, D. *I misteri d'Italia*. Milan: Arnoldo Mondadori Editore, 1978. Caesarius of Heisterbach. *The Dialogue on Miracles*. Trans. H. von E. Scott and C. C. Swinton Bland. New York: Harcourt, Brace and Company, 1929.

Calla, R. S. *Message de Bayside, New York (1975–1976), des jours d'Apocalypse*. St Raphael: Sherbrooke, 1978.

Calvat, M. *Vie de Mélanie, bergère de la Salette*. Paris: Mercure de France, 1919.

Carlier, L. *Histoire de l'Apparition de la Mère de Dieu sur la montagne de la Salette*. Tournai: Les Missionaires de la Salette, 1912.

Carroll, M. *The Cult of the Virgin Mary: Psychological Origins*. Princeton: Princeton University Press, 1986.

———. "The Virgin Mary at La Salette and Lourdes: Whom Did the Children See?" *Journal for the Scientific Study of Religion* 24 (1985): 56–74.

———. "Visions of the Virgin Mary: The Effect of Family Structures on Marian Apparitions." *Journal for the Scientific Study of Religion* 22 (1983): 205–221.

Castella, A. *Maria erscheint in San Damiano*. Hauteville, Switzerland: Parvis Verlag, 1985.

Cawley, T. J. "What Will Happen in 1960?" *Information* 72 (March 1958): 10–24.

Cazzamalli, F. *La Madonna di Bonate*. Milan: Fratelli Bocca, 1951.

Christian, W. A., Jr. *Apparitions in Late Medieval and Renaissance Spain*. Princeton: Princeton University Press, 1981.

———. "Holy People in Peasant Europe." *Comparative Studies in Society and History* 15 (1973): 106–114.

———. *Local Religion in Sixteenth-Century Spain*. Princeton: Princeton University Press. 1981.

———. *Person and God in a Spanish Valley*. 2nd ed. Princeton: Princeton University Press, 1989.

———. "Religious apparitions and the Cold War in Southern Europe." In *Religion, Power and Protest in Local Communities*, ed. E. Wolf, 239- 266. Berlin: Mouton Publishers, 1984.

———. "Tapping and Defining New Power: The First Month of Visions at Ezquioga, July 1931." *American Ethnologist* 14/1 (1987): 140–166.

Christiani, L. *Saint Bernadette*. Trans. P. O'Shaughnessy. Staten Island, NY: Alba House, 1965.

———. *Satan in the Modern World*. Trans. C. Rowland. London: Barrie and Rockliff, 1959.

Cimarosti, A. *La mia Lourdes*. S. Vito al Tagliamento: Edizioni Tipografia "Sanvitesse" Ellerani, 1971.

Colin, R. P. *Berthe Petit, apôtre du coeur douloureux et immaculé de Marie*. Paris: Nouvelles éditions latines, 1967.

Combe, G. *Dernières années de Soeur Marie de la Croix, bergère de la Salette: Journal de l'Abbé Combe*. Paris: Téqui, 1978.

La confidente de l'Immaculée: Bienheureuse Bernadette Soubirous. Nevers: St. Gildard, [1913].

Connor, E. *Prophecy for Today*. Rockford, IL: TAN Books and Publishers, 1984.

Corteville, F. *La Bergère de Notre-Dame de la Salette et le Serviteur de Dieu, Mgr Zola, Évêque de Lecce*. (Paris: Nouvelles éditions latines, 1981.

———. *Pie IX, le Père Pierre Semenenko, et les défenseurs du message de Notre-Dame de la Salette*. Paris: Téqui, 1987.

Costa, H. de la. "Our Lady of Fatima." *Catholic Mind* 49 (1951): 93–98.

Cousins, J. W. "Who's Got the 'Secret'?" *The Sign* 45 (December 1965): 46–47.

Cros, L.-J.-M. *Histoire de Notre-Dame de Lourdes d'après les documents et les témoins*. Vol. 1, *Les apparitions (11 février–7 avril 1858)*. Paris: Beauchesne, 1925.

———. *Histoire de Notre-Dame de Lourdes d'après les documents et les témoins*. Vol. 2, *Les luttes (avril 1858–février 1859)*. Paris: Beauchesne, 1926.

Culleton, R. G. *The Prophets and Our Times*. Rockford, IL: TAN Books and Publishers, 1974.

———. *The Reign of Antichrist*. Rockford, IL: TAN Books and Publishers, 1974.

Culligan, E. J. *The 1960 Fatima Secret and the Secret of La Salette*. San Bernardino, CA: Culligan Book Co., 1967.

———. *The Last World War and the End of Time*. Rockford, IL: TAN Books and Publishers, 1981.

Curicque, J. *Voix prophétiques; ou, signes, apparitions et prédictions modernes*. Paris: V. Palmé, 1872.

Daley, H. *Miracle at Garabandal*. Dublin: Ward River Press, 1985.

Danemarie, J. *Histoire du culte de la Sainte Vierge et de ses apparitions*. Paris: Fayard, 1958.

Dausse, M. *L'homme d'oraison: l'abbé J.-B. Gerin, curé de la cathédrale de Grenoble*. Grenoble: Baratier et Dardelet, 1880.

Deery, J. *Our Lady of Lourdes*. Dublin: Browne and Nolan, 1958.

Delaney, J. *A Woman Clothed with the Sun*. New York: Doubleday, 1960.

Demarest, D., and C. Taylor, eds. *The Dark Virgin*. Freeport, ME: Coley Taylor, 1956.

Des Brulais, M. *L'Écho de la sainte montagne*. 3d. ed. Nantes: Imprimerie Charpentier, 1854.

———. *Suite de l'écho de la sainte montagne*. Nantes: Imprimerie Charpentier, 1855.

Diener, P. G. *Lourdespilger*. Bamberg: St. Otto-Verlag, 1972.

Di Maria, S. *The Most Holy Virgin at San Damiano*. Hauteville, Switzerland: Éditions du Parvis, 1983.

———. *Our Lady of San Damiano*. Bulle, Switzerland: Éditions du Parvis, n.d.

Dinzelbacher, P. *Vision und Visionsliteratur im Mittelalter*. Stuttgart: Anton Hiersemann, 1981.

Dion, H. *Maximin Giraud, berger de la Salette, ou la fidélité dans l'épreuve*. Montsûr: Résiac, 1988.

————. *Mélanie Calvat, bergère de la Salette, étapes humaines et mystiques.* Paris: Téqui, 1984.

Donleavy, A. *The Counter-Revolution for Peace: Words of Warning and Love from the Virgin Mary.* Roslyn Heights, NY: Libra Publishers, 1976.

Dooley, L. M. "Mary and the Atom." *Ave Maria* 75 (22 March 1952): 359–362.

Dozous, Dr. *La grotte de Lourdes, sa fontaine, ses guérisons.* 2d ed. Paris: Chauce, 1874.

Dupont, Y. *Catholic Prophecy: The Coming Chastisement.* Rockford, IL: TAN, Books and Publishers, 1973.

Dupont-Fournieux, Y. *Les derniers jours des derniers temps.* Paris: La Colombe, 1959.

Durand-Lefebvre, M. *Étude sur l'origine des vierges noires.* Paris: G. Durassie, 1937.

Eizereif, H. *Das Zeichen des lebendigen Gottes: Muttergottes Erscheinungen in Marienfried.* Stein-am-Rhein: Christiana-Verlag, 1976.

Engelbert, O. *Catherine Labouré and the Modern Apparitions of Our Lady.* Tran. A. Guinan. New York: P. J. Kenedy and Sons, 1959.

Eparvier, J., and Hérissé, M. *Le dossier des miracles.* Paris: Hochette, 1977.

Estrade, J.-B. *Les apparitions de Lourdes.* Tours: Mame, 1899.

Evans. H. *Visions, Apparitions, Alien Visitors.* Wellingborough U.K.: Aquarian Press, 1984.

Filas, F. L. "What of Lucy's Claims?" *America* 101 (4 July 1959): 490–491.

Fox, R. *Rediscovering Fatima.* Huntington: Our Sunday Visitor, 1982.

Garcia de la Riva, J. *Memories of My Visits to Garabandal.* Trans. Mary of Jesus. Tacoma, WA: Northwest Garabandal Center, 1969.

Gabriel, J. *Présence de la très sainte Vierge à San Damiano.* Paris: Nouvelles éditions latines, 1968.

Gaume, Mgr. *Un signe des temps ou les quatre-vingts miracles de Lourdes.* Paris: Gaume, 1878.

Gebara, I., and M. Bingemer. *Mary: Mother of God, Mother of the Poor.* Trans. P. Berryman. Maryknoll, NY: Orbis Books, 1989.

Gillett, H. M. *Famous Shrines of Our Lady.* London: Walker, 1949.

Gilly de Collières, R. *La Vierge, Messagère de coeur.* Paris: Librairie Plon, 1953.

Girard, C.-R. *Les secrets de la Salette et leur importance: dernièrs révélations sur de prochains événements.* 4th ed. Grenoble: F. Allier, 1872.

Gonzales Dorado, A. *Mariologia popular Latinoamericana de la Maria Conquistadora a la Maria liberadora.* Asunción: Ediciones Loyola, 1985.

González, C. *Diary.* In *Our Lady Comes to Garabandal, Including Conchita's Diary,* J. Pelletier. Worcester, MA: Assumption Publications, 1971.

[Gouin, P.] *Soeur Marie de la Croix, bergère de la Salette.* Angers: Imprimerie de l'Anjou, 1954. English translation: *Sister Mary of the Cross: The Shepherdess of La Salette* (London: Billings and Sons, 1981).

Goubert, J., and L. Christiani. *Les apparitions et messages de la sainte Vierge de 1830 à nos jours.* Paris: Éditions du Veius Colombier, 1952.

Graef, H. *Mary: A History of Doctrine and Devotion*. Vol. 1, *From the Beginnings to the Eve of the Reformation*. New York: Sheed and Ward, 1963.

———. *Mary: A History of Doctrine and Devotion*. Vol. 2, *From the Reformation to the Present Day*. New York: Sheed and Ward, 1965.

Greef, E. de. "Notes sur les faits de Beauraing." In *Les faits mystérieux de Beauraing*, Bruno de Jésus-Marie et al., 31–88. Paris: Desclée de Brouwer, 1933.

Greeley, A. *The Mary Myth: On the Femininity of God*. New York: Seabury, 1977.

Green, C., and C. McCreery. *Apparitions*. London: Hamish Hamilton, 1975.

Grignon de Montfort, L.-M. *True Devotion to Mary*. Ed. The Fathers of the Company of Mary. Trans. F. W. Faber. Rockford, IL: TAN Publishers, 1941.

Guilhot, H. *La vraie Mélanie de la Salette*. Saint-Céneré: Éditions Saint-Michel, 1973.

Guitton, J. *Rue du Bac: ou, la superstition dépassée*. Paris: S.O.S., 1973.

Gustavson, G. J. "Private Revelations and Prudence." *The Priest* 15/9 (September 1959): 713–717.

Guynot, E. *Sainte Bernadette d'après ses contemporains*. 4th ed. Paris: Cerf, 1978.

Halley, T. A. "Apparitions of Our Lady at Fatima." *Ave Maria* 63 (16 February 1946): 199–202.

Hart, H. "Six Theories about Apparitions." *Society for Psychical Research* 50 (1956): 153–181.

Haynes, R. "Miracles and Paranormal Healing." *Parapsychology Review* 8 (1977): 25–28.

Hebert, A. J. *Prophecies: The Chastisement and Purification*. Paulina, LA: privately printed, 1986.

Hellé, J. *Miracles*. Trans. L. C. Sheppard. London: Burns and Oates, 1952.

Herkenrath, J. *Das Jahrhundert der Muttergottes und unsere Zukunft*. Wiesbaden: Credo-Verlag, 1954.

Höcht, J. M. *Fatima und Pius XII*. Wiesbaden: Credo-Verlag, 1959.

Holland, M. "Ballinspittle and the Bishops' Dilemma." *Irish Times*, 21 August 1985. Reprinted in *Seeing is Believing: Moving Statues in Ireland*, ed. C. Toibin, 45–48. Dublin: Pilgrim Press, 1985.

Hume, R. "Fatima in the Headlines." *Marianist* 47 (October 1956): 11–16.

Introduction au Mystère de Tilly. [Luc-sur-Mer]: Association des Amis de Notre-Dame de Tilly, 1973.

Jacobus de Varagine. *The Golden Legend*. Trans. G. Ryan and H. Ripperger. London: Longmans, Green and Co., 1941.

Jameson, M. *Legends of the Madonna*. New York: Houghton Mifflin, 1890.

Jaouen, J. *La Grâce de la Salette 1846–1946*. Paris: Cerf, 1946.

Johnson, E. "The Marian Tradition and the Reality of Women." *Horizons* 12 (1985): 116–135.

———. "Mary and the Female Face of God." *Theological Studies* 50/3 (1989): 500–526.

Johnston, F. *Fatima, The Great Sign*. Rockford, IL: TAN Books and Publishers, 1979.

———. *When Millions Saw Mary*. Chumleigh, U.K.: Augustine, 1980.

José Maria de Dios. *Dios en la Sombra*. Editorial Circulo, 1967.

Kerkhofs, L. *Notre-Dame de Banneux*. Liège: R. Dessain, 1972.

Kondor, L., ed. *Fatima in Lucia's Own Words*. Trans. Dominican Nuns of the Perpetual Rosary. Fatima, Portugal: Postulation Centre, 1976.

Kraljević, S. *The Apparitions of Our Lady at Medjugorje (1981–1983)*. Chicago: Franciscan Herald, 1984.

Kselman, T. *Miracles and Prophecies in Nineteenth-Century France*. New Brunswick, NJ: Rutgers University, 1983.

Kselman, T., and S. Avella. "Marian Piety and the Cold War in the United States." *The Catholic Historical Review* 72 (1986): 403–424.

Küng, H., and J. Moltmann, eds. *Mary in the Churches*. New York: Seabury, 1983. (Concilium 168).

Künzli, J. *Die Erscheinung in Marienfried*. Günzburg-Reisensburg, West Germany: G. Deininger, 1971.

La Douceur, E. *The Vision of La Salette: The Children Speak*. New York: Vantage Press, 1965.

Laffineur, M., and M. T. le Pelletier. *Star on the Mountain*. Trans. S. L. Lacouture. Newtonville, NY: Our Lady of Mount Carmel of Garabandal, 1968.

Lagier, Abbé F. *The Abbé Jots It Down*. Ed. and trans. E. La Douceur. Altamont, NY: La Salette Press, 1946.

Lahart, K. "Miracle in Bayside." *Critic* 33 (1974): 36–44.

Lambertini, G. *Segno dei tempi, i fatti straordinari dei populo di Dio*. Brescia: Magalini, 1973.

Larsen, T. A. "Our Lady's Warning at Fatima." *Ave Maria* (13 July 1946): 39–42.

Lasserre, H. *Les épisodes miraculeux de Lourdes*. Paris: Palme, 1883.

———. *Notre-Dame de Lourdes*. Paris: Palme, 1869.

Laurenceau, J. "L'importance psychologique de l'image maternelle dans les messages de San Damiano." *Études Mariales* 30–31 (1973–1974): 57–66.

Laurentin, R. *The Apparitions at Medjugorje Prolonged*. Trans. J. Lohre Stiens. Milford, OH: The Riehle Foundation, 1987.

———. *Bernadette of Lourdes*. Minneapolis: Winston Press, 1979.

———. "Bulletin Marial." *Revue des sciences philosophiques et théologiques* 48 (1965): 85–128; 52 (1968): 479–551; 56 (1972): 433–491; 60 (1976): 281–345, 451–500; 65 (1981): 123–154, 299–335; 69 (1985): 611–643; 70 (1986): 101–150.

———. *Études scientifiques et médicales à Medjugorje*. Paris: O.E.I.L., 1985.

———, ed. *Lourdes, dossier des documents authentiques*. Vol. 1, *Au temps des seize premières apparitions, 11 février–3 avril 1858*. 2d ed. Paris: Lethielleux, 1962.

———, ed. *Lourdes, dossier des documents authentiques*. Vol. 2, *Dix-septième apparition, gnoses, faux miracles, fausses visions, la grotte interdite, 4 avril–14 juin 1858*. Paris: Lethielleux, 1957.

———, ed. *Lourdes, histoire authentique*. Vol. 2, *L'enfance de Bernadette et les trois premières apparitions, 7 janvier 1844–18 février 1858*. Paris: Lethielleux, 1962.

Laurentin, R., ed. *Lourdes, histoire authentiques*. Vol. 3, *La quinzaine des apparitions*. Paris: Lethielleux, 1962.

————, ed. *Lourdes, histoire authentique*. Vol. 4, *La quinzaine des apparitions: La quinzaine au jour le jour, première semaine, 19 à 25 février 1858*. Paris: Lethielleux, 1963.

————. *Lourdes, pèlerinage pour notre temps*. Chalet: Oeuvre de la Grotte, 1977.

————. *Queen of Heaven*. Dublin: Clonmore and Reynolds, 1956.

————. *The Question of Mary*. New York: Holt, Rinehart and Winston, 1965.

Laurentin, R., and B. Billet. *Année sainte 1983–1984, pèlerinages, sanctuaires, apparitions, redécouvrir la religion populaire*. Paris: Office d'Édition, 1983.

Laurentin, R., and A. Durand, eds. *Pontmain, histoire authentique*. 3 vols. Médiaspaul, 1970, 1977.

Laurentin, R., and H. Joyeux. *Scientific and Medical Studies on the Apparitions at Medjugorie*. Trans. L. Griffin. Dublin: Veritas, 1987.

Laurentin, R., and L. Rupčić. *Is the Virgin Mary Appearing at Medjugorje?* Trans. F. Martin. Washington, DC: The Word Among Us Press, 1984.

Le Hidec, M. *Les secrets de la Salette*. Paris: Nouvelles éditions latines, 1969.

Le Rumeur, G. *Apocalypse Mariale: La Salette et Fatima, Kerizinen, Garabandal et San Damiano*. Argenton-l'Église: Guy Le Rumeur, 1978.

————. *La grande hérésie*. Argenton-l'Église: Guy Le Rumeur, 1971.

————. *Notre-Dame du Carmel à Garabandal*. Argenton-l'Église: Guy Le Rumeur, 1978.

————. *La révolte des hommes et l'heure de Marie*. Argenton-l'Église: Guy Le Rumeur, 1981.

Leuken, V. *Roses from Heaven*. 2 vols. Orange, TX: Children of Mary, 1982–1984.

Ljubic, M. *Erscheinungen der Gottesmutter in Medjugorje*. Miriam Brothers, 1983.

Llorens, E. *Fatima, apocalypsis de Maria*. Barcelona: Balmes, 1974.

Lochet, L. *Apparitions*. Bruges: Desclée de Brouwer, 1957.

Lopez, P. "Le pèlerinage à Fatima: une expression mystique du sacré populaire." *Social Compass* 36/2 (1989): 187–199.

————. "Le pèlerinage à Fatima: un processus de transition entre tradition et modernité à partir d'une situation migratoire." *Social Compass* 33/1 (1986): 91–106.

Luthold-Minder, I. *Ich wurde in Lourdes geheilt*. Stein am Rhein: Christiana-Verlag, 1971.

Lutiis, G. de. "Novi Casi esemplari." In *Studi sulla produzione sociale de sacro*, 120–167. Naples: Liguori Editore, 1978.

Lyons, J. R. "The Message of Fatima." *Action Now* 2 (October 1948): 7–8.

McCafferty, M. "Virgin on the Rocks." *New Statesman*, 13 September 1985, 24–26. Reprinted in *Seeing is Believing: Moving Statues in Ireland*, ed. C. Toibin, 53–58. Dublin: Pilgrim Press, 1985.

McClory, R. I. "TV Report Says Fanatics Run Shrine at Necedah." *National Catholic Reporter*, 21 December 1979, 3, 19.

McClure, K. *The Evidence for Visions of the Virgin Mary.* Wellingborough, U.K.: Aquarian Press, 1983.

McConnon, T. "How America Heard of Fatima." *Mary Today* 57/1 (January–February 1966): 38–42.

McGinn, B. *Visions of the End: Apocalyptic Traditions in the Middle Ages.* New York: Columbia University Press, 1979.

McGlynn, T. "Fatima on War and Peace." *Integrity* 8 (October 1953): 2–8.

———. *Vision of Fatima.* Boston: Little, Brown and Company, 1948.

McGrath, W. C. *Fatima or World Suicide?* St. Meinrad, IN: Abbey Press, 1950.

MacKenzie, R. "Mariology as an Ecumenical Problem." *Marian Studies* 26 (1975): 104–20.

Maindron, G. *Des Apparitions à Kibeho.* Paris: O.E.I.L., 1984.

Maisonneuve, R., and Belsunce, M. de. *San Damiano, histoire et documents.* Paris: Téqui, 1984.

Manifold, D. *Fatima and the Great Conspiracy.* Galway, Ireland: Firinne Publications, 1982.

Manteau-Bonamy, H. "Les interventions de Marie et l'espérance de l'Église." *De Primordiis Cultus Mariani. Actes du Congrès de Lisbonne-Fatima, 1967*, 416–422.

Marchand, A. *The Facts of Lourdes and the Medical Bureau.* Trans. F. Izard. London: Burns, Oates, and Washbourne, 1924.

Marchi, J. de. *The Crusade of Fatima: The Lady More Brilliant than the Sun.* Trans. A. C. Branco and P. C. M. Kelly. New York: P. J. Kenedy and Sons, 1948.

———. *Fatima: The Facts.* Trans. I. M. Kingsbury. Cork: Mercier Press, 1950.

———. *The Immaculate Heart.* Ed. W. Ray. New York: Farrar, Straus and Young, 1952.

———. *Our Lady of San Damiano.* Bulle, Switzerland: Éditions du Parvis, n. d.

Marnham, P. *Lourdes, a Modern Pilgrimage.* New York: Coward, McCann and Geoghegan, 1981.

Martindale, C. C. "The Phenomenon of Fatima." *Dublin Review* 221 (Winter 1948): 121–143.

Martins, A. M., ed. *Novos Documentos de Fatima.* São Paulo: Edições Loyola, 1984.

Martins dos Reis, S. *Fátima, as suas provas e os seus problemas.* Lisbon, n.p., 1953.

———. *O Milagre do Sol e o Segredo de Fátima*, Porto, Portugal: Ediçoes Salesianas, 1966.

Marty, A. *Alerte au monde.* Paris: Nouvelles éditions latines, 1959.

———. *Balestrino.* Paris: Nouvelles éditions latines, 1971.

———. *Le monde de demain vu par les prophètes d'aujourd'hui.* Paris: Nouvelles éditions latines, 1962.

Mazzolari, P. *Viaggio à Lourdes.* Vicenza; La Locusta, 1973.

Meilach, M. D. *Mary Immaculate in the Divine Plan.* Wilmington, DE: Michael Glazier, 1981.

Melton, J. G., ed. *The Encyclopedia of American Religion.* 3d ed. Detroit: Gale Research, 1989.

Meyer, S. J. "The Miracle At Serra da Aire." *Fate Magazine* 3 (July 1950): 26–33.

Michaud, S. *Muse et Madone. Visages de la femme de la Révolution française aux apparitions de Lourdes*. Paris: Éditions de Seuil, 1985.

Michel de la Sainte Trinité. *Toute la vérité sur Fatima*. Vol. 1, *La science et les faits*. Saint-Parres-les-Vaudes: La Contre-Réforme Catholique, 1984.

———. *Toute la vérité sur Fatima*. Vol. 2. *Le secret et l'Église, 1917–1942*. Saint-Parres-les-Vaudes: La Contre-Réforme Catholique, 1984.

———. *Toute la vérité sur Fatima*. Vol. 3, *Le troisième secret, 1942–1960*. Saint-Parres-les-Vaudes: La Contre-Réforme Catholique, 1985.

Miravalle, M. *The Message of Medjugorje: The Marian Message to the Modern World* Lanham, MD: University Press of America, 1986.

Moncoq, Dr. *Résponse complète au Lourdes de M. Zola*. Caen: A. le Boyteux, 1894.

Monin, A. *Notre-Dame de Beauraing*. Bruges: Desclée de Brouwer, 1949.

Montes de Oca, F. *More about Fatima and the Immaculate Heart of Mary*. Trans. J. da Cruz. N.p.: L. Owen Traynor, 1979.

Neary, T. *I Comforted Them in Sorrow*. Knock: Custodians of Knock Shrine, 1979.

———. *I Saw Our Lady*. Knock: Custodians of Knock Shrine, 1983.

Nelson, C. "The Virgin of Zeitoun." *Worldview* 16 (1973): 5–11.

Nicolas, A. *La Salette devant la raison et le devoir d'un catholique*. 2d ed. Lyon: J.-B. Pélagaud, 1857.

Nolan, M. L., and S. Nolan. *Christian Pilgrimage in Modern Western Europe*. Chapel Hill: University of North Carolina Press, 1989.

Noone, P. *Mary for Today*. Chicago: Thomas Moore, 1977.

Northcote, J. *Celebrated Sanctuaries of the Madonna*. London: Longmans Green, 1968.

O'Carroll, M. *Medjugorje: Facts, Documents, Theology*. Dublin: Veritas, 1986.

———. *Theotokos: A Theological Encyclopedia of the Blessed Virgin Mary*. Wilmington, DE: Michael Glazier, 1982.

Odell, C. *Those Who Saw Her*. Huntington, Indiana: Our Sunday Visitor, 1986.

Ó'hÓgáin, D. "A Manifestation of Popular Religion." In *Seeing Is Believing: Moving Statues in Ireland*, ed. C. Toibin, 67–74. Dublin: Pilgrim Press, 1985.

Olivieri, A. *Υ a-t-il encore des miracles à Lourdes?* Paris: Lethielleux, 1970.

Oraison, M. "Le point de vue du médecin psychiatre clinicien sur les apparitions." In *Vraies et fausses apparitions dans l'Église*, B. Billet et al., 123–147. Paris: Lethielleux, 1973.

Orsi, R. A. *The Madonna of 115th Street: Faith and Community in Italian Harlem, 1880–1950*. New Haven: Yale University Press, 1985.

Osee, J. *Call of the Virgin at San Damiano*. North Quincy, MA: Christopher Publishing House, 1977.

Paco, R. *Contributions à l'étude des faits négatifs par la Commission de Santander contre le surnaturalisme des faits de Garabandal*. Blois, France: privately printed, 1968.

Palmer, J. *Our Lady Returns to Egypt*. San Bernardino, CA: Culligan Publications, 1969.

Palmer, J. "Virgin Mary in Egypt." In *Miracles*, ed. M. Ebon, 118–126. New York: New American Library, 1981.

Paul, V. de. *The Days of the Apocalypse, They've Begun*. St Louis: Third Order, [1974].

Pelletier, J. A. "The Fatima Secret in 1960?" *The Messenger of the Sacred Heart* 95 (January 1960): 18–22.

———. *Our Lady Comes to Garabandal, Including Conchita's Diary*. Worcester, MA: Assumption Publications, 1971.

———. *The Queen of Peace Visits Medjugorje*. Worcester, MA: Assumption Publications, 1985.

———. *The Sun Danced at Fatima*. New York: Doubleday, 1983.

Pérez, R. *Garabandal: The Village Speaks*. Ed. A. Orhelein. Trans. A.I.C. Mathews. Lindenhurst, NY: The Workers of Our Lady of Mount Carmel, 1981.

Perry, N., and L. Echeverría. *Under the Heel of Mary*. London: Routledge, 1988.

Petitot, H. *Histoire exacte des apparitions de N.-D. de Lourdes à Bernadette*. Paris: Desclée de Brouwer, 1935.

Pinar, A. del. *Da Fatima a Garabandal*. Rome: Volpe, 1976.

Pope, B. "Immaculate and Powerful: The Marian Revival in the Nineteenth Century." In *Immaculate and Powerful: The Female in Sacred Image and Social Reality*, ed. C. W. Atkinson, C. H. Buchanan, and M. R. Miles, 173–200. Boston: Beacon Press, 1985.

Pour servir à l'histoire réelle de la Salette. Documents. 3 vols. Paris: Nouvelles éditions latines, 1963–1966.

Proudfoot, W. *Religious Experience*. Berkeley: University of California Press, 1985.

Pugh, R. J., and F. W. Holiday. *The Dyfed Enigma*. London: Faber and Faber, 1979.

Puncernau, R. *Los extraordinarios Hechos de San Sebastian de Garabandal*. Buenos Aires: Cruz y Fierro Editores, 1967.

Rahner, K. *Visions and Prophecies*. Trans. C. Henkey and R. Strachan. London: Burns and Oates, 1963.

Ravier, A. *Bernadette*. Trans. B. Wall. London: Collins, 1979.

———, ed. *Les écrits de sainte Bernadette et sa voie spirituelle*. Paris: Lethielleux, 1980.

Rebut, R. *Les messages de la Vierge Marie*. Paris: Téqui, 1968.

Reeves, M. *The Influence of Prophecy in the Later Middle Ages: A Study in Joachimism*. Oxford: Clarendon Press, 1969.

Reju, D. *Le troisième secret de Fatima*. Monaco: Éditions du Rocher, 1981.

Remy. *Fatima, espérance du monde*. Paris: Plon, 1957.

Rennel, D. "Pope of Mary." *Our Lady's Digest* 5 (1950): 148–156.

Ricard, Mgr. *La vraie Bernadette de Lourdes*. Paris: Dentu, 1894.

Robert, J. *Lourdes*. Capbreton: Chabas, 1971.

Rogo, D. S. *Miracles: A Parascientific Inquiry into Wondrous Phenomena.* New York: Dial, 1982.

Rouby, H. *La vérité sur Lourdes.* Paris, 1910.

Rovira, G., ed. *Der Widerschein des Ewigen Lichtes: Marienerscheinungen und Gnadenbilder als Zeichen der Gotteskraft.* Kevelaer: Verlag Butzon und Bercker, 1984.

Ruether, R. *Mary: The Feminine Face of the Church.* Philadelphia: Westminster Press, 1977.

Ryan, T., and J. Kirakowski. *Ballinspittle: Moving Statues and Faith.* Cork and Dublin: Mercier Press, 1985.

Saillens, E. *Nos vierges noires, leurs origines.* Paris: Éditions Universelles, 1945.

Saint Mary's Transfigurations at the Coptic Orthodox Church of Zeitun, Cairo. [Cairo]: al-Mahabba Bookshop, 1969.

Sanchez-Ventura y Pascual, F. *The Apparitions of Garabandal.* Trans. A. de Bertodano. Detroit: San Miguel Publishing Company, 1966.

———. *Stigmatisés et Apparitions.* Paris: Nouvelles éditions latines, 1967.

Santos, L. dos. *Fatima in Lucia's Own Words.* Ed. L. Kondor. Trans. Dominican Nuns of the Perpetual Rosary. Fatima: Postulation Centre, 1976.

Saunders, E. *Lourdes.* New York: Oxford University Press, 1940.

Schallenberg, G. *Visionäre Erlebnisse: Erscheinungen im 20. Jahrundert. Eine psychopathologische Untersuchung.* Aschaffenburg: Paul Pattloch Verlag, 1979.

Seguy, J. "Millénarisme et ordres adventistes, Grignion de Montfort et les Apôtres des Derniers Temps." *Archives de sciences sociales des religions* 53/1 (1982): 23–48.

Servant, M. *Veillez et priez, car l'heure est proche.* Saint-Germain-en-Laye: M. Servant, 1971–1973.

Sharkey, D. *The Woman Shall Conquer: The Story of the Blessed Virgin in the Modern World.* Milwaukee: Bruce Publishing Company, 1952.

Sheen, F. J. *Communism and the Conscience of the West.* Indianapolis: Bobbs Merrill Company, 1948.

Sicam, G. D. *The Grotto Shrine of Our Lady of Lourdes in the Philippines.* Manila: Sicam, 1977.

Souillet, H. *Les apparitions de Notre-Dame à l'Île Bouchard.* Saint-Céneré: Éditions Saint-Michel, 1972.

Staehlin, C. M. *Apariciones: Ensayo crítico.* Madrid: Razón y Fe, 1954.

[Stanford, R.] *Fatima Prophecy.* Austin, TX: Association for the Understanding of Man, 1972.

Stella, P. "Per una storia del profetismo apocalittico cattolico ottocentesco." *Rivista di storia e letteratura religiosa* 4 (1968): 448–469.

Stern, J. "La Salette: bibliographie—état de la question." *Ephemerides Mariologicae* 22 (1972): 337–355.

———, ed. *La Salette, Documents authentiques: dossier chronologique intégral.* Vol. 1, *Septembre 1846–début mars 1847.* Paris: Desclée de Brouwer, 1980.

———. *La Salette, Documents authentiques: dossier chronologique intégral.* Vol. 2, *Le procès de l'apparition fin mars 1847–avril 1849.* Paris: Cerf, 1984.

———. "La Salette vue par Léon Bloy." In *Léon Bloy*, ed. M. Arveiller, 161–170. Paris: Les Cahiers de L. Herne, 1988.

———. "Mélanie Calvat." *Catholicisme*, vol. 7, cols. 1110–1111. Paris: Letouzey et Ane, 1979.

Stevenson, I. "The Contribution of Apparitions to the Evidence for Survival." *Journal of the American Society for Psychical Research* 76 (1982): 341–358.

Suffran, M. *Lourdes; ou, les témoins sont aveugles.* Arrigues-près-Bordeaux: S.N.I. Delmas, 1976.

Swan, H. *My Work with Necedah.* Vol. 1, *Mary Ann Van Hoof's Own Story of the Apparitions of the Blessed Virgin Mary.* Necedah, WI: For My God and My Country, 1959.

———. *My Work with Necedah.* Vol. 2, *The Narrative of the Passion from the Sufferings on the Fridays of Advent and Lent.* Necedah, WI: For My God and My Country, 1959.

———. *My Work with Necedah.* Vol. 3. Necedah, WI: For My God and My Country, 1959.

———. *My Work with Necedah.* Vol. 4. Necedah, WI: For My God and My Country, 1959.

Taves, A. *The Household of Faith: Roman Catholic Devotions in Mid-Nineteenth-Century America.* Notre Dame, IN: University of Notre Dame Press, 1986.

Thurston, H. *Beauraing and Other Apparitions: An Account of Some Borderline Cases in the Psychology of Mysticism.* London: Burns and Oates, 1934.

Thurston, H. "Doubts, Frauds, Confusions." In *Miracles*, ed. M. Ebon, 89–97. New York: New American Library, 1981.

Tizané, E. *Les apparitions de la Vierge: Un enquêteur laïc s'interroge.* Paris: Tchou, 1977.

Todd, E. H. "Mary, Dogma, and Psychoanalysis." *Journal of Religion and Health* 24 (1985): 154–166.

Toibin, C., ed. *Seeing is Believing: Moving Statues in Ireland.* Dublin: Pilgrim Press, 1985.

Torelló, J. B. "Echte und falsche Erscheinungen: Besonnenheit und Offenheit vor der Marienerscheinungen." In *Der Widerschein des Ewigen Lichtes: Marienerscheinungen und Gnadenbilder als Zeichen der Gotteskraft*, ed. G. Rovira, 89–107. Kevelaer: Verlag Butzon und Bercker, 1984.

Treece, P. *Nothing Short of a Miracle: The Healing Power of the Saints.* New York: Doubleday, 1988.

Tridot, A. *San Damiano.* Marquain, Belgium: Jules Hovine, 1982.

Trochu, F. *Saint Bernadette Soubirous, 1844–1879.* Trans. J. Joyce. Rockford, IL: TAN Books and Publishers, 1957.

Turkel, R. R. "Fatima 1960 Jitters." *Information* 74 (January 1960): 33–36.

Turner, F. "Part I: John Paul II and Garabandal." *Garabandal* (July–September 1980): 10–13.

———. "Part II: John Paul II and Garabandal." *Garabandal* (October–December 1980): 15–19.

Turner, V., and E. Turner. "Postindustrial Marian pilgrimage." In *Mother Wor-*

ship, ed. J. Preston, 145–173. Chapel Hill: University of North Carolina Press, 1982.

Tyrrell, G. *Apparitions*. London: Duckworth, 1953.

Ullathorne, W. B. *The Holy Mountain of La Salette*. 9th ed. Altamont, NY: La Salette Press, 1942.

Vallet, A. *Mes conférences sur les guérisons miraculeuses de Lourdes*. Paris: Libraires-éditions, 1937.

Vallet, A., and R. Dubuch. *Les guérisons de Lourdes en schémas*. Paris: Téqui, 1923.

Van Hoof, M. A. *Revelations and Messages as Given through Mary Ann Van Hoof*. Ed. M. Sommers. Necedah, WI: For My God and My Country, 1971.

Visher, L. "Mary: Symbol of the Church and Symbol of Humankind." *Mid-Stream* 17 (1978): 1–12.

Vlašić, T. "The Message of Medjugorje." *Our Lady Queen of Peace* (November 1985): 1–7.

Volken, L. *Les apparitions dans l'Église*. Paris: Salvator, 1960.

Vulliaud, P. *La fin du monde*. Paris: Payot, 1952.

Walne, D., and J. Flory. *The Lady Said*. Chicago: Franciscan Herald Press, 1978.

Walsh, W. J. *The Apparitions and Shrines of Heaven's Bright Queen*. 4 vols. New York: T. J. Carey, 1904.

Walsh, W. T. *Our Lady of Fatima*. Garden City, NY: Image Books, 1954.

Warner, M. *Alone of All Her Sex: The Myth and Cult of the Virgin Mary*. New York: Knopf, 1976.

Weible, W. "Miracle at Medjugorje." Privately printed, March 1987.

Weigl, A. *Mary—Rosa Mystica*. Trans. N. C. Reeves and I. Muske. Essen: J. Bürger, 1975.

West, D. J. *Eleven Lourdes Miracles*. London: Helix Press, 1957.

Winiarski, M. "Where Mother Cabrini Warns against speeding." *National Catholic Reporter*, 12 September 1975, 1–2.

Zaki, P. *Our Lord's Mother Visits Egypt*. Cairo: P. Zaki, 1971.

Zalecki, M. *Notre Dame de Czestochowa*. Paris: Desclée de Brouwer, 1981.

Zeitler, P. E. *Die Herz-Maria-Weltweihe*. Kaldenkirchen: Steyler Verlagsbuchhandlung, 1954.

Zimdars-Swartz, S. "Popular Devotion to the Virgin: The Marian Phenomena at Melleray, Republic of Ireland." *Archives de sciences sociales des religions* 67/1 (January–March 1989): 125–144.

———. "Religious Experience and Public Cult: The Case of Mary Ann Van Hoof." *The Journal of Religion and Health* 28/4 (Spring 1989): 36- 57.

———. "The Virgin Mary: Mother as Intercessor and Savior of Society." In *Seeing Female: Social Roles and Personal Lives,* ed. S. S. Brehm, 69–79. New York: Greenwood Press, 1988.

INDEX